The
INVENTION
of POWER

The
INVENTION
of POWER

POPES, KINGS, *and*
THE BIRTH OF THE WEST

Bruce Bueno de Mesquita

PUBLICAFFAIRS

New York

PublicAffairs
Hachette Book Group
1290 Avenue of the Americas, New York, NY 10104
www.publicaffairsbooks.com
@Public_Affairs

Printed in the United States of America

First Edition: January 2022

Published by PublicAffairs, an imprint of Perseus Books, LLC, a subsidiary of Hachette Book Group, Inc. The PublicAffairs name and logo is a trademark of the Hachette Book Group.

The Hachette Speakers Bureau provides a wide range of authors for speaking events. To find out more, go to www.hachettespeakersbureau.com or call (866) 376-6591.

The publisher is not responsible for websites (or their content) that are not owned by the publisher.

Print book interior design by Amy Quinn.

Library of Congress Cataloging-in-Publication Data

Names: Bueno de Mesquita, Bruce, 1946- author.
Title: The invention of power : popes, kings, and the birth of the West / Bruce Bueno de Mesquita.
Description: New York : PublicAffairs, [2022] | Includes bibliographical references and index.
Identifiers: LCCN 2021033991 | ISBN 9781541768758 (hardcover) | ISBN 9781541774407 (epub)
Subjects: LCSH: Civilization, Western—Christian influences. | Church and state—Europe, Western—History. | Exceptionalism—Europe, Western—History. | Catholic Church. Treaties, etc. Holy Roman Empire, 1122 September 23.
Classification: LCC BR115.C5 B84 2022 | DDC 909/.09821—dc23
LC record available at https://lccn.loc.gov/2021033991

ISBNs: 9781541768758 (hardcover), 9781541774407 (ebook)

LSC-C

Printing 1, 2021

CONTENTS

PREFACE   1

CHAPTER 1: EXCEPTIONALISM   5
  Three Treaties About Power and Money Changed Europe   8
  Think of Popes and Kings as Self-Interested   11
  Short-Term Decisions, Lasting Consequences   15
  Europe: Unexpected Exceptionalism   17
  Europe's Unique Feature   24

CHAPTER 2: TWO SWORDS, ONE CHURCH   27
  *Iconoclasm, the Papal States, and Escape
    from Constantinople*   28
  The Birth of Papal Nepotism   30
  Papal Maneuvers to Increase Political Power   35
  The Struggle over the Investiture of Bishops   39
  The Pope's War with the Holy Roman Emperor   47

CHAPTER 3: THE CONCORDAT GAME   59
  The Terms of the Concordats   60
  The Process of Bishop Selection Before the Concordats   73
  The Concordat Game   78
  Key Implications of the Concordat Game   89

CHAPTER 4: SECULARISM SURGES   95
  *The Game's Third Outcome: Avignon and Rebellion
    Against the Church*   96
  The Church's Changing Use of Punishment   98
  The Secularization of Bishops   104
  The Wealth of Dioceses   107
  Wealth and the Secularization of Bishops: A First Test   107

    Assessing the Expected Costs of Defying the Church   109
    Wealthy Sees for Secular Bishops and Poor Sees
        for Religious Bishops   113

CHAPTER 5: THE ROAD TO PROSPERITY   119
    Maneuvers to Influence Economic Growth   124
    Four Lateran Councils: Combating Secular Economic
        Growth   137
    Secular Maneuvers for Growth   151
    Growth, Crusades, and the Commercial Revolution   155

CHAPTER 6: THE ROAD TO PAPAL SERFDOM
               AND LIBERATION   167
    Gamble on Bishops, Gamble on Vacant Sees   169
    Breaking from the Church: French Wealth and
        the Avignon Papacy   174
    Testing When France Was Ready to Rebel   176
    The Church Contemplates Reform; Protestants Rebel   183
    Art and the Rise of Secularism   195

CHAPTER 7: THE BIRTH OF STATES, THE BIRTHING
               OF REPRESENTATIVE DEMOCRACY   199
    The Concordat: A Step Toward Modern Sovereignty   202
    War and Accountability   210
    War and State Building   216
    The Concordats and Accountable States   218
    Secularism, Wealth, and Parliaments   230
    Rubber Stamps or Real Parliaments   235
    Did Parliaments Help or Hurt Monarchs?   238

CHAPTER 8: TODAY   253
    The Altered Tides of Power   258
    The Concordats and Today's Quality of Life   265
    Innovation and Discovery   280
    Insights for Today   286

ACKNOWLEDGMENTS   293
NOTES   297
BIBLIOGRAPHY   311
INDEX   321

PREFACE

THE PUZZLE THAT THIS BOOK CONFRONTS IS SIMPLY STATED: HOW CAN we explain "Western exceptionalism"? Resolving this puzzle is not merely a matter of historical curiosity. It is of the utmost importance. Its solution will identify strategies to improve life for billions of people today, and it will help quash the misguided and incorrect inferences tied to explanations for Europe's successes based on claims that Europeans are culturally superior, that they are harder-working, smarter people, or that Europe's God and its religions are superior to others'. Those explanations are incorrect. They confuse correlation with causation, often with disastrous consequences. That is why I have spent more than twenty years studying how the competition between popes and kings a thousand years ago led to Europe's "exceptionalism."

It is not my intention to celebrate, denigrate, or deny Europe's accomplishments. Rather, my objective is to explain the strategic, calculated maneuvers of popes and kings that produced those accomplishments. To do so, together we will explore the historical origins of Western exceptionalism as the product of three treaties signed in the twelfth century. We will see as a matter of logic and of evidence that a direct connection can be drawn between those treaties and variations in Europe's secularization, economic growth, commitment to or eventual abandonment of the Catholic Church, and creation of accountable parliamentary government. Those logical connections run neither through religion nor through monarchy, although both were instruments of its realization. The connection to exceptionalism runs through the regulated competition that the three treaties put in place. I conclude by evaluating how those origins and their strategic implications for structured competition might be exploited by others today to secure the best parts of what Europe has achieved.

This investigation of Europe's distinct economic, political, and social evolution is unlike any that has been offered before and, if judged to be right, can help serve as a blueprint for fostering such distinct accomplishments in every corner of the world. Then what seems most exceptional about the West—its tolerance, prosperity, and freedom—might become routine everywhere. That is a tough order, of course, since, as we all know, the high and mighty are not keen to promote tolerance and freedom, although they do not object to prosperity.

Today's powerful leaders are no different on this score from their distant predecessors. Europe's great powers in the Middle Ages, its popes, bishops, kings, and emperors, were not keen to promote tolerance and freedom. Today's powerful people also generally prefer to avoid such policies. But despite a widely held reluctance to encourage freedom and tolerance, some—not all—of Europe's medieval leaders helped create just such a world. They did so not out of any eagerness for it but, rather, out of narrow, self-interested choices made in and of the moment. Thankfully, by following the logic behind what they did (and the evidence that they followed that logic), we can better understand how and why Europe turned out as it did, both for better and for worse. History, after all, is most valuable when it teaches us lessons for the future. I believe the history examined here will do just that. It will show us the way to greater freedom and prosperity across our world while overturning misguided ideas that Europeans somehow were just smarter, more inventive, or otherwise superior to other people.

This book contends that a mostly forgotten or overlooked deal, the Concordat of Worms, signed on September 23, 1122, and its predecessors agreed to by the Catholic Church and the kings of England and France in 1107, laid the foundation for northern Europe to become more prosperous than southern Europe, for parts of Europe to break with the Catholic Church while other parts stuck with it, for some kingdoms in Europe to develop accountable government ahead of other kingdoms, and for science to flower more successfully in some portions of Europe than in others. In short, it laid the foundation for the creation of Western exceptionalism first in France and for the gradual spread of its effects northward and then elsewhere. That exceptionalism, that tolerance, prosperity, and freedom, began to be born and to spread four hundred years before Martin Luther and the Protestant Reformation.

Before plunging into the story of the creation of Europe's exceptional modern record, it is useful to take a moment to explain what this book tries to do, what its origins are, and what, if anything, makes me qualified to write it. My objective is to encourage a reconsideration of what we know about Europe's economic and political development, about its emergence, after hundreds of years of decline following the collapse of the Roman Empire, into societies that were becoming prosperous, tolerant, and accountable and that were slowly, hesitatingly, and grudgingly inventing good governance, transparency, and respect for human rights. Nothing, of course, is absolute. Western societies, whether European or not, are flawed and have a miserable past of tyranny and repression. Yet for all the remaining flaws, people flock to the West from everywhere in the world much more than they flee it, and that is because the West seems to have found the way to provide a good quality of life for its citizens.

While much of the history recounted in this book takes place hundreds of years ago, I aim to show in the final chapter that it is highly relevant today. The impact of the Concordat of Worms and other associated agreements is readily discerned in the differences in quality of life across contemporary Europe. Indeed, I suggest that other parts of the world may still take lessons from the beneficial incentives developed in the concordats—that is, the treaties signed between popes and secular rulers in the twelfth century. In building on those incentives, others, no longer living in a world dominated by popes and kings, may learn to improve their own quality of life in our time and in the future.

Any effort to write such sweeping "big history" is fraught with risks. This is especially true for me since I am not a historian, let alone a medievalist or a specialist on the Concordat of Worms. Undoubtedly, readers will find here and there a wrong date or an error in some other detail of the story. I apologize for such errors. I am sure, efforts to avoid them notwithstanding, that some remain. But I submit that the big story being told here is what matters, and the big story does not depend on anecdotes or on any individual fact. Rather, it depends primarily on quantitative evidence, which I have supplemented with anecdotes to illustrate rather than evaluate the argument. This evidence will address and compare key issues and developments before, during, and after the period of time during which the concordats were most clearly reshaping Europe.

The approach I take to address Europe's successes, mindful of its many past and present failures, is grounded in game theoretic reasoning and the analysis of a broad body of evidence. Those who are interested in more technical details can consult the online appendix at https:// wp.nyu.edu/brucebuenodemesquita/books/. In this book everything is explained in plain English and with straightforward graphs. Developing and explaining important contemporary and historical phenomena through game theoretic analysis and then testing that analysis statistically is what I have been doing as a professor of politics for the past five decades.

Throughout this investigation, history serves as the source of evidence, and the terms of the Concordat of Worms serve as the source of logical implications with which to evaluate the extent to which the modern Western world has been shaped by the deals struck between the church and the Holy Roman emperor and other kings so long ago. I hope that by the book's end you will share my conviction that previous studies missed a very big part of the story of the development of Western exceptionalism and that by understanding the story better we may also be positioned to make all people's lives more exceptional in the future.

1

EXCEPTIONALISM

That which is hath been long ago, and that which is to be hath already been.

—Ecclesiastes 3:15

WE SHOULD ACKNOWLEDGE WHAT SEEMS INCONTROVERTIBLE: PEOple in the West are freer, richer, more tolerant, more innovative, and happier than people just about anywhere else in the world.[1] But then we should also recognize that despite holistic claims of "Western exceptionalism," there is tremendous variation in how well people are doing in different parts of the Western world. Declarations that Westerners are superior are puzzling, offensive, and just plain foolish when looked at over the long drift of history. The explanations for "Western exceptionalism" that rely on claims of superior culture, superior religious beliefs, or superior people cannot withstand even a whit of scrutiny. More plausibly, some scholars, starting with such luminaries as the Scottish economist Adam Smith and the German sociologist Max Weber, say that parts of Europe—England, the Netherlands, and even, for a time, Otto von Bismarck's Germany leap to mind—gained a leg up because they adopted capitalism ahead of others. Yet this belief is far from universal: others, such as Karl Marx and Friedrich Engels, argued that capitalism doomed many Europeans to misery and revolution; they made a case that was persuasive to millions of people in Europe, as well as to major political parties such as the Social Democratic Party (SPD) in Germany, the Labour Party in Britain, and Léon Blum's Popular Front government in France (1936–1940). According to this view, Western exceptionalism is rooted not in capitalism but in its opposite, socialism.

Yet these are only the broadest of arguments. There are also somewhat more detailed cases for exceptionalism. One holds that it resulted from changes in the Catholic Church's understanding of marriage and family and how those changes altered kinship relations and expanded the church's reach.[2] Another says that Europe's success was due to the spread of literacy engendered by Johannes Gutenberg's publication of the Bible in the 1450s,[3] followed not long after by the rise of the Protestant Reformation.[4] Yet here is a third idea that cuts against those two: maybe it was dumb luck. Modern Europe and its Western offshoots might have been created when an Italian, flying the Spanish flag, sailed the ocean blue in 1492, stumbling on the "New World" and the opportunity to benefit from all of its riches.

There are doubtless plenty more theories. I am not, after all, posing a new puzzle. As we will see, events in the fifteenth or sixteenth centuries certainly reinforced and extended the development of European exceptionalism, but those events cannot be the "big bang" that set Europe apart from the rest of the world because Europe's exceptional social, economic, and political course was already well established long before Gutenberg, Luther, and the rise of Protestant Germany. Lots of earlier developments may also have contributed to Europe's remarkable development, but we will see that the path from pre-twelfth-century European misery to "exceptionalism" does not require them. Most importantly, accounts grounded in some variant of "Europeans have a superior culture," "Europeans are harder-working, smarter people," or "Europe's God and religions are superior" will be seen to be misguided and wrong.

There is no good reason to believe that Europeans are inherently smarter, genetically more creative, or culturally superior to other people. It is hard to imagine that Britons, Belgians, or Germans are just smarter, more creative, more tolerant, or obviously superior to

Egyptians, Peruvians, or anyone else. Egyptians looked a lot more capable five thousand years ago than folks living in the territories that today are called Germany or France or England. The Phoenicians of Tyre, Sidon, and Carthage were doing a heck of a lot better than were Belgians or Britons four thousand years ago, and in fact, they were doing better for hundreds of years after the collapse of the Roman Empire. And there is no reason to think that today's Belgians or Dutch are superior to the Chinese, or the Germans to the Austrians, or the French to the Czechs, Argentines, or Nigerians. Every place has had good times and bad times. It is puzzling why western Europe and its settler offshoots are having such a good time now, why some in the West are having so much better a time of it than others, and why, compared to the rest of the world, a lot of the folks in western Europe have been having a better time for nearly a thousand years.

The record of the long-ago past suggests that Europeans were not exceptionally good at just about anything a thousand or more years ago. After the Roman Empire died in the mid-fifth century, today's "exceptional" Europe was a mess that for hundreds of years did little to invent, discover, or improve life's conditions. Rather, Western Europe first began to become the breeding ground for innovation in art, literature, government, and science during what was once mistakenly and derisively referred to as "the Dark Ages," nearly a thousand years ago. Especially beginning with the twelfth century, Europe began to part ways with the rest of the globe, innovating when others stagnated. The leaders of western Europe began grudgingly to reward change and those who created it. In fits and starts, with stumbles as well as massive retreats, with more or less success in different parts of the continent, Europe left much of the world behind in successfully separating religion from government and in promoting secularism, prosperity, freedom, and discovery. Of course, that does not mean that Europe's "success" will continue, nor does it mean that everyone agrees that Europe is more successful rather than just different. Maybe Europeans won't seem better—or different—at these things in a thousand years or even in fifty years, although I am betting on Europe and its settler offshoots to continue to provide a really high quality of life for a long time to come. By the last chapter, building toward it all along the way, it should be clear why I would make that bet. Hint: it has nothing to do with European superiority.

THREE TREATIES ABOUT POWER AND MONEY CHANGED EUROPE

I am going to explore history, logic, and lots of evidence in my effort to persuade you that today's diverse degrees of "exceptionalism" in different parts of Europe are the consequence of three similar, equally obscure deals. The first two were agreed to by the Catholic Church and the kings of England and France in 1107. The main deal—an agreement of less than five hundred words in Latin—was signed on September 23, 1122, and applied to all the kingdoms and territory of the vast Holy Roman Empire. That deal, the Concordat of Worms, like its predecessor agreements, is unknown to almost everyone other than medieval scholars. It did not in any obvious way address the creation of prosperity, freedom, tolerance, or anything else that makes us think the European/ Western world is "exceptional." The agreement signed on that day essentially just said three things.

First, the Catholic Church had the exclusive right to nominate bishops. Second, the Holy Roman Emperor, along with some other kings, had the right to accept or reject whoever was nominated. Third, if the nominee was rejected, then the secular ruler over the relevant Catholic diocese got to keep the bishopric's revenue until an acceptable bishop was nominated and installed.[5]

This hardly sounds like a monumental contract that would change the world, and yet that is exactly what it did. We will see that the reason parts of Europe leaped ahead in prosperity, secularism, religious freedom, and social and governmental accountability is simple: two of Europe's great powers at the time—Pope Calixtus II and the Holy Roman emperor, Henry V—agreed at Worms on how to compete with each other for political dominance by trading money for power and power for money. They accepted the rules of that competition on September 23, 1122, and their deal changed everything.

In ways hardly anyone could imagine at the time, the deal signed in the ancient city of Worms, less than forty miles from modern Frankfurt, transformed the incentives of the Catholic Church, Europe's temporal leaders, its lesser lords, merchants, and peasants for centuries afterward and even up to the very present. The interplay of wealth, secularism, and distance from Rome became critical in ways that had not previously existed for the people in the Catholic dioceses that together defined the map of Europe. The interplay of diocesan money, power, and distance shaped the way the myriad of bishops and monarchs dealt with each other, reshaping the institutions and rules in the kingdoms they made up.

Hard as it must be to believe that a deal agreed to in 1122 changed Europe's economic, political, and social trajectory, it is even more remarkable to realize that the consequences of the logic put into motion at Worms is still at work in today's Europe. As we will see in Chapter 8, some of the most profound differences across European countries today can be tied to the conditions of their bishoprics starting nine hundred years ago. To illustrate that thought, let's pause to look at some surprising current facts whose meaning and causes we can ponder as the logic of the treaty signed in Worms—and its impact on "Western exceptionalism"—unfolds before us.

It seems odd that today's average Belgian works just a few more hours per year than does the average Briton, and yet the typical British worker earns $4,017 less over that year. The discrepancy between work and pay is even more pronounced—and surprising—if we compare the Netherlands and Germany, neighboring countries whose culture and history have been closely intertwined for centuries. Despite their similarities, the average German worked just 1,386 hours in 2019, and the average Dutchman 1,434, giving Germans the equivalent of about one extra week of vacation time. But for that one extra week of leisure, the German earned nearly $6,000 less. That seems like a really heavy price for a little more time off.[6] Why are the Brits making so much less than the Belgians, and the Germans so much less than the Dutch? What's going on here?

Certainly the disparity must have a lot to do with differences in the policies currently followed by these governments. Perhaps it is due to differences in the strength of labor unions or of businesses. Maybe it has something to do with Germany being more Catholic than the

Netherlands. But those religious differences do not help explain why Belgium, a predominantly Catholic country, is doing better today on income than Britain, a predominantly Protestant country. These and other differences across many European nations probably have lots of explanations that come quickly to mind, as well as lots of reasons to doubt those explanations.

Few commentators are likely to suspect that all this has anything to do with the concordats signed in Germany, England, or France in the twelfth century, even though all the countries mentioned—England, Germany, the Netherlands, and Belgium—were subject to those long-ago treaties. Just as surely, it is hard to imagine that today's incomes are related to the selection of Roman Catholic bishops between 1122 and 1309, the years when, for reasons internal to the logic of the concordats, the conditions behind the selection and consecration of bishops fundamentally changed. And yet nearly 38 percent of Dutch bishops between 1122 and 1309 and almost 63 percent of bishops in what today makes up Belgium had worked for their king, prince, duke, or other local ruler before being chosen to head a diocese, while the same was true of only one-sixth of German bishops and of a bit over one-quarter of English bishops during those years. If we ask what percentage of bishops subject to a concordat in the twelfth and thirteenth centuries worked in the secular world rather than the religious world just before becoming a bishop, we discover that the answer predicts today's incomes pretty darn well. Countries that enjoy a better quality of life today—better life expectancy, more-accountable government, and more money—are the same ones that began hiring bishops with a relationship to their kings in the twelfth century. And those differences today can and will be tied directly to the altered incentives created by the Concordat of Worms and its French and English predecessors.

Of course, the correlation between the relations of bishops to kings nine hundred years ago and incomes today in a much broader array of countries than just England, the Netherlands, Belgium, and Germany does not assure causation. The correlation between the "secularism" of bishops so long ago and the leisure time of workers today, for instance, might just be an odd, cute fact. It might have nothing to do with anything important today, like differences in freedom, prosperity, tolerance, health, or innovativeness across the Western world. Or perhaps there was something about what was going on in Europe nine hundred years ago that still matters today. Maybe choices made so long ago laid a pathway to better or worse outcomes today in different parts of Europe regardless of cultural, governmental, or religious similarities then. Maybe it is not just a cute set of facts and coincidental correlations. Maybe to understand "Western exceptionalism" we need to understand the logical, strategic consequences of an obscure deal struck in 1122. If that is true, then we have to reconsider much of what we think we know about the history behind the modern world.

Indeed, we will examine how individual decisions by popes and kings, made for individual advantages, translated into the sorts of macrolevel, high-altitude effects that others have highlighted as the source of "Western exceptionalism." It will be apparent that neither church policy on its own nor decisions by secular rulers outside their competition with the church over power and money were behind Europe's remarkable performance in promoting prosperity, secularism, democracy, religious tolerance, and innovativeness. We will see that it was instead the terms of the concordats, combined with local conditions, that determined the balance of bargaining leverage and policy choices across Europe in ways that shaped what Europe and its Western offshoots look like today.

THINK OF POPES AND KINGS AS SELF-INTERESTED

To evaluate the shifting influence of the church, monarchs, and their nascent states from a strategic perspective, we need to agree on a few ground rules about how we assess hundreds of years of history and the thousands of bishops and kings whose decisions eventually led to Western exceptionalism. I propose that we agree to take a cynical view of human nature, putting aside any optimism we might have about kings and popes (or anyone else) doing what they thought was good for their subjects or what might have been good for the long-term future of their empires and their church, respectively. That is not to suggest that they had anything against helping others; rather, it is to say that whenever they faced a conflict between helping others or helping themselves, we will understand their choices better if we assume that they mostly did what they believed was good for themselves.

That means that they were paying attention to what they believed would be the consequences of their decisions for their future. Kings and popes were playing multidimensional chess against a great many rival kings, bishops, and other opponents simultaneously. They had hard jobs staying in power, keeping track of dangerous, complex challenges, while trying to advance their own interests. Those who were not good at looking ahead probably ended up overthrown and maybe even headed for an early death. Much of the time they just could not safely do whatever they most wanted to do; instead, they constantly had to adjust, choosing their next move and the move after that, considering carefully what moves their rivals would make in response to their doing this or that or something else. It gives us a headache just thinking about thinking so far ahead, but maybe that is why most of us wouldn't want to be a pope or king.

All of that is to say that I rely on game theoretic reasoning where appropriate to offer a plausible, logically structured way of working through and making sense of critical developments that contributed to Europe's later success. "Game theory" is a fancy term for thinking about something all of us do all the time. It helps us ask thoughtfully what people will most probably do when they have to take into account not just what they themselves desire but also what other people want and what others are likely to do. This way of thinking recognizes that what any king, pope, peasant, merchant, banker, or anyone else in the Middle Ages chose to do depended on three things: (1) what the chooser valued, (2) what constraints limited the chooser from going after his or her heart's desires, and (3) what the best decisions were in the face of uncertainty about the situation or the things rivals and allies were prepared to do.

Although what people want—what is in their heart of hearts—might be the product of learned psychological states, the culture within which they were raised, their religious beliefs, or their personal experiences, here the concern is not with the sources of their preferences or desires but, rather, with their strategic maneuvering to advance their objectives when faced with challenges and threats from others whose desires are different from and incompatible with theirs.[7] Thus, in my perspective, individuals are not captives of a certain set of norms and values; rather, they are ready to adjust and alter these considerations when they believe it will improve their lot.

There is a limit to what can be known about how people made decisions hundreds of years ago. Maybe, like Nostradamus in the sixteenth century, they stared into bowls of water to figure out what they thought they should do. Or maybe they sought guidance by looking at the stars or at sheep entrails to figure out the omens and odds of success. Maybe they consulted friends and relatives or authority figures, such as priests or local dignitaries, to help them choose. However they thought about their situation, the ability to plan consciously, to build shelter for warmth and to make tools to hunt and harvest food, is a hallmark of the human experience. One way or another, people have always adjusted what they do in light of the obstacles put in their way. Neither we today nor popes and kings nearly a millennium ago blindly do whatever we want.

We and our Middle Ages predecessors consider the costs, the benefits, the risks, and the uncertainties behind our choices and then, faced with difficult decisions, we do the best we can. Of course, constraints on choices and uncertainty about the situation or the desires of others can always lead to what turn out to be wrong choices. Nevertheless, if we can put ourselves in our ancestors' shoes, taking advantage only of the things they could have or should have known at the moment, then we ought to be able to figure out why they did what they did, making their decisions predictable for us and for them. For instance, with the benefit of hindsight, today's pope might wish that Calixtus II had negotiated a different deal with the Holy Roman emperor in 1122. But Calixtus, like all of us, could only cut a deal based on what he knew and what he believed at the time. To use an anachronistic metaphor, Monday-morning quarterbacking is irrelevant. All of us act only on what we know and what we believe at the moment we must act; we do not get to rewrite history to make things come out better. Indeed, even if Calixtus or Henry V could see what they were building in the distant future, they probably would not have cared. Remember, we are thinking about self-interested people: they are interested in whether their actions are good for themselves and for what they value at the moment—and perhaps for *their* own eternity as well—and not in whoever else their decisions turned out to benefit a year or two later, let alone nine hundred years later. They were not trying to choose for the ages; they were trying to seize the day for themselves.

The game theoretic approach adds one more consideration that we should keep in mind because it is an important departure from how historians tackle the past. Historians are primarily interested in what happened and so, naturally, examine the unfolding of observed events rather than taking a strategically driven look at what did not happen and at how what did not happen influenced what did happen. Other scholars, such as economists, psychologists, and economic historians, are more tuned in to finding out *why* things happened, but their research has given limited attention to the pre-Reformation division of European wealth and power. Game theory requires us always to think about what did not happen—what choices were rejected—at least as much as about what did happen. By paying attention both to what happened and what did not happen, we will see that events played out as they did—quite differently in different parts of Europe—because of the altered incentives created by the concordats.[8]

Once the game theoretic logic is laid out, it will be matched up with a detailed analysis of a large body of information about many thousands of bishops, a few thousand monarchs, and hundreds of dioceses, and it will be complemented with anecdotal or documentary evidence as well. Our dive into history and its available evidence will be designed specifically to evaluate whether the incentives implied by the shifting strategic setting created in 1122 in fact led to fundamental, predictable, and consequential shifts in the behavior of kings and popes and others with a deep stake in the outcome of the contest for power between the secular and the sacred, between Caesar and God.

Don't get me wrong. Major developments are almost never caused by a single event, and this is certainly true of Europe's political, economic, and religious evolution that created the basis for Western exceptionalism. We should not expect a perfect fit between the effects of the concordats and outcomes in every nook and cranny of Europe. Too much else was going on, and it is too difficult to measure key ideas precisely. What we should expect and demand is strong consistency between the argument and the evidence. What will be evident, and maybe surprising, is how much of Europe's evolution was punctuated by the events leading up to the concordats and by the details of the deal struck at Worms and its precursors in England and France.

It is particularly noteworthy how swiftly Europe began to part ways from the rest of the world once the struggle between the church and secular rulers over political control was out in the open by 1046. That year marked a crucial moment that set the Investiture Controversy in motion: the living pope was deposed by the Holy Roman emperor. The struggle begun in 1046 was resolved by the treaty in Worms almost eighty years later. Prior to the Concordat of Worms, Europe was not alone in many of its initial leaps forward (or backward), but from that time onward, its growth began to diverge sharply from that of other countries. Indeed, much of the rest of the world was busy doing remarkable things long before Europe surged ahead yet proved unable to keep up once Europe's strategic environment was reset in September 1122. Europe's cultures had not changed. Its religion had not changed. Its people had not changed. What had changed were the incentives of its secular and its clerical leaders.

Short-Term Decisions, Lasting Consequences

Today, Europe's support for individual rights in every corner of life has made people dream of migrating to the Western world, even risking their lives to share in its freedoms and prosperity. But that is now; it was neither always nor inevitably so. For centuries, and even within the twentieth century, western Europe, like so much of the rest of the earth, was a place from which people fled. They ran for their lives as tyranny threatened to replace freedom and as a privileged few threatened to control and oppress the prosaic many. It is a place whose present special accomplishments did not arise easily, quickly, or cheaply.

Good results do not always follow from carefully laid plans. Indeed, through all the struggles and across all the fits and starts over two millennia that gradually created modern Western exceptionalism, it seems unlikely that anyone had the promotion of freedom and tolerance in mind. Certainly, the fourth-century artist who made the oldest known portrait of the first pope, the apostle Saint Peter, did not contemplate that his or her fresco would be looked upon 1,700 years later not just as a religious (or political) statement but as an artistic one as well.[9] And equally, that artist's approximate contemporary, the sculptor who gave us the bust of the Roman emperor Constantine in the fourth century,[10] would have had no inkling that the followers of Saint Peter would manage to quash secular images like his, along with secular ideas, for many centuries. These artists could not have imagined the part they were playing in the unfolding drama between the secular and the sacred. That drama, against all expectations and despite tremendous efforts to reverse the tide of tolerance, culminated in the modern West. No one a thousand and more years ago, looking to the distant future, would have dreamed of anything like the social, economic, and political contours of today's West. No pope, no king, no philosopher could have imagined, or would have wished for, the range of tolerance that is nevertheless the product of the myriad decisions they made so long ago, decisions that moved the West in the direction of freedom even when powerful efforts to restore intolerance, efforts as recent as Adolf Hitler's and Joseph Stalin's, rose to reverse the now firmer but always fragile course of a tolerant modernity.

To grasp why western Europeans, and their far-flung settler offshoots, more than just about any other people, nurture freedom, innovation, and competition, we must uncover and understand the meticulously calculated, strategically sophisticated decisions that were made by popes, kings, aristocrats, and ordinary people during the so-called age of superstition, a millennium and more ago. That means that after briefly touching on the rest of the world in relation to Europe, we must focus on what was varying *across Europe* at the expense of a more detailed comparison of Europe to the rest of the world.[11] The evolution of what is special about Europe is the product of internal competition and differences in internal choices. Indeed, these dynamics are more potent than any unified decisions about how to cope with forces external to what is now understood as the West, changes such as the expansion of Islam or the arrival of Genghis Khan on Europe's edges, which were described as threats to Europe nearly a thousand and more years ago.

Not that these and other external events were inconsequential. Change is much too complicated to rule out the role of external developments, but the purpose here is to understand how European decisions about life in Europe influenced outcomes, putting aside the important but, I believe, secondary part played by medieval and premedieval Europe's interaction with other parts of the globe. We will come to realize that Europe's exceptionalism can be mostly explained by the conflicts and choices of popes, kings, aristocrats, and common people, conflicts and choices framed by individual, narrow interests and not by destiny, design, or desire.

EUROPE: UNEXPECTED EXCEPTIONALISM

In trying to understand why Europe did so well while other parts of the world did not, we first of all need to know that no one living in the year 1000 would have claimed to be enjoying any such good fortune. Over the previous thousand years, starting roughly with the birth of Jesus, Europe's quality of life had declined sharply; it was the fairly new Islamic world, born at the time of Muhammad's move from Mecca to Medina in 622, that would have looked exceptional. To a first-millennium millennial, the idea that there was something exceptional about Europe would have seemed odd, ill-informed, and maybe even laughable. Only when we look at the second millennium of the Common Era do we see a reason to believe that today's Western world is special.

We can only examine life's conditions in the first millennium with a wide range of uncertainty, as reliable and detailed information is hard to come by for conditions a thousand to two thousand years ago. Still, as a starting place, though not our only starting place, we do have estimates of per capita income for regions of the world that far back in time and even for some individual countries, thanks to the highly regarded Maddison Project, which builds on Angus Maddison's pioneering effort to measure economic development across the world from the time of the Roman Empire to the present.[12]

The Maddison Project's currently available data for much of the world only allow us to estimate regional per capita incomes for three time points between the approximate birth of Jesus and 1500: the years 1, 1000, and 1500. While the Maddison Project offers a smattering of estimates for a few modern-day European countries, with so few time periods it is not possible to form a nuanced understanding of what was happening *within* Europe over that first millennium. Against that limitation, these per capita income estimates exist not only for Europe but for the entire globe. Hence, we can compare Europe to the rest of the world to get a sense of how well—or how poorly—Europeans were doing at different times over the first one and a half millennia after Jesus. That comparison helps set the stage for examining the birth of Western exceptionalism and how different that exceptionalism looks from our perspective compared to what it would have looked like to someone of a thousand years ago.

We should keep in mind as we pore over incomes from long ago that we are living in an extraordinarily prosperous time. Incomes, even after being adjusted for inflation, were vastly lower across the world between the years 1 and 1500 than they are almost everywhere today. Hence, we should not be surprised that the Maddison Project's estimates of average incomes look nothing like modern incomes except, perhaps, in a handful of miserably poor modern countries.

In the thousand years after Jesus, western European per capita income fell from about $600 dollars to only about $425, a drop of about 30 percent.[13] Italy (or rather, the region now known as Italy) saw per capita income drop from about $800 to $450, a monumental, devastating fall of nearly 45 percent.[14] Life, to borrow from the much later view of Thomas Hobbes, was "solitary, poor, nasty, brutish, and short."[15] Yet thanks to the success of the Roman Empire, western Europe had begun the millennium with a distinct advantage. At the dawn of Christianity, the average income in western Europe was thirty to fifty percent higher than in China, India, Africa, the Americas, and in what later became the Islamic world of the Middle East and North Africa. So Europe inherited a big boost in its conditions thanks to the Roman Empire, and it managed to lose that advantage over the long, slow years between Rome's demise around 476 and the dawning of the new millennium.[16]

Of course, big things were happening to Europeans between the years 1 and 1000. The demise of the rich and powerful Roman Empire gave rise to the Byzantine Empire, shifting wealth and power away from Rome and eastward to Constantinople. Christianity was born, oppressed, and then adopted by the Roman Empire as its official religion. That gave Christianity a leg up on the many competitor religions within the empire, and then, as proselytizing Christians spread Christianity's word across the European continent, the Catholic Church expanded its institutional advantage over rival religions and locked in new patterns of family relations that strengthened the church's position as a competitor for spiritual and secular power, converting many and supporting the suppression of resisters.[17] Then too, Christian Europe began to feel challenges as Islam came into existence in the Middle East and as its adherents worked assiduously to spread its word through proselytizing and through conquest. And the Holy Roman Empire was created in 800 to act as a substitute source of protection for Catholic western Europe, at the expense of the Byzantine Empire. As is so often true of those who are chosen to provide protection, the Holy Roman emperor, in rather short order, provided protection at a price. Over time, that price gradually became control over almost every member of the church's leadership. In short, there was a lot of political, religious, and economic churning during the first "Christian" millennium, and that churning was accompanied by widespread suffering from plagues, chaos, and economic hardship.

With the collapse of the Roman Empire, Europe lost its great source of social organization, political stability, and common identity. Times were clearly tough in Europe, but that does not mean that they were tougher in Europe than elsewhere. We can get a glimpse of whether life had become more difficult in Europe than in other parts of the world by putting Europe's economic record in a global context. This global comparison is limited by a lack of data, but there are a few tactics we can use to make do.[18]

Our first chart, Figure 1.1, focuses attention on the four economically top-performing parts of the globe at the approximate time of the birth of Jesus. The figure looks at how four regions—western Europe, the Middle East, Africa, and China—were doing on per capita income in the years 1, 1000, and 1500 relative to the world average at the time, setting the world average as a baseline of 100.

This way of looking at the average person's income on a country-by-country or region-by-region basis gives us an easy way to compare relative incomes and also gives us an easy way to compare how different places were doing relative to the global average over time. It produces some eye-opening views that may give us pause about beating our chests and bragging about how well western Europe, or any other part of the world, is doing right now. As the chart makes evident, looking across long stretches of time tells us that what we see and think today is not what we might have seen, let alone thought, long ago. It also

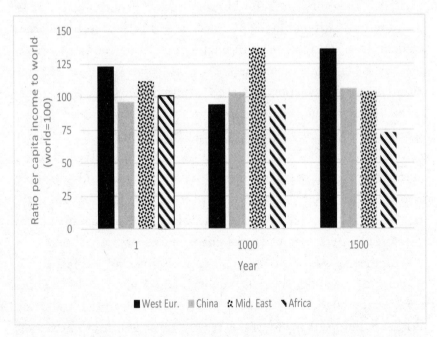

Figure 1.1: Per capita income: Top performers, years 1–1500. The figure divides the Maddison Project's estimate of each region's per capita income each year by the project's estimate of global per capita income in the same year and then multiplies the result by 100. This sets the world's average per capita income equal to 100 and then compares each part of the globe to that baseline. If a region or country scores, say, 110, then its per capita income averaged 10 percent more than the global average in the year in question. Conversely, if it scores 80, its per capita income was only 80 percent of the global average, suggesting a relatively poor material quality of life in that part of the world.

demonstrates that regional or countrywide performance is neither inevitable nor fixed for all time. It makes us want to know whether the forces that got us where we are now have run their course or whether, as I said I would bet, those forces have created lasting success that the rest of the world might adopt and emulate.

Among the notable trends here is the change in the fortunes of the Middle East. Per capita income there exceeded the global average by a whopping 37 percent in the year 1000. The people of China, in second place globally at that time, had a one-third lower income than the folks in the Middle East. At that moment, if anyone had a claim to exceptionalism, it was the people of the rising Islamic world. While the world's regional per capita incomes in 1000 ranged between $400 and $460, the Islamic world's per capita income was about $560. And not only was the Islamic world's income on the rise, but so too was the range of territory it controlled. In the span of a few centuries, the adherents of Islam grew from a tiny minority to a dominant position in North Africa and established significant footholds in Europe. Neither China nor the Islamic world of the Middle East, however, managed to do great things as far as per capita income was concerned during the next five hundred years. They both hovered very slightly above global average income performance, meaning that the people of China had neither progressed nor regressed, relatively speaking, during that half millennium and that the Middle Eastern region, dominated by Islam well before 1500, had regressed mightily from its heady perch of five hundred years earlier. Europe, however, sprang way up.

Was Europe's recovery in 1500 a matter of chance? Were its people suddenly smarter or culturally or religiously superior? Or was something else going on? Was the Islamic Middle East's decline over those same five hundred years just a chance slip down? Was Africa's further descent about to be reversed or was that descent, as we know from our perspective today, part of that region's long decline into relative economic misery? And how about China? We know that China has experienced dramatic economic expansion over the past few decades. When placed in the context of the rest of the world, has it leapt forward?

Figure 1.2 repeats the process that produced Figure 1.1 for the year 2000, replacing Africa with Europe's Western settler offshoots (that is, the United States, Canada, Australia, and New Zealand). They are the world's per capita income champions, and they help us fill in the picture of so-called Western exceptionalism. The figure for the year 2000 helps us address the question of whether the western European economic record in 1500 was just a lucky bounce or whether something particular was going on, something that then spilled over onto Europe's settler colonies in the years and centuries to come.

Figure 1.2 tells a startlingly different story from what we saw in Figure 1.1. For the years from 1 to 1500, no part of the world had a per capita income of more than 140 percent of the global average. Indeed, if we take a look at all the regions of the world, we see surprisingly little variation in per capita income from place to place over the first 1500 years of the Common Era. Of course, there were huge differences in wealth between the rich and the poor, but that does not seem to have produced tremendous global disparities in average per capita income; wealth by region was pretty equally distributed. In a comparison of the whole world—divided into ten regions—the lowest per capita income

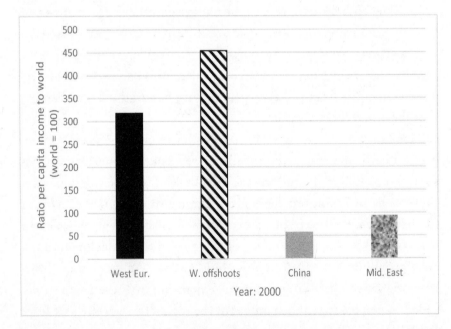

Figure 1.2: Per capita income: Select regions in 2000

score in year 1 was 86 relative to the baseline of 100, and this was the value for what are today's Western settler offshoots of Europe, the countries of Latin America, eastern Europe (those countries that were later part of the Soviet Union), and Japan (areas that are not shown on Figure 1.1). By 1000, the minimum value against the global 100 baseline was 88, attained by what are now the Western settler offshoots, eastern Europe (the states that were later in the Soviet Union), and the countries of Latin America. In 1500, inequality was a bit higher, with the worst performers scoring 71 (what are now the Western offshoots) and 73 (Africa), respectively.

Unlike the chart for years 1 to 1500, the graph for the year 2000 tells a story of enormous income inequality. Figure 1.2 shows that, compared to the per capita income in the Western offshoots, which now is up to 450 percent of the global per capita income average, the rest of the world lags far behind. While Europe's Western offshoots were the top performers in 2000, western Europeans enjoyed a per capita income 3 times larger than the average person. The folks in the Middle East have about the same income as the global average, just as they did five hundred years ago. China, despite decades of rapid economic expansion, found itself in 2000 at a little over half the global average per capita income, much worse than was true for China in 1500 or 1000 or in the year 1. Even using World Bank per capita income data for 2019—the latest available at this writing—China's score is only 89, about 17 percent below its relative income position in 1500, when it scored 106. By 2000, the low score against the global 100-point baseline was 24 (Africa), 47 points worse than the worst performer in 1500. India, at 31 percent of the global average, was second worst, 40 points behind the worst performance by any place in 1500. China is third worst, and the states of the former Soviet Union are next worst at 74, a hair better than the worst-performing region of five hundred years ago. Seeing the pattern in 2000 compared to that of, say, 1500, it is easy to understand how some, focused on correlation without careful thought about causation, would believe that the West is made up of superior beliefs and people. But a wider historical view quickly weakens the case for that view.

EUROPE'S UNIQUE FEATURE

Why Europe became distinct after the year 1000 and not before can be reduced to this surprisingly simple reason: in Europe, the head of religion and the head(s) of state were different people who faced off against one another in long-standing, long-lasting, intense competition for political control. Certainly, the rulers of China and Japan were thought to be gods. In the Mongolia of Genghis Khan (c. 1162–1227), the head of religion as late as 1207 was Genghis's competitor, the shaman Teb Tengerri. Genghis solved the religious and political challenge to his authority by executing his rival and by tolerating, even encouraging, Nestorian Christianity, a religious movement that he understood would be subservient to him.[19] The Mongol code of law, the Yassa, whose writing Genghis seems to have personally overseen, called for unquestioning obedience to the khan, thus making Genghis the supreme ruler, inferior to God but not inferior to any of God's agents on earth.

The Incas and the Mayas (the Aztecs being rather later than the period studied here) likewise had their priesthood, but either the priests were the rulers, as in the Inca tradition, in which the ruler was the son of the sun god, or the priests were subservient to the ruler. In the Mayan case, for instance, the priesthood was drawn from the nobility, whose interests they served. In none of these places were church and state on an equal footing competing with one another. In Europe as well, much of the higher clergy were drawn from the nobility, but for centuries the European clergy and European secular rulers were in a wrestling match for authority, whereas in the Maya world, the religious served the royal elite.

The rise first of the Roman Catholic Church and its pope and then the Holy Roman Empire and its emperor meant that the two swords of power in much of Europe, the one spiritual and the other secular, resided in different hands and were cast in a contest for dominance with one another. The dividing line that Jesus drew—"Render therefore unto Caesar the things which are Caesar's; and unto God the things that are God's" (Matthew 22:21)—lay overwhelmingly in favor of Caesar for as long as the Roman Empire survived. This remained true even as Christianity's influence from the fourth century onward was much greater than it had been during its first three centuries. Despite its adoption as the imperial religion by the late fourth century, still the clergy of the newly named Catholic Church was unquestionably subservient to the emperor until there was no emperor any longer.

Then, certainly by the time of the Iconoclast Movement in the eighth century, the advantage began to swing away from the new Caesar of the day, the Byzantine emperor, moving toward the pope in Rome. Indeed, it is fair to say that for seven hundred years following the death of Constantine, until the rise of Holy Roman Emperor Henry III in 1046, Caesar's portion of earthly power was mostly in retreat. But once Caesar, in the shape of Henry III, removed God's agent, Pope Gregory VI, from his presumably God-given office, the question of what exactly to render unto any Caesar or king and what unto God or God's vicars in the form of the pope, bishops, and priests was once more a fraught affair, one with enormous consequences for the future of the West.

The Catholic Church played a crucial part in the emergence of Western exceptionalism, but it was neither the church's religious beliefs nor its own structure that deserves credit. The monarchies of Europe likewise played a crucial part, but it was not their governance style or their regard (or rather, disregard) for freedom that deserves credit. The credit goes to the competition between kings and popes, monarchies and the church, and monarchs and their subjects, not to any of them on their own. Thus, the story of Europe's exceptionalism is a story of strategic triggers and competitive logic. It is, I believe, a logic that presents a compelling account that explains why Western Europe, despite its poor showing 1000 years after Jesus, became so much richer and freer than most of the rest of the world.

2

TWO SWORDS, ONE CHURCH

Great men are almost always bad men.

—Lord Acton

THE CATHOLIC CHURCH, BORN AS A RELIGIOUS MOVEMENT HOLDING out the promise of eternal salvation for its faithful adherents, began to shift in the eighth century to a more secular, power-seeking, wealth-hungry organization. The drift away from its religious mission resulted from three developments that set the church and its popes on a collision course with Europe's secular rulers. The collision of church and secular interests persisted for centuries, fundamentally reorienting the political, economic, and social conditions across Europe that resulted in the creation of what we know today as the West.

This journey began innocently enough. Its first step was the creation of the Papal States, which gave the church the resources to strengthen its religious mission. But that development also gave the church something less beneficial: a new incentive to pursue power and riches rather than nobler religious goals. With the Papal States under the pope's control, the church tilted in a corrupt, venal, and nepotistic direction. The corruption of the papacy, the second crucial development, coupled with efforts to restore the church to a more religious path, led to the third critical development: the Investiture Controversy, an eighty-year-long clash between the church, kings, and emperors over who had the right to appoint bishops and to invest them with the vast power that bishops possessed. These circumstances precipitated the Concordats of London and Paris in 1107 and the Concordat of Worms in 1122.

ICONOCLASM, THE PAPAL STATES, AND ESCAPE FROM CONSTANTINOPLE

The Papal States were the consequence of a dilemma facing the Byzantine emperor, Leo III, early in the eighth century. At that time, Leo (reigned from 717–741) found his empire facing a dire threat from Muslim invaders. In an effort to quell that threat—which he successfully fought off in 726—and to achieve peaceful relations with his Muslim neighbors, the emperor declared a ban on Christian icons. Without bothering to consult or secure the support of the patriarchs—the popes—in Rome or in Constantinople, the emperor, extending the call in Deuteronomy (12:1–3) to destroy graven images, ordered the destruction of Christianity's most beloved images, including depictions of God, Jesus, angels, saints, apostles, and Mary. This Iconoclast Movement may have eased the emperor's struggle against Islam a bit, but it also weakened his control over the western parts of his empire. His stand against the icons of Christianity challenged the Roman pope's religious authority, opening the door to the assertion of independence by the leader of the western church. Pope Gregory II made clear that he was outraged at Leo's presumption to dictate what was acceptable imagery and religious doctrine for Christians.[1] The pope, perceiving his religious prerogative to have been challenged, balked at the emperor's decree. In response to the imperial order, Gregory wrote to his nominal boss, the emperor:

> You say: "We worship stones and walls and boards." But it is not so, O
> Emperor; but they serve us for remembrance and encouragement, lifting our slow spirits upwards, by those whose names the pictures bear and whose representations they are. And we worship them not as God,

as you maintain, God forbid! ... Even the little children mock at you.
Go into one of their schools, say that you are the enemy of images, and
straightway they will throw their little tablets at your head, and what you
have failed to learn from the wise you may pick up from the foolish. ...
The dogmas of the Church are not a matter for the emperor, but for the
bishops.[2]

With the rise of the Iconoclast Movement and the emperor's embrace
of it, the pope understood that the Byzantine emperor was no longer a
reliable protector of the church. The Iconoclast Movement had revealed
that the emperor was, instead, a threat to the pope's own growing power,
so the bishop of Rome found an innovative solution to the difficulties he
faced. On the death of Pope Zachary and the election of Pope Stephen
II in 752, the emperor in Constantinople had lost control over the selection of the pope in Rome. Now Stephen, the choice of the Roman elite
rather than of the emperor, saw a way to build up the Roman church as
an independent power. To do so, he needed a new, more reliable protector, and he needed more economic security. He found a way to get both
and in doing so eventually led the swords of religious and secular power
to turn against each other in a way he surely did not foresee.

Stephen laid the foundations for a newly independent and temporally
powerful Roman church by striking a deal with Pepin the Short (714–
768, reigned from 751), the ruler of the Franks. He anointed Pepin as
king of the Franks, something no pope had done for any king before.
Stephen also conferred on Pepin the title of *Patricius Romanorum*, a title
invented by Emperor Constantine to honor his most notable military
officers, conferring great legitimacy on him. In return, Pepin's army defeated the Lombards who were threatening to capture Rome.

The lands that Pepin seized from the Lombard king were then given
to the papacy in 756, not long before Stephen died. With this vast
amount of territory added to the Patrimony of Saint Peter (which the
pope had received from Constantine in the fourth century), the pope
and church now controlled a long, large swath of territory running from
the Tyrrhenian Sea on Italy's west to the Adriatic Sea on the east and
from a little south of Rome north to encompass today's province of

Emilia-Romana, bordering on the Republic of Venice. The Gift of Pepin, creating the Papal States, marked a critical moment. Now in possession of extensive territory, the church and pope were well positioned to exercise their independent power. While the church could have used its newfound wealth and power to advance its religious mission, it chose, instead, to use its liberated position for less commendable ends.

The creation of the Papal States denoted a marked shift in the church's territorial endowment and, crucially, its formal entry into the realm of secular sovereignty. It was now unquestionably both a religious and a temporal political player that possessed a large, independent source of wealth. With the creation of the Papal States, the pope was not only head of the western church, as he had been for centuries, but also head of a substantial independent territory governed by him according to his interests. The new papal interests were sometimes complements to the religious mission of the church, but all too often, they were not.

THE BIRTH OF PAPAL NEPOTISM

The gift of land conferred by Pepin on the church fundamentally changed the terms of the office of pope. Now there was enormous tension between the religious and venal motives of popes and those who would control his selection. The key impact resided in a simple fact: the territory of the Papal States belonged to the pope only so long as he was *the pope*. After him, it passed to the succeeding pope and not, as was so often the case with wealth in those times (or our own), to the family of whoever held the wealth. The idea was that the line between the church's ownership of the Papal States and the pope's ownership was sharply drawn, but that line could be blurred if the office of pope remained within the same family, as when Pope Stephen II's brother succeeded him as Pope Paul I. The Papal States were intended as a source of wealth and security for the Roman church and for whoever happened to be the bishop of Rome at the moment. This divide over the control of prodigious wealth precipitated a long struggle to dominate the papacy, one that pitted venal family interests against the church's religious mission, setting up the travails to come over the next few centuries and, in the process, setting the stage for western Europe's exceptional growth.

The birth of the incentives that produced secularism and prosperity in parts of Europe arose quite unexpectedly. As Lord Acton pithily observed in 1887, "Power tends to corrupt and absolute power corrupts absolutely. Great men are almost always bad men, even when they exercise influence and not authority; still more when you superadd the tendency of the certainty of corruption by authority."[3] Unsurprisingly, with the creation of the Papal States, papal nepotism and corruption were boosted as an effective way to blur the lines between what had been rendered unto the church and its papacy and what unto the individual pope. With so much wealth and power on the line, nepotism, murder, and the advancement of family became the hallmarks of the papacy.

The previous religiosity of popes declined so much that the years between 904 and 964 became known as the *saeculum obscurum*, "the unknown or obscure century." During those years and for many years to follow, the papacy was shaped and controlled by powerful families, most notably in the early 900s by the family of the count of Tusculum, starting with Theophylact I (860–924), who ruled Rome from about 905 until his death. Their papal ambition was driven by money and not by spirituality or reverence for God.

The progeny of Theophylact's daughters, Marozia and Theodora, tell a remarkable tale of control over the papacy by the Tusculum family. Marozia's son became Pope John XI at the tender age of twenty. She and her sister, in fact, were the mother, grandmother, great-grandmother, or great-great-grandmother of seven popes spanning four generations. Much of that papal control was the consequence of Tusculum family violence, some of it allegedly perpetrated or instigated by Marozia.

After the death of Pope Formosus in 896—a pope who was strenuously opposed by the Tusculum family—virtually every pope for the next half century was murdered or died under unexplained circumstances. Pope Sergius III, for instance, allegedly conspired with his patron, the count of Tusculum, in the murder of his two predecessors as pope (Leo V, 903–903, and Christopher, 903–904). The allegation is unproven but nevertheless seems credible. Certainly, it is obvious that neither Leo nor Christopher lasted long. It is also obvious that Sergius had both the motive and the opportunity to do them in. Sergius and

Theophylact may have been out for revenge for Sergius's having previously been pushed aside in his quest for the papacy by Holy Roman Emperor Lambert, a great foe of the Tusculum family's power in Rome.

Sergius had been "elected" to the papacy in 898 but was denied the office when Holy Roman Emperor Lambert threw his support behind the man who became Pope John IX (898–900). If being denied his place as pope were not motive enough for murder, Sergius, along with his supporters, then found themselves excommunicated by Pope John.

Pope John died suddenly, under mysterious circumstances. He was succeeded by Pope Benedict IV (900–903), whose own sudden death led to speculation about murder. Then, with the papacy vacant again, Theophylact is said to have imprisoned Pope Leo V and Pope Christopher, providing the opportunity for their apparent murders. Upon the death of Christopher, Sergius finally became pope in 904.[4]

The gruesome procession of murdered popes continued. Pope John X (914–928), like Sergius, was a protégé of the count of Tusculum, who chose him to become pope. Unfortunately for John, Marozia and he eventually had a falling-out that apparently led to his imprisonment and murder.[5] It seems that Marozia was keen for her son to become pope, but alas, at just eighteen years old, he was still too young. Hence, she handpicked Leo VI, who died several months later at age forty-nine, perhaps of natural causes, perhaps not. Then Marozia selected Stephen VII as pope. He also died of unknown causes—and was alleged to have been murdered—just when Marozia judged her son to be of an acceptable age (twenty) to become pope. Across the years, many more Tusculum family members would become pope, enriching their family if not the church. Of course, the story of the Tusculum popes is not typical, but tragically, it was not an alarming example out of keeping with their time.

The popes who owed their position to wealthy, powerful families, like the Tusculums, no longer seemed to be committed to the church's religious objectives. Indeed, most of the popes during the *saeculum obscurum* were utterly lacking in regard for religious conviction, and a great many had not even been priests before becoming pope. With so much at stake, they were in the business of corruption through power rather than being "exceptional" through their superior culture, beliefs, or ability.

If we had not believed Lord Acton's dictum before, his observation was clearly borne out as, for so many popes during the lost tenth century, family ties came to dominate the path to the papacy. The reason to pursue the papacy was to acquire money or power, with family ties the path to both. Religious calling seems not to have played a significant part. Rather, those who could buy control of the church did so. Their corruption made them powerful, and their power then enhanced their opportunities for corruption. Certainly, this linkage between corruption and power seemed to be well understood by the families that led the Catholic Church throughout the dark years after the creation of the Papal States.

The Papal States had made the job of pope extremely lucrative, and that meant the papacy became a job besmirched by nepotism, a common accompaniment to wealth and power. While there were occasional exceptions to this nepotistic, venal, murderous trend among popes, such papacies were few and increasingly far apart.[6] We can see that by evaluating the frequency of nepotism in the selection of popes, starting with the first pope, Saint Peter, and continuing up through 963 when the Holy Roman Empire's base shifted from France to Germany. Looking over this long time span makes it abundantly obvious when the august post of bishop of Rome switched from being the job of sincerely religious leaders to being the position of connected, corrupt individuals.

To evaluate the spread of nepotism, I define the degree of papal nepotism as increasing as specific family-related characteristics of popes piled up. These critical characteristics are (1) whether the pope had been preceded in the papacy by a close relative, such as his father, brother, uncle, great-uncle, or grandfather; (2) whether the pope, when he was selected, already had a close relative who was an archbishop, cardinal, or bishop; (3) whether the pope came from a wealthy, powerful family, such as the Orsinis or Tusculums, with a history of influence over the selection of popes; and (4) whether the pope, after his selection, designated close relatives as cardinals (that is, what became known as cardinal-nephews), putting them in line to have a good prospect of be-coming pope in the future.

Figure 2.1 plots papal nepotism based on the proposed indicator of its prevalence. The level of papal nepotism that actually occurred per quarter century is reported from "none" to "very high" (at least ten elements of nepotism occurred). Hence, the dots in the graph show the total amount of papal nepotism in twenty-five-year blocks. The solid black line displays the best prediction of the level of nepotism over time such that the average differences between the solid line and the actual degrees of nepotism are minimized.[7] The graph reports the level of papal nepotism, starting in the early first century, with Saint Peter, the first pope, and continuing through 963, with Pope John XII (955–963). The year 963 also marks the rise of the Ottonian dynasty under Holy Roman Emperor Otto I. The Ottonian dynasty greatly ex-panded the power of the office of Holy Roman emperor, first held by Charlemagne—son of Pepin the Short—in 800 and created by Pope Leo III to provide a replacement protector for the church once it had divorced itself from the Byzantine emperor. The essential fact of note in the graph is that papal nepotism really took off after the creation of

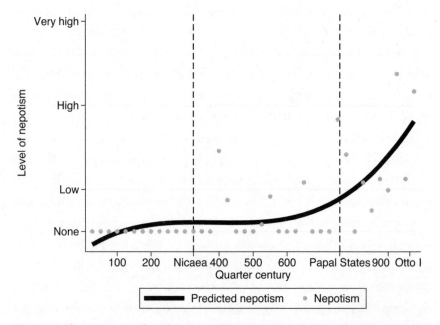

Figure 2.1: The occurrence of papal nepotism: From Saint Peter to Pope John XII

the Papal States and, except for a few brief exceptions, was essentially nonexistent before then.

PAPAL MANEUVERS TO INCREASE POLITICAL POWER

Once papal nepotism began to accelerate, popes were chosen for their ability to deliver power, prestige, and wealth to their families. The youngest was only twenty, well below the canonical age—that is, the minimum age, set by church law, at which one could be a bishop, which is the completion of the thirtieth year. Some men were not even priests when they were elevated to the papacy. And yet, regardless of youth, inexperience, and a dearth of training, the individual elevated to the papacy had extraordinary powers, powers that may even have been greater than those of a king or emperor. The Caesars of the church were unrivaled in their monopoly control of salvation. And what did that monopoly mean in practical, political, and economic terms?

Monopoly opens the door to higher prices. So it was with the price of forgiveness through penance to ensure the eternal life promised by the church. The church had realized early on that it could allow sinners to buy forgiveness, their indulgences coming in cash rather than in personal sacrifice and suffering. As one thoughtful scholar observed of this cash-for-forgiveness system, "Recidivism was always possible, and the commutation of sentence by payment of cash perpetuated the notion that salvation could be bought."[8] The money flowing in from the sale of forgiveness was significant. With its monopoly power over penance and other privileges, the church was encouraged onto a path of corruption and inefficiencies that could not be sustained when confronted with competition.

With its monopolistic power growing and its entrenched hierarchical structure assuring the church's leaders that they only needed to have support from a small group of people, their "winning coalition," the men at the top, no longer dedicated to the church's religious mission as their forefathers had been, instead followed what are today established principles for those who govern with low accountability and concentrated authority.[9] What do those established principles tell us?

All leaders, whether religious or secular, naturally want to stay in power. They can do so only if they manage relations correctly with two groups of people. One, the pool of people who have at least a nominal say in choosing their leaders, constitute what modern government theory calls "the selectorate." Because all bishops, for instance, were nominally elected by their local Christian community, that community was part of their selectorate. The selectorate's say about filling bishoprics, however, depended on approval by others, such as the local metropolitan bishop, and so their decision by itself was not binding. A portion of the selectorate, which government theory refers to as "the winning coalition," is the group of people whose support is essential for a leader, such as a bishop, a pope, a king, or an emperor, to come to and remain in power.

As long as the members of that coalition were kept happy, they would remain loyal, sticking faithfully to their leader's side and doing what they could to prevent rivals from deposing him. In exchange for their loyalty, the pope, bishop, king, or emperor, like any other form of leader, rewarded them with privileges and opportunities for enrichment. If denied sufficient rewards, their loyalty might waver. If any of their essential support were lost, the incumbent could expect to be overthrown and replaced by someone else. This means that to remain in power, the incumbent had to raise revenue and spend it wisely to keep the loyalty of his winning coalition. What makes a coalition stay loyal?

Wise spending means providing enough benefits that one's coalition of essential supporters believe they are better off with the incumbent than they would be by throwing their support to someone else. It turns out that the amount of revenue that must be spent to survive in power depends on how big a selectorate a ruler has and on how big a coalition he or she needs. If the coalition is a small proportion of the selectorate, as has been true in the Catholic Church to varying degrees since 325, then a smaller portion of revenue has to be spent to keep the coalition's loyalty. If, as in a more accountable government, the coalition is both large itself and a large portion of the selectorate, more needs to be spent. And, of course, any money left over after spending what is necessary to beat back challengers and secure loyalty can be used at the discretion of the ruler, maybe for the good of his or her followers and maybe to support a sumptuous lifestyle.

For a ruler to retain power, the share of money that he or she must spend on the good of *all* subjects depends neither on their subjects' needs nor on the ruler's sentiments. Rather, it depends on the size of the coalition and its expected loyalty. To keep coalition members loyal, the ruler must offer benefits at least as good as the best credible offer a rival could make. Of course, a would-be ruler can promise the stars, but once in power he or she has every incentive to shuffle the coalition to keep the least costly members, replacing any who are too demanding or are deemed insufficiently trustworthy.

Coalition members get two types of rewards. They get what economists call public goods, goods that benefit everyone (in the case of the church, the prospect of eternal salvation). They also get private benefits that are targeted just to members of the coalition (such as opportunities to engage freely in corruption or, in the case of the higher medieval clergy, special religious privileges and opportunities for opulent lifestyles). These special, private benefits are expensive. Hence, as the coalition grows and special benefits have to be doled out to more recipients, private rewards begin to be nudged aside, replaced by general policies—public goods—that benefit all. This has two consequences.

First, as the coalition grows, its members get fewer special benefits, so the ruler has to spend more revenue to keep their loyalty, compensating them with more public goods to replace the more prized private benefits that have been cut back. Second, coalition loyalty is weakened, because as the coalition makes up a bigger percentage of the selectorate, it is less risky for members to abandon the incumbent since they are likely to be needed by the ruler's successor too. Conversely, especially when the coalition is small relative to the selectorate, as it is in the Catholic Church, loyalty is strong. A small coalition gets most of its rewards in the form of exclusive private advantages that induce loyalty and that are affordable for the incumbent because only a few people have to be paid sumptuously. When the coalition is small and the selectorate is large, it is very risky for a member of the coalition to gamble on throwing support to a rival since the chances of being in the successor's coalition depends on how many are needed and how big a pool they are drawn from. Thus, as the papal coalition shrank—as it did in later periods, as we will see—then the lifestyles among the church's leaders became resplendent and, as expected by the principles that have just been reviewed, the church drifted farther away from choosing its leaders by the will of the people and clergy and more toward an autocratic, nepotistic dictatorship. Thus, the powerful leaders of the church became seekers of personal aggrandizement. The church shifted from an organization whose leaders were prepared to become martyrs, willing to face death rather than compromise their beliefs, to an organization whose leaders had greatly weakened religious convictions and greatly enhanced interests in the acquisition of land and power.

The leaders of the church knew how to exploit their greatly improved political situation. Kings now looked to the pope to anoint them, granting them the valuable imprimatur of the church. Pepin the Short had been the first so honored and legitimated. After him, anointment by the pope was almost a necessity for any legitimate ruler. Coronation, accompanied by anointment, called for kings and Holy Roman emperors to declare loyalty to the church and to promise to protect it. In a time when oaths were taken extremely seriously, deviating from the assurance of fealty was an important matter, one that could involve excommunication and, in the event of death during excommunication, deprivation of the great promise of Christianity—eternal salvation. This was a power unique to the pope. He alone could legitimate a ruler, even a usurper, by crowning him. It was a power not exercised lightly.

The pope sought benefits for the church (and through it, himself) in exchange for legitimation of rulers. He demanded and obtained protection for the church by the lay leaders of Europe. He also demanded, and obtained, payments of money given directly to the papal see, such as Peter's pence, to facilitate the church's operations and to supplement its other—soon to be growing—sources of revenue. How extraordinary a change in stature the pope and the church had undergone from the martyred popes of Christianity's earliest times! And how extraordinary that change was when we remember that as the papacy exercised these unique powers, its highest post was captured as a family business. The apostolic power of the pope, as the successor to Saint Peter as bishop of Rome, was now accompanied not by anything like personal holiness but, rather, by nepotism and greed. That departure from holiness not only did not go unnoticed in Europe, but it also began to stir up trouble. With the church controlled by powerful families, Holy Roman emperors, especially during the tenth and eleventh centuries, began to ask, Why should they not, once again, as in the times of the Roman and Byzantine emperors, control appointment to the papacy and all of its exceptional assets?

THE STRUGGLE OVER THE INVESTITURE OF BISHOPS

Power, money, and family advantage were the temptations that fell upon the newly empowered and enriched church thanks to the deal that resulted in the creation of the Papal States. Now, in ways not true before, there was something really valuable to fight over beyond the church's religious mission. Now control over the bishops of the church was more important than at any time since the collapse of the Roman Empire. Now new prospects were introduced for the assertion of Catholic hegemony in the secular as well as the sacred domain.

In the first few decades after securing the Papal States, the church, not yet beset by the demands of the soon-to-be created Holy Roman emperor, understood that the moment was at hand to seize authority over the choice of bishops in the West, thereby liberating itself from secular jurisdiction. After all, those who occupied the posts of bishop across Europe were the most important individuals defining the nexus between spiritual and secular authority. They alone were the overseers of the path to salvation and to harmony or discord between the church and the temporal powers of the day. As the distinguished historian Jörg Peltzer, aptly put it:

> The bishop . . . was the spiritual leader of the people and the clergy and exercised the supreme jurisdictional authority over ecclesiastical matters in his diocese. The bishop was also a secular lord . . . exercising influence well beyond his diocesan borders. Thus combining spiritual and secular powers the bishop was a focal point for the flock, the local ecclesiastics and the pope, the aristocracy and the ruler; his election was of great interest to many people.[10]

Control over the selection of bishops proved to be difficult exactly because every bishop embodied both spiritual and temporal power. Few among those imbued with authority, whether that authority's source was the secular or the spiritual sword, were content to defer to the wishes of others in conferring the awesome power that a bishop had over the people in his see, over forgiveness, over the assessment of rectitude, over the actions of even the highest lords, over the sacraments, and, ultimately, over the expectation of salvation. With great variation in the political status of local lords, monarchs, and clergy, bishops were chosen through a variety of practices.

When the time came to elect a bishop, in principle "the consent of the laity was absolutely necessary to render it valid," although in reality the laity were often subject to pressure to acquiesce to the wishes of others, such as their metropolitan bishop, the local lord, or the king.[11] In modern parlance, many bishops were chosen through rigged elections. The days when bishops were elected by the people over the objections of the local or higher clergy, as Bishop Cyprian of Carthage was in the mid-third century, had mostly passed. The office was just too valuable and too powerful to be left to the people to fill.

Everyone understood that control over bishops was a crucial determinant of the balance between church and "state," between what was rendered unto temporal rulers and what was rendered unto the church, if not unto God. Thus, the method by which bishops were selected depended on the customs or practices in different locales and at different times. Bishops might have been chosen through local election; or they might have been appointed by church authorities, by local secular authorities, or by monarchs; or they might have been selected by other practices. The office of bishop might have been filled in recognition of a candidate's religious calling, spiritual vision, or, alas, the deepness of his pockets, the post being sold to the highest bidder.

In this "Wild West" period of bishop selection, even the choice of the most influential bishops, like the patriarchs (popes) of Rome and Constantinople, was generally outside the control of the church. The bishop of Rome had depended for two centuries on the favor of the Byzantine emperor for his job. By the mid-eighth century, however, that was no longer true, as the Byzantine emperor was occupied with managing the threat to his empire from Muslim invaders. Under these circumstances, as we have seen, the power of the pope in Rome grew tremendously.

Papal hegemony was near its peak when Theophylactus of Tusculum was elected as Pope Benedict IX in 1032. Theophylactus was the son of Alberic III, the duke of Tusculum, and the nephew of Pope Benedict VIII. He was, unsurprisingly, his father's candidate but was opposed by Giovanni de' Crescenzi-Ottaviani, a member of the great family of competitors of the Tusculums, the Crescenzis. Alberic allegedly bought enough votes for his son to win, but the friction between the families continued and with it, the descent of papal prestige as the church lost its domination over prochurch "public" discourse.[12] Eventually, well into his papacy's first interlude, Benedict IX had pretty much lost the backing of the people of Rome. He fled the city, chased away by a popular uprising against him in 1044.[13]

After considerable infighting, Giovanni managed to get himself elected (anti)pope even though Benedict IX was alive and well. Giovanni named himself Sylvester III and managed to hang on to the papacy from January 20, 1045, until March 10 of that same year. Theophylactus—that is, Benedict IX—was not inclined to take his usurpation lying down. He excommunicated his rival, drove him from Rome in March, and reestablished himself as pope. Sylvester returned to his bishopric in Sabina. The records show no evidence that he made any attempt to retake the papacy after his expulsion. So now the church had, depending on whose camp one was in, either two living popes or one pope and one antipope, each having been deposed against his will and each having succeeded, albeit through corruption, in securing election to the papacy.[14]

Benedict's return to the papacy was, by his own devising, short-lived. Less than two months after his return to Rome, he *sold* the papacy to his godfather, Johannes Gratian. Why he did so and why his godfather agreed to make the purchase are important for an understanding of the subsequent effort to control the papacy by the Holy Roman emperor. One well-regarded nearly contemporaneous account, written about twenty years after the events, explains what happened during the Synod of Sutri, called by the German king and soon-to-be Holy Roman emperor, Henry III, specifically to address the sale of the papacy to Gratian, now called Pope Gregory VI. The account states:

> The cause of this assembly was three Popes who were all alike living at that time. For the first of them abandoned the see by reason of an unlawful marriage which he contracted; he retired by his own will rather than by the pressure of any opposition. Wherefore, while he was still living in the flesh, the Romans conspired together and set up another Pope. The first, however, sold his office for money to a third, because in his wrath he refused that one subject to him should have it. To be brief, they were all judged in this synod, and deposed; and Suitger, bishop of Bamberg, a man worthy of the see, was chosen by the whole council of clergy and people.[15]

According to this nearly contemporaneous account, Benedict IX had married, an act contrary to the norms of the time for the pope and an act that certainly would have alienated his subjects in Rome. Whether he married or not is contested, but there is no doubt that he sold the papacy, a shocking act even in his time. Gratian, a man reputed to have been deeply religious, acknowledged that he paid a large sum for the office of pope so as to get his godson to abandon the position in favor of someone—himself—who would try to return it to a more religious calling. Purchasing the papacy, or any ecclesiastical office, however, is the sin of simony.

Although many accounts at the time indicate that Gregory VI was well received as pope by Henry III, it is also clear that Henry recognized that Gregory's simony created the opportunity to impose a German pope who could be expected to be loyal to him. Thus, less than a week after Gregory's deposition, Bishop Suitger of Bamberg became the new pope (Clement II), marking the beginning of a sequence of German popes. Alas, Clement died less than ten months after assuming his office. The cause of death was lead poisoning, perhaps because he drank too much German wine, which contained lead, or more likely, because his wine was intentionally laced with lead, as modern forensic medicine indicates.[16]

Benedict's act of selling the papacy and Henry's act of deposing Gregory and imposing Clement launched the Investiture Controversy over who had the right to choose bishops. Thus, in Benedict's and Gregory's fall we have the overt beginning of the great struggle between imperial and papal authority, a struggle that nominally ended in 1122, would resurge in 1302, and in important respects did not end until 1648. The actions of Henry III, Benedict IX, and Gregory VI triggered a turning point in the history of the church, in the history of the Holy Roman Empire, and in the history and trajectory of Europe. That last new direction persists to this day, although, of course, no one at the moment would have recognized what was to follow for the next thousand years.

With Benedict having resigned, Sylvester's legitimacy never acknowledged, and Gregory deposed by Henry, three questions dominated the day:

1. Who should control the selection of bishops, including the highest bishop of all?
2. What cause could justify the removal of a bishop, including the highest bishop of all?
3. Who could depose a bishop, including the highest bishop of all?

These were not new questions. They had been critical concerns for the church's leaders when Emperor Constantine seized control over the appointment of bishops across the Roman Empire in the first quarter of the fourth century. The answers to these questions had swung briefly in favor of the church after it became the official religion of the Roman Empire in the late fourth century. The determination of the choice of bishops swung again in favor of the secular powers of the day when the Byzantine emperor asserted the right to choose even the pope in Rome, only to abandon that power in 752. That these questions were being asked once again was indicative of the declining power and prestige of the papacy and the great struggle that ensued to restore that power and prestige on the part of the church and to suppress that power, if not the prestige of the pope, on the part of the Holy Roman emperor and his allies.

Given the great power of bishops as the critical link between the competing secular and religious domains, the first and third questions are especially pertinent if we are to understand the approaching pivotal moment embodied in the Concordat of Worms eighty years later. How these questions were to be settled was the foundation of the struggle between church and state, between the pope and the emperor, that was so important in the creation of modern Europe's exceptionalism.

The claim that bishops were vicars of Christ dates back at least to Saint Ignatius's Epistle to the Magnesians, which declared around 100 CE, "Your bishop presides in the place of God."[17] But by the time of the Investiture Controversy the pope had come to claim that he, perhaps even more so than other bishops, was God's primary agent on earth, that he was *Vicarius Christi*. This claim was made into canon law a century later by Pope Innocent III (1198–1216). Certainly only God could remove the pope, and at least from Innocent's time, the pope unambiguously was the only person with the right to remove bishops. But in the eleventh century, the Holy Roman emperor contended that he was emperor thanks to the grace of God, who had chosen him above all others, and that therefore he too had authority to remove bishops, including even the pope.

The Council of Nicaea's canon 4 had seemingly provided a definitive answer to the first question, at least in the eyes of a prochurch faction. As the anonymous author of the influential *De ordinando pontifice* (On the establishment of the pope) argued in 1048, "Who elects the one that we work for? Those who stand closest to the church; if he is not called by the bishops, he is not received immediately by the church; if so, he is not legitimate, because for the ordination of a bishop, according to the council of Nicaea, all bishops of the province should be convoked and meet and if not, there has to be written consent."[18] In this view, not even the Holy Roman emperor could install a bishop who was not chosen by the bishops of the church. The Council of Nicaea also suggested an answer to the third question, and it is here that all the troubles between kings and church come into full focus.

For hundreds of years, as the Roman Empire contracted and died, the church had been the dominant authority. Again we turn to *De*

Ordinando Pontifice for the argument on who can depose a pope. The anonymous author reminds his readers—remember he is writing in 1048 when the issue is front and center—of an argument made by Emperor Constantine:

> O' pious Emperor Constantine, you who obeyed the holy Pope, Sylvester, you who lowered your head as he blessed you, say what you have apparently learned of the higher honour of the office of the bishop from the synod of Nicaea: "You," he said, "cannot be judged by anyone because you alone are reserved for the judgement of God; bishops are namely called gods, and cannot therefore be judged by men."[19]

The author of *De Ordinando Pontifice* was not alone in arguing that kings could not remove popes. The case was also made by Bishop Wazo of Liège (985–1048, bishop from 1041 until his death): "Therefore, since you have been pleased to ask for our opinion, it is that Your Sublimity should refrain from placing someone in the office of a person who is still alive, since this is permitted neither by divine nor human law, and the holy fathers have laid down both in words and writing that the pope is to be judged by no one unless by God himself."[20] These and other arguments in support of the church echoed the sentiment expressed in 1 Corinthians 2:15: "But he that is spiritual judgeth all things, yet he himself is judged of no man." The Holy Roman emperor and a faction of church leaders saw it differently.

The emperor, in removing the pope, had demonstrated the potential for secular authority to trump the ecclesiastical in the selection and in the removal of the highest church official. The church rebelled at the emperor's claim to have the right to remove or to select the pope. Starting with Bishop Suitger in his capacity as Pope Clement II and then really gaining steam after his sudden death, a faction of the church's leaders launched a powerful reform movement intended to forge a less corrupt and more religious church. They intended both to strengthen the church and to stop the secular authorities from interfering in the selection of the pope or, indeed, any church official. They sought to re-establish the church as a great independent power in Europe. And of course, that reformist bent was also consistent with their ambition to more effectively consolidate political power in the hands of the papacy rather than sharing it with secular rulers, whether local, such as the Tusculum family, or international, such as the Holy Roman emperor.

A synod was called in 1059 at which the church's leaders set down rules for selecting popes through what came to be the College of Cardinals. Their ostensible motivation was to control the usurpation of control over the church through simony. Their remedy, as distinguished papal historian Bernhard Schimmelpfennig has noted, was to back "free elections—again with recourse to the ideals of the church—which, in the case of the bishops, were to take place among 'the clergy and the people,' and in the case of the abbots, among the monks of the cloister."[21] Thus, for the election of the pope, the members of the synod introduced a quasi-representative electoral system in which selected bishops, representing the community of bishops, who themselves indirectly represented their diocesan Christian communities, were given the authority to select the pope.[22]

The synod of 1059 was a critical moment in the struggle between the church and secular rulers. Among the many distinguished church leaders who participated in setting the synod in motion and making it transformative, one stood out then and stands out today for his role in trying to put the church back on a more independent and pious path. Hildebrand of Sovana, later to be Pope Gregory VII (1073–1085), was a former student—and loyal admirer—of Johannes Gratian, that is, Pope Gregory VI, whose deposition in 1046 began the Investiture Controversy. Hildebrand had already proven himself to be an indispensable reformer by the time of the 1059 synod. He was central to the ouster of the antireformist pope Benedict X (1058–1059), brother of Benedict IX. To depose the pope, Hildebrand worked closely with Gerard of Burgundy, ensuring that Benedict would quit and that Gerard would be elected Pope Nicholas II (1059–1061), thereby assuring an intense, reformist bent at the top of the church. Nicholas, of course, convened the synod of 1059. More than a decade later, when Hildebrand himself was elected pope, he engaged in a no-holds-barred campaign to settle whether the church and its new quasi-representative political system was in control of its own fate or whether it was, as it had been for much of the time from Emperor Constantine at least to the eighth century and then again up to Gregory's own time, subject to the wishes of secular rulers.

In Gregory's view, no one could become a bishop, invested with the religious symbols, signs, and meaning of that post, who was selected by any other than the church. As Abbot Abbo of Fleury explained:

> The Holy Spirit has said through the mouth of the blessed Pope Gregory "that that benediction shall turn for them into a malediction who is thus promoted to be a heretic, and by this malediction he shall have no profit who thinks for the sake of money to invade an office in the church." The custom has now grown so much that laymen sell bishoprics.... And if you ask them who made them bishops they will answer quite freely, saying "I was recently ordained by the archbishop, and gave him a hundred shillings to have episcopal consecration."[23]

Contrary to Gregory VII's firmly stipulated view, some authorities, both secular and religious, used diocesan vacancies as opportunities to sell bishoprics for their own profit. Now such acts were declared to be outrages that could—and did—result in excommunication even of kings and emperors. The bitter battle over to whom the church hierarchy owed their loyalty eventually produced diplomatic agreements between kings and pope over the appointment of bishops. But before diplomacy could prevail, the emperor and the pope were essentially at war with one another.

THE POPE'S WAR WITH THE HOLY ROMAN EMPEROR

To strengthen the church in its fight against the Holy Roman emperor, Pope Gregory VII shrank the size of the coalition of supporters he and his successors needed to hold their offices. They made the new, emerging College of Cardinals and cascading "representative" bodies of authority in the church into a *more* autocratic regime, quite different from the early principle of bishop selection by the people and the clergy. To apply the principles I laid out earlier: the fewer people needed to make someone pope and the more narrowly defined the group from which they were drawn, the lower the risk that outsiders could successfully interfere with the workings of the church and the interests of the incumbent pope. Figure 2.2 displays the shifting number of supporters needed to form a winning coalition sufficient to select a pope. The vertical axis—the size of the coalition—is expressed as the number of persons needed, depicted on a logarithmic scale. The logarithmic scale is required because otherwise everything after the Council of Nicaea would look essentially as if it were zero compared to the large coalition needed to pick the bishop of Rome before 325.

Before the Council of Nicaea, the group whose support was required to select the bishop of Rome included, at least in principle, a majority of the local Roman Christian community. After Nicaea, that required group was greatly diminished to include essentially only the metropolitan bishops and, possibly, just the local metropolitan and the emperor. Through the mechanism of the metropolitan's veto, Roman Emperor Constantine had made the nascent church of his time into a small-coalition, autocratic regime that would do his bidding in exchange for the great benefits, including exorbitant salaries, he bestowed on the church's leaders.[24] During the rise of the Holy Roman Empire, starting

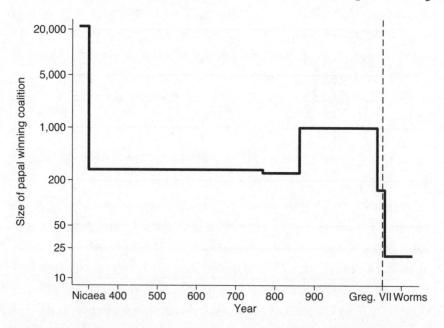

Figure 2.2: The papal winning coalition: How Much Gregory VII reduced it!

after 800, the required papal coalition became somewhat larger, perhaps as the church found it necessary to incorporate some imperial interests as part of the price it had to pay for the emperor's guarantee of the church's security.

When Gregory VII became pope in 1073, as Figure 2.2 highlights, he almost immediately greatly diminished the coalition of backers on whom he needed to rely. Initially, there was a decrease from around a thousand to about two hundred needed votes, and then, a few years into his papacy, he instituted a further diminution in the pope's winning coalition, bringing it down to about twenty-five, a remarkable decrease in just a handful of years.

Gregory, even before he became pope, had already formed a coalition within the papal curia. That coalition pushed through the establishment of a College of Cardinals whose members would eventually be truly responsible for choosing the pope and whose membership shrank as its power grew. This new institution could be—and was—used to shore up loyalty to Gregory's reformist agenda and to squeeze out imperial influence. And as befits the leader of a more autocratic regime that depended on the support of fewer people to sustain itself, Gregory and his successors understood that the cardinals, the curia, and other papal legates had to have their rewards. As Schimmelpfennig put it with regard to the period from Gregory VII to the time of the Concordat of Worms and beyond, "More frequently than in the two preceding epochs [of larger winning coalitions], popes rewarded their supporters with privileges—especially exemptions—and in so doing changed the structure of the church to their advantage."[25]

Undoubtedly, Gregory VII's reformist actions before and during his papacy were a response to the emperor's interference in the deposition of Gregory VI. That, of course, was the purpose behind Gregory VII's reformist movement: to diminish "outsider," secular influence over the purpose, the functions, and the wealth of the church.[26] The reduced coalition introduced by Gregory VII persisted through the signing of the Concordat of Worms in 1122 and a while beyond that.

The extent to which the reduced coalition of essential supporters were themselves wedded to the clerical or the secular interests of the day depended on the pope's ability to eliminate as prospective bishops, archbishops, and cardinals those who owed allegiance to temporal rulers rather than to the Catholic Church. Indeed, to look ahead for a moment, this division in the selection of bishops between those loyal to the church and those loyal to their lay leader would be the central mechanism by which the concordats of 1107 and 1122 would resolve the battle over the investiture of bishops. And it was the incentives created by this division of loyalties, rather than cultural, religious, or other sources of superiority, that would in turn produce Western exceptionalism.

Naturally, given the great importance of family ties as a source of loyalty, nepotism was one of the best ways for church leaders to weed out rival perspectives. If, however, the imperial side were successful at reining in the church's power, then papal nepotism should have declined with the rise of the Ottonian dynasty of Holy Roman emperors. Declining nepotism would be a pretty clear signal that imperial efforts were working to undermine the threat the church represented to the emperor's secular authority. If the balance of power favored the church, then the church should have successfully fought to use nepotism to assure internal loyalty to the pope. The combination of a smaller required coalition

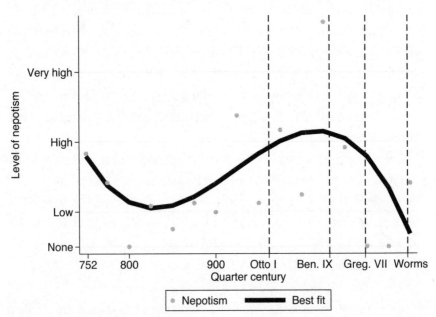

Figure 2.3: Nepotism: Loyalty to pope versus Holy Roman emperor

and increased assurance that the church's leadership would be drawn from loyal backers could have been a key recipe for improving the odds that the pope could have strong backing in the struggle with the Holy Roman emperor.

Figure 2.3 picks up our examination of nepotism just as Pope Stephen II and King Pepin the Short struck their deal in the eighth century. The figure highlights the years 963, when Otto I became Holy Roman emperor; 1032, when Benedict IX became pope; 1073, when Gregory VII became pope and launched his reform movement; and 1122, when the Concordat of Worms was signed, ending the Investiture Controversy.

The solid curved line in the figure represents the best-fitting approximation of the level of nepotism for each quarter century. The actual degree of nepotism is depicted by the gray dots. The graph indicates that nepotism, after a brief decline at the start of the internal struggle over papal domination, was then on the rise for a long stretch until the emergence of the Ottonian dynasty of Holy Roman emperors. This is also what we saw in Figure 2.1. Then, as we have discussed, the emperors sought to rein in the papacy's growing potential to be a political threat, and as Figure 2.3 makes clear, they were slowly, but surely, successful. Between the rise of Otto I as Holy Roman emperor and the selection of Benedict IX as pope, the papacy's nepotistic awards to family members rose, but then nepotism suffered a serious backlash and went on the decline starting with Benedict IX's selection as pope, precipitating the start of the Investiture Controversy, and continued its recession at least until the struggle over who controlled the investiture of bishops was resolved in 1122.

The reduction in papal nepotism following Henry III's deposition of Gregory VI is consistent with the idea that the balance of power had shifted toward the emperor and away from the pope. As the balance seemed to swing sharply in favor of imperial interests with the deposition of Gregory VI and the imposition of a German pope, Clement II, the church's leaders responded by fighting back through the reform movement. As Figure 2.3 demonstrates, the Investiture Controversy indeed was a critical turning point in the political battle for control. Power had swung to the emperor, but for how long?

The graph of nepotism between 752 and 1122 is consistent with the idea that the dispute over control of the appointment of bishops was underway before Hildebrand's efforts of the late 1050s, let alone his intense efforts during his rule as Pope Gregory VII, between 1073 and 1085. Although historians of this period often argue that the controversy was a clash of personalities between the pope and the emperor, it seems that it was, indeed, a struggle over control of bishops as essential political figures in Europe.[27] Nepotism was in retreat during the Investiture Controversy, but it certainly was not dead before the signing of the Concordat of Worms. Whether it would be dead or would be resurrected during the interlude of the concordats remains to be seen.

As loyalty was under attack within the papal succession, the pope was emboldened in his reform movement, which was aimed, in part, at diminishing the influence of the Holy Roman emperor in matters pertaining to the church's leaders and its policies. Gregory VII reiterated and expanded upon the view of Pope Nicholas I (858–867) that the pope could judge secular rulers. Gregory's expansion of this idea included the notion that the pope alone had the authority to choose and to depose even emperors.[28] And so he did. Gregory VII excommunicated Holy Roman Emperor Henry IV in 1077 and again in 1080. Indeed, Henry was not done being a thorn in the church's side even after Gregory died. Henry was excommunicated again in 1091, in 1094, and, together with his son, soon-to-be Holy Roman Emperor Henry V, yet again in 1102.

So intense was the conflict between Gregory and Henry that Gregory's foes accused him at the time of trying to provoke a popular uprising against the emperor. Beno, cardinal priest of Santi Martino and Silvestro, for instance, offering the equivalent of the first mean tweet, told those who had sworn loyalty to Gregory, "He is perverse, to whom you gave your oath. He is wicked, and a perjurer, and a criminal; you do not owe fidelity to him. This indeed, my lord pope, we read in your writings, this indeed, we have heard carried throughout the world by your evangelists."[29] It clearly is not an exaggeration to suggest that in a series of letters and pamphlets—hundreds of them—exchanged between their respective propapal and proimperial parties, the pope and the emperor would both try to foment a revolutionary uprising against the other.[30]

As Guido of Ferrara, a loyal follower of Henry IV, wrote of Hildebrand (whom he rarely referred to as Pope Gregory):

> First then, it is proven that his manner of life was contrary to the rule of the Holy Fathers. That he also promoted this, we shall show in the proper place. From a boy he followed secular business and paid attention to military affairs. He involved himself in many killings. He polluted himself with sacrilege. He tied himself up with perjuries. In addition, he set sons in arms against their parents, set vassals against kings, aroused servants against their masters, and throughout the world destroyed the peace of the Church.

As if this were not sufficient, in his long polemic condemning Gregory, Guido goes on to lay the war in Saxony and other tragedies of the time squarely at Gregory's feet:

> It is agreed then that he can be called a murderer or a perjurer.... He was guilty on all these counts ... in that he gave orders for Rudolf [of Swabia], to be set up as king against his own lord, despite the many oaths of loyalty that bound him. He absolved all the other German magnates from their oaths of loyalty owed to King Henry, and roused them, by letters and by frequent legations, to go to war with him. In this he truly polluted himself with sacrilege, since he sent them the money which [Saint] Peter's devotees had given to the Church, to stir them up to even greater hatred.[31]

The war of words and deeds between the pope and the emperor had become intense indeed. The pope was losing on the nepotism front. Did he have other tools at his disposal to win at least the people, if not the emperor, over to his side? One way we can check out the shifting power to control the people might be teased out by using a different yardstick, one independent of nepotism, to assess the balance of church and imperial power during the same years covered by Figure 2.3.

There are several ways we might estimate and illustrate the rise or decline of church hegemony. We have already seen Gregory VII's

effort to reassert his authority by shrinking his coalition of loyal backers so as to concentrate church power in his hands, but that measure,
like nepotism, was tied directly to internal church decisions and so is
not a fully independent metric. I suggest we look at the distribution of
Christian and non-Christian artwork in Europe between the creation
of the Papal States and the settlement of the Investiture Controversy
at Worms in 1122. Artwork has always been an important indicator
of prominence in the public sphere, a vehicle for communicating the
importance of rulers and events.[32]

Indeed, in a world in which few could expect to ever cast their eyes
on their rulers (and that world spanned virtually all of human history
until only the past few decades), it was statues, mosaics, frescoes, and,
later, paintings that conveyed rulers' eminence and greatness. As the
Christian historian and commentator Eusebius (263–339) observed
of Roman Emperor Constantine, "[He] held in subjection all the to-
parchs, ethnarchs, satraps and kings of barbarian nations of every
kind. These spontaneously saluted and greeted him, and . . . they hon-
oured him at home with pictures of him and dedications of statues,
and alone of emperors Constantine was recognized and acclaimed by
them all."[33]

The church understood from its beginnings that it could spread the
message of its power by commissioning and disseminating Christian
art and other subjects clearly associated with Christianity. As it grew in
power, it undertook to further promote itself by limiting and even, when
possible, extinguishing non-Christian images, whether they were secular, mythological, or pagan.[34] Can we observe empirically whether any
such effort to suppress secular imagery was successful? Naturally, any
such measurement can only be imperfect. Still, I believe it is possible
to create a plausible approximation of the shifting power of Christian
and secular interests over a long sweep of European history. To do so I
use the images of European art found in the leading contemporary art
history textbooks.[35] I assume the authors did not choose what to include
based on anything like the thesis I have put forth; rather, I assume they
sought to depict the important, influential images of different times and
from different places in Europe. My contention is that the important,

representative, or influential art of Europe will also display the relative power of Christian and secular—imperial—sources.[36]

Figure 2.4 displays, by quarter century, the percentage of European artwork whose primary theme was non-Christian or secularly oriented art rather than religious, Christian imagery. The solid black line shows a statistical estimation of the best-fitting curve for the individual observations, which are shown as gray dots for each twenty-five-year period. As in Figure 2.3, vertical demarcations note the beginning of Otto I's reign as Holy Roman emperor, the selection of Benedict IX as pope, and the election of Gregory VII as the reformist pope who led the Investiture Struggle. Thus, Figure 2.4 parallels and highlights the periods emphasized in Figure 2.3 on nepotism. Both figures give us ways to examine the relative power of the secular sphere and of the church during the time when the competition between church and state came to a boil. Figure 2.4 begins at the crucial moment in 752 when the Byzantine emperor lost the right to choose the bishop of Rome and ends in 1122 when the signing of the Concordat of Worms officially ended the dispute over the appointment of bishops.

As is evident in Figure 2.4, the proportion of non-Christian or secular art dropped steeply starting about forty or fifty years after Charlemagne's coronation in 800 as Holy Roman emperor, gradually driven to nonexistence until the start of the Investiture Struggle over who could choose bishops. Charlemagne, and his son, Louis the Pious, coruled from 813 until Charlemagne died in 814. Louis died in 840. But Louis's reign was torn by civil war between his sons Lothair I and Charles the Bald, a conflict that culminated in the division of the Carolingian kingdom and the creation of Germany as the new seat of the Holy Roman empire. Naturally, with the Carolingian monarchs at loggerheads, the church was temporarily advantaged in its pursuit of political influence, as suggested in Figure 2.4 by the decline in secular art starting in mid-century. Still, even amid its troubles, the Carolingian dynasty generally demonstrated loyalty and devotion to the teachings of the church, facilitating the church's efforts to boost its authority across Europe. As I. S. Robinson reports, "The fact that only the priests could administer the sacraments on which Christian society depended set them apart from

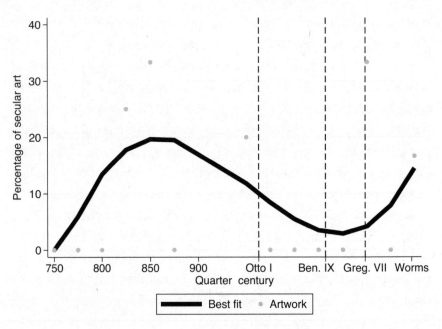

Figure 2.4: Christian representation in art rises before the Investiture Controversy and then declines.

the rest—the legal aspects of this separation appear in Carolingian legislation—and exalted them above the laity."[37] That exaltation was not to last long or go unmodified. Once Benedict IX became pope, the situation changed dramatically.

After Benedict's election in 1032 and continuing at least until the Concordat of Worms in 1122, secular imagery began to make a comeback, diminishing the proportion of art that was about Christian subjects, suggesting a diminution in the church's and pope's power to control the narrative of the time, much as we saw with the decline of nepotism during the Investiture Controversy. During the height of the Investiture Controversy starting in 1046 and ending with the signing of the Concordat of Worms in 1122, secular art was resurrected to become about one-fifth of the art as recorded by the present-day leading art history textbooks.

Figures 2.3 and 2.4 highlight what everyone who was paying attention knew in 1032: Theophylactus's election as Pope Benedict IX was fraught with difficulties. In the wake of his selection, papal nepotism, which had been thriving, began to collapse, and secular art, which had become all but nonexistent, began to recover. Benedict's selection clearly marked a crucial turning point; treating the papacy as a family business had gone too far! The secular sword, in the hands of the Holy Roman emperor, was pulled from its sheath and wielded with a strong hand and an outstretched arm to limit the power of the church.

Benedict IX's election highlighted the mounting displeasure of the Holy Roman emperor with the dealings of the church. By the time Benedict sold his papacy to his godfather, the urge to recapture control over the highest church appointments had become irresistible for the emperor, and by the time Hildebrand became Pope Gregory VII, the church's willingness to tolerate the emperor's interference was at its end. Indeed, the dispute between Emperor Henry IV and the pope over whose sword was the more powerful had no parallel. The emperor himself was not reluctant to condemn the pope. He spoke out directly against Hildebrand in a series of letters. For instance, in a letter of January 24, 1076, three years into Gregory's papacy, Henry wrote:

Henry, king not through usurpation but through the holy ordination of God, to Hildebrand, at present not pope but false monk.

Such greeting as this hast thou merited through thy disturbances, inasmuch as there is no grade in the church which thou hast omitted to make a partaker not of honour but of confusion, not of benediction but of malediction. For, to mention few and especial cases out of many, not only hast thou not feared to lay hands upon the rulers of the holy church, the anointed of the Lord—the archbishops, namely, bishops and priests—but thou hast trodden them under foot like slaves ignorant of what their master is doing. Thou hast won favour from the common herd by crushing them; thou hast looked upon all of them as knowing nothing, upon thy sole self, moreover, as knowing all things. This knowledge, however, thou hast used not for edification but for destruction; so that with reason we believe that St. Gregory, whose name thou has usurped for thyself, was prophesying concerning thee when he said: "The pride of him who is in power increases the more, the greater the number of those subject to him; and he thinks that he himself can do more than all."[38]

The Investiture Controversy, prompted by Benedict IX's sale of the papacy to his godfather and his godfather's willingness to buy it and become Gregory VI, had exploded into a war of words between the imperial and papal factions. And if those words were to be believed, the controversy had erupted practically into open warfare. The imperial side declared Hildebrand, that is, Pope Gregory VII, to be a false pope and proceeded to elect and install a new antipope. Gregory VII and his loyal followers denied the antipope, excommunicated the emperor, and produced a monumental conflict that is sometimes described as Europe's first revolution.[39] The struggle over whether worldly, secular rulers or the church and pope had the right to determine who would hold clerical positions, including bishoprics, persisted for decades without a solution. When it was officially, if not truly, resolved, it set into motion the transformation of Europe's political structure; altered the incentives of kings and popes; invented newly defined domains of power for popes, for kings, and even for peasants; and inaugurated the march toward modern, "exceptional," Europe. It is to those changes that I now turn.

3

THE CONCORDAT GAME

The one elected ... may receive the regalia from thee.

—Pope Calixtus II

POPE GREGORY VII DIED IN 1085, BUT THE WAR OF WORDS OVER THE investiture of bishops did not die with him. It did not die when Emperor Henry IV breathed his last breath in 1105. Nor was it settled easily and quickly once Henry's son became the new emperor, Henry V. Instead, the dispute escalated into open warfare between the church and the imperial government. Much else was going on across Europe that was of deep importance and could have competed to be the main story of the time, but investiture was the issue that would dominate the eight decades between the deposition of Gregory VI and the signing of treaties in France and England in 1107 and in Germany in 1122.

We must not overlook the other great religious battle that was happening before and during the early phases of the Investiture Controversy: the East–West schism. This profound division within the Catholic world between the Roman Catholic Church and the Orthodox Church began when Pope Leo III made Charlemagne Holy Roman emperor in 800, making him a substitute for the Byzantine emperor in the west. It culminated with the split between the Roman Catholic Church and the Orthodox Church in 1054. But that split—still a source of tension to this day—was a fait accompli by the time Henry IV and Gregory VII were at each other's throats. By the start of the twelfth century, the struggle over the selection of bishops within the Roman Catholic world was surely the headline news.

The procedure for appointing bishops was finally resolved between the church and the kings of England and France in 1107. Pope Paschal II, after an aborted effort to resolve the controversy over the investiture of bishops with the Holy Roman emperor in late 1106, traveled to France to settle the matter with the kings of France and England.[1] Progress had been made and a policy outlined for the broader settlement of the dispute, but nevertheless, the controversy persisted and was not settled between the empire and the church for another fifteen years. Finally, following the outline of the agreements with the English and the French, the Investiture Controversy was resolved when the Concordat of Worms was accepted by both the pope and the Holy Roman emperor.

To flesh out how the concordats rearranged incentives, resulting in the promotion of greater secularization and economic growth in some parts of Europe and not in others, we need first to examine the substance of the agreements in England, France, and Worms. Then we can begin to assess the details that reveal the fundamental strategic implications and consequences of the concordats. Those implications and consequences will then be tested against the record of history.[2]

THE TERMS OF THE CONCORDATS

Both England's King Henry I (reign 1100–1135) and France's King Philip I (reign 1060–1108) signed significant diplomatic agreements with Pope Paschal II (papacy from 1099–1118) designed to resolve the struggles between religious and secular powers over the appointment of bishops, the first but not the last such agreements. In the Concordat of London, Henry agreed to a (temporary) transfer to the church of regalia—that is, rights, especially property rights, that were recognized as solely the king's in his capacity as king (or the rights, including rights to revenue, of a diocese's secular ruler as the temporal lord of the see). The regalia of greatest importance in the terms of the concordat was control over diocesan land and its income once a bishop nominee had sworn fealty and pledged homage to the king. Philip signed much the same deal. In so doing, both agreed to a transfer of diocesan revenue from their hands to the church's hands once an acceptable bishop was consecrated, and not before.[3] Thus, if a bishop nominee was unacceptable to the crown, then the see remained vacant, an interregnum ensued during which there was no bishop, and the king retained the revenue from the bishopric. In so pledging, the kings of France and England accepted concordats that foreshadowed the terms agreed to later in the Concordat of Worms.

The French and English deals made bishops essentially into vassals of the secular ruler who presided over the diocesan territory where they were to serve. This vassalage was achieved by requiring homage and fealty to the king as preconditions that the bishop nominee had to satisfy in order to receive ecclesiastical investiture and, with it, the rights enjoyed by a bishop of the Catholic Church. Thus, the church gained the right of nomination and investiture, but at a heavy price in terms of the bishop's obligations to his secular overlord. What was at stake was no less than whether the bishop—the essential bridge between church and state—would act as the agent of the secular or the spiritual sword. The question the agreements required to be asked was, Would the bishop, nominated by the clergy but requiring the approval of the crown, do the king's bidding or the pope's?

While the agreements with the English and French crowns paved the way for a broader settlement of the controversy, getting to an agreement by 1122 was far from easy or amicable. To put it mildly, things did not go smoothly after these first deals were struck. Barely had the ink dried on the Concordat of London, signed on August 11, 1107, than the English king regretted having made the deal. He was angry that he had conceded to the church exclusive power over the choice of bishops in England when kings in Germany and elsewhere did not face equivalent constraints on their control over the church in their lands.[4] King Philip seemed to have warmer relations with the church and Pope Paschal II. He seems not to have articulated regrets over his deal with the church. In fact, he offered his kingdom as a suitable location for a meeting between the pope and the Holy Roman emperor to work out their own differences.

Both the pope and the emperor agreed to take up Philip's offer. But the meeting certainly did not go well. We are lucky to have a detailed, often firsthand account of that meeting and subsequent developments from the pen of Suger (1081–1151), secretary to the abbot of St. Denis in 1106 and later, in 1118, himself abbot of the monastery at St. Denis. Lest anyone believe it is hyperbole to speak of the dispute over investiture as having escalated from a war of words to a genuine war of force, here is a critical excerpt from Suger's eyewitness report:

> The universal and supreme pope Paschal . . . his mitre on his head in the Roman fashion, he came to the venerable home of St. Denis. . . . There King Philip and the Lord Louis met him with compliments and vows. . . . The lord pope . . . consulted them familiarly on the state of the church and, flattering them delicately, he prayed them to render assistance to St. Peter and himself . . . to resist boldly tyrants and the enemies of the church, above all the Emperor Henry. They gave him their hands as witness of their friendship, aid and counsel, put their realm at his disposal, and sent with him to Chalons to meet the imperial legates . . . The Archbishop of Trèves spoke for them [i.e., the imperial party]. He was a well-bred and agreeable man, rich in eloquence and wisdom, fluent in French; he made an apt speech, offering the lord pope and his court the greetings and cooperation of the emperor, saving the rights of his kingdom. Then in accordance with his instructions, he said: "This is the reason why I was sent by my lord the emperor. In the days of our ancestors and of the holy and apostolic to imperial law, all elections should proceed thus: before a public election took place, the name of the favoured candidate should be mentioned to the emperor, and if the person was suitable, he would give his assent before the election; then an assembly was held according to canon law, and by the request of the people, at the choice of the clergy and with the assent of the suzerain, the candidate was proclaimed. After being consecrated freely and without simony, he would go to the emperor for the regalia, to be invested with the ring and staff, and to take the oath of fidelity and homage. There is nothing odd about

this. It is exactly the way in which cities or castles or marcher territories or tolls or any other gifts of the imperial dignity are conferred. If the lord pope will accept this, the kingdom and the church will remain together in prosperity and peace to the honour of God."

To this the lord pope replied, after reflection, through the mouth of the bishop of Plaisance: "The church which has been redeemed and set free through the precious blood of Christ ought in no way again to be imprisoned. If the church cannot choose a bishop without consulting the emperor, then it is servilely subjected to him, and Christ died in vain. Investiture with the staff and ring, since these things belong to the altar, is a usurpation of God's rights. If hands consecrated to the body and blood of Christ are to be placed between laymen's hands, bloodied by the use of the sword, in order to create an obligation, then it derogates from ordination and from sacred unction."

When the stiff-necked legates heard this and similar things, with German impetuosity they ground their teeth, they grew agitated, and if they could have dared to do so safely, they would have vomited their insults and wounded others. They cried, "This quarrel will not be ended here but in Rome, and by the sword."[5]

The meeting in France ended not with an agreement between the pope and the emperor but, rather, with the threat by the emperor's agents that imperial forces would march on Rome, sword in hand, and have their way. And alas, that was what happened just a few years later. Before the sword was raised against the pope, but in the face of the dire threat that it would be raised, it appeared that a deal was in the offing. Paschal and Henry struck a truce at Sutri that called for bishops to surrender their control over all imperial fiefs—that is, the church would lose a great source of diocesan revenue (the candidate "would go to the emperor for the regalia") in exchange for the emperor's agreement to concede the right to investiture to the metropolitan bishops and their coprovincial bishops.

So strong was the clerical resistance to this settlement that Paschal was compelled to renege on the terms of the truce. Henry appeared at St. Peter's Basilica expecting to be coronated by Paschal on February 12, 1111, but, instead, he found that the pact they had struck had unraveled. Perhaps fearing the rebellion of the bishops, Paschal refused to go ahead with the coronation.[6] What happened next is best left, in all its critical detail, to Suger's words, reporting on this fateful day in February 1111:

> The emperor, in the second year after his return home, collected together an enormous army of thirty thousand men.... He set out for Rome. There he very convincingly pretended to peaceful aims, put aside the investiture dispute, made all sorts of fine promises about this and other things and, in order to be allowed to enter the city, which would otherwise have been barred to him, he used flattery and feared not to deceive the supreme pontiff, the whole church, even the King of Kings.... Then the lord pope celebrated thanksgiving mass, offered the body and blood of Jesus Christ, then broke the Eucharist, and the emperor received it and made his communion.... The lord pope had scarcely taken off his episcopal regalia after the mass, when with unexpected wickedness of Teutonic fury, inventing grounds for a breach, broke forth in passion. Drawing their swords and rushing out as if filled with frenzy, they met the Romans, naturally unarmed in such a place; they shouted and swore that they would capture or slay the whole Roman clergy including bishops and cardinals and, the final height of insanity, they did not fear to lay hands on the lord pope himself... injuring him much.

Henry took prisoner not only the pope but also thirteen additional bishops. Neither the bishops nor the pope were released until Paschal, under compulsion, acquiesced by declaring that the emperor had the right to the investiture of bishops, an acquiescence that obviated the reformist struggles of the preceding several decades. Paschal's declaration was abhorrent to the bishops of the church, who even accused him of heresy for agreeing to it. Hence, the agreement was overturned by the Lateran Synod of 1112, leaving the church and the imperial regime at loggerheads. A resolution of the Investiture Controversy still remained up in the air, not to be resolved for another decade.[7]

Finally, in 1122, the emperor and the pope came to terms, albeit again not without huge resistance to the agreement in its aftermath.[8]

According to the Concordat of Worms, the Holy Roman emperor, Henry V, and the pope, now Calixtus II (1119–1124), resolved that the right to nominate bishops resided in the hands of the church through the efforts of the relevant metropolitan bishop and the bishops under the metropolitan who generally sought and received advice from their cathedral canons. The agreement also resolved that the right of investiture resided in the hands of the church and not the hands of the emperor. Because the interpretation of the Concordat of Worms is so central to the analysis that follows, I quote it here in its remarkably brief, but transformative, entirety:

(a.) Privilege of Pope Calixtus II.

I, bishop Calixtus, servant of the servants of God, do grant to thee beloved son, Henry—by the grace of God august emperor of the Romans—that the elections of the bishops and abbots of the German kingdom, who belong to the kingdom, shall take place in thy presence, without simony and without any violence; so that if any discord shall arise between the parties concerned, thou, by the counsel or judgment of the metropolitan and the co-provincials, may'st give consent and aid to the party which has the more right. The one elected, moreover, without any exaction may receive the regalia from thee through the lance, and shall do unto thee for these what he rightfully should. Be he who is consecrated in the other parts of the empire (i.e. Burgundy and Italy) shall, within six months, and without any exaction, receive the regalia from thee through the lance, and shall do unto thee for these what he rightfully should. Excepting all things which are known to belong to the Roman church. Concerning matters, however, in which thou dost make complaint to me, and dost demand aid,—I, according to the duty of my office, will furnish aid to thee. I give unto thee true peace, and to all who are or have been on thy side in the time of this discord.

(b.) Edict of the Emperor Henry V.

In the name of the holy and indivisible Trinity, I, Henry, by the grace of God august emperor of the Romans, for the love of God and of the holy Roman church and of our master pope Calixtus, and for the healing of my soul, do remit to God, and to the holy apostles of God, Peter

and Paul, and to the holy catholic church, all investiture through ring
and staff; and do grant that in all the churches that are in my kingdom
or empire there may be canonical election and free consecration. All
the possessions and regalia of St. Peter which, from the beginning of
this discord unto this day, whether in the time of my father or also in
mine, have been abstracted, and which I hold: I restore to that same
holy Roman church. As to those things, moreover, which I do not hold,
I will faithfully aid in their restoration. As to the possessions also of
all other churches and princes, and of all other lay and clerical persons which have been lost in that war: according to the counsel of the
princes, or according to justice, I will restore the things that I hold;
and of those things which I do not hold I will faithfully aid in the restoration. And I grant true peace to our master pope Calixtus, and to
the holy Roman church, and to all those who are or have been on its
side. And in matters where the holy Roman church shall demand aid I
will grant it; and in matters concerning which it shall make complaint
to me I will duly grant to it justice. All these things have been done
by the consent and counsel of the princes. Whose names are here ad-
joined: Adalbert archbishop of Mainz; F. archbishop of Cologne; H.
bishop of Ratisbon; O. bishop of Bamberg; B. bishop of Spires; H. of
Augsburg; G. of Utrecht; Ou. Of Constance; E. abbot of Fulda; Henry,
duke; Frederick, duke; S. duke; Pertolf, duke; Margrave Teipold; Margrave Engelbert; Godfrey, count Palatine; Otto, count Palatine; Ber-
engar, count. I, Frederick, archbishop of Cologne and archchancellor,
have given my recognizances.[9]

The terms of the Concordat of Worms were binding on the pope, the
Holy Roman emperor, and the secular rulers of the kingdoms of Burgundy and Italy, who at the time, as it happens, was the same Henry,
the Holy Roman emperor. The terms agreed to at Worms differed in
certain ways related to the timing and expectations of physical presence
during consecration from the specifics applied to the kingdoms of Burgundy and Italy as well as from the conditions stipulated in the earlier
agreements with the kings of England and France. But, as the following
description of the deal with England and France in 1107 makes clear,

the essential terms were the same in 1107 as they were fifteen years later in Worms:

> Pope Paschal held a council to work out a settlement of the Investiture Controversy with the Holy Roman emperor. His plan was to go to Germany after his council. But the pope did not go to Germany after the council, though the German court still expected him. Instead, he went to France.... While there, he settled the Investiture Controversy in France and England by making compromises that permitted the kings of those countries to participate in choosing bishops but not to invest them. The agreements with France and England rested on the analysis of the *episcopatus* and regalia offered by Ivo of Chartres ten years earlier. The agreements permitted the kings to invest bishops with the regalia *after* they had been consecrated. This was a true compromise of the disputed points because it recognized the secular character of the regalia and the rights of kings in them.[10]

As I believe is evident, the difference across the agreements are not consequential for the analysis here and its implications for the rise of Western secularism and prosperity. For our purposes, the core common parts of the three agreements involved acceptance of the idea that investiture was the sole right of the church and acceptance or rejection of nominees was the right of the relevant king, who could withhold the regalia, including the revenue from the diocese, pending his acceptance of the nominee and the nominee's pledge to defend the monarch through the lance.

The terms for Burgundy and Italy, as for England and France, just like the terms for the Teutonic elements of the Holy Roman empire, required that the regalia be transferred after consecration of the new bishop. The essential feature of all of these agreements was that the ruler could say no to the church's nominee, and as long as no nominee was consecrated, the regalia remained in the possession of the crown. The retention of the regalia before consecration and its transfer after consecration is the feature of the Concordat of Worms and its predecessor agreements with England and France that altered the political balance of power. Control over the regalia was the price that the emperor and the kings of France and England extracted in exchange for conceding the church's exclusive right to the investiture of bishops.

Holy Roman Emperor Henry V certified in the text that he was signing "by the consent and counsel of the princes." Their consent indicated that the concordat would bind future emperors as well. They were in a unique position to do so. The position of prince-bishop, created more than a century earlier, tied the interests of the church and empire closer together as the individuals occupying this position ruled simultaneously as princes over secular domains and as bishops in the dioceses that overlapped with the prince's secular territory. This arrangement formally obliterated the notion codified by the church at the Council of Chalcedon in 451 that no bishop was to "occupy himself in worldly engagements."[11] Yet in practice, the prince-bishops were princes first and bishops only secondarily with many of them having never pursued religious training and with nearly all of them interested in advancing the welfare of their families and the riches and power of the territory they controlled. These prince-bishops formed a nexus between the empire and the church, acting most of the time on behalf of the worldly pursuit of wealth and power rather than on behalf of the church's religious mission.

It is reasonable to infer that by obtaining the consent of the prince-bishops, Henry indicated that the man, Henry, who occupied the position of emperor was signing not on his own personal, individual behalf but, rather, in his capacity as the Holy Roman emperor. In this way, Henry invoked the concept of the king's two bodies (Henry the man and Henry the emperor) and indicated that he was speaking on behalf of the person who had been consecrated as emperor "by the grace of God," and with the approval of the princes of the empire as well, rather than as a mere individual.[12] This important distinction proved consequential later when a faction in the church argued unsuccessfully that the concordat was only binding as long as Henry was alive.[13]

The terms of the Concordat of Worms, like those of its predecessors signed in 1107, established that secular authorities had the right to accept or reject bishop nominees. If a nominee was accepted, he took an oath of homage to the emperor (or other relevant ruler in accordance with the several concordats) that included a promise of military support when called for, and only then was he installed as bishop. That the bishop nominee was required first to take the oath of homage before investment with the rights and powers of a bishop was particularly noteworthy at the time. After all, Pope Calixtus II, in his capacity as Archbishop Guido of Vienne a decade earlier called a synod of French and Burgundian bishops in Vienne that excommunicated Henry V exactly because he had compelled Paschal II to accept such terms, which were judged to have "jeopardized the liberty of the Church."[14]

If the nominee was rejected, then during the time of the interregnum, the temporalities—that is, inter alia, the property and income from the diocese ceded to the church in fief by the emperor (or other relevant secular ruler)—would go to the lay ruler, as he would not yet have transferred control of the territory to a new bishop and the church. This separation of spiritual and temporal interests was the core of the compromise that had been proposed by Ivo, later bishop of Chartres, during the time of Gregory VII at the height of the Investiture Controversy. It was also the very idea that had been condemned by the church when Paschal II met with the emperor. Recall what the bishop of Plaisance, speaking on the pope's behalf, responded when this was proposed in 1107: "If the church cannot choose a bishop without consulting the emperor, then it is servilely subjected to him, and Christ died in vain." What a powerful statement: "and Christ died in vain." How could so powerful a rejection, just fifteen years later, have vanished? Troubles for both the emperor and the pope had made it possible for them to agree to that which indicated that "Christ died in vain." Now that very deal was put into effect.[15]

Many critics at the time of the agreement recognized that the concordat, in resolving the Investiture Controversy, had formalized terms that may have brought momentary peace between the two swords of power but that did so by weakening the longer-term position of the church. Bishop Adalbert of Mainz, for instance, feared that the terms of the concordat that allowed the Holy Roman emperor to be present when a bishop was selected meant that, as he put it, "the Church of God must undergo the same slavery as before, or an even more oppressive one."[16] Arnold of Brescia objected that the church's control over the diocesan regalia (that is, income in fief while a bishop was in place) had been made dependent on secular approval of the nominee. He contended that this meant the secularization of the church and necessitated its excessive involvement in worldly affairs.[17] Arnold's objections proved both to be correct and to have dire consequences for him. He was subsequently hanged for his opposition to and criticisms of the concordat and for his many other criticisms of church practices at the time.

The essential understanding of the power implications of the Concordat of Worms was well summarized by the canon regular Hugh of St. Victor (1096–1141). He contended, "With regard to earthly possessions, earthly princes ... sometimes concede only utility to a church, sometimes both utility and power"—that is, merely the economic use of the land in question or "a grant of secular jurisdiction over the subjects inhabiting the lands conferred upon a church."[18] Although such French ecclesiastics as Hugh of St. Victor and Bernard of Clairveaux were agreeable to the exchange of regalia for approval of the bishop nominee, other canons regular were hostile to the deal. Gerhoh of Reichersberg, for instance, initially resisted, arguing that the regalia, at least from dukes, counts, and others below the monarch, should be declined, as they clearly belonged to the secular world and not to the church.[19] But eventually even Gerhoh came around in his thinking. By 1142 he agreed, as the pope had done for two decades, that the church should accept the regalia, and he argued that they should be administered by judges drawn from the secular, not the ecclesiastical, domain.[20] His views had come around to those of Hugh of St. Victor. The deal conceded "secular jurisdiction over the subjects inhabiting the lands conferred upon a church," a great secular gain at clerical expense.

The principles enshrined in the concordats gradually became accepted doctrine from the perspective of much of the church's intellectual leadership. Even many recalcitrant clerics came around to the view that bishops owed homage and fealty to their secular ruler. Furthermore, the church had agreed to trade away some of its notional political power over diocesan territory in exchange for money and the return of church property, as promised by Holy Roman Emperor Henry V in the

Concordat of Worms. In the process, the clergy gained greater, but still limited, practical say in the selection of bishops and abbots. In return, temporal rulers gained a veto over the choice of bishops and monetary leverage with which to improve the chance of enforcing their interests at the expense of the church.

It cannot be doubted that Calixtus II understood that he was making a poor long-term deal—under coercive pressure—that could prove disastrous for the future of the church and its popes. The church's chroniclers emphasized the concessions made by Henry V and greatly underplayed those granted by Calixtus. As the eminent historian Robert Benson noted, "The official biography of Calixtus in the *Liber pontificalis* and the papal records in the *Liber censuum* reveal the full text of Henry's charter, but bypass the Calixtinum."[21] Thus the record at the time emphasized the gains of the church, including the important rights of nomination and investiture and the material benefits in the form of Henry's promise to return to the church the property that he and others had taken from it. At the moment, of course, the concordat brought a temporary solution to a grave crisis and offered avenues by which the papacy and other church leaders might, for a while, gain greater leverage over ecclesiastical offices than they had enjoyed for hundreds of years. Furthermore, the concessions that Calixtus granted, and the objections to it that soon followed from people like Arnold of Brecia, were somewhat offset by the fact that in the short term the pope and other senior church leaders retained bargaining power and regained assets that had been alienated during the long struggle that began with Emperor Henry III and was finally settled with Henry V.

Then too, we must recognize that the church was not devoid of tools to protect its interests against the damage that could be—and would be—done by the concordat. In addition to the proposal power that was conceded to the church's leaders, popes had an arsenal of punishment tools at their disposal with which to try to rein in the harm the church was eventually likely to suffer from the deals. They could challenge a secular leader's credibility through harsh public declarations, as Pope Gregory VII had done in his public criticisms of Emperor Henry IV and his followers during the Investiture Controversy. They could absolve

subjects of the oaths they had given on behalf of the ruler, as Pope Innocent III did to the subjects of England's King John in 1208. They could
excommunicate the secular ruler or his entire domain as Pope Boniface VIII did when he challenged the right of any king—and France's
Philip IV in particular—to challenge his decrees, excommunicating
him in the process. They could interdict specific territories (dioceses)
controlled by a temporal ruler, denying those territories' people access
to some or all of the sacraments, thereby potentially even denying them
the hope that they would eventually enter into heaven, an approach followed by Pope Innocent III in his conflicts with France's King Philip II.

Even if a secular ruler was not religious (an unlikely circumstance
in those highly religious times), he would surely have been mindful
that the church was the monopoly provider of salvation in the eyes of
his subjects and that its support was therefore essential for his political
well-being. All this meant that the Concordat of Worms, along with its
predecessor agreements, had created a new institutional environment
between church and state in response to the fact that Europe, seemingly
unlike the rest of the world for most of human history, was divided between the power of its Catholic leadership and its temporal rulers.

The preservation of the regalian temporalities in the hands of the
secular ruler was one of the most fundamental changes in church-state
relations. This newly instituted condition critically shaped the conflict
between religious and secular leaders over the next several hundred
years. It overrode canon 25 agreed to in 451 at Chalcedon. That canon
stated, "Forasmuch as certain of the metropolitans, as we have heard,
neglect the flocks committed to them, and delay the ordinations of bishops the holy Synod has decided that the ordinations of bishops shall take
place within three months, unless an inevitable necessity should some
time require the term of delay to be prolonged. And if he shall not do
this, he shall be liable to ecclesiastical penalties, and the income of the
widowed church shall be kept safe by the steward of the same Church"
(that is, the church's chosen financial manager of the diocese's temporal
accounts).[22] During the eleventh and twelfth centuries, the church, an
enormous landholder in its own right, derived substantial revenue and
sustained its churches, parishes, and many clergy through its diocesan

income. Control over these revenues was a highly significant matter.[23] As such, the logic of the three concordats should have meant a change in church-state relations for the signatories, and it did.

From the perspective of the church, the agreement at Worms appeared to restore its often-eroded rights to select bishops and abbots. Proposal power was placed back in the church, as had been true at the start of the Council of Nicaea and only intermittently after that. And when the selection of a nominee to fill a bishopric was contested among the provincial bishops, then in practice (though not decreed in the concordat) the pope often made the choice himself, free to override the metropolitan's point of view. This was surely a winning position for the bishops of the church and especially for the pope. The nomination aspect agreed to at Worms fostered greater centralization of church authority in the hands of the pope while at the same time restoring the lapsed rights of local bishops and their metropolitan to advance the names of candidates for local offices.[24]

The winning aspects for the church and the pope, however, were more than overwhelmed by the political concessions that were made to the Holy Roman emperor and the other monarchs covered by the concordats. For these temporal rulers, the improved bargaining leverage translated into a huge gain in their secular authority and in a shift in the balance of power away from the church and toward their interests, although, of course, that shift, anticipated by many at the time, nevertheless took a long time to unfold.

The Process of Bishop Selection
Before the Concordats

To work out more thoroughly what the implications of the concordats were, we need first of all to think about how bishops were chosen before the concordats. With that information in hand, we can sort out the strategic meaning embedded in the deals agreed to in 1107 and 1122. Working through the altered incentives institutionalized by the concordat (which I will now generally refer to in the singular to highlight their essential similarity regarding the transfer of regalia and pledges to secular rulers) will allow us to see how state sovereignty, the secularization of Europe, the distribution of wealth, and the bargaining power of temporal rulers vis-à-vis the church were intertwined.

Before the Investiture Controversy was resolved, bishop selection generally followed one of three patterns:

1. The local community and clergy nominated and elected a bishop (*a clero et populo*) who was then accepted or rejected by the local metropolitan or archbishop.[25]
2. The metropolitan put a candidate forward who, if elected by the local clergy and Catholic community (often doing so in deference to the metropolitan's wishes), was then consecrated as the bishop of the diocese.
3. A secular ruler, whether an emperor, king, duke, count, or some other powerful local family, put a candidate forward who was then either accepted or rejected by the church leaders, usually the local archbishop in consultation with his clerical advisers, generally accompanied by a rubber-stamp approval by the local community and clergy.

Of course, as is well known, in each of these systems there was the possibility of simony—the buying and selling of bishoprics.

How often any one of these three means of choosing bishops was used is hard to know at this remove in time. However, no matter which selection method was used, the revenues from the bishopric continued to flow to the church, regardless of whether or not there was a bishop in place. That, as we know, was not true during the period of the concordat. Hence, before the concordat, there is no institutional reason to think that bargaining power and the alignment of a bishop were systematically related to the wealth of the diocese, at least not beyond the magnitude of the price a simoniac would pay for a particular bishopric. In contrast, both bargaining power and the alignment of candidates for a bishopric, whether with the church or with the lay leader, should have been crucial once the concordats were accepted.

The terms of the concordat altered how bishops were selected in two fundamental ways. First, it established the church unambiguously as the nominator of candidates, a circumstance that sometimes arose before the concordat, but not always, and not as an institutionalized, agreed-upon procedure. Second, the concordat gave the secular ruler veto power over the nominee and the right to retain the diocesan revenue during an interregnum. In the preconcordat years, by contrast, that income flowed to the church whether a bishop was agreed on or not, and the secular ruler did not have an institutionalized veto.

In a time when agreement on a new bishop did not influence the transfer of money from the lay leader of the diocese to the church, what might have shaped which of the three preconcordat procedures was followed? One clear factor would have been the temptation to engage in simony. It is a safe bet that many would-be candidates were eager to become a bishop in those dioceses where the post was expected to be highly lucrative. In such sees, the opportunity to enrich oneself by committing the sin of simony would have been awfully tempting for whoever had the say in choosing the new bishop. In poorer bishoprics, in contrast, it seems more likely that religious men with prior religious training would have been chosen. They, of course, were less likely to be able or willing to bribe their way to the office of bishop. But they probably did not face serious competition from richer men.

Wealthier men, seeing little prospect of extracting a good income from a poorer diocese, were probably not especially inclined to buy their way into the job, or if they were, then they were probably prepared to pay only a small price. Hence, poorer dioceses—the most common type of bishopric—were probably more likely to follow the first selection process, relying on the local clergy and Catholic community to identify a worthy candidate, or at least a not-terribly-wealthy simoniac when there was not much beyond religious interests at stake. Wealthier sees, by and large, would have been more likely to follow the latter two processes for picking a new bishop.

To put all this more simply: the more wealth there was in a bishopric, the more it made sense for a wealthy person to try to buy power there.

If the local community and local clergy chose and elected a candidate, they would have had no obvious collective mechanism by which to sell the office of bishop. Even if they could, as a group their interest would have resided more strongly in advancing their prospects for salvation—a highly valuable benefit believed to be available to all of them—rather than in getting their small portion of a bribe that was offered to the whole community in exchange for nomination as bishop. Certainly, the chance at eternal life, which retained its value no matter how many other people received it, was believed to be, in modern parlance, a public good available to all, whereas committing the sin of simony, though translating into some money for the members of the community, put salvation in jeopardy.[26] So, when selection was done *a clero et populo*, we can be pretty confident that the preference would have been for a candidate who was religiously inclined and that the diocese was likely to be poor.

Powerful secular or religious authorities, such as kings and archbishops, probably would not have relied on the local community in such an important matter if, indeed, the diocese were of sufficient value that a simoniac would pay them a handsome price to be chosen as bishop. Selling or buying the office of bishop made sense if the post was expected to be profitable. Of course, the post could be lucrative for the buyer and for the seller without regard to whether the buyer's or seller's policy preferences leaned toward the secular or religious. All that mattered in the preconcordat times was that the buyer—a simoniac—gained access to what he wanted by enriching the seller. He might have wanted money, as with the Tusculum family's influence over the selection of bishops of Rome. But, as the case of Gratian (Pope Gregory VI) indicated, the simoniac might have wanted religious influence. The preconcordat selection process simply did not create a mechanism by which the church and secular authorities bargained over the exchange of money and power. The see's income flow was not at stake.

Hence, what we can infer with some confidence is that before the concordat there was no reason to tie the bishop's secular or religious leanings to the diocese's wealth. In poorer dioceses where the income potential was low, as an empirical matter we should expect that bishops before the concordat were men whose interests were overwhelmingly aligned with the church's policy goals and religious mission. In wealthier dioceses, in contrast, there probably would have been a somewhat more mixed bag of secularly and religiously inclined bishops than was true in poor bishoprics, but the difference is expected to have been small and not the driving force behind appointments.

Indeed, our expectation that diocesan wealth did not shape bishop selection before the concordat is borne out by the evidence. To see that this is so, I use diocese-level trade-route information and the diocesan land's caloric productivity potential as two means to estimate the wealth of each bishopric in Europe. I categorize each bishop as preferring to follow the policies of the church or the diocese's secular ruler—that is, as religious or secular—based on the job he had before becoming bishop. I probe bishop biographies to ascertain whether they worked for the secular ruler or for the church before becoming bishop. Chapter 4, where we more thoroughly investigate the alignment of bishops during the concordat period compared to before and after, provides more details on the process of estimating wealth and the secular or religious alignment of bishops. Here we do not yet need the details.

Figure 3.1 shows us how bishop alignments were distributed before the concordats. Bishoprics not on major trade routes or with land that was below average in its potential to produce calories are classified as

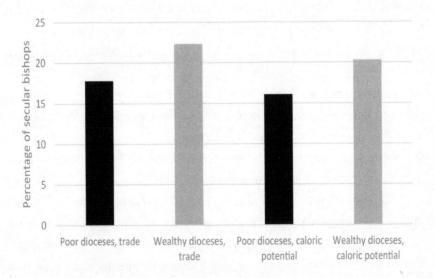

Figure 3.1: Dioceses and secularism, from 325 until signing of concordats

poor, while dioceses on major trade routes or with above average caloric potential are considered to have been wealthy. The two solid black
bars show the percentage of secularly aligned bishops across all poor
dioceses in the years from 325 to the signing of the relevant concordat.
The gray bars show the secularism of bishops in sees that were wealthy
during the same time period.

Secularly inclined bishops always had a small advantage in wealthier bishoprics, but nevertheless, religiously inclined bishops dominated
and the secularism advantage in wealthier places is not statistically
meaningful. Before the concordat period, in fact, diocesan wealth was
not an important element in sorting out the type of bishop candidate—
secularly leaning or religiously leaning—chosen to hold this powerful
office. What, then, in contrast, should we expect when the terms of the
concordat were in effect?

THE CONCORDAT GAME

Once the Investiture Controversy was resolved by the concordat, the
procedure for appointing bishops was completely altered. Whereas before the concordat, the people, the church, or the secular ruler might
have had the first move, the secular ruler never officially had the final
move in which he could agree to or veto the bishop nominee. Once
the treaties with France, England, and the Holy Roman Empire were
in place, however, the church moved first, usually meaning nomination
by the relevant metropolitan bishop, sometimes his cathedral chapter,
or sometimes the pope. Then the Holy Roman emperor, another designated monarch (depending on the specific agreement), or in practice,
the monarch's agents or other possessors of regalian sees, in the form of
local dukes, counts, or other lords, could accept or reject the nominee.
If accepted, the nominee was invested with the rights of a bishop. If rejected, the income from the diocese went to the secular ruler rather than
the "widowed" church and the see remained vacant until the church
nominated someone acceptable to the temporal leader. Once the nominee was consecrated, the subsequent income from the diocese was controlled by the bishop and the church. Thus, the concordat, in principle,
put explicit procedures in place for the selection of the most powerful

members of the church. In doing so, it also created new incentives that derived from the change in who controlled a diocese's income in the event of an interregnum between bishops.

The rules for the selection of a bishop are sufficiently critical to make it worthwhile to connect them directly to the relevant text from the Concordat of Worms so that when we turn them into a game theoretic analysis, we will understand exactly the source for every claim. Here, then are the rules:

1. The church nominates a bishop to fill a vacant see. (As stated by Henry V: "In the name of the holy and indivisible Trinity, I, Henry, . . . for the healing of my soul, do remit to God, and to the holy apostles of God, Peter and Paul, and to the holy catholic church, . . . that in all the churches that are in my kingdom or empire there may be canonical election and free consecration.")

2. The king accepts or rejects the nominee. (Calixtus states, "If any discord shall arise between the parties concerned, thou [that is, the king], by the counsel or judgment of the metropolitan and the co-provincials, may'st give consent and aid to the party which has the more right.").

3. If the ruler accepts the nominee, the nominee is invested and the income from the diocese flows to the church. (Calixtus declares, "The one elected, moreover, without any exaction may receive the regalia from thee." Henry promises in return that there will be "all investiture through ring and staff.") If the king rejects the nominee, the king retains the regalia, meaning in particular that he retains control over property and, crucially, control over revenue generated from the income from the bishopric until a nomination is made that is accepted by the king.

As was true before the concordat, a nominee for bishop might have been a church loyalist or a royalist. He might have fallen anywhere on the scale from most pious and religiously devoted to most worldly and secularly oriented. But now there was a tremendous change in the consequence that followed if a nominee was rejected. Before the concordat, rejection of a nominee by whoever could do so certainly meant that the see remained vacant for a while, but as a practical matter, that had no major consequence in terms of the revenue flowing to the church. Vacancies were terrible things because they meant a lack of leadership and guidance in the event that something new and unexpected arose. But whether a bishop was in office or not, the lesser clergy carried on, and the routine, expected policies of the diocese probably continued to be carried on as they had been before. Indeed, the continuity of policy—in favor of the church or of the secular ruler, depending on the previous bishop's alignment—was probably unaltered by a vacancy before or after the concordat was put into place. But once the deal was struck at Worms (or London or Paris), a vacancy meant a loss of revenue to the church, whether the recipient of at least part of that income had been the local church, the metropolitan bishop, or the pope in Rome. The money that would have flowed to the bishopric now remained under the control of the secular ruler. That meant that picking a nominee was a truly critical decision, because if the wrong person were chosen—from the point of view of the temporal leader—a vacancy and loss of revenue would result for the church.

Deciding whom to choose was not easy. Even if the relevant metropolitan bishop or, a bit later, the pope was in a position to be confident of getting his pick, he still faced a challenge. No one could really be sure what a bishop's future alignment might be, just as today presidents of the United States cannot be sure how a Supreme Court nominee's alignment will evolve once he or she is on the bench. Shifting and uncertain local conditions, an individual's privately held inclinations, and many other factors would have contributed to uncertainty about a bishop's alignment once he made it through the vetting process and was granted what was often a lifetime job in the chosen diocese.

Still, bishop nominees were generally drawn from people whose prior records suggested how loyal they and their policies could be expected to be to the church, the pope, or the ruler.[27] Looking at their prior work records and whose interests they had served in the past, it is not hard to imagine that rulers and popes frequently knew enough about would-be bishop candidates that they had little difficulty in forming an opinion about which prospective bishop nominees would be loyal to the one or the other. They would surely have been wrong some of the time, but given that picking a bishop was a big decision with high stakes, they probably chose carefully and correctly most of the time.

To illustrate the sort of information that would have been readily available and that would have shaped choices, consider the selection of Dietrich I von Hengebach (1150–c. 1223), bishop of Cologne from 1208 to 1212, and Anthelm (1107–1178), bishop of Belley from 1163 until his death in 1178 and venerated as a saint since 1607.

Dietrich, in his late fifties when he became the archbishop of Cologne, a major and extremely important clerical post, was not yet even a member of the clergy. He was not ordained as a priest until May 24, 1209, five months *after* his consecration as archbishop. Though we cannot know for sure, the weakness of his clerical background (he had been selected to be a pastor when he was sixteen) certainly suggests he was unlikely to be someone thought to be in the pope's camp. More tellingly with regard to his anticipated alignment, Dietrich was the openly preferred choice for archbishop by the then king of Germany, Otto IV (1175–1218). With Dietrich's backing, Otto became Holy Roman emperor in 1209. Having been the choice of the politically powerful Otto, it is no surprise that Dietrich indeed proved to be loyal to him rather than to the pope. Pope Innocent III in fact excommunicated Otto in 1210 and Dietrich in 1212. When Dietrich refused to accept his excommunication, Innocent then placed Dietrich under interdict.[28] It seems pretty clear from Dietrich's background that he was unlikely to work out to be a reliable supporter of the pope's interests when those interests clashed with Otto's goals.

In contrast to Bishop Dietrich, consider Anthelm bishop of Belley.[29] Anthelm was consecrated as bishop of Belley by Pope Alexander III in 1163, at fifty-six years old. What had Anthelm been doing to gain the pope's attention? Unlike Dietrich, Anthelm had spent his life in religious devotion and religious service. Anthelm had been a monk for many years, was briefly a hermit, and from his early thirties had served as the prior of Grande Chartreuse, the principle monastery of the Carthusian order of which he was a member. While in that position, he defended

Alexander in the pope's conflict with the antipope Victor IV, who had the backing of Holy Roman Emperor Frederick I, Frederick Barbarossa. Anthelm's life before he was made a bishop had signaled that he was a papal loyalist, unafraid to oppose even the choice of the emperor. It seems a safe bet that Anthelm, in his time, was expected to be aligned with the pope and church (which, indeed, he was), just as Dietrich was expected to be a royalist (which, in fact, he was).

As suggested by the stories of Dietrich and Anthelm, we would expect the church to have preferred religiously aligned bishops, and kings, also pursuing their own interests, to have preferred secularly aligned nominees. Thus, following the death of a bishop, the church's first decision, and probably the most important following the logic of the situation created by the concordat, was to select a candidate to fill the vacant see and get the revenue flowing to the church's coffers again. In practice, this choice was sometimes made by the metropolitan of the diocese in question, sometimes by a larger church body in consultation, and often with consideration for the pope's wishes and interests. Rather than speaking of the church or the metropolitan, I will encapsulate the process as the choice of the pope, recognizing, of course, that this is shorthand for the broader set of clergy involved in the decision.

Naturally, the process of choosing a bishop begins when a see becomes vacant because of the death, transfer, or (infrequently) resignation of the bishop. Rejection of a nominee, as we know, meant the relevant secular ruler—sometimes the Holy Roman emperor, sometimes a king, and sometimes a local lord, but generally referred to from now on, for convenience, as the king—got to keep the income generated by the diocese, but that benefit did not come for free. The pope had plenty of leverage to induce secular leaders to find the church's nominee acceptable. As Henry IV and Henry V learned, the pope could and did excommunicate even emperors. Furthermore, the pope could interdict the diocese in question or even a broader portion of the ruler's territory, denying the residents essential sacraments. The pope could use his bully pulpit to encourage sermons and public screeds against the ruler, much as had happened throughout the Investiture Controversy. So, saying no to the pope meant more money for the king but also had political costs. If those costs were large enough or the revenue from the see small enough, then the king would be inclined to say yes to the pope's nominee, and as a consequence, the pope would be inclined to nominate someone expected to be closely aligned with the pope's interests.

As the income from a diocese rose, or the pope's ability to inflict costs that were enforced by the local clergy against the king decreased, the king's inclination to say no to a nominee thought to be a papal loyalist should have increased, and so should have the pope's incentive to pick someone more aligned with the ruler. That way, the pope avoided an interregnum during which the see remained vacant, and he would at least be assured of getting the income from the diocese even if he could not assure himself of a bishop expected to be strongly loyal to him. If the expected cost of rejecting a bishop nominee got really small and the income from the bishopric got really large, the king might no longer have an incentive to trade income for political leverage. Even if the pope gave him a bishop expected to be completely loyal to the king, the money from the diocese might have been of greater value to the king than having a bishop in place and avoiding papal punishment.

Either the "outside option," leaving the see vacant, or the "inside option," agreeing to fill it with someone who had no concern for the church's interests but, rather, cared only to advance the king's interests, would mark a radical break from the church. During the Protestant Reformation that started in 1517, some monarchs in parts of Europe exercised the outside option. They rejected even the idea of appointing Catholic bishops and used the establishment of a new religious order to keep more money for themselves. Under similar circumstances, as demonstrated in Chapter 6, the French king, choosing the inside option, began the Avignon papacy in 1309, assuring himself and his heirs for an extended period that no less a figure than the bishop of Rome would do their bidding even when doing so was costly to the church. Wherever wealth had grown sufficiently great, such outcomes were sustainable, meaning that the church's political leverage had pretty much vanished, perhaps compelling it, at least in locales that followed the outside option, to behave more like a religious institution than a political one. If, when, and where the church faced such conditions, nepotism within the church is expected to have diminished markedly as the victory of secular power came to overwhelm the worldly interests of the clergy. The interlude during which the concordat was in effect constructed the struggle that would eventually take the church back to its religious roots, but before that could happen, the strategic implications of the concordats would have to run their course.

Naturally, the selection process could go on indefinitely as popes and kings, operating in an uncertain environment, searched for the right nominee. The church leaders, especially the pope, would want to bring forward candidates who deviated from his interests as minimally as possible. Kings would want to accept the most loyal bishop they could induce the church to offer them—that is, one who would follow the king's preferred policies rather than the pope's. A vacant bishopric meant more money for the king, but it also meant nonmonetary costs inflicted by the pope and a continuation of the agenda pursued in the diocese before the vacancy occurred. An interregnum in a see meant less money for the pope, but at least in those sees where there had been a papal loyalist as bishop, policies that may have advanced the pope's interests would persist. Interregnums, like the selection of bishops, meant trade-offs for both kings and popes. Whoever cared more intensely about the trade-off between money and policy would blink first. Each gained some advantage and each suffered some losses when no bishop was in place, just as they did when one was agreed upon. Hence, the concordat created subtle incentives and maneuvers. The solution to the concordat game's strategic setting can help us uncover some of these subtle implications.

To make clear the implications of the concordat game, let me provide an intuitive, reasonably rigorous account that helps clarify the strategic environment, hopefully without getting too technical.[30]

In a simplified view of the contest to pick a bishop, the pope nominates either a secularly inclined or a religiously inclined candidate to be bishop.[31] The king then either agrees to the pope's choice or rejects him. If he accepts the pope's nominee, then the candidate swears loyalty to the king, is consecrated, and receives the regalia, including revenue from the diocese, from the king. If the king rejects the proposed candidate, then the king retains the regalia, including the revenue from the diocese, but risks being punished by the pope, a very costly and painful result if the punishments are successfully carried out. Of course, if the king agrees to the candidate, then the pope and the church get whatever value they attach to that person as bishop, remembering that their value is lower if the person is secularly oriented rather than religiously aligned, and they get the revenue stream from the king's regalia until the next time the diocese is vacant. Conversely, if the king turns down the nominee, then the church gets the continuation of whatever policies the previous bishop had implemented in the bishopric and the church loses the income from the diocese for as long as the diocese remains vacant.

If we think about the king's point of view in this simplified, intuitive representation of the concordat game, then we realize that just three circumstances could arise. To see that this is logically so, recall that kings move last and, all else being equal, always want a secularly aligned bishop. The pope, moving first, likewise all things being equal, always want a religiously aligned bishop. All things, of course, are never equal, and that is where the interesting details lie. So the three potential circumstances, from the king's point of view, are these:

1. In a *poor bishopric*, a nominee who will do the king's bidding (a secularly aligned nominee) is preferred to a nominee who will be in the pope's pocket (a religiously aligned nominee), but a religiously inclined nominee is better than no bishop if the available revenue from the bishopric is less than the political and financial cost of defying the pope.

2. In a *middle-class bishopric*, having a secularly aligned nominee is better than keeping the diocesan revenue (minus the costs inflicted by the pope), but the revenue minus costs is still better for the king than agreeing to a religiously aligned bishop who will follow the policies preferred by the pope.

3. In a *wealthy bishopric*, the diocesan revenue is so large relative to the costs the pope can successfully impose on the king that the king would rather reject even a papal nominee expected to be loyal to the king, let alone one who would do what the pope wanted, and just keep the revenue. In this third case, the king just wants the

money no matter whom the pope nominates; this is the extreme version of the outside option in which an interregnum is essentially a permanent condition rather than a bargaining device to get a bishop who is completely committed to the king's interests.

Consider the first situation, in which the see to be filled is, relatively speaking, poor. If a diocese is sufficiently poor or the costs of defying the pope are sufficiently high, then the king, though wanting a secular bishop, will agree to a religious bishop even though such a bishop is his second choice. The minimal extra income from a poor bishopric is not worth enough to the king to risk the wrath of the pope by rejecting the pope's nominee. So in the first case, the king will accept a nominee whether the candidate is thought to be secularly oriented or religiously inclined. The pope has every reason to figure this out, so, realizing that he can get his way, the pope will nominate a religious loyalist, and that person will be accepted and become the pope's agent in the diocese.

Now imagine that the pope and the king face the second circumstance. In this case the vacant diocese is wealthy enough that the value—what Hugh of St. Victor referred to as the "utility"—of the income, even after bearing the cost that the pope could inflict on the king (the pain and suffering the pope could impose on the king and his subjects), was worth more to the king than dodging the cost by agreeing to a religiously oriented bishop. With sufficient revenue at stake, the king will reject a nominee who is believed to be a papal loyalist but he will accept a candidate who is expected to be committed to the king's interests. The pope, of course, would rather have a bishop who would do whatever the pope asked him to do, but in this circumstance, when the revenue from the bishopric is a significant attraction to the king, getting a papal loyalist is just not an option for the pope. So the pope's choice is either to nominate a secularly inclined bishop to whom the king will agree so that the church at least gets the diocesan revenue, or to pick a papal loyalist and get neither a bishop in place nor the money from the see. By picking a secularly leaning bishop, the church at least gets the significant money from the diocese. Picking a religiously inclined nominee means that the pope and the local diocesan community forego the see's revenue in exchange for the continuation of the previous bishop's policies. Of course, unless the diocese has recently enjoyed a spurt in its wealth, the previous bishop will have been the king's man, at least after the concordat has been in force for at least one generation of bishops. (The average bishop's tenure, given life expectancies in the twelfth and thirteenth centuries, was about thirteen years.) Thus, in all likelihood, the pope, however reluctantly, will nominate a royalist as bishop in this case, and the king, of course, will accept the nominee.

Finally, in the third case, the diocese is so wealthy that the king is in a position to say no regardless of whom the pope nominates. Ignoring for the moment the value of maintaining the diocese's previous policies, we see that whether a bishop will be loyal to the king or the pope is heavily dependent on the cost the pope can impose and on the wealth the diocese generates for whoever controls it. If the wealth is sufficiently great, then lay leaders would have no interest in turning that money over to the church even if doing so gets them a favorable bishop, unless, of course, their personal religious devotion was sufficiently strong. In the absence of strong personal devotion, wherever the third case arises, it is likely that the king no longer cares about striking a bargain with the pope. Indeed, if the king has neither a need nor an interest in striking a deal with the pope, one way to avoid the costs the church might inflict on him is to abandon the church and its religion altogether. That is what happened with the advent of the Protestant Reformation in northern Europe in 1517. Alternatively, with sufficient wealth at stake, the king in the third case could exercise the inside option, agreeing to the appointment of bishops who would do exactly what *he* wanted. The Avignon papacy in France, beginning in 1309, is such a case. There was no concern about differences in royal policies and church policies because, under the constraints of the inside option, even the pope was the king's agent.

Throughout our assessment we should realize that the pope could always refuse to offer a desirable nominee, just as the king could reject any nominee. That tells us that the risk of an interregnum depended in part on the urgency the pope felt to arrive at the "right" sort of nominee. That urgency depended on just how attractive the existing policies in a diocese were when balanced against the quality of bishop the pope could get and against the value of the revenue the diocese generated. So whether the pope put up with an interregnum should have depended on how much he valued gaining or maintaining political control over diocesan policies compared to the value he put on the income that was being foregone during an interregnum. That, in turn, was at least partially a function of how large or small the diocesan income was. In a low-income bishopric, the pope would have been more prepared to accept an interregnum, all else being equal, than in a wealthier diocese. There was just not a big revenue loss, and the pope could use time to pressure the king into giving the church a bishop closer to the sort of bishop it wanted. We will see that this was the case when we investigate the likelihood of interregna in Chapter 6.

In the concordat game's first case—that is, in sufficiently poor sees—the church retained virtually all the bargaining leverage over the choice of a bishop. In the third case—that is, in sufficiently rich bishoprics—the king had great political and economic leverage within the diocese regardless of who the church nominated. In the middle case, popes and kings were compelled to trade political influence for income, creating a new institutionalized bargaining environment. The three cases, taken together, shift the advantage to the church in poorer dioceses and to the king in richer dioceses, also creating new incentives over the stimulation or inhibition of economic growth as a means to secure political control. All of this is happening—at least in the logic of the concordat game—without any need to invoke cultural, racial, or other differences across the peoples in different parts of Europe. It is happening with some attention to the personal religious commitments of individual rulers and the pressures they might face from their subjects due to the punishments the church might try to impose in this or that bishopric. And it is happening overwhelmingly because of the new incentives created by the concordat, incentives that emphasize trading church power away to secular rulers in exchange for some of their money.

Before the concordat, kings still favored secularly oriented bishops and the church still favored religiously oriented bishops, but there was no trade-off between political leverage and money. Whether the bishop followed the political dictates of the king or the pope, the money from the diocese went to the church. Whether a bishopric had a bishop or was vacant, the relevant portion of the diocese's money went to the church. Once the concordat resolved the Investiture Controversy, money and political influence were pitted against one another in a way that had not been true before. Whereas the preconcordat environment provided no special incentives to promote—or hinder—economic productivity and development, the deal signed on September 23, 1122, like its predecessors in France and England, most assuredly did. Kings now had a reason to stimulate economic growth as the pathway to greater political control over their territory. Popes now had a reason to limit economic growth wherever they could to mire dioceses in the first case—the case of poor bishoprics—in which the church's influence was greatest.

KEY IMPLICATIONS OF THE CONCORDAT GAME

The logic of the strategic game created by the Concordat of Worms tells us that wealthier dioceses should have gotten bishops more aligned with the king than the pope after the concordat was signed as compared, on average, to the alignment of bishops prior to the resolution of the Investiture Controversy. In addition, poorer sees should have gotten fewer secularly oriented bishops than did wealthier bishoprics. That, of course, is why kings would have had a greater interest in improving economic performance than had been true before the concordat was signed. And since the pope's leverage would be decreased in wealthier dioceses, he had an incentive to limit growth so that diocesan wealth did not pass the threshold at which the king, rather than the pope, would have gotten a loyal bishop. That is, the church would have been happy for a diocese to enjoy income-generating economic growth as long as that growth did not move the bishopric from the first case to the second or third, from a prochurch bishop to a proking bishop. A high-income see was a win for the secular ruler whether he kept the money or used it to get a loyal bishop, with all the political advantages that implied. The situation for the church was more complicated.

Unlike lay leaders, the pope and the church did not continue to be better off as a bishopric became richer and richer, nor were they strictly worse off as diocesan income grew. For them, each diocese had a unique "optimal" level of revenue: below that level, the pope's and church's welfare was increasing as revenue increased, but past that income point, the pope's and church's welfare was diminished as diocesan revenue continued to increase. Where that optimal diocesan income fell, from the perspective of the pope, depended on whether the lay ruler or the pope placed greater weight on the diocese's policies compared to its income. If the king valued policy over money more than the pope did, then the pope could tolerate what were from his perspective bad, secular policies in exchange for more money. Conversely, if the pope prized policy over money more than the king did, then the king would be more reluctant than the pope to give up money, and the pope could get his way only if the diocese's revenue was relatively smaller than when the king cared more about policy outcomes than he did about income.

The incentives created by the concordat drove a wedge between the interests of secular authorities and those of the church. Secular rulers had unequivocal incentives to support policies that increased local economic development because such policies increased the power of secular political authorities relative to the church. The church, by contrast, had at best mixed incentives. In sufficiently poor dioceses, secular rulers had little enough bargaining power that the church benefited from the increase in income it consumed when a bishop was in place. But as parts of Europe became wealthier, the church's loss of bargaining power from increased local income, and the associated loss in political authority, more than offset the benefits. The church probably could anticipate this loss of bargaining power and, thus, had incentives to limit economic development even in dioceses below the optimal wealth level. The church very much wanted to keep bishoprics within the first case of the concordat game wherever they could. This could be done by maintaining and promoting relative poverty. Kings wanted to move their territory out of the first, low-income case, thereby creating added power for themselves in their competition with the church over policy and money. This would prove to have profound consequences not only for economic development but also for the promotion of accountable government— the creation of parliaments—as a way to incentivize a work ethic that motivated the effort needed to generate wealth and the power that accompanied it.

The logic of the game also tells us that the pope could use punishment strategies like excommunication as a political tool to thwart his loss of power in wealthier places. That means that we should expect that he shifted the way he used his punishment tools once the concordat was in place. The concordat forced him to bargain with kings over money and policies, and the punishment of recalcitrant kings was a readily available instrument to limit the king's bargaining power, at least up to a point. Effectively exercised punishment could increase the odds that the secular ruler over a diocese would agree to a bishop more closely aligned with the pope, whereas low-cost or ineffectively implemented punishment would fail to discourage rulers from insisting on a bishop aligned with their interests.

To sum up, the logic behind the terms codified in the Concordat of Worms provides several predictions that are readily tested against the record of history. We can see how Europe was expected to change with regard to secularism, the distribution of wealth, the distribution of political clout, and the rise of rival religions as a consequence of whether a diocese or region was poor, moderately wealthy, or very rich and of whether, following on its initial economic circumstances in 1107 or 1122, it became poorer, grew slowly, or became richer faster during the long years that the terms of the concordat were operative. These predictions, enumerated here, are tested in the chapters to come:

1. The concordats gave secular rulers greater bargaining power in wealthier dioceses so that whenever a bishop needed to be chosen, the wealthier the diocese was, the more likely it was that the newly selected bishop was aligned with the interests of the secular ruler rather than the church as compared either to poorer dioceses during the time of the concordat or the same dioceses before the signing of the concordat.

2. During the period in which the Concordat of Worms was in effect, the church could diminish the bargaining power of lay leaders provided it could credibly implement punishments against

secular rulers. Hence the approach to punishment used by the church should have changed while the concordat was in force as compared to punishments before the resolution of the Investiture Controversy.

3. The relationship between a diocese's wealth and the frequency of interregnums depended on the relative salience that popes and kings attached to gaining political control or gaining revenue from each diocese in their respective domains. Hence, all else being equal, interregnums should have been more common before the concordats were signed than after, since beforehand there was no trade-off between diocesan revenue and a bishop's loyalty. Once the concordat was operative, there should have been fewer interregnums, but those that occurred should have been more likely in poorer dioceses, where less money was at stake, and in sees where it was easier for the church to implement punishments against secular rulers.

4. The concordats drove a wedge between secular and church rulers with respect to economic development. Secular rulers had unambiguous incentives to foster economic development. Church leaders had incentives to limit economic development to curtail their loss of political power. Hence, not only should wealthier places have obtained more secularly inclined bishops, but those bishops should have helped foster policies favorable to economic growth, creating an economic separation between places that had more religiously aligned bishops, and so remained relatively poor, and places that had more secularly oriented bishops, and so became relatively rich.

5. Wherever lay rulers had more bargaining leverage than the church and the pope, those lay leaders should have promoted greater economic growth, and that economic expansion should eventually have generated sufficient prosperity that large swaths of dioceses—kingdoms—moved into the third case of the concordat game. In the third case, when there was so much wealth that kings were no longer interested in trading it for political power, we should observe a break with the Catholic Church, creating the prospect of

such events as the extreme inside option, the Avignon papacy, or the outside option, the Protestant Reformation.

6. Reaching a bit beyond the concordat game, I later outline a bargaining game in the shadow of coercive threats to go along with the concordat game and test the following claim: To foster greater economic growth, rulers would have had to incentivize local lords, merchants, laborers, and peasants to improve productivity. To do so successfully, kings would have had to make concessions to some of their subjects so that those subjects would share in the benefits they were creating. One important mechanism for this was to create new, accountable political institutions, like parliaments, that gave subjects a say in how the wealth that was the product of their economic efforts was used. Parliaments, then, would have been created more often in those places that were subject to the concordat's terms, especially as wealth grew.

7. Today's Western exceptionalism should be more discernible in those parts of Europe that fell into the second and third cases of the concordat game and should be less discernible in those parts of Europe that fell into the first case—the poor-diocese case—or that were not parties to the game.

Together, these implications offer us a straightforward pathway from the contest between kings and popes during the Investiture Controversy to the emergence of greater prosperity in some parts of Europe than in others, to the rise of secularism in the wealthier dioceses compared to poorer ones, to the way the effects of secularism and growing prosperity worked together to destroy the Catholic Church's monopoly over salvation, and to the way the resolution of the Investiture Controversy translated into more representative and more democratic government in some parts of Europe than in others. Taken together, the implications of the concordat game suggest that the contract signed by Pope Calixtus II and Holy Roman Emperor Henry V on September 23, 1122, was a pivotal—maybe *the* pivotal—moment in the creation of Western exceptionalism. We have seen the argument. Now it is time to see the evidence!

4

SECULARISM SURGES

That the government may be increased. And of peace there be no end, ...
Through justice and through righteousness From henceforth even for ever.

—Isaiah 9:6

THE GREAT POWERS OF TWELFTH-CENTURY EUROPE HAD SETTLED their eight-decade battle over who would control the selection of bishops, coming to terms in England and France in 1107 and in the Holy Roman Empire in 1122. The church agreed to sacrifice some of its control over the life of emperors, lords, and even the most ordinary of their congregants. Monarchs and lesser lords sacrificed some money they otherwise could have had as the price for greater political control over their territory and their subjects. The church's sacrifice was implicitly limited to wealthier places according to the concordat's logic. That was mostly true as well for the sacrifice of rulers who controlled lucrative regalia. Each side in the eighty-year-long dispute tried to limit the price it paid by manipulating who was chosen as bishop wherever and whenever a vacancy arose on its turf. Now that we know how the concordats should have influenced maneuvers and outcomes, we can investigate how, where, and when the treaties of 1107 and 1122 reshaped the distribution of political power across Europe. Did the concordat matter? If so, did it matter in the way the concordat game predicts it should have? Or, as so many have thought, was the concordat only a small piece of whatever changes took place in Europe over the next few hundred years?

To begin to evaluate the ways in which the concordat altered the balance of power between the church and nascent, developing states across Europe, we need to compare the selection of royalists or church loyalists as bishops depending on whether the bishoprics were relatively wealthy or poor while the concordat was in force. We know what the selection process looked like before the concordat, but we will now also need to assess how different each diocese's secularism was before the agreement compared to during it.

To analyze the concordat's impact, we need to know two more pieces of information: (1) When did the terms of the concordat cease to be the operative or discernible rules shaping the selection of bishops—that is, when and where did bishop selection shift into the concordat game's third outcome? (2) What observable factors shaped the costs that rulers paid if they defied the pope's wishes in choosing a bishop?

THE GAME'S THIRD OUTCOME: AVIGNON AND
REBELLION AGAINST THE CHURCH

The seeming end of the concordat's immediate, observable impact happened twice: once starting in 1309 for France, and a second time, beginning in 1517, for much of the Holy Roman Empire. In between those two events the distribution and existence of wealth was redefined and recalibrated by the economic and human shock brought about by the Black Death that began in 1347 and lasted until about 1351, leaving Europe devastated, with about 30 percent of its population dead and with too few farmers to grow crops and too few laborers to rebuild the economy. As we will see in Chapter 6, but for this monstrous plague, it is likely that the outside option—a secular break with the church—would have been exercised long before 1517 across much of northern Europe. Barring the shock of the plague, the logic of the concordat would have in essence set its own timetable for its demise. Even though the concordat had no explicit sunset clause, the treaty's logic dictated that it would end once wealth expanded sufficiently for signatories to have entered the third case.

The treaty's logical outcome came first to fruition in France, the very country whose King Philip I had come forward in 1107 to try to promote reconciliation between the emperor and the pope, thereby helping create the very idea of a concordat. Remember the third scenario we examined: a diocese or a country full of dioceses became sufficiently wealthy that kings were in a position to keep both control over bishops and the money generated by their regalian sees. Under those conditions, the king no longer needed the concordat's rules and bargaining incentives to assure his growing political power. That is what happened first in France in 1309 and then in the northern portions of the Holy Roman Empire starting well before 1517.

France was rapidly becoming the wealthiest kingdom in Europe during the twelfth and thirteenth centuries. Its attainment of considerable wealth during these years facilitated the creation of the Avignon papacy in 1309, thereby creating the bookends that defined the span of the concordat. After the deal was agreed to by the French monarch in 1107, it was adhered to by his successors until the time of King Philip IV, who by 1309 had rendered the concordat's terms moot. Philip captured control over the choice of popes. Hence, for an extended period beyond 1309, the pope was chosen to be loyal to the French monarch, meaning that it was no longer possible to distinguish between bishops who were royalists and those who were aligned with the church. The two simply became one and the same.

Throughout the Avignon papacy, popes were French and the seat of church power (the curia) resided in Avignon rather than Rome.[1] The Avignon papacy prevailed from 1309 to 1376, resumed as the Western Schism (the period when there were rival claimants to the papacy) in 1378, and ended in 1417 with the Council of Constance. During that period, some of the Avignon popes can be said to have acted fully on behalf of the French king. Others, such as the first, Clement V, understood the importance of survival, so he frequently, as necessary, succumbed to the king's pressures. As James Stephen, writing in 1855, observed, "The Popes were little more than vassals of the French monarchs at Avignon."[2] Since the Avignon papacy turned the pope and his bishops on secular matters into agents of secular rule, the beginning of the Avignon papacy in 1309 can be taken as demarcating the end of the period in which the concordats discernably defined relations between religious and secular authorities.[3] During that two-century interval, the parts of Europe that were covered by the concordats shifted from a balance of power that favored popes to one that favored secular rulers, especially larger, wealthier ones, who tended to be kings. The age of kingly deference to the pope's choices and decisions that was theoretically enshrined in the Concordat of Worms had ended.

If the concordat game yielded the consequences we expect from it, then who was chosen as bishop mattered greatly in terms of the enforcement of church policies or royal objectives. According to the game, the choice of bishops depended on the exchange of money for power and also on the church's ability to credibly threaten to punish lay leaders who were perceived to have disobeyed the pope's and church's dicta. We now know when the impact of the concordats should have started and when its discernible impact should have ended. Now we need to better understand how the church used its punishment tools to provide it with a countermaneuver to the growing influence of the secular domain. I will illustrate how punishments were used by the church so that we can begin to think more strategically about the difference between the power to threaten a punishment and the power to enforce one. After illustrating the shifting uses of punishments by the church, we will consider in more detail how to measure a bishop's alignment, diocesan wealth, and the expected magnitude of punishment.

THE CHURCH'S CHANGING USE OF PUNISHMENT

Money provided kings with leverage that could be used to get the bishops they wanted *if* enough money was at stake in the diocese. Popes also had plenty of leverage *if* they could count on the clergy to carry out their orders. Rulers with little money had to take whomever the church offered to fill bishoprics. Popes with few loyalists in a diocese could impose a sentence on the secular ruler, but they could not count on that sentence being carried out by clergy who were in the ruler's pocket.

In a time when religion was central to everything in life, when the good and bad outcomes in life were attributed to God rather than to science or random misfortune, the church's ability to punish must have carried great weight. For those who believed in the promise of eternal salvation, as surely almost everyone in Europe did in the twelfth to fourteenth centuries and beyond, the pain of being excommunicated or interdicted must have been great indeed. But that pain might be mitigated if, for instance, the local bishop chose not to carry out the orders from Rome, as happened when King Philip II of France (1179–1223; also known as Philip Augustus) found his realm interdicted by Pope Innocent III.

King Philip married Agnes of Merania (1175–1201) in 1196 over the objections of Pope Celestine III (1191–1198). In Celestine's eyes, this marriage was a problem because Philip was already married. He had married Ingeborg of Denmark (1174–1237) on August 15, 1193, and requested an annulment on August 16. The annulment was denied, and when the king ignored the pope's ruling, he was excommunicated. When the excommunication failed to pressure Philip into restoring Ingeborg as queen, the new pope, Innocent III, interdicted Philip's realm.

The dioceses of twenty-five bishops were subjected to the interdict, creating a potential disaster for France and a natural experiment for us. Each of the twenty-five bishops had to choose sides. Would they enforce the interdict, demonstrating their loyalty to the pope, or would they ignore it, showing their alignment with the king? We know for sure what eighteen of them did. Five bishops are known to have sided with the pope. They were from the bishoprics of Senlis, Soissons, Amiens, Arras, and Paris. Only one among these five, Eudes de Sully (bishop of Paris, 1197–1208), had a background that made Philip expect him to be loyal. Eudes was then severely punished by the king.

Thirteen bishops are known to have sided with Philip. Of these, twelve were either Philip's blood relatives or his close personal associates.[4] They were exactly the sorts of bishops who were secularly aligned and therefore could be expected to ignore church efforts to punish their patron, the king.

Two lessons were implied by the French experience with interdiction: (1) The pope and church could not count on their ability to inflict costly punishments if the local bishops were loyal to the secular ruler rather than to them. (2) Knowing they could not count on the punishment strategies of the past, the pope and church probably modified the way they used punishments to gain additional leverage after the concordat altered relations between popes and rulers. The changed circumstances dictated that the church would try to punish recalcitrant kings to induce the selection of more religiously aligned bishops, and they also dictated that where there was sufficient wealth, these efforts would prove ineffective.

To see whether popes were prepared to try to punish secular rulers for political defiance rather than for violations of Christian belief, I turn to Figure 4.1.[5] The figure shows, by century, the distribution of politically motivated excommunications compared to religiously motivated excommunications associated with heresy as well as other, particularistic, excommunications associated with, for instance, marriage disagreements or insubordination by inferior clerics to superior clerics. The graph looks at all significant excommunications from the birth of Christianity until the end of the fifteenth century, just before the time of Martin Luther (1517). Naturally there is some degree of judgment associated with the classification of major excommunications, as these actions are rarely identified explicitly as due to politics or to behaviors outside heresy. And then, too, some excommunications applied to groups of people, such as cardinals who voted for an antipope or whole towns that defied the pope's or local bishop's wishes. These are estimated as between one and five excommunications in each case to avoid overcounting. With these caveats in mind, we see that the figure shows that excommunications before 1046—that is, before the Investiture Controversy was launched by Henry III's deposition of Pope Gregory VI—were primarily the result of internecine church battles over what were accepted teachings, with just a smattering of other causes related to individual personal peccadilloes. Heresy, which placed one's eternal soul in jeopardy, was the nearly exclusive source of excommunication before the church's struggle shifted from competition among internal factions to competition with secular rulers. Then, faced with a threat to its temporal political power, the church used excommunication *politically* in an effort to secure the hegemony of its spiritual sword over the secular sword.

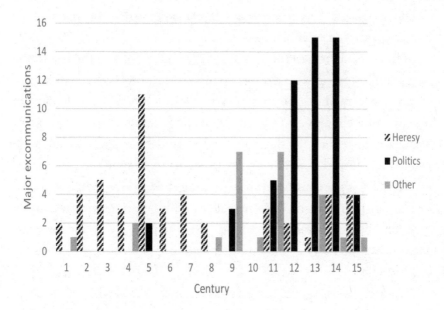

Figure 4.1: Reasons for excommunications: Heresy, politics, or other

The church's shifting reasons for excommunication tell the tale of a political institution struggling against the growing bargaining power and competitive influence of secular rulers, especially during the years that the concordat was in effect, that is, between 1122 (or 1107 in France and England) and the rise and persistence of the Avignon papacy, which rendered the distinction between the interests, or at least the choices, of rulers of the church and the ruler of France moot. Before the Investiture Controversy, over a span of ten centuries, barely any monarch or other significant political—nonreligious—figure experienced excommunication. Even during the century of the Investiture Controversy, 50 percent of excommunications were for religious offenses, with about 35 percent applied to such major political luminaries as the Holy Roman emperor. Yet during the interlude of the concordats, covering the twelfth, thirteenth, and fourteenth centuries, 78 percent of excommunications were aimed at secular rulers and only 13 percent concerned heretical teachings. This is all the more remarkable given that this was the time of such reformist—heretical—movements as the Waldensians, the Cathars, the followers of Henry of Lausanne, and others. The church had not relaxed its efforts against these movements. It just appears that way because the church magnified its efforts against kings.

In the years between the signing of the concordat and the rise of the Avignon papacy, popes used their punishment powers against kings to an unprecedented degree. Where a monarch's control over the flow of money threatened to cost the church its political leverage, punishment was a way to reduce the damage. But for punishment to be effective it had to be enforced. As France's Philip Augustus's experience illustrates, where bishops were more loyal to the king than to the church, the declaration of punishment was one thing and its enforcement was quite another. Th declaration of an interdict by the pope by no means guaranteed that the costs of the interdict were imposed on the ruler or his subjects.

Interdicts were terrible things. Marriages were forbidden. Babies might be denied baptism. Horrible, eternal consequences could follow denial of these essential Christian rights. Interdicts could mean unbelievably painful deprivations for its victims, but those deprivations didn't necessarily follow if the local clergy, firmly in the pocket of the lay leader, ignored the church's orders, as happened for most of the subjects in Philip Augustus's France. That tells us that we have to worry not only about the order of excommunication or interdictions but also about the church's ability to carry out the order and inflict the intended pain. History is replete with examples in which church efforts to punish were powerful indeed, but it is also full of examples where such efforts failed.

The story of King John's decisions in England in 1215 to accept the Magna Carta, the great charter, and then to renege on it provides a useful illustration of what we see in Figure 4.1 about the use of papal punishments as a political tool after the Investiture Controversy, rather than a religious tool in pursuit of adherence to catholic doctrine. As we review the case, we must remember that King John was never accused of heresy, but he did stand accused of taking money away from the church for his own benefit. That was certainly bad behavior, but it was not uncommon for kings to try to take church wealth, and it had previously been uncommon indeed for a monarch to be excommunicated for such an offense. As Figure 4.1 reminds us, it was uncommon for kings to be excommunicated before the Investiture Controversy, but it was remarkably common throughout the interval that a concordat was operative.

The dispute between King John and Pope Innocent III was no small affair. It helped shape the eventual dispute between John and his barons and, through that dispute, the very stability of the English crown. John's conflict with the pope was, in fact, precisely a battle over the selection of a bishop. The case concerned who was to be the archbishop of Canterbury. Under the terms of the Concordat of London, the church—through the pope—had the right to nominate whomever it wanted to fill the important post of archbishop of Canterbury. But equally, under the terms of the concordat, King John had the right to say no, which he did.

John's refusal to accept Stephen Langton as archbishop of Canterbury angered the pope. He then vigorously used the punishment hammers at his disposal to try to get John to accept the new archbishop. John had earlier plundered the English churches, seizing their wealth for his own political purposes. In 1208, Innocent interdicted John's kingdom to force him to make restitution. This failed, so Innocent excommunicated John in 1209. This effort too failed to alter John's behavior. Finally, the pope signed an order of deposition in 1212, nullifying all previous oaths of loyalty to John. The pope actually declared that John, elected king by the barons in 1199, was not a legitimate king so no one owed him any of the protections and services they had taken oaths to provide, a heavy hammer indeed. The pope was inviting the very barons who had elected John to get rid of him, and they heard the message loud and clear.

With their oaths to John nullified and their displeasure, especially with his tax policy, at a peak, the barons rose up against John, confronting him with the Magna Carta at Runnymede. The pope's nullification gave the barons cover, but it was John's increased taxation, not papal punishment, that prompted them to rise up against their elected king. John, having been compelled to sign the Magna Carta, and so promising to give the barons a greater say in their governance, finally capitulated to Innocent's demand that Langton be accepted as archbishop of Canterbury. Compared to the implications of the Magna Carta, John saw Langton as the lesser evil. The pope, now having gotten what he wanted, condemned the Magna Carta and backed John against the barons, triggering England's First Barons' War (1215–1217).

The pope seems not to have been a fan of the Magna Carta, but he was willing to use his leverage to encourage the barons as a means to achieve his own objective. Once Innocent got John to approve of Langton, the barons were abandoned, and John protected his authority against the threat of the charter and made a tentative peace of convenience with the pope. The battle between the church and the monarchy had been as much over political clout as had the struggle at Runnymede between the king and his barons. Religious differences never seemed to be front and center. As was so often true, many of the battles between church and state and between kings and subjects—including the battle with the barons at Runnymede—was more about money and power than about rights. Indeed, the vast majority of the conditions in the Magna Carta are about who owned what, about power and money, and not about freedom and representation. But freedom and representation were the vehicles to lock the king into the material concessions called for by the charter. With the charter pushed aside thanks to John's acquiescence to Innocent, the battles over representation in government were still to come. First the concordat had to stimulate enough economic growth to create leverage for subjects toward their lords and kings.

Popes clearly were ready to fire the arrows of punishment that were in their quiver to try to make rulers do what they wanted, including the selection of prochurch bishops. Rulers with leverage—those who presided over wealthy dioceses—also had to be prepared to translate their leverage into the selection of proking bishops, leaving the church mostly with loyal bishops in poorer sees where the king didn't have a lot of bargaining power. Now it is time to find out if that is what happened.

THE SECULARIZATION OF BISHOPS

Working out the big picture of the impact of the concordat requires us to look at a vast number of decisions about the selection of new bishops. It also means we need to know something about the relative wealth of a large number of dioceses all across Europe, across a tremendous number of years. Today, thanks to the incredible amounts of information available online, with a bit of analysis it is possible to capture the necessary data. In fact, as briefly suggested in Chapter 3, I have assembled relevant information on as many Roman Catholic dioceses as I could, including 286 that were subject to and so should show the influence of one of the concordats and 327 that were not. I refer to the dioceses that were subject to a concordat as being covered. The concordats covered the dioceses in the modern states of Germany, Austria, France, Belgium, the Netherlands, most of Italy from the Papal States northward, and England, as well as the dioceses of Basel (Switzerland), Lebus (Poland, from 1125), Wrocław (Poland), Gniezno (Poland), Poznań (Poland), Lavant (Slovenia, after 1228), and Olomouc (Czech Republic). The rest of Europe, including, for instance, Spain, Portugal, Sicily and much of southern Italy, the Veneto region (a region of Italy that included the port of Venice with its extensive maritime trade), Russia, and the remainder of eastern Europe, were not subject to the concordat. These provide an excellent source of information, a sort of control group against which we can measure the impact the concordat had.

I look at as many of these dioceses as possible each time they got a new bishop, starting in the year 325 and ending as late as 1700 for some of the later analyses. Of course, each diocese had many bishops over the long time period we will look at; we will especially emphasize the period from the Council of Nicaea (325) to the beginning of the Avignon papacy (1309), which marked the end of the "Worms interlude" or the "concordat interlude," and on to 1517, when Martin Luther launched the Protestant Reformation.[6] And also, naturally, the number of bishops about whom we have the required information swells with the passage of time, so in particular we will have a lot of information from about 700 forward.

Not only will we evaluate what was going on across hundreds of individual dioceses and across a thousand years and more, but we will do so with at least some information on about eighteen thousand Roman Catholic bishops and with critical alignment information on more than four thousand of them.[7] That's a lot of data, and it should give us some confidence that the correlations we will see, coupled with the relationships predicted by the concordat game, if consistent with expectations, are not just the product of dumb luck but are probably close to a proper explanation of what was going on to change Europe's future. If secularism spread in the way the concordat game leads us to expect, then in its spread we are looking at the beginning of the growth of Western exceptionalism. And if we see that, then we will be in a good position to look at the rest of the implications of the concordat for the other big pieces of Western exceptionalism: prosperity, religious tolerance, representative government, and the growth of science and of innovation. And if these parts are also consistent with the predictions from the concordat game, then we gain increasing confidence that it is the rules, incentives, and strategic changes created by the concordat—and not cultural, psychological, ethnic, racial, religious, or other factors—that were and are the main causes of Western exceptionalism.

Indeed, we will also gain confidence that the famous thesis of Max Weber, that Protestantism created northern Europe's work ethic and its prosperity, is backward. Instead, we will see that the terms of the concordat incentivized a more successful work ethic in northern Europe than in southern Europe, and we will see that that work ethic, in turn, contributed to the rise of the Protestant Reformation, turning Weber's argument on its head.[8]

The first pivotal factor to be explained concerns the alignment, whether secular or religious, of each bishop. As touched on earlier, this alignment was determined by studying the available biographies of bishops to ascertain what sort of work they did before becoming a bishop.[9]

The biographies I consulted yielded the necessary information to classify a bishop as religious or secular for 4,253 bishops between the years 325 and 1700, regardless of whether they were from dioceses subject to a concordat or not. Of these, 2,709 were bishops between 325 and 1517, the years of greatest interest here. Of the bishops in sees that were subject to the rules of a concordat, 76 percent were religiously aligned; the remainder were secular.[10] The ratio is similar in places that were not subject to a concordat—the "control" countries mentioned earlier. Recall that during the Avignon papacy, the pope was the agent of the French king in nonreligious matters, and so even when a bishop with a "religious" background was chosen, especially between 1309 and 1417, he was probably expected to be loyal to the secular authority who chose the pope.

We should be aware that some dioceses have no relevant data and so there are plenty of bishops who are completely missing simply because records could not be found. There is, however, no reason to believe that missing information reflects any more than losses through fires, disasters, wars, and other destructive forces over the very large number of years investigated here.[11]

THE WEALTH OF DIOCESES

Thanks to the Old World Trade Route Project, historical maps of Europe, and economic histories, for every diocese in Europe, we can make a trade-route approximation of whether it was wealthy or not.[12] Although charting access to trade routes is a crude way of estimating wealth, watching the effects of changing trade patterns year by year gives somewhat more insight. Those dioceses that were consistently on major trade routes probably accumulated a lot of wealth, and conversely, those on a trade route for only a small percentage of their existence presumably accumulated less wealth.[13] I will make use of this cumulative wealth approximation in later chapters. As a secondary indication of diocesan wealth, I will also take advantage of some pretty nuanced information about diocesan wealth from a totally different perspective: the potential of the land in each diocese to produce crops with higher or lower calorie content.[14]

WEALTH AND THE SECULARIZATION OF BISHOPS: A FIRST TEST

Analyzing the impact both of trade routes, a source of wealth that varied in response to a myriad of factors, and of land caloric potential, a source of wealth that was constant, we can start to see how the effects of the concordat played out. Figure 4.2, based on the land's caloric productivity potential, supports the expectation that wealthy bishoprics had more-secular bishops during the years of the concordat and that poor ones had more-religious bishops. The black bars show the average percentage of bishops who were secularly oriented in the dioceses that had high caloric potential—that is, the wealthy sees. The gray bars depict the average amount of secularism in poorer dioceses. The two bars to the right in the figure show the average amount of secularism for wealthy and poor dioceses during the period the concordats were in effect. The bars on the left show the same information for the period before the onset of any concordat. As is evident, only well-to-do dioceses during the interlude of the concordats had meaningfully more secularly oriented bishops. The level of secularism for the wealthy dioceses during the concordat is both statistically and visually significantly greater than for any of the other three categories of bishoprics.[15]

The caloric potential evidence is reassuring for the claims made by the concordat game, especially because the land's physical potential to generate wealth cannot have been caused by the choice of bishops, so we are clearly looking at evidence where there is only one possible direction of causality: better land could yield greater agricultural productivity and, with it, greater local wealth and greater secularism.

Trade-route information can change with time, so now we are just about ready to put our attention squarely on that way of approximating

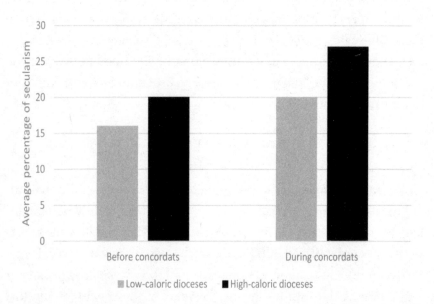

Figure 4.2: Caloric potential and secularism: Before and during the concordats

wealth. One task remains before we do that. We need to resolve when a ruler would have believed he or she was at risk of high costs being imposed by the church for not doing what the pope wanted—for example, for insisting on a secularly oriented bishop.

ASSESSING THE EXPECTED COSTS
OF DEFYING THE CHURCH

The concordat game requires us to take into account the expected magnitude of costs that the church could impose on vexatious lay rulers. Unfortunately, we cannot know how one lay leader differed from another in their personal sensitivity to being excommunicated or having their realm interdicted. We just do not and cannot know what was in their heart. Still, even if we assume that all rulers were eager to avoid enduring the costs the pope might inflict, it is possible to distinguish broadly between those who expected to suffer significant enforced costs from the church and those who expected to suffer lower enforced costs or no enforced costs at all.

While the cost of religious punishments inflicted on lay rulers could be terribly painful, the *expected* impact of the imposed cost depended on the church's ability to *enforce* its chosen punishment. Once again we are reminded that Pope Innocent III's efforts to interdict Philip Augustus's realm failed to be enforced almost everywhere that Philip had a bishop who was loyal to him rather than to the church. And we should remember too that Dietrich I von Hengebach, the archbishop of Cologne, ignored his excommunication by Innocent III in 1212 when he could count on the Holy Roman emperor—also excommunicated— to stand by him. As such, specifically mindful of these and many other such experiences, we can apply a standard approach from the study of war to estimate where the church's enforcement power was weak.

We know that before the advent of modern technology, the ability to project power and carry out costly threats, like the ability to invade a faraway foe or capture and imprison or execute a distant rival, diminished over distance. So we can rely on the distance of a diocese from Rome as a rough proxy for the pope's ability to enforce and exact punishment. Even excommunication functions this way, as the pope has to count on local clergy and the local population to shun their king, which may or may not be in their interest.

Anecdotal evidence for the period between 1122 and 1517 suggests that distance is a good proxy for the power of enforcement.[16] For instance, the success or failure at punishing heretics during the interlude between the concordat and the run-up to and start of the Protestant Reformation illustrates how powerful distance was in dampening the church's ability to enforce its punishment decrees.

Consider, for instance, why the church was unable to stop many of the reformers/heretics who were precursors to the Reformation, such as Peter Waldo or John Wycliffe, but it successfully stopped Girolamo Savonarola, Jan Hus, and many others in the years after the concordat was signed and before Martin Luther nailed his theses to the church door. The distance proxy sorts out where the church found it easy to stop heretics and would-be heretics and where it did not. Naturally there may be other explanations for the church's success or failure in each case, but the reformer/heretic's distance from Rome seems like a pretty strong explanation.

Savonarola, hanged and burned in 1498, preached against the corruption of the church and sought to establish Florence as the City of God. Even before he encouraged the overthrow of the powerful Medici family in Florence, his actions and his preaching had aroused the opposition of Pope Alexander VI. Alexander tried to silence him but failed. Then the pope tried to win him over with an offer to make him a cardinal. That too failed. Savonarola resumed his sermons, including personal attacks on the pope's way of life as well as on the excesses of the clergy and other powerful people. The pope threatened to excommunicate Savonarola and to interdict Florence, thereby inflicting costs on the people in Savonarola's City of God. That did it. Savonarola stuck to his views, but the people turned against him. He and two loyal friars were tried, convicted, hanged, and burned.[17]

Like Savonarola, Jan Hus was seen as a fundamental threat to the church's authority. From his base in Prague he had become rector of Charles University and an advocate of many of the ideas put forward by the English reformer John Wycliffe. Hus's ideas were widely accepted in his home kingdom of Bohemia, including by King Wenceslas IV. That was not good news for the pope. Hus's ideas were most decidedly not accepted by the Catholic Church. Prague was placed under interdict because of Hus's teaching. In an effort to help the king and the people, so many of whom were loyal to him and his ideas, Hus left the city to relieve the pressure of the interdiction.[18] However, that was not the end of the problems his teachings and his political views fomented. Since Hus was pretty far from Rome and enjoyed the support of his own government, support that shielded him from a terrible fate, he kept pushing his ideas, endangering himself further by also speaking out against the Holy Roman emperor's influence in Bohemia, a risky undertaking indeed.

King Wenceslas's brother, Sigismund, became king of Germany in 1411 (and Holy Roman emperor in 1433). From his position in Germany he wished to diminish the strife between the church and the empire as well as to resolve the festering schism between the pope in Avignon and the pope in Rome. With that in mind, Sigismund supported the Council of Constance, which in fact in 1417 ended the papal schism that had followed on the official end of the Avignon papacy in 1376. The schism was not the council's only concern. There was plenty of worry about the growth in heretical teachings that threatened the authority of the already weakened papacy after its century of woes going back to the rise of a French-loyalist pope in 1305.

Hus was a source of concern that Sigismund hoped to correct. Sigismund saw to it that Hus was offered safe passage to attend the council and explain his perspective. Hus foolishly agreed, perhaps believing that his good relations with Wenceslas would assure his safety with Sigismund. Hus went to Constance, putting himself in reach of the church despite the great distance from Rome. The safe passage was violated, Hus was condemned as a heretic, and he was burned at the stake in 1415. Had he not believed in the promise of safe passage, it seems likely that his distance from the clutches of the pope would have saved him, as it seemingly had done before he went to Constance.

In contrast to Savonarola and Hus, John Wycliffe died of natural causes at the age of sixty-four in 1384. He too preached against the excesses of the clergy and also against many of the teachings of the church, just as Savonarola and Hus would do later. But Wycliffe was not condemned as a heretic in his lifetime, although he was so condemned at the Council of Constance, three decades after his death. True, his body was exhumed and burned at the stake in 1428, but we might reasonably suspect that this was a much less painful experience than that suffered by Savonarola or Hus.

Similarly, Peter Waldo, the founder of the Waldensians in Lyon, escaped the ultimate wrath of the church. His movement, begun in 1173, just a half century after the Concordat of Worms had been signed, encouraged lay preaching and poverty for all preachers. Within a decade, Waldo was excommunicated and declared a heretic. But unlike Savonarola or Hus, both more than two centuries later and both within relatively easy reach of the church (foolishly in Hus's case), Waldo, long before the troubles that brought the church's leaders to Constance, fled farther north to Germany, where he could be and was protected from condemnation.[19] His movement spread and eventually became a part of the Calvinist Protestant movement. Distance from the reach of Rome may have been the key difference in the respective fates of Savonarola, Hus, and Waldo.

Distance alone did not guarantee safety. In fact, a considerable number of heretics were condemned and burned at the stake in London and Paris and even as far from Rome as Sweden. Yet many heretics who were far removed from Rome, like John Wycliffe, managed to survive into old age, whereas those more proximate to Rome, such as Peter of Bruys (d. 1131), Gerard Segarelli (d. 1300), Fra Dolcino (d. 1307), Cecco d'Ascoli (d. 1327) and others, were more likely to be judged to be heretics and were then either killed by mobs (like Peter of Bruys) or burned for their beliefs (like Gerard Segarelli, Fra Dolcino, and Cecco d'Ascoli). It was very hard to escape the church's grasp if one was close to the church's seat of power or if, like Jan Hus and his colleague Jerome of Prague, one chose to put oneself within the church's grasp. In this regard we should not forget that Martin Luther was offered safe passage to Rome and declined it, undoubtedly confident that once he was within the pope's reach, the safe passage would be rendered meaningless. With the apparent importance of distance as a source of expectations about how painful the church could make deviation from its interests, I use distance from Rome in kilometers as a proxy for costs. I treat the analysis that uses this noisy indicator as secondary since, of course, different leaders will have viewed, for instance, the cost of their excommunication quite differently independently of how far a diocese was from Rome.

We are now ready to muster a great deal of evidence to answer the first key question about the birth of European exceptionalism. The concordat game instructs us that once the concordat was signed, there should have been an expansion in the number of secularly oriented bishops in wealthier dioceses, moving Europe away from intellectual domination by the Catholic Church and toward a more secularly oriented view of the political—and then the economic and then the spiritual—world.

We will want to view the evidence with some humility, recognizing how extremely difficult it is to measure any of the things we want to know at such a huge remove in time. That is not to make excuses; none are needed. The evidence very strongly reinforces the implications of the concordat game despite all the challenges of trying to test its nuanced implications. It is just to say that we will do well to remember all the crucial things we do not and cannot fully know. We do not know which dioceses were wealthy even though they were not on trade routes. We do not know whether, for reasons not apparent to us across time and space, some local rulers might have preferred a religious bishop, or whether they were subject to the influence of people who did. So what we really want to see is that a *disproportionately large* number of secularly oriented bishops are appointed in wealthy places compared to poor places once a concordat is accepted. We also want to see that this is especially true compared to two control groups: dioceses before the concordat, and dioceses after the concordat was signed but not subject to it, just as we saw when we looked at caloric potential and secularism.

WEALTHY SEES FOR SECULAR BISHOPS AND POOR SEES FOR RELIGIOUS BISHOPS

Let us begin by looking at the big picture of the swing in the secular alignment of bishops over a long swath of time. Figure 4.3 reports the proportion of bishops who were secularly aligned, comparing alignments during the interlude the concordats were operative to the alignments in the preconcordat epoch that starts in 325 and runs through 1107 or 1122, depending on which agreement applied. The black bars show the percentage of secularly aligned bishops in wealthy sees and the gray bars show the percentage of secularly leaning bishops in poor bishoprics. The figure, which only investigates dioceses that were eventually covered by the concordats, tells a clear story in keeping with the secularization implications of the game.

While wealthier dioceses, on average, were a bit more likely than poor bishoprics to have secularly oriented bishops before the concordat, the dramatic difference in favor of the appointment of secularly aligned bishops arises only for the wealthy dioceses during the period from the concordat to Avignon. The difference is sharp whether we look at poor and rich dioceses during the interlude of the concordat or we compare secularism in wealthy bishoprics across the two time periods.

Once the concordats were operative, wealthy sees had approximately twice the odds of getting a secularly aligned bishop as did poor bishoprics during or before the concordat, and they were about 50 percent more likely to get a secularly aligned bishop during the time the

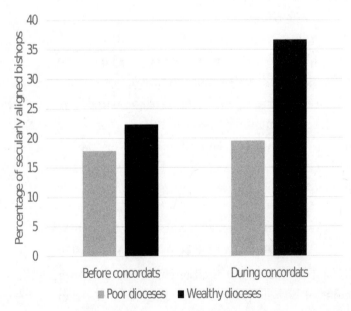

Figure 4.3: Percentage secular bishops by wealth, before and during the concordats

concordat was in effect than was true of wealthy sees before the resolution of the Investiture Controversy. These differences are very unlikely
to be due to chance.[20]

The concordat game, of course, tells us that a wealthy lay leader's improved bargaining leverage vis-à-vis the pope might have been offset
by the costs the pope could inflict on the ruler if the pope were denied
a bishop to his liking. We have discussed a way of trying to evaluate
whether the expected cost was likely to be high enough to get the ruler
to agree to a religiously oriented bishop even when he wanted a secularly inclined one. Now we can probe how well distance from Rome explains the choice of secular or religious bishops.

What do we see when we take into account how far each diocese is
from Rome? It turns out that among wealthy bishoprics, being far from
Rome meant that 38 percent of the people chosen as bishop were secular, twice the odds of secular bishops in distant, wealthy, covered dioceses before the concordat.[21] What is more, being far from Rome also
meant that many more poor dioceses got secular bishops than was true
if they had been close to Rome—twice as many in fact, implying that
the dividing line between wealthy and poor, between more bargaining
leverage and less bargaining leverage, improved for kings as they got far
away from the pope's reach. Being far away apparently meant that the
costs rulers expected to suffer were reduced enough that less wealth was
needed for them to expect a net gain from using their political leverage.[22]

In contrast, if the diocese was very close to Rome—within five hundred kilometers—so that Rome's ability to inflict costs was substantial,
then it turns out that nearly zero secularly inclined bishop were chosen
in wealthy, covered dioceses before or during the concordat. So while
wealth generally boosted the odds of secularism, it seems that high
costs diminished those odds substantially, netting a greatly reduced
likelihood of choosing a secularly oriented bishop close to Rome. As expected, when a diocese was very far from Rome, then the expected cost
apparently was relatively small and so carried little weight in discourag-
ing the selection of secular bishops in dioceses with money and power at
stake. The evidence thus far is consistent with the expectation that the
concordat had a dramatic, stimulating impact on the secularization of

bishops in wealthy locations, especially when those locations were far enough from Rome that they supported the expectation of low costs from defying the pope. This observation carries implications for the rise not only of secularism but also of economic growth and anti-Catholic movements far from Rome, as explored in the coming chapters.

Without getting too bogged down in details, it will be helpful for us to do two more bits of investigating before concluding confidently that the terms of the concordats fostered a significant boost in secularism at the church's expense. One demanding test of the game's claims is for us to repeat what we have already done, but now comparing the effects for bishoprics that were not covered by any of the concordats to what we already know about those that were covered. Doing so allows us to evaluate whether wealthy places in general were becoming more secular or whether those wealthy dioceses that were not subject to the concordat's rules behaved differently from those places that were covered by the treaties.

In fact, what the evidence reveals is that for dioceses that were not covered by the concordat, neither rulers over wealthy sees nor those over poor sees during or before the concordat behaved differently from each other in the selection of bishops. Among bishops in poor bishoprics between the years 325 and 1309 that were not subject to a concordat, 85 percent were religiously inclined. The comparable percentage for wealthy uncovered dioceses was 78 percent religiously oriented bishops, a difference that is not statistically meaningful. It seems that wealth did not prompt rulers of uncovered bishoprics to insist on secular bishops, just as poverty did not limit the occasional choice of secular bishops. Only the bishoprics subject to the rules of the concordat demonstrated the altered choice patterns—picking more secularly inclined bishops in wealthy sees and more religiously oriented bishops in poor dioceses— during the years of the concordats.[23] It seems that Europe's exceptionalism starts with the concordats and starts in the wealthy covered sees, especially those that were far from Rome.

We should do one more tough test before deciding that the concordat game seems to be right about the growth of secularism thanks to the bargaining leverage that rulers gained in wealthier bishoprics. We have

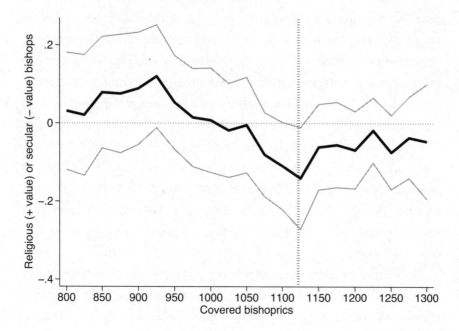

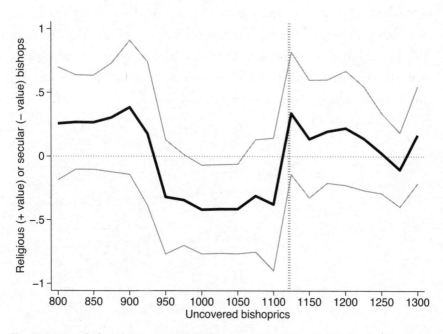

Figure 4.4: Level of secularism among bishops in covered and uncovered bishoprics

seen that the effects were only realized in covered bishoprics, but we do not know, except for a broad-swath comparison, whether the timing of the rise of secularism was intimately dependent on when the concordats were signed. To check whether the concordat really influenced the rise of secularism, I repeated the analysis used to construct Figure 4.3, but now assessing the level of secularism among bishops in each possible 187-year period between the years 800 and 1517 (e.g., 800–987, 801–988, . . . 1330–1517) to see whether the rise of secularism was especially noteworthy during the 187 years that the concordat of Worms was in effect. Figure 4.4 shows the results. The first panel probes the impact of the concordat on secularism for all covered sees, and the second replicates the analysis for uncovered bishoprics.

The results strongly indicate that the peak level of secularism in fact happened during the 187 years between the signing of the concordat and the start of the Avignon papacy and that this is only true for signatories to a concordat.[24] That is exactly what the concordat game indicates should be true.

What is more, secular leanings were taking hold especially across the wealthier sees in the covered kingdoms of France and the Holy Roman Empire but not in the dioceses of the uncovered kingdoms across Spain, Sicily, the Veneto region, Portugal, Scandinavia, or eastern Europe. The times, it seems, they were a-changin'!

5

THE ROAD TO PROSPERITY

Solomon says that "idleness teaches a man to do many evils."

—Geoffrey Chaucer, "The Tale of Melibee"

DURING THE VERY PERIOD THAT THE CONCORDATS WERE IN EFFECT, Europe experienced an explosion in economic growth. Lots of explanations have been offered for that growth. The incentives created by the concordat is certainly not among them.[1] In fact, some have argued the opposite: that the concordats had nothing to do with economic developments across Europe.[2] Instead, the explosion in economic growth has been attributed to completely unrelated phenomena.[3] The earth's climate was warming, making growing seasons longer.[4] New developments in technology, like the heavy plow and the vertical water wheel, and the development of corporations and banking institutions made it possible to improve productivity.[5] The commercial revolution saw a flowering of trade, with merchants bringing exotic products from far away and textiles, tools, lumber, and other products from not so far.[6] All of these were important contributors to Europe's growth, but none explain why northwestern Europe grew faster and grew more than the rest of Europe. The incentives set into motion by the concordats do explain these differences. It is these variations in growth that are also the foundation of the differences in the emergence of exceptionalism between northern and southern Europe and between western and eastern Europe.

How, in a time of so many improvements, might the concordat have made an unnoticed and yet major difference in economic growth? The evidence in this and the next chapter is going to show us that the concordat did indeed play an outsize part in differentiating the rates of economic expansion in different parts of Europe. It is easy to see how it did so if we think about what we have learned so far and what it would have meant to a political leader or to a church leader at the time.

We know, and kings, princes, and other nobles surely knew better than we do, that the ability to compete successfully against the awesome authority of the Roman Catholic Church was greater in wealthier dioceses than in poorer ones *if* they had signed on to a concordat. As the evidence has shown us, secular leaders at the time had figured out that they could get people appointed as bishops—that is, appointed to be among the most powerful people in their world—who would be more loyal to them than to the church. They could succeed in securing such bishops provided that the diocesan territories they controlled were worth enough that it would hurt the church to lose the revenue from them. So wealthier covered bishoprics got more secularly aligned bishops and poorer dioceses got more religiously aligned bishops. From the pope's perspective, these same facts and implications meant that if there were more relatively poor dioceses, then he would control the policies implemented in more parishes, more churches, more cathedrals, and, ultimately, more palaces and castles across Europe's bishoprics that were subject to the concordat. Wealth meant secular power that hurt the church's authority.

Lay leaders who could make more of their territory wealthy could get greater political clout. Likewise, the pope and church could gain greater political control by making bishoprics poorer, or at least not wealthier, once the concordat took effect. Indeed, the deal struck at Worms initiated synergy between the advancement of secular political interests and the promotion of economic development. No longer was it the case that a king could expand his power only through war and marriage.[7] While not obviating the urge for conquest and territorial expansion, the concordats instigated a politically beneficial reason for monarchs to alter their policies and forge compromises with some of their subjects in order to promote economic development. After all, the logic of the concordat dictated that papal influence over local religious, social, political, and economic policies would be diminished wherever substantial diocesan income could be transferred—or withheld—by the local ruler, depending on who was nominated to become bishop. Europe's temporal rulers had secured an opportunity to gain a great advantage over God's vicar on earth, provided they could generate enough wealth to obtain leverage and could withstand church punishment well enough to act on their enhanced bargaining power. By inventing new ways to increase their wealth, they were inventing a new source of power for themselves. Hence, monarchs and other secular leaders who were subject to the terms of a concordat looked for ways to make the dioceses within their territory wealthier, whereas the leaders of the church sought ways to limit the expansion of wealth so as to protect the church's leverage over temporal rulers.

As we now know, both as a matter of the logic of the concordat game and as a matter of the evidence from many hundreds of years of history, before the concordats were accepted, neither the wealth of a diocese nor its distance from Rome mattered much in terms of the odds of choosing a bishop who was thought to be in the pocket of the diocese's secular ruler or under the control of the pope and church. But once the deals over bishop nominations and transfer of regalia were signed, that changed. The concordat induced horse-trading. In earlier times, kings imposed bishops in some places, local communities chose their bishops in others, and metropolitan bishops and their advisers picked new bishops in still other places. Once the concordat was signed, kings and church leaders were compelled, implicitly or explicitly, to negotiate over the choice of bishops. For perhaps the first time, how loyal a bishop was expected to be toward king or pope depended—by mutual consent—on how much money could be swapped in exchange for a bishop's political loyalty and the policy alignment it implied.

How the horse-trading between money and political control changed Europe depended on just two factors according to the concordat game:

wealth meant greater secular power, and distance from Rome meant greater secular ability to avoid severe papal punishments. We have seen that this was true in terms of bishop appointments, but it would be nice to establish that we can see this effect in other ways as well. Figure 5.1 returns us to the view of secularization that is portrayed by the frequency of artwork with primarily nonreligious subject matter. Using the distribution of religious and secular artwork, we ask whether a completely independent means of evaluating secularization also supports the contention that the concordat promoted the bargaining power of lay rulers at the expense of the church.

Figure 5.1 tells a powerfully supportive story for the secularizing influence exerted by the Concordat of Worms. During the interlude between the Concordat of Worms in 1122 and the Avignon papacy in 1309, we see that far away from Rome secular topics dominated the production of artwork, whereas closer to Rome, hardly any paintings, sculptures, frescoes, or friezes were about primarily secular subjects. True, within five hundred kilometers of Rome there was a small burst in the creation of secular works of art, accounting for about 20 percent of art production as captured in contemporary leading art history textbooks, but these were primarily works commissioned by

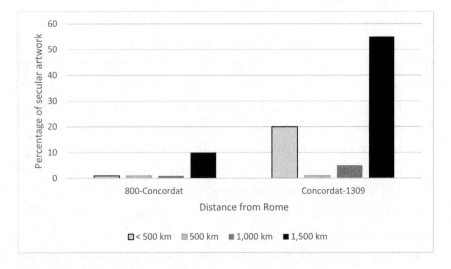

Figure 5.1: Proximity to Rome and secularization of art

popes in their quasi-secular, sovereign role as the ruler of the Papal States. Other than the objects the popes commissioned in this context, virtually nothing close to Rome portrayed subjects that were not religious. Far from Rome, about 50 percent of art between 1122 and 1309 focused on temporal, nonreligious subjects. In contrast, secular art made up only 10 percent of artwork in the years between the creation of the Holy Roman Empire in 800 and the signing of the Concordat of Worms.

The concordat game, however, tells us more than that secularism would be on the rise; it also tells us that wealthy dioceses would become more prevalent far from the pope's reach than close to it, with their bishops' orientation reinforcing that expectation. Hence, we should expect that southern Europe, mostly in close proximity to Rome, would face clerical efforts to hold down its economic growth. That, of course, was a big challenge for the church, particularly in Italy where city-states, especially on the coastline, were deeply embedded in the shipping and trading economies that stimulated their growing wealth.[8]

Northern Europe, in contrast, should have been relatively resistant to the pope's threats, especially in those dioceses where he failed to get a prochurch loyalist as bishop. Indeed, parts of northern Europe, if sufficiently successful economically and sufficiently insulated from papal punishment, would fall into the third case in the concordat game—that is, some realms in northern Europe would be especially well positioned to break from the church. In the third case, kings would either control who was chosen as bishop or they would take the "outside option," not caring about bishops and keeping the substantial amount of money at stake rather than making a deal with the church. In such places, one should expect that kings would defy the church by backing a movement against the church's political authority. Of course, such a movement erupted in 1517 when Martin Luther, beyond the grasp of the church, began the Protestant Reformation. But the movement away from church domination over matters sacred and secular had long been afoot. Since the struggle for control—the horse-trading between money and political power—were core themes taken up in England and France and at Worms, an important place to begin our analysis of how the treaties in 1107 and 1122 drove changes in prosperity is with illustrations of the ways the church tried to limit growth and the countermoves made by kings to stimulate their economies.

MANEUVERS TO INFLUENCE ECONOMIC GROWTH

To evaluate whether the expected economic consequences happened during the Worms-to-Avignon interlude, I turn first to a general assessment of the difference in economic expansion across Europe's dioceses that were subject to the terms of a concordat, an assessment based on whether dioceses' first post-signing bishop of a known type—the first bishop with an informative biography—was secularly or religiously aligned. This will show us hard evidence that where the church's interests dominated, economic growth was sluggish, whereas where secular interests dominated, growth was relatively brisk. That hard evidence will be followed by a detailed assessment of specific maneuvers by the church to limit growth and by additional, nuanced tests of the implications of the concordat game for differences in economic expansion.

According to the incentives for the church and kings under the concordats, where the first bishop of a known alignment was religiously inclined, policies should have been designed to limit economic growth. Such a restriction on growth should have improved the odds that the church would maintain long-term political clout in the diocese. Conversely, where the first bishop was secularly aligned, he should have nudged the diocese toward policies, such as expanded trade, that would promote economic growth so as to further the king's interests at the expense of the church's. Testing this hypothesis takes a bit of calculation, but the results are very convincing.

On average, those dioceses that appointed a secular bishop following acceptance of the concordat grew by 10.0 percent over the years from signing to 1309. For covered bishoprics whose first post-signing bishop was religiously oriented, average growth was 3.83 percent. This enormous difference is not only statistically important but also has large substantive implications for the foundation of Western exceptionalism.

Because each of these values—10.0 percent and 3.83 percent—represents the average estimated growth rate assessed for different types of bishops and their sees over approximately a 150-year span, from when the first post-signing bishop's alignment was estimated to the close of the concordat interlude, we can compound the difference in the two percentages over the approximately six 150-year intervals from signing to the present time.[9] This gives us the expected percentage difference in wealth today between covered dioceses that started the concordat interlude in the early twelfth century with a secular bishop and covered sees that started with a religious bishop. The difference is substantial. The bishoprics that were initially secularly leaning after 1122 (or 1107 in England or France) that were covered by a concordat should be about 42 percent wealthier today, all else being equal, than those sees whose initial bishops were religiously inclined after becoming subject to a concordat.[10] Of course, many other things happened along the way that will have made some locales do even better and others do worse, but this difference is the sort of advantage that is readily inferred by extending the logic of the concordat game to contemplate how secularism could have been used to stimulate wealth creation as the pathway to greater political control in the secular sword's struggle with the church. In Chapter 8 we will see that wealth differences today across Europe are indeed substantially related, as suggested by these results, to developments during the period of the concordats.

Since we already know that wealthier dioceses were more likely to get secular bishops, perhaps the projected 42 percent economic advantage is just what would have happened anyway to wealthier places. Against that supposition we can compare what was happening to the expansion—or contraction—of trade routes in the uncovered dioceses of Europe. Here too we can find the first post-1122 diocesan bishop who was identifiably secular or religious and calculate the change in the percentage of dioceses on trade routes for those that began the concordat interlude with a secular or a religious bishop exactly as we did for covered sees. Those dioceses that were not covered and that started off the concordat interlude with a secular bishop experienced, on average, zero economic growth as estimated by the change in trade-route prevalence. Their rulers did not have the economic-growth incentives engendered by the concordat. Their wealth was essentially irrelevant to their bargaining leverage over the selection of bishops since they did not retain revenue in the event of an interregnum when that revenue otherwise would have gone to the church.

Among those uncovered sees that began the concordat interlude with a religiously inclined bishop, average growth was 5.2 percent, or a 36 percent growth advantage when compounded, holding all else equal, for uncovered *religious* dioceses compared to uncovered secular dioceses to the present time. In turn, that translates into about a one-third advantage in wealth today for the secularly aligned covered sees compared to the better-off, religiously aligned uncovered bishoprics. In contrast, comparing covered religious sees to uncovered ones, the growth difference projected to today would only be 8.5 percent—noticeable, but nothing like the difference between the religious and secular signatory sees. Church-dominated bishoprics just did not grow nearly as much as secularly aligned ones.

I do not want to make too much of the "growth" differences, as I am using rather crude information—trade-route expansion—to estimate economic performance over extended periods. Still, the differences during the interlude of the concordats are real, and trade-route expansion was surely associated with better economic performance. And we now know that such expansion greatly favored the dioceses that were subject to a concordat and that started off with a secularly oriented bishop who would have worked to promote the lay leader's interests. In contrast, those bishops who would have promoted the church's policies—the religiously leaning bishops—would have been incentivized according to the game's logic to limit growth. The pattern in the trade-route record is what the concordat game leads us to expect.

With the crude growth analysis in hand, we can now examine two additional economic implications of the concordats regarding subsequent church behavior. First, we saw that the church lost bargaining power, and hence political control, in places where the person holding the position of bishop was a secular loyalist who, as bishop, controlled significant economic resources. Under these conditions, the pope and his curia were incentivized to shift the locus of resources away from local bishops and toward the pope as a means to partially offset declining leverage over secularized dioceses. Second, the treaties drove a wedge between the incentives of church and secular leaders with respect to economic development. Consequently we should observe the Catholic Church adopting new policies after 1122 that were designed to restrict economic growth. Conversely, kings and other lay leaders should have introduced new policies that encouraged investment and other means to stimulate their local economies. These two implications can be explored first by examining historical evidence on the different strategies employed by secular rulers and church leaders, and then we can turn to more-general evidence to see the patterns uncovered across thousands of decisions.

The concordats put the church in a new, unfamiliar, and difficult position. It obviously had lost some control over its revenue stream. The church's leaders had no intention of taking the new constraints passively. They looked for ways to stem the losses. Popes began to adopt new policies to offset the dangers they faced. Their revenue flow, for instance, was put at risk by the abandonment of canon 25 passed in 451 at the Council of Chalcedon. As noted in Chapter 3, this canon stated, in part, "The income of the widowed church shall be kept safe by the steward of the same Church." Now, under the terms of the concordat, not only did the money not remain with the church when a see was vacant (widowed), but even when the see was filled, the revenue might be in the hands of a secularly inclined bishop who would not use much of it for the benefit of the pope and church. To correct for this fundamental shift in access to money, popes endeavored to shift church revenues away from dependence on local, diocesan money that was paid to the administrators in each bishopric, altering the revenue flow so that more of it was paid directly to the pope's administrators. If the pope could succeed in doing this, he could at least partially mitigate the increase in bargaining power that secular leaders in wealthier dioceses had gained. By diverting funds away from bishops, the pope gave himself an independent income source that helped weaken the political losses the church suffered when monarchs threatened to withhold revenue until the pope did as the king desired.

One crucial example of the pope's shift of revenue toward himself and away from lay leaders arose with the creation or adoption of entrepreneurial and other new monastic orders. The Cistercians, for instance, were created in 1098 and were, by the early twelfth century, centered in Cîteaux, Burgundy, under Bernard of Clairveaux. They secured favors and privileges from the papacy that insulated them from the local demands of bishops and lay leaders by the start of the French concordat. The Knights Templar, created in 1118, were recognized by the pope in 1129 and exempted from taxation in 1139. The Knights Hospitaller were recognized by Pope Paschal II in 1113, just after he had been compelled to back down on a potential resolution of the Investiture Controversy in 1111 that culminated in his facing the political wrath of both the Holy Roman emperor and his own bishops. Here were new orders—military and money making—that were unlike most of their predecessors among monastic orders both in elements of their mission and in their unusually close ties to the papacy.

These new orders and their privileges did not arise in a vacuum. The recognition of these and other monastic orders by the pope coincided with the repeated—almost continuous—selection of schismatic antipopes by the Holy Roman emperor. These antipopes, of course, were competing for control over church revenue. The Holy Roman emperor, by creating antipopes, had found a clever secular institutional maneuver to strengthen his hand in competition with the pope by cutting off the "real" pope (as determined by the later church or by part of the church at the time) from financial support. That the new, entrepreneurial orders were organized and recognized by the "real" pope in this period seems hardly coincidental or benign. Certainly Bernard of Clairveax's support for Innocent II, rather than for the antipope Anacletus II, played a part in the papacy's support for the Cistercians, including the election of the Cistercian monk Bernardo Pignatelli as Pope Eugene III in 1145.

The example of the Cistercians was far from unique. Apparently with the intention of thwarting the impact of imperial maneuvers to capture control over papal revenue and to secure political leverage over bishops, the pope initiated a new set of quid pro quo policies. These policies seemed designed specifically to privilege the new, entrepreneurial monastic orders in exchange for their financial and political support for the pope. Popes Paschal II (1099–1118) and Innocent II (1130–1143), for instance, not only exempted monks from tithes but also granted these new monastic orders protection against taxation by secular authorities and even by their own—now more frequently, secularly aligned—local bishops.

Just how effective the papal effort was in diverting funds away from secular lords and their secularly aligned bishops can be seen by comparing the probability of being governed by a secular bishop in dioceses covered by the concordat that contained at least one Cistercian monastery and in covered dioceses that did not include Cistercian monasteries. The Cistercians, of course, were not only hardworking; they were highly productive, and they were adopters of the latest labor-enhancing technologies of the day. Thus, they were generating substantial revenue that was contributing to the wealth of the sees in which they were located. If a significant portion of their revenue was secured by local secular interests, that certainly could have damaged the pope's and church's objectives in those dioceses. Conversely, if the pope could channel a chunk of the Cistercian's earnings his way, that revenue could diminish the prosecular economic and political impact of the concordat.

Stretching a bit beyond the direct implications of the concordat game, it is notable that nearly 40 percent of the time, the bishoprics that contained Cistercian monasteries had bishops who were aligned with the local secular elite, thereby representing a significant threat to the church's determination of how local revenue would be used. In contrast, only 19 percent of bishops in covered dioceses that did not have Cistercian monasteries were secularly aligned. The probability that this difference occurred by chance is vanishingly small.[11] So it's safe to conclude that through the grant of privileges to monastic orders like the Cistercians, the pope assured himself of a substantial income flow from their sees. That income flow meant that the pope had mitigated some of the financial risks imposed by the concordat even if the king rejected the pope's bishop nominee(s) or got a secularly oriented bishop who would spend the bishopric's revenue to advance the king's interests at the pope's political expense. It seems, indeed, that the favored status given to the new monastic orders by the pope served to protect his revenue and may even have diminished the bargaining leverage that a secular ruler might otherwise have derived over how diocesan revenue was used.

Furthermore, these new monastic orders, created, expanded, or adopted in the wake of the Investiture Controversy, were not mendicant orders like their predecessors. They had no need to beg. Their entrepreneurship meant that they not only produced substantial revenue but also served as a catalyst for reconceiving the value and dignity of hard labor. These new monks did not eschew labor oriented toward money making as, for instance, the Benedictines had. Although labor was an essential element of the Benedictine monk's life, it was performed as a penance for their sins rather than as a desirable, well-regarded behavior in its own right.[12] The new orders, such as the Cistercians, were redefining the place of labor, entrepreneurship, and wealth in medieval Europe. To understand how, let us first consider the low opinion that was generally attached to labor and laborers and then see how the entrepreneurial orders helped change those views.

Today we respect entrepreneurship, hard work, and, perhaps excessively, those who make a lot of money. We seem to have internalized what the eminent sociologist Max Weber described as the Protestant-inspired work ethic, what Weber called the very "spirit of capitalism." But in preconcordat Europe, unlike today or unlike in the world in which new entrepreneurial orders were emerging, the church had routinely promoted the idea that moneymaking through labor was base. As Gratian of Bologna, a famed compiler of the church's canon law, pointedly noted in about 1140, "There were two kinds of christians: first, the clergy who are truly kings and who cannot be compelled to action of any kind by any temporal power; secondly, the laity who cultivate the earth, who give in marriage and whom the clergy lead towards the truth."[13]

Those who chose the clerical life—the superior life—embraced poverty, at least in theory, and renounced whatever worldly possessions they had. The scriptures provided ample reason for detesting labor and embracing a life that excluded it. Indeed, practically from the beginning, starting with the expulsion of Adam and Eve from Eden, labor had

been highlighted as punishment. Recall the sentence to which Adam—
and all future humanity—is condemned in Genesis 3:17–19:

> Cursed is the ground for thy sake; in toil shalt thou eat of it all the days
> of thy life. 18 Thorns also and thistles shall it bring forth to thee; and
> thou shalt eat the herb of the field. 19 In the sweat of thy face shalt thou
> eat bread, till thou return unto the ground; for out of it wast thou taken;
> for dust thou art, and unto dust shalt thou return.

The church, before the treaties were signed, certainly had a poor opinion of labor, but it did not actively denigrate it nearly as much as was done
immediately following the signing of the concordat. Then church policy
shifted to a more aggressive orientation that especially favored retarding
secular economic development and the attendant rise of secular authority. For instance, during the twelfth century, the church began to revise
its views on menial labor in order to limit the spread of newly invented
or adapted efficiency-enhancing, growth-producing machines.[14] As E.
M. Carus-Wilson observed, the development of the fulling machine "was
as decisive an event as were the mechanization of spinning and weaving
in the eighteenth century."[15] Fulling machines, blast furnaces, and other
then-new inventions meant, for instance, that more woolens and more
steel could be made for the export market. That meant that as productivity rose with the spread of efficiency-enhancing machines, tradesmen,
merchants, bankers, and other craftsmen and service-oriented workers
also began to grow in influence as their numbers expanded to fill rising
demand. Indeed, the merchant class and townspeople were emerging as
a new center of power: "The multiplication of different kinds of producers
and traders as well as of specialised administrative officials, led to enlarge-
ment and reworking of the received 'pictures' of the channels of power
and of the relative importance and distinction of roles in society," all serving as threats to an established hierarchy of clergy at the top and laborers
at the bottom.[16] Thus, though these and many other important inventions,
technologies, guilds, and occupations in the years of the concordat interlude became a great boon to economic productivity, they were not accomplishments celebrated by the church.

Relying on Proverbs 16:27–29 or on the admonition often attributed to Saint Jerome to "engage in some occupation, so that the devil may always find you busy," the church revived and promoted the view that idle hands are the devil's workshop. As machines gave workers more leisure time—more idle hands—the machines and their impact on labor and productivity were denounced. That the church viewed productive—secular—economic activity as a base activity until well into the Middle Ages is well summarized by the economic historian Jacques Le Goff's observation, "How often the Middle Ages must have witnessed the inner drama of men anxiously wondering whether they were really hastening toward damnation because they were engaging in a trade suspect in the eyes of the Church. The merchant comes naturally to mind."[17] By opposing both the spread of machines and increased labor productivity, the church seems to have been trying to reduce a key driver of economic development; it seems to have resisted any rise in a moneymaking work ethic.

With the birth of the new entrepreneurial orders as a means to hinder the erosion of the church's economic and political situation, however, its view of labor was compelled to change. Religious and devout these orders were, but they were also devout moneymakers. Indeed, the new, entrepreneurial orders were hardworking, like the Benedictines, but unlike the Benedictines, they were unwilling to execute such traditional charitable activities as performing burials or hearing confessions. For them, living under the protection of the pope, hard labor was not penitence; it was the good behavior that God had recognized before the expulsion from Eden. As stated in Genesis 2:15: "And the Lord God took the man, and put him into the garden of Eden to dress it and to keep it."

The new orders took a new view of labor; they had a strong moneymaking work ethic hundreds of years before the Protestant Reformation. The change in orientation they espoused took hold neither easily nor quickly, but take hold it did. Some attribute its eventual success to the emergence of improved technologies that fostered an improved economy. Surely that is correct, but those who attend to technological improvements without consideration of the political setting within which they arose too often ignore the strategic interdependence between the church's need for changes that would strengthen its hand against the rise of secular power and the concomitant urge by kings to discover new ways to enrich their lands and wrest greater control of them away from the church by improving their economies.

The new institutional arrangements created by the concordats led to essential changes in economic relations and economic interests. Le Goff, for instance, reminds us that "manual labor was restored to a place of honor with the Carthusians *and particularly the Cistercians* [emphasis added] . . . The founding of new orders makes clear that something had changed, that a mutation had occurred in the Benedictine spirit, for why else would such new rules be necessary?"[18] The answer proffered here for why new rules were necessary is straightforward: the pope needed new sources of money to protect his authority in the age of the concordats. Hence the church came to respect labor within the *ecclesiastical* domain of entrepreneurial orders even as it acted aggressively to stymie growth in the *temporal* world.

When it came to the secular world, the church looked for ways to protect itself against the expanding power of kings and local lords. For instance, during the period of the concordats, lords of the manor from time to time insisted on the remeasurement of church lands to better assess local church wealth. The church sought to undermine this practice, thereby protecting its wealth. As Robert Bartlett reports, a Cistercian monastery in Mecklenburg directed, "If the lords of the lands [i.e., the dukes of Mecklenburg] ask what is the number of *mansi*, care should be taken to dissimulate as much as possible."[19]

By dissimulation and direct transfer of authority, the new orders were freed from the local control of their bishops. That made them into an entirely new layer of prospective influencers in the politics of the twelfth century and beyond. Indeed, the new orders did become sources of great influencers over church policy and actions—such as Bernard of Clairveaux, a Cistercian pope maker—as well as sources of new church revenue. We should not forget that the church itself was not bereft of direct revenue sources in addition to the great value the new orders brought to the pope. The church owned about one-third of Europe's land, and from the late 1400s onward, it was a major exporter of alum, which was essential as a fixer of dyes to wool. Furthermore, the church, along with its new entrepreneurial orders, became a voracious user of the many technological innovations of the period. Vertical waterwheels and windmills, for example, were first applied on church lands, especially the lands of the newer monastic orders under papal control. In addition, the church exploited new business technologies, becoming even wealthier through leadership in industry and banking.

The church, not satisfied with economic maneuvers alone, recognized the importance of maintaining a strong hand against the rising authority of kings and lesser lords. With the Second Crusade at hand, the church strengthened and greatly expanded the rights and privileges of its own military orders, particularly the Knights Templar, the Knights Hospitaller, and the Teutonic Order. The church now had its own army, and a superbly courageous army it was. The pope's soldiers fought in the belief that they were assured of eternal salvation, the great promise that Jesus had made to the faithful. These brave knights, especially the Knights Templar, were superbly trained and disciplined, somewhat akin to modern-day US Special Operations Forces. Their courage was remarkable and their death rate in battle was extraordinarily high. Their influence grew larger as they became powerful and extremely wealthy, especially as they and other Catholic military orders became the great bankers of Europe, exempted by the church from taxes and guaranteed by the church the right to move freely across borders.

That these church knights were created *to fight secular power*, and not just the Muslim rulers of the Holy Land, is made clear enough by Abbot Bernard of Clairveaux, perhaps the greatest ecclesiastical mind of his time and certainly the most influential Cistercian abbot. It was his arguments that fostered the recognition of the Knights Templar in 1129 at the Council of Troyes, convened by Pope Honorius II. Bernard believed that those who did not live by God's laws were damned and that those who took pride in living by God's laws were also damned for the mortal sin of pride. (Quite literally, he believed, You're damned if you do and damned if you don't.) Bernard promoted the sacred benefits of holy military orders. He described the typical Templar knight in the early twelfth century thus:

He is truly a fearless knight and secure on every side, for his soul is protected by the armor of faith just as his body is protected by armor of steel. He is thus doubly armed and need fear neither demons nor men. Not that he fears death—no, he desires it. Why should he fear to live or fear to die when for him to live is Christ, and to die is gain? Gladly and faithfully he stands for Christ, but he would prefer to be dissolved and to be with Christ, by far the better thing. Go forth confidently then, you knights, and repel the foes of the cross of Christ with a stalwart heart. Know that neither death nor life can separate you from the love of God which is in Jesus Christ, and in every peril repeat, "Whether we live or whether we die, we are the Lord's." What a glory to return in victory from such a battle! How blessed to die there as a martyr!

In contrast, here is Bernard's description of secular knights and their motives for waging war:

What then, O knights, is this monstrous error and what this unbearable urge which bids you fight with such pomp and labor, and all to no purpose except death and sin? You cover your horses with silk, and plume your armor with I know not what sort of rags; you paint your shields and your saddles; you adorn your bits and spurs with gold and silver and precious stones, and then in all this glory you rush to your ruin with fearful wrath and fearless folly. Are these the trappings of a warrior or are they not rather the trinkets of a woman? Do you think the swords of your foes will be turned back by your gold, spare your jewels or be unable to pierce your silks? . . . Then why do you blind yourselves with effeminate locks and trip yourselves up with long and full tunics, burying your tender, delicate hands in big cumbersome sleeves? Above all, there is that terrible insecurity of conscience, in spite of all your armor, since you have dared to undertake such a dangerous business on such slight and frivolous grounds. What else is the cause of wars and the root of disputes among you, except unreasonable flashes of anger, the thirst for empty glory, or the hankering after some earthly possessions? It certainly is not safe to kill or to be killed for such causes as these.[20]

The Knights Templar, having proven their mettle in combat, gradually shifted their function as the Crusades faded into the past. They shifted from being the pope's army to becoming one of Europe's great banking organizations. This was especially true after the church acted to restrict secular access to money by imposing a ban on usury, that is, on making a profit from lending money. While the church endeavored to restrict lay access to funds for construction and investment starting in 1139, it had no shortage of funds for such undertakings on its own part. Rather, it became the source of demand for new construction as it entered a period of great expansion in church and cathedral building, as can be seen in Figure 5.2.[21]

While great cathedrals and other important church structures had been built from the church's earliest times, as Figure 5.2 makes clear, such building was concentrated in the parts of Europe that were covered by the concordats (the black squares) and not elsewhere (the grey circles), and that concentration overwhelmingly occurred between the signing of the concordats and the rise of the Avignon papacy. Great cathedrals, like great works of art, were profoundly powerful statements

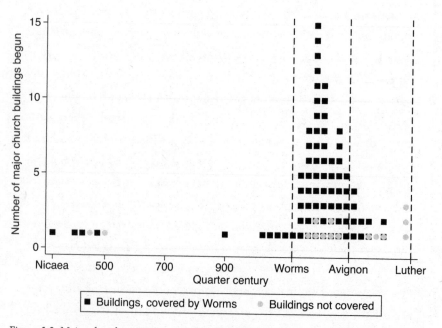

Figure 5.2: Major church construction from Nicaea to Luther

of grandeur, authority, and eminence. Surely many factors influenced the disproportionate construction of such monumental edifices in dioceses covered by a concordat, but it seems likely that one factor was the competition that the concordat helped organize between the spiritual and the secular swords, a competition not fostered outside the domain of the concordat. Thus, in pursuit of its mission, the church was also an intimate beneficiary of and agent for construction-driven economic expansion within its own realm during the high Middle Ages, especially where it faced institutionalized rivalry from kings during the Worms-to-Avignon interlude. At the same time, the church strove to limit economic expansion in the secular world.

The growing wealth of the church contributed to the rising stature and influence of the pope as he struggled to sustain and expand church authority even as the terms of the concordats promoted the eventual erosion of the pope's position. It is widely agreed that the period of greatest papal influence fell between the papacy of Innocent III (1198–1216) and that of Boniface VIII (1294–1303), whose efforts to save the church from the threats of the temporal world led to the capture of the papacy by France's King Philip IV, "Philip the Fair" (as in handsome, not just). During the interlude before Boniface's conflict with Philip plunged the church into vassalage, however, the clergy set out in a series of Lateran councils to limit the economic development that threatened its bargaining power and political standing. We began this chapter with evidence of a large difference in economic growth over the span of the concordats by comparing trade-route expansion in dioceses that started the period off with a secularly leaning bishop to trade-route expansion in dioceses that started the period off with a prochurch, religiously leaning bishop. Now, in probing essential features of the Lateran councils, we can see how they served as a central part of the church's strategy to weaken the rising secular world while trying to preserve its stature as a great political force.

FOUR LATERAN COUNCILS: COMBATING SECULAR ECONOMIC GROWTH

Following the Concordat of Worms, the church convened four Lateran councils at which new canon laws and new Christian practices and

obligations were promulgated. The first, presided over by Pope Calixtus II, began in March 1123. Lateran I first of all ratified the Concordat
of Worms. But it did much more, and much of what it did was aimed,
whether intentionally or by happenstance—we cannot really know—at
constraining secular action and strengthening the ecclesiastical world
in the wake of the concordat.

During the First Lateran Council, the church made celibacy mandatory for the clergy. As stated in its canon 3 and canon 21: "We absolutely
forbid priests, deacons, and subdeacons to associate with concubines
and women, or to live with women other than such as the Nicene Council (canon 3) for reasons of necessity permitted, namely, the mother, sister, or aunt, or any such person concerning whom no suspicion could
arise," and "We absolutely forbid priests, deacons, subdeacons, and
monks to have concubines or to contract marriage. We decree in accordance with the definitions of the sacred canons, that marriages already
contracted by such persons must be dissolved, and that the persons be
condemned to do penance."[22]

The embrace of celibacy may have had a gloss of purity and chastity
about it, but the canons constructed to enforce celibacy served an alternative purpose as well: celibacy was about putting money in the church's
coffers rather than in the hands of secular rivals.[23] Apparently, when it
came to the church's monetary interests, even existing marriages carried no weight: "[they] must be dissolved." Difficulties in implementing
and enforcing the rulings at Lateran I led to a clarification at the Second
Lateran Council (1139), in which the church further ensured that it, and
not any family or other secular venue, would be the beneficiary of any
deceased bishop's estate, or in fact, the estate of any cleric. As stated in
Lateran II's canon 5:

> The goods of deceased bishops are not to be seized by anyone at all, but
> are to remain freely at the disposal of the treasurer and the clergy for the
> needs of the church and the succeeding incumbent. . . . Furthermore, if
> anyone dares to attempt this behavior henceforth, he is to be excommu-
> nicated. And those who despoil the goods of dying priests or clerics are
> to be subject to the same sentence.[24]

By imposing excommunication on violators, the church raised the costs faced by families or monarchs if they tried to seize the "personal" property of dead or dying clerics. Canon 4 at the First Lateran Council was also designed to limit lay access to any church wealth or property:

> In accordance with the decision of Pope Stephen, we declare that lay persons, no matter how devout they may be, have no authority to dispose of anything belonging to the Church, but according to the Apostolic canon the supervision of all ecclesiastical affairs belongs to the bishop, who shall administer them conformably to the will of God. If therefore any prince or other layman shall arrogate to himself the right of disposition, control, or ownership of ecclesiastical goods or properties, let him be judged guilty of sacrilege.

The council, in the aftermath of the negotiated agreement at Worms, passed twenty-two canons, several of which appear designed to limit the authority of lay leaders through an elaboration of costly punishments and an assertion that whatever seemed to belong to a member of the clergy instead belonged to the church. Numerous canons declared actions to be anathema—that is, subject to excommunication—while others called for interdiction as the appropriate punishment. Several of these seemed to be aimed at restricting the power of secular rulers vis-à-vis the church.

For instance, canon 9 may have been intended to rein in the authority that secularly aligned bishops exerted. It stipulates, "We absolutely forbid that those who have been excommunicated by their own bishops be received into the communion of the Church by other bishops, abbots, and clerics." Presumably, bishops, abbots, and clerics aligned with the pope and church would have been disinclined, in any event, to receive back into the Christian communion someone who had not been absolved of their misbehavior by the bishop who had excommunicated them. But a lay-leaning bishop might very well have done so if the misbehavior related to doing the king's bidding at the expense of the church, much as we saw in the case of the bishops of France who were blood relatives of King Philip II. They, recall, refused to obey the pope's interdict, whereas the French bishops who came out of the pope's "court" did obey it.

Lateran I's first two canons spoke directly to the church's resistance to the common practices of buying and selling church offices and to the assignment of individuals to clerical posts by the laity outside church procedure. Canon 1: "Following the example of the holy fathers and recognizing the obligation of our office, we absolutely forbid in virtue of the authority of the Apostolic See that anyone be ordained or promoted for money in the Church of God. Has anyone thus secured ordination or promotion in the Church, the rank acquired shall be devoid of every dignity." And canon 2: "No one except a priest shall be promoted to the dignity of provost, archpriest, or dean; and no one shall be made archdeacon unless he is a deacon." Here the council sought to eliminate the selection of clerics by lay leaders, which was the very power indirectly conferred on them through the right to reject a nominee to be bishop or abbot under the terms of the concordat. This ruling of the Lateran Council would subsequently be explicitly rejected by England's Henry II in the Constitutions of Clarendon (1164). He asserted that the right to designate a candidate for a clerical benefice—a position with pay—fell under the English tradition of advowson and that his regime, and not the church, would take precedence in such matters.

So unsuccessful were the church's efforts to shore up its position and lock in new sources of income and wealth following the signing of the concordat that Lateran II, held in 1139, repeated much of the canonical subject matter covered in Lateran I. The church found it necessary to reiterate its condemnation of simony, to forbid marriage by the clergy (extending that prohibition to nuns as well) and to draw sharp lines between the claimed authority of the laity—including kings—and the clergy. In Lateran II's canon 10, for instance, the council proclaimed, "We prohibit, by apostolic authority, that the tithes of churches be possessed by lay people where canonical authority shows these were assigned for religious purposes. For whether they accept them from bishops or kings, or any person whatsoever, let them know that they are committing the crime of sacrilege and incurring the threat of eternal damnation, unless they hand them back to the church." Apparently lay

leaders were working to impoverish the church, and apparently secularly oriented bishops were advancing that effort, hence the statement,
"whether they accept them from bishops or kings . . . they are . . . incurring the threat of eternal damnation."

In an effort to weaken lay claims to control and to shore up the
church's authority, Lateran II also returned to the theme of banning the
right of any lay person to choose who would fill any clerical vacancy. At
this time, wealthy people had proprietary chapels and more powerful
lords and kings also had churches to which they had customarily appointed clerics; Lateran II sought more vigorously to end this practice,
which they had already condemned at Lateran I. In doing so, however,
they laid bare their own corruption, not only opening the door to battles
with subsequent temporal rulers but also exposing themselves to rising condemnation among reform-minded clerics for the practices they
themselves had declared corrupt.

Canon 16, in an effort to eliminate control over clerical appointments
by the laity, declared:

> It is undoubtedly the case that since ecclesiastical honours depend not
> on blood-relationships but on merit, and since the church of God awaits
> successors not on the basis of any right of inheritance, nor according to
> the flesh, it requires virtuous, wise and devout persons for its administra-
> tion and the distribution of its offices. Therefore we prohibit, by apostolic
> authority, anyone to exercise a claim over or to demand, by hereditary
> right, churches, prebends, provostships, chaplaincies or any ecclesiastical
> offices. If anyone, unjustly and guilty of ambition, dares to attempt this,
> he will be duly punished and deprived of the object of his suit.

Pope Innocent II, who presided over the Second Lateran Council and
who had been Calixtus II's ambassador at the resolution of the Concordat of Worms, could readily make a claim such as this. The canon
condemned nepotism as a way to denounce secular claims to a hereditary right to appoint church officials. But the canon's impact was un-
derstandably limited, given the prevalence of nepotism in the church
hierarchy.

Innocent had not come to his office through nepotism, although his
ascent as pope was extremely controversial. The antipope Anacletus II
had driven Innocent from Rome and had designated Innocent as the antipope. Innocent's claim to be pope was only recognized after the intervention of powerful lay and clerical leaders, with the Cistercian Bernard
of Clairvaux leading the way. While Anacletus came from a powerful,
pope-making, nepotistic family, the Pierleoni, Innocent II (born Gregorio Papareschi) had no such powerful familial ties. Still, Lateran II's
declaration against nepotism must quickly have fallen on deaf ears,
given that it had no beneficial impact on the church's own practices.

Figure 5.3 shows the frequency of nepotistic ties (ranging from none
to fifteen—the highest level) among popes, starting just before the Investiture Controversy and carrying on beyond where we left off earlier
to reflect the swings in papal nepotism during the periods of the four
Lateran councils and on through the Avignon papacy and its ultimate
termination at the Council of Constance in 1417. The figure belies the
canonical renunciation of clerical nepotism, "It is undoubtedly the
case that . . . the church of God awaits successors not on the basis of

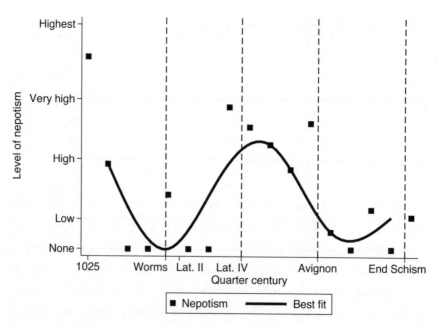

Figure 5.3: Did Lateran II's condemnation of nepotism succeed?

any right of inheritance, nor according to the flesh." Instead, the figure shows that as the papacy struggled to sustain its power, nepotism rose dramatically between the signing of the concordat and the conclusion of the Fourth Lateran Council. It then went into decline as the papacy came increasingly under the sway of lay power, eventually being subjugated by the king of France through the years of the Avignon papacy.

Lateran II's efforts to restrict the authority and influence of kings and lesser secular leaders was not limited to the maneuvers already described. Perhaps most important, the participants in Lateran II strove to limit the ability of secular leaders to invest in economic expansion. Most critically, the council issued a new ruling regarding money lending by imposing a ban on usury. Canon 13 stipulates:

> We condemn that practice accounted despicable and blameworthy by divine and human laws, . . . namely, the ferocious greed of usurers; and we sever them from every comfort of the church, forbidding any archbishop or bishop, or an abbot of any order whatever or anyone in clerical orders, to dare to receive usurers, unless they do so with extreme caution; but let them be held infamous . . . and, unless they repent, be deprived of a Christian burial.

Enforcement of the ban on usury, however, proved problematic. The church reiterated the ban at the Third Lateran Council in 1179, expanding the punishment beyond usurers to those who might have extended a Christian burial to them. Canon 25 at Lateran III declared:

> Nearly everywhere the crime of usury has become so firmly rooted that many, omitting other business, practice usury as if it were permitted, and in no way observe how it is forbidden in both the Old and New Testament. We therefore declare that notorious usurers should not be admitted to communion of the altar or receive Christian burial if they die in this sin. Whoever receives them or gives them Christian burial should be compelled to give back what he has received, and let him remain suspended from the performance of his office until he has made satisfaction according to the judgment of his own bishop.[25]

The ban, despite the expanded costs for ignoring it, failed to take hold. The church recognized the difficulty it faced in determining whether a lender *intended* to commit usury—that is, to sell time that he could not own. As the canonist Hostiensis observed, only God "questions the heart and not the hand."[26] To deal with its failure to discern intent—what was in the heart—the church shifted its enforcement efforts away from canonists and into the hands of parish priests. The logic was simple: while human law might fail to recognize a usurious loan, God knew whether a lender intended to make a profit, to "sell" time, no matter what subterfuge was used to mask the return. Therefore, anyone having made such a profit and failing to make restitution was condemned by God.

The Fourth Lateran Council (1215) greatly improved the mechanism for enforcing the ban on usury. In particular, Lateran IV's canon 21 stipulated, "All the faithful of both sexes shall after they have reached the age of discretion faithfully confess all their sins at least once a year to their own (parish) priest and perform to the best of their ability the penance imposed."[27] In making annual oral confession mandatory for all Catholics, the church took a bold step both to promote belief in the prospect of any individual's salvation and to provide priests with the greatly enhanced opportunity to uncover usurers. The requirement of confession before one's own priest assured that the person confessing was likely to be known to the priest hearing the confession, and therefore, the priest was likely to know whether the person's activities were suspect.

With the introduction of mandatory confession, the church undertook to ensure enforcement. It promoted the spread of confessors' manuals with specific instructions for dealing with merchants and others likely to have engaged in usury, which, remember, at the time meant any lending for profit and not, as today, for an exorbitant profit. As Le Goff reports, based on his analysis of confessor's manuals, "Significantly, the first confessors' manuals to be translated into vulgar tongues . . . were acquired principally by merchants." These manuals were important for them at least in part because "they reflect the pressure brought to bear on the Church by men engaged in given types of work."[28] And the work that most put one's salvation at risk was the sale of time—that is, the business of educators, who charged for conveying knowledge that belonged to all, and of moneylenders, who charged for the time a borrower used money, time that, again, belonged to all. As expressed in Luke 6:35, "lend, hoping for nothing again."

The risks and costs for usurers—that is, bankers, Jewish and Muslim moneylenders (who were already treated horribly), and many merchants—had been raised, so naturally, the expected rate of return from money lending had to rise commensurately to reflect the increased risk.[29] The upshot was to make loans scarcer and costlier, thereby slowing economic development and the rise of secular political power relative to what it otherwise would have been. Making money expensive and money lending risky were certainly potentially terrific ways to slow economic growth, particularly in the secular world, as the ban on money lending was less relevant to the church's ability to spend. The church was better able to continue to borrow, even after the ban on usury, and, critically, it was also less dependent on financing for construction.[30] Cathedrals and churches were often built with free labor, acquired through the granting of indulgences for sins in return for good works or through the in-kind payment of tithes.[31] For instance, the historian Robert Swanson notes that, "indulgences played a role in the construction, alteration or rebuilding of a number, if not most . . . important church buildings."[32]

The concordat game implies that church actions, such as the ban on usury, were designed to shore up the church's political position by limiting the secular world's opportunities to invest and to promote economic expansion. This is not, however, how most scholars have thought about the ban. They have given scant attention to its political implications. There are those who argue that the ban on usury was simply economically ineffective in practice. The distinguished sociologist Rodney Stark, for instance, contends that "*usury* had become essentially an empty term."[33] If the ban was an empty threat, however, it was because bankers had found ways around the rule and because several monastic orders, most especially the Templars by this time (when many of their practices were condemned by canon at Lateran III), were apparently more interested in their own political power and economic well-being than in religious dicta. They participated in usurious lending to their own benefit and, indirectly, as noted, to the enrichment of the papacy.

Seemingly contrary to the perspective I am offering, such scholars as Stark and the noted historian John Gilchrist contend that the church *was* interested in promoting economic growth and made active efforts to do so. But upon a bit of inspection, we discover that they come around to something akin to the very argument made here. The concordat game suggests that the spread and expansion of wealth were the pathway by which church authority could be undermined. Stark and Gilchrist, for instance, attribute a large positive role to the church in Europe's remarkable economic expansion in the period between the eleventh century and the fourteenth century while also arguing that the inconvenient ban on money lending was irrelevant.[34]

Views like these, which support church efforts to stimulate economic growth, turn out to conflate the inventiveness, the intellectual rigor, and the entrepreneurial spirit of *individual clergymen* with the policy stance of the church's senior leadership and their changes in canon law, especially the consequences of the four Lateran councils, including the ban on usury. Furthermore, as with the burst in secular artwork close to Rome that we saw in Figure 5.1, these views fail to distinguish between the secular and religious concerns of many clergymen. Indeed, Stark's own defense of the church's support for economic growth concedes that to the extent church officials refrained from standing in the way of economic growth, it was because of their secular, rather than their religious, interests. As he observes, "The worldly aspects of the medieval Church were an endless source of scandal and conflict, culminating in the Reformation. But they paid serious dividends in the development of capitalism."[35] Of course, this is consistent with the implication of the concordat game that where clergy were acting as the agents of the secular ruler, there were strong incentives to promote economic growth, thereby strengthening lay leaders' political standing at the expense of the church. The church's rules were designed to make secular economic expansion difficult. The ambitions of some individual clergy and the commitment of many to their secular lord were on the side of growth. Popes and canon law during the period of the concordat were not.

Economists also seem not to have reflected on the political incentives that might have been behind the ban on usury. Looking at the world through the lens of what made for efficient economic policy, they miss the way the concordat created interdependence between political power and economic growth. As, for instance, Robert Ekelund and his coauthors report, "Paradoxically, the most outwardly economic directive of the medieval church, the doctrine of usury, has proven most resistant to purely economic explanations."[36] The incentives created by the Concordat of Worms, however, provides a strong *political* explanation: a ban on usury was a way for the church to use religious policy to pursue its political interests relative to secular leaders by curtailing economic development outside monasteries and other ecclesiastical institutions, thereby limiting the secularization of European dioceses.

We can probe these claims with some evidence from the period. Figure 5.4 looks at the number of constructions begun fifty years before and fifty years after the introduction of the enforceable ban on usury at the Fourth Lateran Council. The figure distinguishes three types of construction. The first type, in the first pane, is the number of castles that were built for powerful, wealthy people in the secular realm, such as kings, princes, and influential families. The second pane shows the results for two types of nonsecular building starts. The gray bars show the number of constructions built on behalf of the Roman church, such as we saw in Figure 5.2. These were mainly churches and cathedrals, the latter, of course, being grander and more expensive undertakings. The white bars show the number of castle constructions by powerful people who operated in the religious realm—that is, castle constructions undertaken by bishops, archbishops, and the occasional abbot.

Because there were so many more opportunities for powerful secular people to build castles, the graph's panes are separated to make it easier to see the critical difference across the secular and religious constructions. However, before investigating what the figure tells us, a cautionary word is in order. We have dates for the start of construction for a little more than one thousand castles, but many more castles were

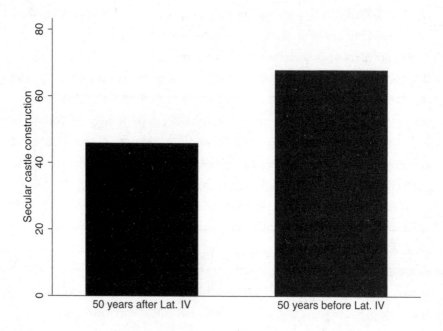

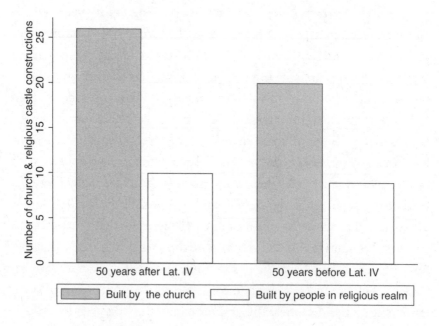

Figure 5.4: Changing castle and church construction: Before and after the usury ban

built. There are data on the existence of more than ten thousand castles. Some of them were decorative structures—really palaces—built well after 1550 and so are irrelevant; some of them were built long before 750 and amounted to little more than a mud heap or an easily defeated wooden structure and so also are irrelevant. But there are also a great many for which no dates are known by which we can pin down when construction began. If, for some reason, these castles of unknown dates are systematically biased in terms of whether their construction began before or after the ban on usury, then they could alter what we discover by looking at those castles for which dates are known. We will just have to live with that degree of uncertainty.

Comparing the two solid black bars in Figure 5.4 shows us that castle constructions by the secular elite decreased markedly fifty years after Lateran IV imposed an enforceable usury ban as compared to the fifty years before. The gray bars reflect the same time periods, but they compare construction starts for major church buildings before and after the implementation of an effective ban on money lending. As we can see, church construction increased following the ban. Likewise, albeit only by a little, "religious" castle construction increased during the fifty years after the Fourth Lateran Council compared to fifty years before. Similar results are observed if we look at the change over one hundred years after Lateran IV compared to one hundred years before it or, indeed, over just about any other equal time periods on either side of the ban on usury.

The figure makes evident that before the ban on usury, secular castle construction was thriving. Immediately after the ban went into effect, however, such construction dropped sharply. In contrast, when we look at construction of cathedrals, churches, and castles built for bishops and other religious figures, we see that the ban on usury did not slow down spending on great edifices. It seems evident that the ban was an effective policy for limiting investment specifically in the secular domain.

We can also look at church construction from an alternative perspective. Rather than assessing the number of such construction projects, we can assess their size. Thanks to data generously provided by Eltjo Buringh and his colleagues, we know how many cubic meters of church and cathedral construction took place each decade.[37] Their data show unabated growth in church construction, with approximately seventy-six million square meters built in the half century prior to the usury ban and approximately ninety-five million square meters built in the half century after the usury ban. Clearly, church construction was not slowed down the way secular castle construction was.

The impact of the change in castle construction is especially meaningful because castle construction was no small activity. Castles were very expensive structures, making their construction a pretty good indicator of the builder's resources and ability to secure credit. Because castle construction was very expensive and often would have necessitated loans to pay labor and secure materials, which sometimes had to be imported over considerable distance, the rise or decline in such construction is probably well correlated with the impact of the ban on usury on the cost of credit. As the architect and builder of Beaumaris Castle, Master James of St. George, noted regarding the construction he was overseeing in 1282:

> In case you should wonder where so much money could go in a week, we would have you know that we have needed and shall continue to need 400 masons, both cutters and layers, together with 2,000 less skilled workmen, 100 carts, 60 wagons and 30 boats bringing stone and sea coal; 200 quarrymen; 30 smiths; and carpenters for putting in the joists and floor boards and other necessary jobs. All this takes no account of the garrison ... nor of purchases of material. Of which there will have to be a great quantity.... The men's pay has been and still is very much in arrears, and we are having the greatest difficulty in keeping them because they have simply nothing to live on.[38]

With castles costing upwards of thousands of pounds, a fortune at the time, Figure 5.4 is consistent with the inference that the ban on usury greatly slowed temporal, lay construction. It seems banning usury served an important political purpose.

Many of Europe's great cathedrals were being built during the very time that the ban on usury was operative and that secular castle construction collapsed. Chartres Cathedral was finished in 1220, five years after Lateran IV. Building on Reims Cathedral began in 1211, before the Fourth Lateran Council but after an ineffective ban on usury promulgated in 1139 and reiterated in 1179. It was finished in 1275, a remarkable case of rapid turnaround. Its construction ran throughout the period of the ban on usury. The great cathedral in Cologne was begun in 1248, at the height of the ban. It seems the ban created fewer constraints—in terms of recruiting labor or acquiring materials—for cathedral construction or for the building of castles for bishops than it did for secular castle builders. But then, as noted earlier, the church could and did more easily command free labor to help with construction, and it had plenty of access to money to pay for materials. Both labor and materials did not come so easily or cheaply to secular projects, as the quotation from Master James of St. George reminds us.

It seems, indeed, that the Roman Catholic Church was hard at work in Europe devising new rules, new laws, and new norms aimed at limiting economic growth. That is just what we should expect they would do once the concordat rewrote the terms of the balance of power between lay rulers and church leaders, tying the new balance of power between the secular and sacred domains to trade-offs between money and political authority. Now we ought to have a look at how the church's secular competitors fought back.

SECULAR MANEUVERS FOR GROWTH

Secular rulers had different incentives from the church, and they were no less innovative in erecting institutions to grasp political control and to increase wealth. The decades immediately after the Concordat of Worms, for instance, saw a dramatic expansion in the amount of productive land being worked in Europe, with the expansion instigated by lay leaders and their secularly aligned bishops. The activities of Archbishop Wichmann of Magdeburg (1152–1192), for instance, exemplify the efforts to clear new lands and then colonize them to improve productivity. Wichmann was a close ally of Holy Roman Emperor Frederick Barbarossa (1155–1190) and an adversary of Pope Alexander III (1159–1181). Even at his elevation to become a bishop he was well known to be

a favorite of the laity. His elevation to bishop was opposed both by Pope
Eugene III (1145–1153) and Pope Anastasius IV (1153–1154). He was
an archbishop who should have—and did—follow the expectations of
the concordat game that clergy leading prosperous dioceses would do so
on behalf of their secular lord, even at the expense of the church.

The secularly oriented Archbishop Wichmann was committed to
economic expansion as a means to enrich himself and to increase his political clout. He made colonization and development of the assarted—
cleared—lands on the fringe of his diocese a great attraction for landless
peasants. As the economic historians Edwin Hunt and James Murray
report, "The attractions were considerable: freedom from forced labor
on castles or the lord's land, and possession of large amounts of fertile
land in return for reasonable rent." The new villages that were created
advanced Wichmann's economic vision: "[The locatores] will settle new
colonists there, who will drain the marshy grasslands, which are pres-
ently good for nothing but grass and hay, and plow them and sow them
and make them fruitful."[39]

As efforts to assart tracts of land spread across Europe, so too did secular prospects for economic prosperity, both for the lords who owned
the land and for the peasants who occupied it, developed it, and farmed
it. The secularly aligned Wichmann was but one example. Even more
dramatic was the decision by thirteenth-century Flemish counts to
launch a major land-reclamation undertaking that, as we know with
hindsight, made the Netherlands one of the wealthiest, most secular,
and most powerful lands in Europe. And, as Hunt and Murray observed,
without reference to the critical impact of the concordat, "The resulting
property . . . remained subject to the *regalian rights* [emphasis added] of
the count, even that which passed into the possession of a monastery."[40]

Europe's economy took off not only because of the physical development of new land in the hands of secular rulers, but also thanks to the
flowering of secular institutions such as arose in England and France,
institutions that were designed to encourage development. Consider,
for instance, the series of legal reforms introduced by King Henry II
(1133–1189) in England during the mid-twelfth century. Henry coun-
tered papal economic strategies with an expanded curia regis (loosely,

the central government administration) and four important writs. The first two provided important incentives for a tenant farmer's commitment to the land he farmed and to improving its productivity. The first writ (*assize of novel disseisin*) protected the property right of the tenant farmer, and the second (*assize of mort d'ancestor*) protected inheritance rights, including the tenant farmer's family's right to remain on the land after he died. These popular writs helped secure the property rights that are essential to economic growth while also enhancing the king's credibility as the person who would protect the common man in matters of property.

The third and fourth writs (*darrein presentment* and *utrum*) dealt with restrictions on ecclesiastical rights. *Utrum* established the king's primacy in determining whether a dispute belonged in his secular courts or in the church's ecclesiastical courts. Prior to Henry, there was a presumption in favor of the jurisdiction of the ecclesiastical courts. *Utrum* reversed this presumption among litigants in England, and the period of which I write was a litigious age. The writ of *darrein presentment* addressed Henry's interest in protecting the tradition of patronage that gave landowners the benefit of presenting or selecting clerics for appointment in their proprietary churches. This ran counter to the efforts of the church to take all such influence away from the secular domain, as is evident from the rulings in Lateran II (1139) and III (1179). In *darrein presentment*, as in *utrum*, Henry challenged church authority, and as in the first two writs, he sought to protect a property right that, in this case, the church was trying to usurp for itself.[41]

Henry accompanied the effort behind the writs with the introduction and spread of the jury system to replace trial by ordeal. Trial by ordeal was the process by which innocence or guilt was determined through the presumed intervention of God. Two common ordeals, both supervised by the church and its local clergy, involved cold water or hot iron: the accused was submerged in cold water or forced to hold a red-hot iron rod. Failure to stay submerged for a prescribed period of time was taken as proof of guilt, as was the inability to hold the iron for a specified period. Henry sought to ensure "victory of a reasoned, rational mode of proof over the old irrational appeals to God or the obscure forces of nature."[42] Efforts similar to Henry's are also found at the same time in France and elsewhere on the Continent, where there is also impressive evidence demonstrating that the stringency of trials by ordeal may have been strategically manipulated by the local clergy.[43]

In attacking trial by ordeal, Henry simultaneously asserted the superiority of his secular rules and worked to deprive the church of a substantial portion of its discretionary revenue. No wonder the church wanted to prevent the rise of secular power. Probably not coincidentally, the shift to a jury system from trial by ordeal also weakened church institutions and income. Trials by ordeal were supervised by the clergy, who were well compensated for their participation. For instance, two priests are known to have been paid ten shillings for blessing the ordeal pits near Bury St. Edmunds in 1166. At the time, a worker's daily wage was about one penny, and a villein and his entire family could be purchased for twenty-two shillings.[44] So much political pressure was raised against trials by ordeal that the Fourth Lateran Council, in its canon 18, banned them, at significant economic loss to the church and, especially, local clergy.

The French king, Philip Augustus, was not to be outdone by his rival in England. Indeed, so sharp were Philip Augustus's efforts to assert his autonomy that Pope Innocent III struck back, interdicting his domain. Although the pope's explicit complaint was Philip's marriage without papal agreement to the annulment of his first marriage, an important political motive involved Philip's reluctance to back the pope's choice for Holy Roman emperor. In a period of intense struggles between church and state, nothing suited the pope's interest more than control over the power of the emperor.

Furthermore, the kings of England and France sought new ways to raise revenue, often making claims on the very resources the church was trying to redirect away from parishes and dioceses and toward Rome. In England, King Richard (the Lionhearted) significantly increased taxes, including from church property. His successor, John, went so far as to seize church lands. Philip IV followed a similar path in France, prompting a backlash from Pope Boniface VIII that led to war. Philip sought to punish the church economically by cutting off essential exports to

Rome. He also diminished the influence of the church at court by establishing a bureaucratized, more merit-based administrative system that is sometimes described as the beginning of modern government.[45] These and other maneuvers by European secular leaders followed the logic of the concordat game and set the stage for a complete break from the church, where such a break could be achieved at relatively low cost.

As secular rulers expanded their institutional repertoire, Pope Boniface VIII made what proved to be a failed effort to reestablish the church's political control. In 1296 and 1302 he issued the bulls *Clericis laicos* (1296) and *Unam sanctam* (1302). The first of these bulls prohibited the clergy from paying taxes to lay leaders without church approval. The second bull declared that the pope could depose anyone, including kings, but could not be deposed by anyone other than God. Not surprisingly, Boniface's effort to restore church authority produced a backlash. He was overthrown by France's King Philip the Fair, who then launched the Avignon papacy, thereby shifting control of the papacy to France for nearly one hundred years.

Everything we have seen reminds us that the competition put into motion by the concordats was intense. Popes found ways to constrain economic expansion even as temporal leaders found an equally large array of maneuvers to stimulate growth. Every king understood that he gained greater political control at the expense of the church in dioceses that enjoyed prosperity, and therefore he sought everywhere to stimulate economic growth. Indeed, at the time the deal was struck at Worms, many religious thinkers foresaw a grave risk that lay rulers would win the long-term competition that the concordat was supposed to resolve. Now it is time for us to resolve how the battle for economic development unfolded. Most especially, we want to know where the secular sword prevailed, and where the church prevailed.

GROWTH, CRUSADES, AND THE COMMERCIAL REVOLUTION

We know that the wielders of the temporal sword had strong incentives to promote economic growth, but we must also acknowledge that events and actions motivated by the church's interests could also have served as stimulants for economic expansion. If they did, then we must explain why the pope and his bishops agreed to pursue those actions at the very time that economic expansion threatened the church's political leverage.

The singular set of church-motivated events that might have most threatened the economic status quo were the crusades against Islam aimed at liberating, capturing, and controlling Jerusalem.[46] Four crusades took place during the Investiture Controversy and the interlude of the concordats, spanning the periods 1096–1099, 1147–1149, 1189–1192, and 1202–1204. The First Crusade, initiated by Pope Urban II, was motivated by a desire to help the forlorn Byzantine emperor, who had lost a large part of his empire to the Seljuk Turks. This crusade saw the capture of Jerusalem and much of the Holy Land by the crusaders, but their success was to last less than a century. Saladin, leader of a North African/Middle Eastern empire centered in Egypt and Syria, retook Jerusalem in 1187.

The church's efforts to reassert its influence in the Holy Land against the triumphs of Islam necessitated the raising, transporting, feeding, and arming of massive numbers of common soldiers, knights, princes, and kings. While much of the economic burden fell on the secular warriors, whose participation assured the forgiveness of their sins, the church too had consequential expenses to address. Indeed, by the Fourth Crusade, initiated by Pope Innocent III, the church's own need for the economic means to wage the crusade led Innocent to impose a 2.5 percent tax on the clergy's revenue. Of course, we should bear in mind that this burden would have fallen more heavily on secularly aligned clergy, who at that time represented about 40 percent of bishops in wealthy dioceses. About 80 percent of bishops were in poor dioceses and were overwhelmingly religiously aligned. They, therefore, would have paid little, although they might have still felt the payment keenly.

The large crusader armies that moved across Europe to the Middle East, some by land and others by sea, may have affected local politics and caused the creation of new trade routes to satisfy the demand for the goods and services needed to support these armies. Yet evidence—both narrowly conceived over a brief time window around the occurrence of each crusade, and broadly conceived over the span of the years from the

start of the concordats to the start of the Avignon papacy (with equivalent findings if we extend the time to the beginning of the Protestant
Reformation in 1517)—shows us that the dioceses traversed by the crusader armies seem to have neither stimulated nor retarded the creation
of new trade routes. The church, however, seems to have successfully
limited the advent of secularly aligned bishops in those few wealthy sees
on the crusader routes. In the remaining, vast majority of dioceses that
were not on crusader routes, secularism and trade expansion continued
in accordance with the incentives of the concordat.

To begin, let us compare the number of bishoprics on trade routes
up to five years before a crusade to five years after the crusade. This
zoomed-in, narrow focus reveals no net change in the number of
wealthy dioceses across the three crusades that occurred between 1147
and 1204. The Second Crusade saw an increase of 6 dioceses on trade
routes out of 378 dioceses within five years after the crusade compared
to five years before, but the Fourth Crusade saw a loss of 6 sees on trade
routes out of 383 between 1197 (five years before the start of the Fourth
Crusade) and 1209 (five years after its end). The Third Crusade experienced no change in the number of bishoprics on trade routes up to five
years before compared to up to five years after. It seems that during
the roughly sixty years between the start of the Second Crusade (the
first during the concordat period) and the end of the Fourth, there
was no net change favoring the creation or elimination of trade routes.
Thus, the evidence suggests that the crusader routes did not act as
more than transitory sources of economic stimulation and so were
consistent with the church's long-term economic interest in limiting,
or at least not encouraging, economic growth.

The Crusades were, of course, very important events. They mobilized
enormous armies that traversed specific portions of Europe—mostly
across the eastern reaches of the Holy Roman Empire, parts of western
Europe that provided routes to the sea, and across Italy—on their way to
do battle. Although so far we have not seen evidence that the Crusades
created new trade routes, we should probe a bit more deeply to be sure
that the concordat's effect in promoting secularism and wealth holds up
even when we correct for the religious purpose behind the Crusades. I

make that correction by identifying the precise dioceses through which the crusader armies traveled, recognizing that the crusader routes differed from one crusade to another. Hence, I treat those armies as having had a lasting impact on those bishoprics they went through from the start of the crusade that brought the army to the see until the end of my calculations in 1517.[47] What do we find?

It turns out that the Crusades did not produce more sustained trade than had existed elsewhere or before. However, the Crusades did limit the rise of secularism in the decided minority of dioceses that the crusader armies went through. Despite being on trade routes, the crusader dioceses had no more secularism than the average see. In comparison, the much larger group of dioceses that were not on crusader routes but were wealthy produced vastly more secular bishops than was true in the typical, non-trade-route dioceses or on the few diocesan routes that the crusader armies traversed. Of course, a great percentage of the crusader routes passed through what is today Italy, close to Rome, where the pope could exercise effective control. The Crusades themselves did not diminish secularism among concordat-signatory territories that were off the crusaders' routes, nor did they influence the growth in trade routes in the sees the crusader armies passed through on their way to battle. Rather, the Crusades only limited secularism's rise in the minority of bishoprics that the crusaders literally traveled through.

Europe's economic growth was not, of course, solely the product of the changed incentives put into motion by the concordat, and the Crusades were not the only important development that could have provided an alternative explanation for growth in European wealth and secularism. Well before the Concordat of Worms, starting around 950, Europe's economy was bolstered by the rise of the Commercial Revolution. The Commercial Revolution was sparked by a marked growth in trade, an impact that lasted until the start of the Industrial Revolution many hundreds of years later.[48] Within the time frame of interest here, the rise of the Commercial Revolution overlaps with the period that the Concordat of Worms and its French and English precursors were operative (and before the plague of the mid-fourteenth century temporarily reversed the expansion of trade), so it is possible that the patterns in economic expansion are due to the Commercial Revolution and are only incidentally associated with the period of the concordats.

As far as I know, no discussions of the Commercial Revolution suggest that the expansion of trade routes had anything to do with the shifted incentives of church leaders and secular rulers once the concordats went into effect. Instead, the Commercial Revolution is understood to have spread along the pathways of commerce, both overland and maritime, wherever trade with the east stimulated commercial interests.[49] It could easily have spread from the Kingdom of Sicily, not subject to the concordat, which had many fine ports and produced export goods, especially wheat and wine. It could have spread across Spain and Portugal, also not subject to a concordat, with their many potential overland routes and ports giving access to the markets of North Africa and the East. Lots of parts of Europe, covered and uncovered, seemingly had good conditions for supporting the expansion of trade. Yet the evidence indicates that there were important differences in the expansion or contraction of trade routes across Europe as a function of whether the locales—the dioceses in our computations—were covered by the concordats or not and, if so, whether they were religiously or secularly aligned.

If what we have argued and seen so far regarding the linkage between wealth and secular power is correct, then the covered dioceses that were wealthy should have attracted secularly aligned bishops, which, as we know, they did. Those secular bishops, in turn, would have supported growth-oriented policies that benefited their lay leader. The logic of the concordats tells us that the Commercial Revolution's impulses should have interacted with the incentives put into place by the treaties. That means that secularism should have reinforced the economic impact of the Commercial Revolution, and the Commercial Revolution should have reinforced the growth of secularism.

It is difficult to separate the extent to which wealth induced greater secularism from the extent to which secularism induced greater wealth during the Commercial Revolution. Still, we do observe that economic expansion was strongly correlated with the secularization of dioceses, with causality possibly running both ways. In fact, Europe's religiously aligned, covered dioceses primarily experienced trade-route contraction (or trade-route contraction led to more religiously aligned bishops) once the Investiture Controversy was resolved by the concordats. Secularly aligned dioceses, in contrast, had their ups and downs once the Commercial Revolution began and until the concordats went into effect, but once the concordats were signed, either this set of dioceses saw dramatic trade-route expansion or dramatic trade-route expansion reinforced the secularization of bishoprics. Meanwhile, the uncovered dioceses lost trade routes during the concordat period despite the Commercial Revolution.

Just how strong the association is between economic expansion, type of bishop, and the concordats, as implied by the game, is readily demonstrated with a couple of comparisons. To give each type of diocese its best shot at being treated equally during the span we are interested in, I begin the comparison between covered, religiously dominated, and covered, secularly dominated dioceses at the time—right as the reformist party secured the papacy in the hands of Gregory VII in the eleventh century—when these two types of dioceses were exactly equal on trade-route prevalence, at about 37 percent. From their position of equal trade-route prevalence, a century into the Commercial Revolution, we can then look at how that prevalence changed by the end of the concordat interlude in 1309.

The covered dioceses that were dominated by religiously oriented bishops ended the concordat interlude with just around 28 percent remaining on trade routes, a decrease of 25 percent from when they and secular sees were equal on this indicator. In contrast, the covered dioceses that were dominated by secularly inclined bishops ended the period with 40 percent on trade routes. So, from a starting place with no difference in their trade-route prevalence, the two types ended up with a 12 percent spread between them, with the secularly aligned dioceses faring better. Either the Commercial Revolution interacted with the concordat incentives to shift the secularization of wealthy sees, or secular bishops did more than religious bishops to promote growth under the impulses of the Commercial Revolution. For our purposes it is not critical which way causality runs. What is critical is that the impact of the Commercial Revolution demonstrably depended on the incentives put into play by the concordats.

The uncovered dioceses, by the way, further reinforce the account that says the concordats fundamentally changed the rules of the game. The uncovered dioceses started out with a disadvantage, with only about 18 percent of these sees having been on trade routes whereas the two types of covered dioceses were starting out equally at about 37 percent. From their 18 percent starting place, the uncovered dioceses declined to only about 5 percent by the end of the concordat interlude, a tremendous drop from their already poor starting place. And this was true despite the expansionist tendencies brought about by the Commercial Revolution.

The evidence tells us that the effects of the Commercial Revolution varied as a function of the institutionally induced changed incentives brought about by the concordats. Other scholars look elsewhere to explain Europe's economic growth and the differences in where economies took off and where they did not. Some—such as those who attribute differences in growth to the development of movable type, the printing press, and the introduction of Gutenberg's Bible, or those who zoom in on the Protestant Reformation as the stimulant for differential economic growth—are looking at developments well after Europe's regions had already diverged in their relative prosperity.[50] Others highlight alleged aspects of European superiority. The superiority claims, embedded in religious or cultural differences, seem inconsistent with the evidence.[51] Why didn't "superiority" produce these effects all through the period of the Commercial Revolution, or before? If, as some argue, Catholic commitments to innovation prompted the growth associated with exceptionalism, then why was it that the dioceses that did best were secularly aligned rather than religiously aligned?

Others point to shifts in family ties and marriage rules introduced by the church starting in the fourth century and still being made as late as the eleventh century. This is an inadequate explanation if we want to account for variations in economic, political, or social performance across Europe. The changed church rules and their presumed consequences did not vary markedly between places that secured secular bishops and places that secured religious bishops during the concordat period, yet the type of bishop seems to have dramatically influenced subsequent economic or trade expansion.[52]

Still others focus on the period when representative assemblies—parliaments—began to blossom across Europe. Where such assemblies arose, the argument goes, they naturally acted to protect property rights, which, in turn, stimulated economic growth.[53] The first hints of the creation of parliaments appear shortly after the signing of the Concordat of Worms, although that event is not considered by those who tie growth to the rise of governmental accountability. We will examine how the Concordat of Worms *stimulated* the institutional incentives both for economic growth and for the establishment of representative parliaments in Chapter 7. There we will see that growth and accountable government seem to have a common causal pathway that runs through the concordat.

My contention is simple: earlier research, by ignoring the terms and implications of the concordats, misses an important part of the explanatory story behind differences in economic expansion across Europe and differences in the rise of accountable government, and therefore it misses a fundamental explanation of why parts of Europe surpassed the rest of the world in prosperity and in the development of political and human rights and why other parts lagged behind.

The concordat game indicates that the most secularized dioceses were primed to promote economic growth. We have seen evidence that is consistent with that contention, but we can and should probe that contention more deeply. Particularly, we should ask whether the concordats were shaping Europe's economic divisions and its economic future. We should expect that the combination of distance from Rome, meaning low costs for defying the pope, and strong secular influence during the interlude between the concordats and the Avignon papacy combined to further stimulate progrowth economic policies.

Figure 5.5 displays the cumulative average change during each prior half century in the percentage of years that a diocese was on a trade route, reporting that cumulative average change over each twenty-five-year interval. The cumulative changes by diocese category indicate my approximation of economic growth for each type of diocese. The figure compares the estimated economic record of religious and secular dioceses based on their proximity to Rome.[54] The figure covers the years from the start of the Commercial Revolution in 950 through to the start of the Protestant Reformation in 1517. The long span of time is divided into two broad segments for ease of display and to highlight the factors of greatest interest.

The factor of greatest interest in Figure 5.5, as in all the assessments in this chapter, is differences in economic growth as a consequence of diocesan conditions and incentives under the concordats. The idea is that the longer a see was on a trade route, the greater its accumulation of wealth and therefore the greater its economic growth. A decrease in the percentage of years on a trade route suggests economic contraction.

The black bars in the graph show us the percentage of dioceses experiencing economic growth during the interlude that the concordats were operational. The gray bars evaluate the percentage of dioceses experiencing economic expansion for the years from 950 to the start of the concordat and from 1309 to the Protestant Reformation. The dioceses are divided into those that were near to or far from Rome, and within each distance category they are further

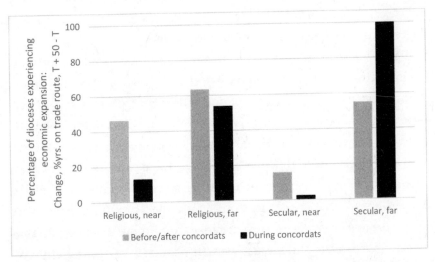

Figure 5.5: Economic expansion over fifty-year periods given prior diocesan secularism

divided by whether the bishops over the relevant time interval were predominantly religiously or secularly aligned. Thus the figure asks and answers, How well did dioceses do in our rough estimate of economic growth depending on the alignment of their bishops and depending on the ease with which the pope could punish recalcitrant rulers?

Unlike our investigation of the decision to nominate and choose a secular or religious bishop, here we can and should look more deeply into the impact of secularly oriented or religiously oriented bishops, since now we are interested in their impact on future economic performance. A bishop's impact, of course, should depend on whether he was inclined to follow the king's policies or the pope's. But it should also depend on how long he was in office, since a bishop who lasted for only a few months or even only a year or two could not have had the same policy impact as one who dominated his diocese, whether as a prochurch or a proking bishop, for many years. Hence, I now define the secularism of dioceses in each quarter century as the average percentage of the time they were governed by secularly aligned bishops. This way I extend the earlier estimate of whether a chosen bishop was expected to be aligned with the lay leader or with the church by treating every year the bishop was in office as either secular, if the bishop was the secular type, or as religious, if the bishop was the religious type. Of course, the cost indicator—distance from Rome—does not change over time, but the degree of diocesan secularism or religiosity does.

Figure 5.5 supports the implications of the concordat game for shifting incentives regarding economic growth. The impact of secularism on economic expansion during the period of the concordats is substantively (and statistically) very strong. First, the economic growth graphed by the black bar for far-from-Rome secular bishoprics during the Worms interlude towers over all the other bars in the figure. These sees grew economically much more than any other category of diocesan locales. Second, we see that greater proximity to Rome by itself decreased economic expansion, while greater distance from Rome increased it. Thus we see that the second-largest growth occurred where the church's reach was weakest, far from Rome, even when the appointed bishop was expected to be aligned with the pope. Leaders presumably wanted to strengthen themselves wherever they could. Being far from Rome greatly helped in advancing that ambition, and being close to Rome, being easily punished by the pope, did not. Finally, we see that secularism in the years before and the years after the concordat (and before the Protestant Reformation) did not support economic growth, and neither did religious alignment when compared to secular, distant dioceses. Growth was most clearly focused primarily in distant secular sees during the interlude of the concordats.

Unfortunately, we cannot say whether the evidence in Figure 5.5 means that secular bishops stimulated growth or that growth attracted secular bishops. It is too difficult to separate the temporal sequence of change with the information that is available. But both directions are consistent with the concordat game's implication that wealth enhanced secularism and secularism enhanced wealth. According to the game, kings always wanted more wealth, as it gave them more power. Hence, during the period the concordats were in force, where a king was wealthy, he gained more power by securing a secular bishop, and where he had a secular bishop, he expected the bishop to stimulate economic growth.

Thus, we see that the intertwined political and economic struggles between the church and nascent states led to the overthrow of the church's interests where the costs of resisting the church's will were low and wealth was relatively high. The concordats incentivized the church to find ways to slow economic growth and incentivized kings to stimulate growth wherever they could. Where economic expansion took place—far from Rome, especially in territories where the interests of the ruler and the bishop were aligned—Europe's population swelled as well. Growing prosperity meant that vast amounts of land needed to be and were assarted to improve food production. Remarkable new machinery was invented to enhance labor productivity, further enriching those parts of Europe that were best at evading the iron fist of the church. All of these developments meant that parts of Europe were closing in on sufficient secularism and sufficient wealth to enter the final consequence implied by the concordat game. Those regions that were closer to Rome and dominated by religiously aligned bishops failed, on average, to enjoy economic expansion. In contrast, those dioceses that were secularized and far from Rome enjoyed expanding prosperity well before the Protestant Reformation. Those parts of Europe were positioned to divorce the Catholic Church. Now we are ready to look at the evidence in greater depth on differences in economic expansion and how they related to regional decisions to succumb to, try to capture, or try to divorce the Catholic Church.

6

THE ROAD TO PAPAL
SERFDOM AND
LIBERATION

*The spiritual and the temporal are different
spheres which ought not to be confused.*

—F. A. Hayek, *The Constitution of Liberty*

T HE CONCORDAT PREDICTABLY STIMULATED SECULARISM IN WEALTHY
places and not in poor ones. Because diocesan wealth made secular power grow, especially during the concordat interlude, lay leaders
naturally acted on their new incentive to encourage economic growth.
At the same time, the church sensibly adopted policies designed to restrict economic growth. Christian beliefs did not make the church oppose improvements in economic conditions. Rather, the problem with
growth was that it translated into more secular power, which was bad
for the church as a political institution. So the Catholic leadership did
what they could to limit economic expansion in order to protect their
interests. And lay rulers did what they could to get richer. Indeed, we
should expect that the rich got richer and the poor, not so much. That,

indeed, is just what happened. We must now ask, What happened in these much wealthier dioceses?

The third outcome of the concordat game indicates that if a see got much richer, so that revenue from the diocese, after adjusting it downward by subtracting the cost of irritating the pope, was more valuable to the secular lord than even the benefits derived by getting a loyal bishop nominee, then that lord would reject the constraints imposed on him by the terms of the concordat. He would no longer have a reason to be open to trading revenue to the church in exchange for political influence over the bishopric's policies. He simply no longer needed the deal. Rulers presiding over really wealthy dioceses could have their cake and eat it too. The pope might have given such a ruler a strongly royalist bishop, but even that might not have been enough for the king to sacrifice his local income in exchange for the church's cooperation. The lay leader in this circumstance could keep the money and secure his political rights either by taking his outside option, divorcing from the influence of the church, or by pursuing his inside option to its fullest, making bishops adhere strictly to his interests even when those interests deviated from those of the church. Indeed, he might pick bishop nominees himself and get them accepted by a compliant church, turning the deal struck in Worms on its head, bringing it to a complete end.

Any of these actions, of course, was a very big step for a lay leader to take. Such rulers almost certainly believed in the teachings of the church, but the extreme inside option—or even more so, the outside option—required that a king be willing to stop caring about whatever short-term or even eternal threats the church brought to bear against him and maybe even his soul. If he were willing to accept these risks, then a king could afford to take the extreme inside option, just as King Philip IV did in France when he captured the papacy in 1309 and made the pope beholden to him. Or a sufficiently wealthy king could take the outside option, as many rulers did in northern Europe when, in the 1500s, they embraced the rebellions against the church led by people like Martin Luther and John Calvin.

Wherever the credible pursuit of both political and economic power was in the offing, Europe's economic, political, and religious landscapes should have been expected to be on the threshold of monumental changes. Those changes would end with the church no longer a major political power in Europe, with its monopoly over salvation shattered, and with the emergence of a new world of sovereign states and the flowering of secular art, literature, and science. But to get there, first we must work out—and demonstrate with evidence—how church and papal temporal power fell so far.

Gamble on Bishops, Gamble on Vacant Sees

To grasp the changes that were afoot, it is useful to go back in time before going forward to the Worms-to-Avignon interlude and beyond. The biggest shift in the incentives behind the selection of bishops resided in the changed revenue implications if a diocese had no bishop in place to attend to the diocese's religious business. The Council of Chalcedon asserted that the church's revenue from a diocese continued to flow to the church whether a see was vacant or not. The resolution of the Investiture Controversy changed that arrangement by leaving the secular ruler's regalian rights, including the right to the diocesan revenue, in his hands until a bishop acceptable to the church and to the ruler was installed. That shift in rules raised the church's stakes for nominating the wrong type of bishop—that is, a bishop who would be rejected by the secular ruler.

There was always a risk that the church would nominate an unacceptable bishop after the concordat was signed. As the concordat game assumes, the church and pope could not be certain about the exact degree of policy alignment a secular ruler required from a bishop nominee, nor could they be sure of how loyal a nominee would be to the pope's or the king's agenda once he was installed in office. The prevalence of uncertainty meant that there was always a chance that a bishop too weakly or too strongly aligned with the pope would be nominated. Nominating someone who was too weakly aligned with the pope and who was more strongly aligned with the king than the king required was a loss for the church, to be sure, but no king would reject such a nominee. Such an error would not have resulted in a vacant see and a loss of revenue. However, if the nominee was too strongly aligned with the church to satisfy

the ruler's needs, then the nominee would be rejected. Before the concordat, before kings had an institutionalized veto over bishop selection,
that gamble over the required alignment of a candidate to be bishop,
from a revenue perspective, was irrelevant to the church. Whether a
chosen bishop was aligned with the local Christian community, the
metropolitan, the pope, or the relevant secular lord, the money still
flowed to the church, so there were no economic ramifications from the
failure to quickly fill a vacant bishopric. Although a vacant see meant
a consequential loss in religious function, there were still priests and
other religious figures to fill the void, carrying on the policies that had
guided the diocesan choices of the previous bishop.

Hence, before the concordat raised the financial stakes from diocesan vacancies, we should expect that interregnums were more commonplace than after the deals had been signed. Once the agreement was
signed, in contrast, the church's revenue loss in the event of a vacant see
was greater than it had been before. In particular, once the concordat
was agreed to, the church's willingness to gamble and err on the side
of picking a bishop nominee who was too favorable to the church to be
accepted by a local leader should have fallen markedly in bishoprics that
were wealthy and/or in dioceses situated far enough from Rome that
the ruler's exposure to papal punishment was minimized. Vacant sees
had become a potentially significant cost to the church and were, therefore, to be avoided under the terms of the concordats in dioceses with a
lot of revenue at stake, unless, of course, the previous diocesan bishop
had been loyal to the church and the pope cared more about policy than
money.

Consider how different the gamble was for the pope and church
during the interlude between the concordat's signing (1107 or 1122)
and the eruption of the Avignon papacy (1309) as compared to after
Chalcedon (451) and before the concordat. Once the concordat was in
place, denying the king what he had sufficient leverage to secure meant
a high probability that the king would reject the bishop nominee. That
would not have mattered much economically for the church when it
came to poor dioceses that were close to Rome. In those places, there
was little money at risk, and the pope could afford to be more aggressive

in choosing bishops more to his liking because the ruler's proximity made him a relatively easy target for punishment. What is more, once the Papal States were established, many of the dioceses that were close to Rome were under the pope's sovereign control—he was both their secular ruler as well as head of the church.

It seems that popes and the church had reasons to be more cautious about putting up the wrong type of bishop in dioceses that were wealthy, far from the pope's influence, or both. Secular wealth and diminished risk of real punishment, all else being equal, should have made popes reluctant to gamble on losing access to significant money by nominating a papal loyalist in the vain hope that the king would agree to someone the king did not want. If a diocese was rich, it behooved the church to choose a bishop pleasing to the king. If the diocese was rich and distant from Rome, it even more behooved the church to give the king the bishop he wanted, lest the king reject the nominee, precipitating an interregnum with its associated loss of revenue for the church as well as of some important religious function. We see, then, that the concordat game gives us some expectations, albeit not very strong expectations, about the odds of an interregnum given high or low revenue and high or low costs for irritating the church officials who were the relevant nominators, particularly the pope, and it also tells us that the chances of such vacant bishoprics would look different before the concordat and once it was in force. Now it is useful to check the evidence to see if this implication is borne out, as it will help guide our thinking about where and when rebellions against the church were most likely.

Evaluating the risk of an interregnum requires that we measure whether or not an interregnum occurred following the death, resignation, or departure of each bishop. This would seem to be simple; we just need to look for the times when a vacancy occurred. But, alas, it is not that easy. The gravest problem in assessing interregnums arises because it is not possible to tell the difference between interregnums and situations where the names and dates of bishops have been lost to history or are lost in the records I inspected. Hence, it is close to impossible to know for sure whether an interregnum occurred or whether we just do not know about bishops who might have presided during the years of a seeming vacancy. This alone means that we must interpret the assessment of interregnums with considerable caution. And then too, even with this caveat in mind, there are other difficulties in evaluating when interregnums occurred.

I have recorded, to the extent available, the year in which each diocese was filled following a vacancy, but the exact date when each bishop was consecrated is unknown for many European bishops, although the year of their designation as bishop is generally known. Hence, to be reasonably confident that an interregnum occurred, a full calendar year must have passed between the death, resignation, or removal of the bishopric's previous bishop and the installation of the new bishop. If less than a year passed, then the diocese is treated as having had no interregnum. Thus, a bishopric that became vacant in, say, 1100 and was filled in 1101 is treated as having had no interregnum. Since information more precise than the year of the bishop's installation generally is not known, this means that a vacancy of as little as a day and, in principle, as much as one day shy of two years is coded as having had no interregnum.[1] By counting interregnums only if more than a year has passed, we also overcome some of the problems that arise with forgotten or unknown bishops, many of whom may have served for such a brief time that their term has been forgotten or was not recorded.

With these cautions in mind, I use the information available on nearly twelve thousand transitions from one bishop to the next between 451 and 1517 to assess whether an interregnum happened. I divide the dioceses of Europe into four categories:

1. Those that were poor (not on a major trade route) and close to Rome (less than the median distance of 1,115 kilometers from Rome).
2. Those that were poor but far from Rome.
3. Those that were wealthy and close to Rome.
4. Those dioceses that were wealthy and far from Rome.

Figure 6.1 displays the observed probability of an interregnum for each of the four categories of dioceses over time.

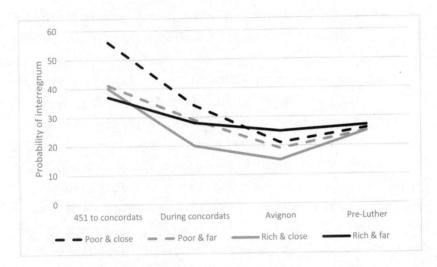

Figure 6.1: Interregnums, wealth, distance: From Worms to Luther

Figure 6.1 provides a few striking findings that draw attention to how decision-making changed because of the conditions agreed to in the concordat. First, interregnums were commonplace before the concordat regardless of diocese type. The proportion of interregnums between the departure or death of one bishop and the installation of the next bishop was between about 35 percent and 55 percent depending on wealth and proximity to Rome. Once the concordats were signed, however, only dioceses that were relatively poor and close to Rome had even a little over a 30 percent chance of an interregnum. Distant sees and wealthy sees all had fewer interregnums. As expected, the odds of an interregnum in this group of sees is well below the preconcordat or poor and close diocese experience.

Once the concordats were operative, the willingness to gamble on nominating someone as bishop who might be unattractive to the secular ruler, or simply sitting on a vacant bishopric without nominating anyone, remained commonplace *only* in bishoprics where the pope could expect to have maximum leverage—that is, in dioceses that were poor and close to Rome. The poor nearby sees, of course, are the very places in which the pope had no need to trade money for policy control: he could have both. The error rate, that is, the chance of experiencing an interregnum, was far lower—and statistically significantly lower—once the risk and cost associated with picking the wrong person or of picking no nominee was heightened by the terms of the concordat.

Moving forward in time in Figure 6.1, we see a sharp temporal decline in the range of dioceses in which the pope could afford to gamble on getting someone leaning more favorably in his direction. While it remains true that papal toleration for interregnums was stronger in dioceses that were poor and proximate to Rome, the degree of such tolerance is dramatically reduced once the French king turns the pope into his vassal during the Avignon papacy. Then, slowly but steadily, interregnums begin to resume. The likelihood of interregnums declined after the concordats were signed for all categories of dioceses, signaling as well the decline in the pope's power and control over his own bishops. Given that we know that these periods were accompanied by an increase in secularly inclined bishops, it is evident that gambling on getting a religious bishop was on the way out; acquiescing to the wishes of kings was on the rise.

BREAKING FROM THE CHURCH: FRENCH WEALTH AND THE AVIGNON PAPACY

Wealth begot secularly inclined bishops, and secularly inclined bishops, working with their lay leaders, seem to have begotten greater diocesan wealth. Growing wealth was a recipe for entry into the game's final, rebellious case in which rulers could dare to turn their back on the church's secular influence. France, whose boundaries then were similar to today's, was Europe's first rich, organized country.[2] As such, it was likely to be the first candidate to rebel against the church's influence. It did so throughout the Avignon papacy (1309–1376), followed, after a brief break, by the Western Schism (1378–1417). Did it rebel in accordance with the logic and the incentives set up by the concordat?

Figure 6.2 helps us visualize the substantial difference between France's wealth, as measured by the percentage of its dioceses that were on major trade routes, and that of the rest of Europe. The figure divides the rest of Europe into two groups: countries other than France that were covered by the concordats ("Wealth in concordats" in the figure) and those that were not subject to the new rules for picking bishops ("Wealth not covered"). As is evident, at the time of Charlemagne and for more than two centuries after the creation of the Holy Roman Empire, France fell in the middle on trade-route prevalence, below the rest of Europe that eventually would be covered by the concordats and above those parts of Europe that would not be subject to a concordat. The portion of Europe that did not participate in the concordats—much of eastern Europe, Spain, Portugal (with much of Spain dominated by Muslim regimes at the time), the area around today's Venice, and today's Italy south of Rome—was collectively notably poorer, as judged by trade-route prevalence, around 800 but, along with France, was rising quickly, while the rest of Europe stayed relatively level regarding trade-route prevalence. France, alone, passed the rest of Europe around the time the Investiture Controversy began and kept on rising until about 1200 and then flattened out. An observer watching Europe at the time that Charlemagne was first given the title of Holy Roman emperor would have had little reason to think that France would become the wealthiest part of Europe in a few hundred years.

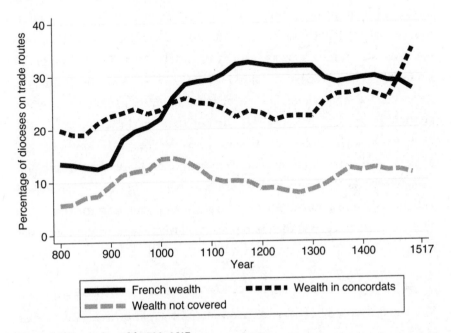

Figure 6.2: Europe's wealth: 800–1517

By the turn of the millennium, however, anyone watching growth would have bet against Germany and Italy and might have bet instead on France or on what became the portions of Europe that were not subject to a concordat. Both these areas were booming. Some of Europe's economic engines outside of France, such as the Veneto, would have looked like a promising bet. But despite the reasonable expectations of an observer before the millennium, the next few centuries saw the uncovered parts of Europe mostly decline in wealth, falling behind large portions of Europe that were subject to the rules of the concordats. France, however, had a totally different experience. France was far ahead according to the trade-route indicator of economic development. It seems with hindsight, and it could well have seemed to a careful observer by early in the 1100s, that France was positioned to be the first region in Europe with a credible chance to break free from the church's political influence.

France's wealth surely took many of its dioceses out of the first outcome of the concordat game by the reign of King Louis VI (died 1137). Dioceses that had been poor appear to have become wealthier, maybe even wealthy enough to have been transported into the third feasible outcome, in which rulers no longer felt a need to make deals with the church over the selection of bishops. This shift into the third outcome of the game could have begun to arise as early as the interval between the reigns of Louis VII (1137–1180) and Philip IV (1268–1314). With the limited indicator of wealth available for the years studied, we cannot know when enough dioceses were sufficiently wealthy that the third outcome of the game—a break from the church—was possible. We can, however, use the evidence across hundreds of years of history to evaluate why the Avignon papacy happened when it did, whether its occurrence might have been anticipated by an astute observer even at the time, and how the rise of the French rebellion against the church was tied to the logic of the concordat game.

TESTING WHEN FRANCE WAS READY TO REBEL

The Avignon papacy had punched a hole in papal power, making the pope, at least for a time, once again dependent on a king for his selection, much as had been true under the Roman and Byzantine emperors. That urges us to address two critical questions: (1) Was a rebellion against the church inevitable given France's great economic advantage during the years from the twelfth century onward? (2) If so, when was the optimal time for such a rebellion to occur? The logic creating the final outcome of the concordat game, the extreme inside option, the vassalage of the church and its pope, or the outside option, the abandonment of the church and its pope, gives us the necessary roadmap to answer both questions.

The odds that a country's worth of dioceses would rebel against the church depended on their enjoying substantial wealth. We cannot know exactly when France had that much prosperity, but we can find out when its dioceses were so much wealthier than the rest of Europe that they were good candidates for rebellion. To do so I create a variable—I called it Avignon—that assigns a 1 to each French diocese every quarter century and a 0 to all other dioceses. Then, every quarter century, starting in 950, at the beginning of the Commercial Revolution, and concluding in 1648, when the Thirty Years' War ended, statistical methods are used

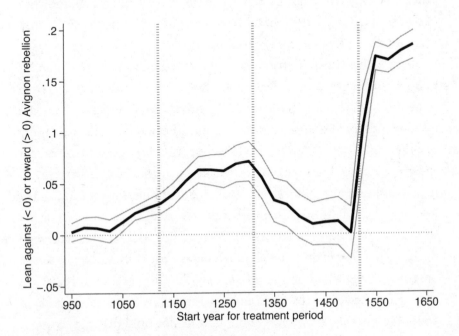

Figure 6.3: Diocesan wealth and the rise of the Avignon papacy

to evaluate how well we can predict each diocese's value (0 or 1) on Avignon just by knowing the percentage of French dioceses on trade routes compared to that percentage for all other sees in that twenty-five-year period. Figure 6.3 displays this comparison.[3]

The solid black line in Figure 6.3 shows us the estimated relative advantage in trade-route prevalence that France enjoyed over the rest of Europe each quarter century. The light gray lines denote the range within which we have 95 percent confidence that France's true wealth advantage fell. Whenever the projected advantage has a positive value, there was a tilt *in favor* of rebellion.

As we see in Figure 6.3, the risk of the Avignon rebellion against the church, though in the positive, plausible, range from 1050 onward, spiked much higher, meaning it was increasingly likely, precisely as the Avignon papacy arose. Rather remarkably, the tilt in favor of the Avignon rebellion reaches its two highest points in the exact quarter century (1300–1325) in which the Avignon papacy began and just one quarter century earlier than that, in 1275–1300. During the quarter century from 1275 to 1300, Philip IV and England's Edward I were occupied fighting a war with each other. The data used to estimate the likelihood of rebellion is uninformed of that fact, telling us that but for their war, Philip IV might have broken with Boniface VIII even earlier than he did.

The positive tilt in favor of starting a rebellion against the church's political influence diminishes noticeably as soon as there is a French pope in Avignon ready to do what the French king desires, so we can no longer discern a meaningful difference between secularly leaning or religiously leaning bishops. Of course, the data used to construct the graph do not know this or any related historical facts. The urge to rebel continues at a diminished level, finally falling into the antirebellion region in the 1400s. Then, it turns upward dramatically just as the Protestant Reformation comes on the horizon, another fact unknown to the test. The risk of a French rebellion against the church just keeps on growing right up until approximately the time of the Thirty Years' War, which began in 1618 and ended with the Treaty of Westphalia in 1648. Hence, the test in Figure 6.3 tells us not only that the Avignon papacy started at the "right" time but also that France would fall back into the Catholic fold well before Martin Luther initiated the Protestant Reformation and would then again be supportive of rebellion for the rest of the time covered by the figure. We can only speculate, with hindsight, whether this might have been an early-warning indicator of the antichurch secularization France saw during its revolution, still 150 years in the future. It is fun to speculate about that hint in the graph, but of course, it is just that, fun speculation.

The test in Figure 6.3 and the historical evidence about wealth on which it is based pointed the finger at the time of Philip IV as a highly likely period for a French rebellion to have happened. In fact, Philip was already challenging the pope's influence in France nearly a decade before the formal launch of the Avignon papacy.

Philip ordered the arrest of Bernard Saisset, bishop of Pamiers, for instance, in October 1301 while the bishop was serving as the pope's legate in negotiations with Philip over the king's attempt to reclaim his regalian revenue from a diocese with a suspended bishop. The arrest outraged the pope, who called a council two months later that condemned the actions of the French crown. Furthermore, Boniface reiterated the position, which he had stated in September 1296 in a message to Philip, *Ineffabilis amor*, that anyone, including King Philip, who seized a clergyman or his property was subject to excommunication.

The battle between the French king and the pope continued to escalate. When in 1302 Boniface issued *Unam sanctam*, which declared that the pope could depose any lay person, even a king, Philip took it as an indefensible assault on his power. His chancellor, Pierre Flotte, threatened the pope, telling him that papal power was only verbal whereas the king's power was real. Philip, working to derail Boniface's assertion that the French king held his office at the pleasure of the pope rather than God, called a meeting of the Estates General "to rally them to his support in the defense of the liberties and honour of France."[4]

Philip went on to issue a statement in response to the position staked out by the pope:

Let your high folly know (*Sciat tua maxima fatuitas*) that we are not subject to anyone in temporal affairs, that collation of vacant churches and prebends belongs to us of royal right, that their revenues are for us, that collations made in the past or to be made in the future are valid and we shall strenuously protect those who hold them. Those who believe otherwise, we hold to be fools and madmen.[5]

Philip's position, driven by his claim of a God-given right to the power enjoyed by the monarch of France and, of course, therefore also to its revenue, could not have been more different from the pope's perspective. In *Ausculta fili*, issued in December 1301, before Philip's statement, the pope warned the French king:

We want you to know that you are subject to us in spiritual and temporal matters. The collation of benefices and prebends is none of your business. And if you have custody of temporalities during vacancies, you should reserve the income for those who succeed to the offices in question. Should you have collated, we declare the act null; if it has taken place, revoke it. Those who believe otherwise, we hold to be heretics.[6]

The verbal exchanges between Boniface and Philip, notably strongly focused on money matters and ecclesiastical appointments, escalated unabated. Finally, in September 1303, with Philip now literally at war with the pope, Boniface was taken prisoner while he vacationed in Anagni. He was rescued—or released—a few days later and died shortly thereafter, but of course his death did not bring an end to the struggle for control between church and king. Instead, Philip expanded the conflict to reach far beyond his personal dispute with Boniface. He seized on the dispute to expand his power at the expense of the church, culminating in the launch of the Avignon papacy. Arnold of Brescia's prediction that the pope would be enslaved had come true.

But what about the other major kingdoms that were subject to the terms of the concordats? Maybe their monarchs were just as ready as France's Philip IV to rebel against the church at the end of the thirteenth and the beginning of the fourteenth centuries. We can check that possibility by repeating the test in Figure 6.3, but this time making the covered dioceses of Italy and then those of England the effect of interest by creating, respectively, the variables Italy Rebel (all Italian bishoprics equal 1; all others, 0) and England Rebel (all English sees equal 1; all others, 0) to see if and when they might have rebelled. Figure 6.4 replicates the exact process used to create Figure 6.3 but now for these two different kingdoms. Later we will repeat the process for the dioceses that, in fact, rebelled starting in 1517 by choosing the outside option, the adoption of Protestantism. When we do that it will be interesting to look back at Figure 6.4 to see what the pattern looked like for England. We may infer an answer to the question of whether England's King Henry VIII had any religious or "national" political qualms with the Catholic Church, or whether his divorce from it was purely for personal advantage, as surely everyone believes.

Figure 6.4 tells a straightforward story. Between 950 and the start of the Avignon papacy, Italy never looked like a candidate to rebel against the great influence of the Catholic Church. Such a condition arose later, and at a more muted level than was true in France, right around the time of the mid-fourteenth century Black Death, a most unpropitious time for rebellion. That muted rebellious urge, based on wealth in Italy, perhaps in keeping with the efforts of such heretics as Savonarola (executed in 1498), experienced a sharp diminution as the fifteenth century drew to its close and as the Protestant Reformation was about to begin.

The picture was much the same in England. According to the figure, any revolutionary zeal was even damper than in Italy and, again, began to arise at an inauspicious time: the Great Famine of 1315–1322 struck England especially severely and was followed shortly by the Black Death that swept across England starting in 1348. Of course, England did break from the church in 1533, when the pope denied Henry VIII's request to divorce his wife even as the figure suggests that the weak antichurch, rebellious spirit, as indexed by wealth, was leaving England. But we should remember that at the start of the Reformation, Henry was a staunch defender of the church, even receiving the title Defender of the Faith (*Defensor fidei*) in 1521.

It seems that France's Philip, like several of his predecessors, had reasons to come into conflict with the church, but unlike them, he was

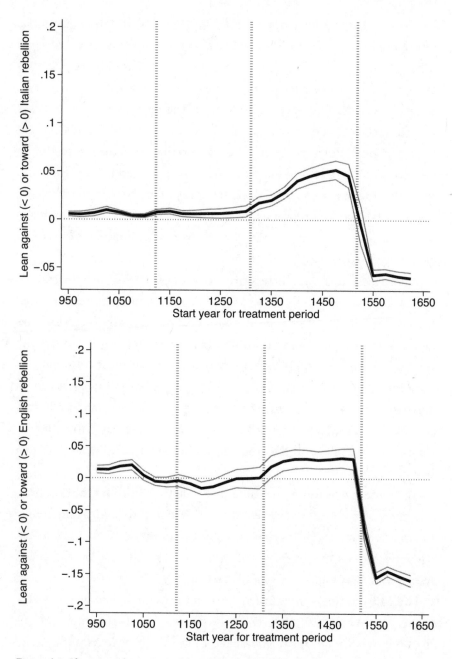

Figure 6.4: Changes in diocesan wealth and the likelihood of rebellion in Italy and England

willing to fight the church with all his substantial might. By contrast, the displeasures of the rulers in England and Italy did not begin to amount to enough for them to contemplate rebellion. And when, according to the wealth evidence and the concordat game, they might have been ready to use the inside or outside option, the times were inauspicious indeed for doing so.

THE CHURCH CONTEMPLATES REFORM; PROTESTANTS REBEL

Any thoughtful clergyman or lay leader in Philip IV's time would have understood that Philip was a threat to the political standing of the Catholic Church even if he did not realize that that risk was the product of the conditions created by the concordat. That same thoughtful clergyman or lay leader in medieval Europe would have also understood that the church's political power depended on the dual beliefs in eternal salvation and in adherence to the Catholic Church's practices and teachings as the one and only path to that salvation. The Avignon papacy and the Western Schism marked the first secular efforts to enact the third case of the concordat game, but they had not challenged the fundamental ideas behind the church's claim to be the monopoly provider of eternal salvation. Perhaps the ideas needed for the outside option just did not yet exist or were not prominent enough to have captured Philip IV's imagination. Hence, he turned the pope into his vassal rather than abandoning Catholicism and its church entirely. The French popes were still the religious leaders of the church during the Avignon papacy even though their temporal power was diminished. The church's leaders fully understood the threat they had escaped, at least for the moment, when the Western Schism ended. But a succession of popes proved unwilling to concede any of their newly recovered power as a way to prevent similar threats in the future.

To be sure, many leaders of the church understood that internal reform might yet save the papacy and the church from the forces put into motion by the concordats. An effort to advance such a goal was central to the church's rebellion at the Council of Constance against the century-old rebellion in France. The resolution of the papal schism at the Council of Constance reunified the church under a single, elected pope, but it also introduced a new risk to the authority of the pope through its conciliar movement. The idea behind conciliarism was that the pope would no longer have veto power over church policy. Rather, he would receive policy guidance from a representative body, an ecumenical council, designed, as a practical matter, to prevent the further weakening of the church as had occurred during the Avignon papacy and the Western Schism. The idea drew sufficient interest that it was a focal point of the Council of Basel (1431–1449), at which papal supremacy was restored and the threat—or liberalizing reform—of the conciliar movement was laid to rest, at least for a time.

We may understand the conciliar movement, in part, as the church's effort to protect itself, albeit certainly not wittingly, from the third outcome of the concordat game. Had the conciliar movement succeeded in creating a representative church rather than the authoritarian, even dictatorial, church that functioned under papal domination, then perhaps the greatest risk to church power, the Protestant Reformation (at the time less than a century into the future), might have been avoided. But this was not to be. Thus it was that the conciliar movement failed to wrest control away from the pope and place it in an ecumenical council. Popes, for their part, now needed to find ways to shore up their position as the expansion of wealth in parts of Europe continued to threaten their authority, contributing to stirrings of rebellion beyond the frontiers of France. But here too they failed, more out of the drive of personal interests than out of a commitment to the religious principles under which they governed.

To be sure, the church loosened its papal stranglehold on reform ever so slightly once the Protestant threat to its religious supremacy was undeniably underway. Not until the Council of Trent, really a series of councils between 1545 and 1563, begun just before Martin Luther died in 1546, did future popes face a larger, slightly more accountable, electorate drawn from among the cardinals (often cardinal-nephews) they appointed. The conciliar movement launched at the Council of Constance yielded only a small increase in the papal winning coalition, the number of supporters among the cardinals required to elect a pope. A larger increase followed the Council of Trent, at which, in its early phases, the church made an unsuccessful effort to reconcile with the spreading movement of Protestant "heretics" in Germany and, to a smaller extent, in France. By the end of the council, no concessions had been made to the Protestants. Even the hope of an easily understood Bible was quashed. Instead, Saint Jerome's Latin translation of the Bible—an effort initiated by Pope (Saint) Damasus I in the fourth century to make the Bible *more* accessible—became the inaccessible official translation of the scriptures, reinforcing the Catholic hierarchy's view that ordinary, lay people should only understand God's teaching through the church's clergy. The divide with the Protestants that might have been avoided, or at least mitigated, was instead cemented to protect the interests of the popes who led the church after the Council of Constance and up to and during the Council of Trent. This was a short-term fix for the church that protected popes who, alas, proved more interested in their own luxurious lifestyles, nepotism, and alleged debauchery than in the long-term interests and unity of Christendom.

Figure 6.5 makes clear that even as conciliarism encouraged a modest improvement in papal accountability to a very tiny number of Christians—those in the slightly expanded College of Cardinals—following the Council of Constance, the failure of conciliarism to stick supported the return of nepotism to papal affairs. Once again, the papacy became a family business. From the Avignon papacy until the end of the Western Schism, although not eradicated, papal nepotism was at a low level. To be sure, we should not construe this to mean that the church had revised its views away from nepotism. Rather, popes were selected to be loyal to the French king; their personal, family relations were not his primary concern. The Avignon popes by and large certainly lived to excess and sought to advantage their families. It was just that they did not get to inherit the papacy from their relatives or pass it on to their heirs. But once the Council of Constance was convened and the church was out of the grasp of the French king, papal nepotism made a vigorous return.

With the papacy returned to Rome, and mostly to Italian hands, nepotism resumed with a burst of energy supported by the competition between such prominent families as the Colonnas, the Borgias, and the Medicis. The latter two families, in particular, controlled the papacy on and off for much of the fifteenth and sixteenth centuries. Their popes

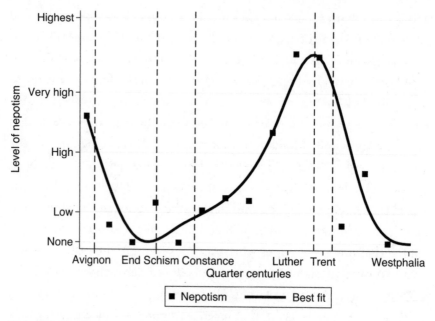

Figure 6.5: Papal nepotism, Avignon to Westphalia

lived opulent and often corrupt lives, acted as political agents for their families, and seem only secondarily, at best, to have focused on religious interests as the motivator of their action.

The burst in nepotism after the Council of Constance lasted for more than a century and did not return to its pre-Constance level for nearly two centuries. By the time of the Council of Trent, the papal winning coalition, requiring a two-thirds majority of the enlarged College of Cardinals, increased apace, doubling in size from what it had been at the time of the Council of Constance. Whether because of the increase in the required size of the papal winning coalition, the Protestant Reformation's objections to the lavish lifestyles and corrupt practices of the church, similar objections by Catholic reformers ("heretics"), introspection, or something else, papal nepotism went into a steep decline following the Council of Trent. By the time of the Thirty Years' War, nepotism was close to eliminated in the papacy, apparently returning the selection of the pope to the same religious considerations as had dominated that choice before the creation of the Papal States.

It seems that after the mid-seventeenth century, popes were no longer men seeking to enrich their families and to corrupt the church for that purpose but were, instead, men of religion, as had been true of the earliest popes. And like those early popes, the post-Trent popes were men of greatly diminished political power who were also facing religious competition as they had in Roman times. Out of the serfdom of Avignon and the Protestant competition that followed it, the leaders of the church emerged as men liberated to practice their religion instead of pursuing temporal power.

As every pope surely understood, those monarchs who became rich enough would not take direction and would not horse-trade with the church or its pope anymore. In Philip IV's case, not having a better idea, he had taken political charge of the church. A different idea, however, was lurking in the reformist "heretics" who sought to change the church's teachings and practices. These reformists were spread across Europe, and those among them who were in wealthy places far from Rome were protected thanks to the leverage of their princes and kings and the limited ability of the church to punish its foes. The combination of wealth and sufficient distance from Rome fertilized new ideas, first of a religious nature and later of a scientific nature, that could and did jeopardize the spiritual as well as the temporal power of the church.

Putting ourselves in the shoes of a hypothetical clergyman or lay leader of the Middle Ages, we can think about which dioceses across Europe were experiencing economic expansion and which were not. We can do so with information that in principle could have been inferred or known at the time. As astute observers, we would have noticed that the wealthiest parts of Europe by far included those dioceses that were 1,000 to 1,500 kilometers from Rome, including much of what today is France as well as significant portions of today's Germany. As we know, French dioceses were first in line to rebel against church domination. The German and Germanic sees, such as in today's Switzerland, were next in line, and indeed, they proved to be essential for the Protestant Reformation.

The dioceses that were farthest from Rome also include German dioceses, Scandinavian sees, and a great many others that were parts of kingdoms that became Protestant during the sixteenth and seventeenth centuries. Their secular rulers did not grow wealthy enough to break from Rome until shortly after the Council of Constance. An observer looking at the bishoprics that were closer to Rome would have noticed that they were neither wealthy enough nor distant enough to gamble on breaking from the church. They seem not to have been close to entering the third outcome of the game. Thus, our hypothetical observer looking across Europe's landscape over a long swath of time might have seen a hint that something akin to the Protestant Reformation could have happened in the territories of the bishoprics that were farthest from Rome, as their economies had begun to grow rapidly enough to possibly enter the third equilibrium outcome of the concordat game during the late fifteenth and early sixteenth centuries.

Indeed, other than the dioceses within a thousand kilometers of Rome, Europe seemed to be growing economically as it entered the time of the Black Death, the bubonic plague that killed almost one-third of all Europeans. Following a pause in growth, these more distant parts of Europe resumed their economic expansion. This extensive growth outside Rome's more proximate region should have been an ominous sign to the pope and church, one that would have called on reforms such as were proposed in this period during the conciliar movement. But, as we know, those reforms were not instituted and, in fact, had been outright rejected by the time of the Council(s) of Trent.

Instead, the church appears to have adopted a strategic approach designed to preserve its power while following policies that kept the average diocese within five hundred kilometers of Rome relatively poor, much as those parts of Europe still are to this day. One piece of the church's strategy appears to have been the creation of new sees that were close to Rome and that would follow the pope's bidding.

Naturally, new dioceses had to form as regions became Catholic. Because the church managed to secure itself in Scandinavia rather late— genuinely Scandinavian bishoprics were all but nonexistent before the twelfth century—we might well expect that the greatest growth in the establishment of dioceses would have been far from Rome. Furthermore, as the extensive programs to assart new land indicates, population growth coupled with growing wealth were especially happening in the parts of Europe that were distant from Rome, lands where the adoption of the heavy plow in the tenth century, around the same time as the arrival of Catholicism, expanded food production to support a larger population.[7]

Yet the actual pattern of diocesan expansion cannot be supported by a normal economic or demographic account of what was happening across Europe. Rather, it is in the areas that were closest to Rome, where Catholicism had been longest established, that there was the greatest proportionate (and often, absolute) expansion in the establishment of new dioceses, especially up to the start of the Avignon papacy, when diocese creation fell to the hands of a servile French papacy. By the 1370s, with a pope, if not *the* pope, returned to Rome, the expansion of dioceses in the neighborhood of Rome resumed. Just before the concordat, there were only about 40 to 50 bishoprics within 500 kilometers of Rome; by the start of the Avignon papacy, there were 75, a 50 percent increase in a region without new conversions. The next-largest expansion was a close contest between the sees that are more than 500 kilometers but less than 1,000 kilometers from Rome and those that are more than 1,500 kilometers from Rome. The farthest regions expanded from about 100 bishoprics at the start of the concordat interlude to around 130 by 1309, a 30 percent increase. The number of bishoprics in a band more than 500 but less than 1,000 kilometers from Rome grew from about 75 to 90 during the same years, a growth of 20 percent. The number of fairly close-in sees continued to expand, increasing 67 percent by the time of Martin Luther, even though we are talking about a region in which Catholicism was well established. The regions of Europe that were 1,000 or more kilometers from Rome barely saw any further increase in their diocesan representation between 1309 and 1517.

It seems surprising that the neighborhoods closest to Rome were experiencing a substantially larger proportionate expansion in the number of sees, despite their smaller geographic area, than any of the more distant regions. What was going on to make the parts of Europe that were most securely in the pope's camp expand the number of their dioceses so much more than the rest of Europe? And what was happening to the size of dioceses as threats to the church's political power were growing? The answers to these questions suggest strategic maneuvering by the church as its political position eroded.

The average distant diocese, more than 1,500 kilometers from Rome, occupied about ten times more square kilometers than those sees that were closest to Rome. Indeed, the farther one got from Rome, the larger the average size of bishoprics in square kilometers. This could not have merely reflected differences in population or population growth. After all, the population of the Papal States plus the city-states of Italy combined came to about 6.25 million in 1500 whereas France and the Holy Roman Empire each included about 16.5 million people.[8] Why, then, was there such an explosion in the number of bishoprics close to Rome when population was larger and growing especially rapidly far from Rome? What strategic purpose might have been served by the creation of new dioceses that were poor and easily within the reach of the pope's outstretched arm? A simple, Occam's razor sort of answer to these questions is that the church needed to protect its political position as wealth and population grew far from Rome. Distant, secular rulers were growing into threats against the church's political power, weakening the church as these rulers lost interest in and incentive to comply with the pope's wishes.

Having put ourselves in the shoes of a thirteenth- or fourteenth-century observer, now it is time to put our own shoes back on, taking advantage of the knowledge we have about how the Concordat of Worms changed history. Let's have a look at Figure 6.6. The figure reminds us that shortly before the concordat was signed, today's Protestant Europe (the solid black line), far from Rome and the pope's reach, today's Catholic Europe (the dashed gray line), and today's France (the dashed black line) were all about equal in trade-route prevalence. But by some time between the Fourth Lateran Council (1215) and the start of the Avignon papacy, that was no longer true. By the mid-fifteenth century, it was looking like no contest: today's Protestant Europe was pulling way ahead of the rest of Europe other than France. The facts about trade-route expansion, at least, seem to tell us that Protestant Europe's wealth took off compared to Catholic Europe's wealth starting long before Martin Luther and the Protestant Reformation. The economic incentives

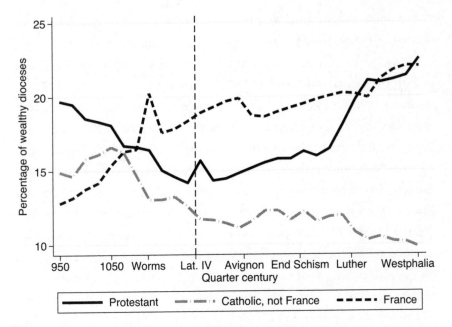

Figure 6.6: Protestant economic expansion and Lateran IV: The end begins.

institutionalized by the concordat seem to have created an intense work ethic in those parts of Europe that avoided severe papal punishments long before the so-called Protestant work ethic came to be.

Whether rulers chose the new Protestant religion or stuck with Catholicism depended, of course, on a great many issues beyond proximity to Rome and the wealth within their reach. Also weighing heavily must have been considerations of their domestic political situation and, for the faithful, concerns about their eternal salvation. The expectation of relatively low costs for deviating from the pope's wishes was important but probably not sufficient to explain decisions to break from the Roman church. Certainly, looking at diocesan distances from Rome, the indicator of costs, reminds us that even in the farthest reaches of non-Orthodox Europe, a significant portion of sees remained Catholic. As Germany and other distant locales teach us, even for places more than two thousand kilometers from Rome, still some dioceses remained Catholic as of 1600, and indeed, are still Catholic today. Thus, while the evidence overall is strongly consistent with the thesis proposed here, that thesis clearly is not the whole story.

For one thing, in much of Europe—maybe all of Europe by the century before Luther—decisions about religious affiliation were surely not made only by individuals and not even by local secular rulers. Much of Europe was already consolidating into larger kingdoms and states, meaning that, for instance, had the French king chosen Protestantism, then just about all of France would probably have been Protestant. Indeed, by the time of the Council of Trent, France included many who adhered to Protestant beliefs. Their presence created a challenge for the French king, who ultimately chose to remain Catholic, as therefore did France. The French king successfully resisted further rebellion, but England's Henry VIII certainly did not resist; he initiated the abandonment of the Catholic Church in pursuit of his own personal gain. His religious decision swept up all the English other than those most willing to take risks, as he imposed huge costs on those who did not subscribe to his decision to abandon Catholicism and who would, therefore, not accommodate his wishes.

As time passed following the signing of the concordats, much of southern Europe—those parts closest to Rome—remained poor, as Figure 6.6 reminds us, and they remained loyal to the church. But far away in the north, far from the pope's grasp, vast territories had become rich enough to gain political clout and, at some point, rich enough to enter the final phase of the concordat game by breaking with the church, just as Philip IV had done in France. As Figure 6.6 demonstrates, well before Martin Luther nailed his ninety-five theses to the church door, the signs that someone like Luther and something like the Protestant Reformation were on the way were clear enough.

Of course, Luther's ideas launched the Protestant Reformation, but there had been many would-be reformers before him: men like Waldo, Wycliffe, Savonarola, and Hus. The Concordat of Worms produced the economic and political conditions for breaking with the church, dissolving its monopoly over salvation and, with that, crushing the church's hope for hegemonic religious—or political—power in Europe. It is in this window of time that, in Europe, the value of the material present surpassed that of the eternal future. But, as with the timing of the Avignon papacy, the very fact that there were so many reformers leaves us with the question, When did the parts of Europe that joined the Protestant Reformation enter the period of the third outcome of the concordat game? As with Avignon, I conduct tests designed to approximate an answer to this question.

Figure 6.7 shows the results of the tests. As with the previous tests for France, Italy, and England, the factor of interest, the factor plotted in Figure 6.7, is the statistically measured impact of diocesan wealth each quarter century in differentiating between the dioceses that became Protestant and those that did not. The solid dark line plots, over quarter centuries, the impact of wealth as a way to distinguish and predict the dioceses that became Protestant Europe from the rest of Europe, and the lighter lines show the 95 percent confidence interval, estimated for each quarter century as well. The figure gives us a way to estimate when there was sufficient diocesan wealth in what is today continental Protestant Europe to contemplate beginning the end of Catholicism's monopoly on salvation according to the third outcome anticipated by the concordat game. Of course, someone also had to have the idea of breaking from the church. The statistical test can tell us when such an

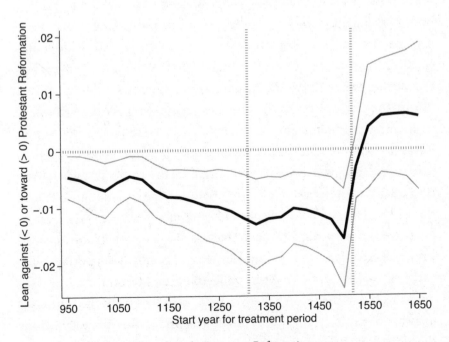

Figure 6.7: Changing wealth predicts the Protestant Reformation.

idea could take hold, but not when such an idea—an idea like Martin Luther's—would arise.

As with the Avignon analysis, the focus is on two considerations: (1) When is the weight of the push exerted by changes in wealth sufficiently positive that all, or at least most, of the confidence interval is also within the positive range? (2) When is the estimated weight of the influence of wealth at its peak positive value, denoting the optimal time for a break from the Catholic Church according to the implications of the concordat game? Despite the limitations of our measurement of wealth between 950 and 1650, we see that at the time between the Investiture Controversy and the start of the Avignon papacy (the first dotted vertical line) the line that shows the influence of wealth and the confidence intervals around it are all well within the negative range, leaning against the Reformation during the quarter centuries when France's Philip IV was positioned to rebel against the church. During that interlude, as we now know, the evidence shows that neither England, Italy, nor any of northern Europe that today is Protestant was in a position to break away from the Catholic Church, even though France was and did.

As we also know, following the initiation of the Avignon papacy, both England and Italy had a near-zero probability of rebellion. When it comes to the Holy Roman Empire and its surrounding kingdoms that eventually chose to be Protestant, they too tilted against rebellion during the period of the Avignon papacy and the Western Schism. But by the last quarter of the fifteenth century, the wealth advantage plotted in the graph begins to climb steeply toward the positive—pro-Reformation—region. The upper confidence interval supports rebellion for the first time exactly in the first quarter of the 1500s, just when Martin Luther took the risk of rebelling. Between the end of the 1520s and the 1550s, the estimated weight in favor of rebellion reaches its approximate peak. Seen strictly through the lens of the figure, it looks as if the launch of rebellion was risky but feasible and generally supported in the early 1500s, became less risky by midcentury, and remained a little risky until the end of the graph, when, as it happens, although the analysis is unaware of this fact, the Thirty Years' War ended the risk, establishing the long-term survivability of the Protestant rebellion.

Between the graphic results for England and for northern Europe, it is evident that the late 1400s and early 1500s were a ripe time for a big hunk of Europe—all of that hunk far from Rome—to find a new way to escape the political influence of the Catholic Church. Those who had reformist ideas and were close to Rome in that period, men like Girolamo Savonarola, failed to carry the day. Those who had the ideas and could avoid the church's punishment—those who were far from Rome—succeeded. The figures tell us that the opportunity simply did not exist, outside France, during a propitious time for rebellion until the post-plague mid-1400s, when the door began to open to allow rebellious ideas to come together with the interests of Europe's powerful lay leaders.

The moment of opportunity beyond France started at the time of famine and plague in England and arose in the north of the continent just in time for Martin Luther. He seized the day in a way no one had before, his ideas stuck, and Catholicism's monopoly on salvation was broken. Luther's ideas and the ideas of other reformers spread, and they won the day in much of northern Europe. The divorce that Luther implicitly advocated was successful, giving shape to the rise of the sovereign-state political system, the focus of Chapter 7.

ART AND THE RISE OF SECULARISM

I have argued that the controversy over investiture and its resolution in the Concordat of Worms marked the beginning of the end of church religious and political dominance in wealthier parts of Europe, where there was a concomitant rise of secular authority. In an important sense, this political process reached its apex in the Avignon papacy and in a climactic reversal of church fortunes with the Protestant Reformation. Of course, many events, such as the widespread crop failures that produced the Great Famine that began in 1315 and the subsequent bubonic plague that created the Black Death, especially along the overland trade routes of Europe, had dramatic effects on European economics, politics, and religion in the two hundred years between the Avignon papacy and the Reformation. Nonetheless, as we continue to attempt to understand patterns of economic, political, and religious development in Europe, the account here suggests that we need to consider the role played by institutional incentives, like those created at Worms, that affected the interplay of these domains well before the dramatic events surrounding the Protestant Reformation that have occupied much of the attention of historians and economists of the period.

The clashes of the previous two hundred years had undermined the church's sacred legitimacy and monopoly over salvation, to the benefit of local secular rulers. The new ideas about religion and secularism, damaging to the church and beneficial to temporal rulers, were paralleled in the arts as religious art's prevalence nose-dived. Figure 6.8 brings our previous views of the distribution of artwork forward from the beginning of the Commercial Revolution to the end of the Thirty Years' War. The figure reiterates what we found when we looked at the distribution of interregnums, at the distribution of wealth, and at the collapse of nepotism. What we see in the figure is that secular art gradually makes up a larger and larger percentage of Europe's art. Secular power is proclaimed as images of kings and queens, as well as images of everyday life, come to replace the religious art that was dominant before the concordat. In addition, if we divide the distribution of artwork by

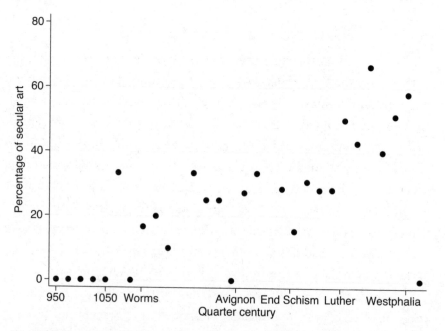

Figure 6.8: The decline of the church: Secular art flourishes.

distance from Rome, we see clearly that the quantity of religious art-work initiated close to Rome declines but then enjoys a revival after Martin Luther, whereas religious artwork is all but extinguished once we are far from Rome. Far from Rome we see the flowering of Flemish depictions of ordinary life and German and Dutch portraiture of common people as well as well-to-do patrons of the arts. Sacred images are just about all gone.

As monarchs embraced their liberation from the pope and the attainment of greater power, they faced new challenges to their authority thanks to the very reforms they had instituted. Nationalism had been appealed to in France and in England as they fought one another, and it had also been invoked to resist the pressures that Boniface VIII brought to bear. To achieve their secular ends, both Philip in France and Edward in England had found it beneficial to make concessions to their subjects. Now the birth of legitimate claims by the monarch's subjects came back to bite rulers, putting Europe on the road to representative, more accountable government. It is to that subject that we turn in Chapter 7.

7

THE BIRTH OF STATES, THE BIRTHING OF REPRESENTATIVE DEMOCRACY

God made man from the beginning, and left
him in the hand of his own counsel.

—Thomas Aquinas (Ecclus.
15:14), *Summa theologica*

WHEN POPE BONIFACE VIII ISSUED THE BULL *UNAM SANCTAM*, HE provoked outrage on the part of France's King Philip IV, but he did much more. Europe was at that very time experiencing the beginnings of a new political theory of governance, one that suggested that rulers ruled for the good of, if not with the consent of, the people. The French Dominican monk Jean Quidort was an early proponent of this movement. In his powerful treatise *De potestate regia et populi* (On the power of kings and popes), written in opposition to *Unam sanctam*, he reasoned from the very outset that "when considering the nature of royal government the following definition of the correct sense of the word kingdom should be known: it is the government of a perfect or self-sufficient community by one man for the sake of the common good. . . . 'For the sake of the common good' is included in the definition to distinguish it from oligarchy, tyranny and democracy, in which the ruler seeks nothing but his own good, especially in a tyranny."[1]

Quidort was not alone in articulating new ideas about the accountability of government. Thomas Aquinas (1225–1274) had argued even earlier that, to use a modern term, *sovereignty* in temporal matters resided with the people and their temporal rulers and not with the church. A few decades later, Dante Alighieri argued vigorously for citizen sovereignty in *De monarchia* (1310–1313), and perhaps even more vehemently, Marsilius of Padua, in his *Defensor pacis* (1324), reasoned that the power to govern resides in the hands of the people and not in the hands of the church or pope. In one way or another, these big ideas all preached that temporal, secular matters were to be rendered unto Caesar, leaving religion to the religious. Such ideas as Quidort's and Marsilius of Padua's did them no good. Quidort died, under the threat of excommunication, a few years after he wrote his treatise in defense of Philip IV and in opposition to Boniface VIII. Marsilius of Padua was rewarded for his ideas by being declared a heretic in 1327. Wisely, as his arguments supported the Holy Roman emperor at the expense of the pope, Marsilius spent the latter part of his life far from Rome, in Munich, where he died in 1342 still charged as a heretic.

Thus, between the beginning of the concordat interlude and through the end of the Avignon papacy and beyond, we see the emergence of a new political theory that separated the power of the church, and began to separate the power of kings, from the power of the people. Perhaps coincidentally, perhaps not, these new ideas began to flower at just the time that our tests in Chapter 6 suggest the times were becoming ripe for rebellion against the old, preconcordat ways, in which the church exercised great influence over every aspect of life, sacred or secular.

The new ideas about governance conferred on citizen-subjects at least a theoretical say in how they were to be ruled. This would prove to be a remarkable departure from past practice, one that would reshape the political world to our time and surely well beyond it. It would be the final, critical, concordat-induced prong in the creation of European exceptionalism, shifting governance increasingly into the hands of representative bodies rather than of solitary rulers. But these new ideas were distinctly at odds with the understanding of the responsibilities of government that was held by monarchs and by popes.

Popes, following on the heels of the Council of Constance (1414–1418) and its conciliar movement, acted as if they were "princes by concentrating on rebuilding their control in the Papal States." "Under the threat of the extreme conciliarism of Basel [they] were concerned not to dominate secular monarchs but to enlist their support . . . The papacy presented conciliarism as a common danger to monarchy both secular and ecclesiastical."[2] Governing on behalf of the earthly well-being of their subjects seemed to be a remote, even dangerous idea to many lay and clerical leaders; governing based on the consent of the people would have occurred to few indeed. They were accustomed to ruling on their own behalf and for the benefit of their inner circle of most loyal and well-rewarded supporters. Yet rule with the consent of at least a somewhat broader group of people, especially powerful lords and rich merchants, was becoming the new normal, expanding inner circles and changing how governance worked. Indeed, by the time of the Council of Basel and the pressures of the conciliar movement, parliaments— national assemblies—were creeping up across parts of Europe, especially those parts that had signed a concordat. This was not happening because of any "superiority" among western Europe's people—it was not happening everywhere in western Europe—or because of any enthusiasm for accountability among Europe's rulers.

Resistance to the new theories of governance notwithstanding, the conditions and incentives created by the Concordat of Worms set into motion the realization of more accountable government, government in which kings answered not just to God but to some of their subjects as well. That impact was to come from the enhanced bargaining power of lay leaders who presided over wealthier territory and the concomitant rise in secularism that weakened the church in those wealthier places while strengthening the hand of local territorial rulers and other local influential subjects of kings and even of the Holy Roman emperor.

THE CONCORDAT: A STEP TOWARD MODERN SOVEREIGNTY

Monarchs in the Middle Ages differed from other nobles in two essential respects. First, they, or their ancestors, had a widely accepted, credible hereditary claim to be first among equals, to be above dukes and other nobles through "superior blood" granted to them by God; or second, they successfully proclaimed themselves to be monarchs because they could muster greater military force than any rivals. With such force they could lay claim to being in the highest position by dint of conquest or by the credible threat of conquest with all its dire consequences for those who resisted.

William, duke of Normandy, for instance, had only the thinnest claim to the English crown following the death of Edward the Confessor in 1066. William's claim came down to his assertion that Edward had promised him the crown, a promise not witnessed by any credible source. Maybe Edward had indeed promised William the crown, and maybe he had not. It did not matter because William had a ready pathway to fulfill the alleged wish of the deceased monarch. What William had, as demonstrated decisively at the Battle of Hastings, was greater military power than his rival, the new English king, Harold II. Once ensconced, the duke of Normandy, now the king of England, adopted a stronger view of hereditary rights as distinct from "promised" rights to succession: when William died in 1087, he was succeeded by his son William as King William II.

Although England, following on its earlier, pre-Norman traditions, continued to elect its king at least through the reign of King John, the monarchy had nevertheless been established based on power and certainly not based on the will of the people. The same pattern prevailed across much of Europe. Holy Roman emperors, for instance, were officially elected by the prince-electors, although, as in the English example, heredity played a critical—though not a decisive—role. France through Philip Augustus also nominally elected its king. In practice, though, the living king designated his successor—usually his eldest son—who then was dutifully elected to the office, as Philip was, becoming a sort of coking until his father died. While this pattern of elevation to the crown through family ties continued after the concordats were signed, a part of the monarch's function changed in ways that were essential for the gradual establishment of sovereign states in the modern sense of the term and for the separation of the monarch's interests as a "tyrant," to borrow Quidort's terminology, and as an individual with responsibilities and accountability to the community over which he or she presided.

The Concordat of Worms granted a fiduciary responsibility to the secular ruler over diocesan territory. This fiduciary responsibility was the obligation to retain or cede control over territorial regalia on behalf of all the subjects living within the territorial boundaries in which a new bishop was needed to advance and protect their religious interests. This responsibility could neither be sold nor kept within the ruler's family in the event that succession passed to another family. In creating this fiduciary responsibility, the signatories of the concordat marked the start of the modern, territorial, sovereign state by tying the ruler's interests as a ruler, rather than as an individual, to the wealth of the territory he or she controlled. Where the territory had great value, the leader in control of the regalia could shape future policies that influenced the welfare of everyone within those dioceses whose borders were confined to the ruler's domain. In that sense at least, the secular holders of regalia—strictly in their capacity as the holders of the temporalities of the territory— were emerging sovereigns, the source of policy, and the source of peace or conflict with the church.

The rights and obligations conferred on the ruler by the concordats, a fiduciary responsibility that was a new feature of temporal rule, foreshadowed the terms of sovereignty set out in the Treaty of Westphalia in 1648, half a millennium after the resolution of the Investiture Controversy. For lots of good reasons, the modern state-centric international system is generally thought to have originated with the resolution of the Thirty Years' War in the Treaty of Westphalia, both because the treaty is thought to have introduced the idea that states have sacrosanct borders, and because it conferred legal obligations and rights on any sovereign. But as with so much previous thinking, the impact of the concordats seems to have been given scant attention other than with respect to their impact on secularism's rise, a feature that has been noted by some.[3] Generally, politics between monarchies prior to 1648 are understood as having been governed by feudal and family ties with what we might think of as "considerations of state" being less of a factor. As a modification of this view, we can see that the concordats created a unique economic and political competition between the Catholic Church and the Holy Roman emperor, the king of France, and the king of England. That competition implied the invention of the modern sovereign state, secure in its own borders.

To comprehend the role the concordats played in creating modern, state-centric European politics, it is useful to review the essential features of the Treaty of Westphalia that posit fundamental elements of sovereignty. Then, we can compare them to the terms of the concordats. We will see that the terms in the concordats that established rules for appointing bishops established a property right that adhered to sovereign territory with defined borders. This property right placed the king in a new fiduciary role regarding the territory in his domain that was carved up as regalian sees. And we will see that this property right fostered competition that necessitated diplomacy and occasional wars to establish the new political order. The property right established at Worms in 1122 and in England and France in 1107—the right of kings to accept or reject bishop nominees and the right, when the post of bishop was vacant, to the income that previously had belonged to the church from the territory defined by each diocesan domain—gave impetus to the end of feudalism and was essential to the rise of the modern, territorially based state system. In this view, the Treaty of Westphalia marks a critical point along the way, but the modern state system had been set in motion five centuries earlier in those kingdoms that subscribed to a concordat.

The Treaty of Westphalia contains more than one hundred articles laying out the terms and conditions under which the Thirty Years' War ended.[4] Most of these articles allocate valuable resources among aristocrats or restore valuables lost by some members of the nobility to others during the war. But a few articles pertain directly to the establishment of territorial sovereignty. Some central examples of these articles highlight this important feature of Westphalia. Consider Articles 64, 65, and 67, for instance:

[Article 64] And to prevent for the future any Differences arising in the Politick State, all and every one of the Electors, Princes and States of the Roman Empire, are so establish'd and confirm'd in their antient Rights, Prerogatives, Libertys, Privileges, free exercise of Territorial Right, as well Ecclesiastick, as Politick Lordships, Regales, by virtue of this present Transaction: that they never can or ought to be molested therein by any whomsoever upon any manner of pretence.

[Article 65] They shall enjoy without contradiction, the Right of Suffrage in all Deliberations touching the Affairs of the Empire; but above all, when the Business in hand shall be the making or interpreting of Laws, the declaring of Wars, imposing of Taxes, levying or quartering of Soldiers, erecting new Fortifications in the Territorys of the States, or reinforcing the old Garisons; as also when a Peace of Alliance is to be concluded, and treated about, or the like, none of these, or the like things shall be acted for the future, without the Suffrage and Consent of the Free Assembly of all the States of the Empire: Above all, it shall be free perpetually to each of the States of the Empire, to make Alliances with Strangers for their Preservation and Safety; provided, nevertheless, such Alliances be not against the Emperor, and the Empire, nor against the Publick Peace, and this Treaty, and without prejudice to the Oath by which every one is bound to the Emperor and the Empire.

[Article 67] That as well as general as particular Diets, the free Towns, and other States of the Empire, shall have decisive Votes; they shall, without molestation, keep their Regales, Customs, annual Revenues, Libertys, Privileges to confiscate, to raise Taxes, and other Rights, lawfully obtain'd from the Emperor and Empire, or enjoy'd long before these Commotions, with a full Jurisdiction within the inclosure of their Walls, and their Territorys: making void at the same time, annulling and for the future prohibiting all Things, which by Reprisals, Arrests, stopping of Passages, and other prejudicial Acts, either during the War, under what pretext soever they have been done and attempted hitherto by private Authority, or may hereafter without any preceding formality of Right be enterpris'd. As for the rest, all laudable Customs of the sacred Roman Empire, the fundamental Constitutions and Laws, shall for the future be strictly observ'd, all the Confusions which time of War have, or could introduce, being remov'd and laid aside.

Article 64 establishes territoriality and the right of the state to choose its own religion, as well as the right to noninterference by other states in any of these matters. Under Article 65 sovereign authority is further spelled out. This article establishes that neither the Catholic Church nor the Holy Roman Empire can make or negate alliances made between sovereigns for the purpose of protecting their respective nation's security. In a similar manner, Article 67 establishes that sovereign states can determine their own domestic policies, free from external pressures and "with a full Jurisdiction within the inclosure of their Walls, and their Territorys." A review of the major innovations of the treaty makes clear that the new system emphasized territoriality and policy control within a nation's border. Borders, rather than fealty, became a critical institutional feature that defines where sovereign authority is exercised. Feudalism, by contrast, defined authority in terms of a hierarchy of personal relations, with only loose reference to territorial rights.

Borders are a natural source of conflict because shifts in their location expands or contracts sovereign authority.[5] Because each state's territorial borders define a domain within which its rulers have sovereign authority over the use of force, acting in a fiduciary role for their citizen-subjects, international law has come to view all states, whether large or small, whether autocratic, monarchic, or democratic, as legally equivalent entities.[6] This understanding of the role of the state seems almost natural and inevitable, yet important parts of its origins are anything but the natural state of affairs. Those origins, however, did not emerge in 1648. They can be traced to the property right granted by the Concordat of Worms to kings as fiduciaries in vacant, territorially defined, clearly bordered bishoprics.

The concordat, long before the Treaty of Westphalia, set into motion the development of important institutions of the modern sovereign state as a natural product of the strategic maneuvering that we have already investigated between the Catholic Church and European kings over political control within their domains. It established a new dynamic process, thanks to the institutions it created that stand in sharp contrast to the general accounts of institution building found in prior historical and political economy investigations.[7]

The choice to transfer regalian rights established by the concordat created an inalienable right that secular rulers possessed because of their position as ruler and not as a personal, individual right. Thus, the ruler over the defined territory of a Catholic bishopric, strictly in the capacity as lord over the territory, had the sole authority to decide whether the territory's income remained in his or her possession or was transferred to the church in exchange for an acceptable bishop. If the revenue was retained, then the lord bore the cost of not having a bishop and possibly, as well, any costs imposed by the church on the lord or on the lord's subjects. Conversely, the lord had the sole ability—as lord—to negotiate with the church, especially when the diocesan revenue was substantial, to reach agreement on a bishop nominee in return for greater control over the policies implemented within the diocese's defined territory— that is, within its borders. This right to shape policy within the defined borders of a diocese may well have been the "antient Rights, Prerogatives, Libertys, Privileges, free exercise of Territorial Right . . . by virtue of this present Transaction" referred to in Article 64. And that territorial right would have been greatly expanded when, as was so often the case, a king presided over large territories that included many dioceses, each governed by the king but also governed by the church.

As king, the individual holding the office could turn "state" lands over to the consecrated bishop in fief in each see under the monarch's temporal control. In doing so, the ruler was shaping a critical part of the policies that would govern the people living within the bishopric, acting in a sovereign capacity as the one and only person with the right to withhold the regalia or transfer them in exchange for a negotiated agreement with the church on who would implement the locally construed interest of the church and of the lay ruler. With veto power over the selection of the church's agent, the concordat implied that the secular ruler and his government were first among equals vis-à-vis the church.

Because of the fiduciary responsibility over regalian rights that was established by the concordats, the land controlled by the king or by a local lord was not, at least with respect to church-state relations, the king's or the lord's personal property in the usual sense of that term. Rather, it was only as the secular ruler over a bishopric that the temporal official could demand defense from the bishop (through the lance), and it was as a sovereign that the ruler could accept or reject the choice of bishop, with all that implied about policies within the diocesan borders. The concordat, after all, stipulated the obligations the bishop had to the king—as king—in exchange for receipt of the temporalities—that is, the regalia and, most particularly, the money earned by the see. That obligation, through the oath of *homagium*, included serving the monarch in times of war. As stated in the Concordat of Worms, "The one elected, moreover, without any exaction may receive the regalia from thee through the lance, and shall do unto thee for these what he rightfully should." This and the other promises contained in the terms of the concordat were the promises of emperors (or kings) in their *titular* role and not merely the promises of a person named Heinrich (Henry), who happened also to be the Holy Roman emperor, or a person born Guido of Burgundy who, in 1122, happened also to be called Calixtus, the pope. No one else, without the authority granted by the Holy Roman emperor or the French or Burgundian or Italian ruler or the English king as *sovereign*, could fulfill the terms of the concordat in determining who would become bishop or who would receive the diocesan lands in fief. No one else was granted by the church authority over all who resided in territory subject to the terms of the concordat. As Hugh of St. Victor observed at the time, the agreement at Worms conceded "secular jurisdiction over the subjects inhabiting the lands conferred upon a church"—that is, the rights of a sovereign over defined territory.

The arrangement stipulated by the concordat may well have marked the beginning of the implementation of the notion that the king had two bodies, one as a sovereign monarch or lesser lay leader and the other as the individual he was.[8] Thus, the agreements in 1107 and 1122 implied the formal separation of a king's personal interests from his state interests, making the king the sovereign of a nascent, territorial state much as stipulated five hundred years later in the Treaty of Westphalia's Article 67 when it proclaimed that the one presiding over a territory, such as one or many dioceses, would have "full Jurisdiction within the inclosure of their Walls, and their Territorys." Naturally, the agreement reached in Westphalia went much further than the one accepted in Worms in that it renounced the obligation to transfer regalia that was essential to the impact of the concordats, but its essential emphasis on territorial sovereignty and right to defense (as the concordat required defense through the lance upon the secular ruler's demand) codified what had been established by 1122. Between 451 (the Council of Chalcedon) and 1122 (the concordat) and culminating in 1648 (the Treaty of Westphalia), the king's secular, sovereign claim over regalian revenue went from no claim to a partial claim—during a diocesan vacancy whose likelihood and length the monarch could control—to a full claim. If we follow the money, it is evident that the concordat is a major monetary break with the past, a break that by the Treaty of Westphalia had evolved into full sovereign control over revenue. Arnold of Brescia, in the twelfth century, had seen what was to come: sovereign, secular rulers had won the competition between the secular and sacred sword. Only time was needed to make that victory obvious to others.

Because of the deals made in the early twelfth century, such high-ranking rulers as kings and emperors now had powerful reasons to effectively manage not only any subsequent territorial competition with the church but also competition with their local lords, who might have exercised control over specific diocesan territories and, therefore, exercised local control over the decision to retain revenue or transfer it to the church in exchange for political leverage. To the extent that monarchs controlled dioceses within their realm as regalian sees, they also had increased bargaining leverage in the relationship between church and state in those dioceses. To the extent that local dukes or other lords owned the territory on which a diocese sat and had regalian rights regarding the bishopric, the selection of the local bishop required a bargain with the church that was acceptable to the local secular ruler, whose local authority might have trumped that of the monarch with regard to this decision.

Possession of such regalian rights by the rulers of princedoms and duchies was common. This was true, for instance, of the rulers in the

Duchies of Brittany, Normandy, Pomerania, in parts of Bohemia, and on and on, giving these leaders bargaining leverage with both the church and the monarchs who nominally ruled over them. To offset such local leverage, monarchs, acting under the incentives institutionalized by the concordat, naturally tried to expand their influence over the portions of their realm whose sees were not under their direct control, thereby improving their own political power. They had two pathways to achieve that objective: costly conquest, or contractual agreements crafted with local lords. Such agreements would transfer some of a local lord's authority to the monarch in exchange for the monarch's granting some institutionalized political and/or economic gain for the local lord. Such deals were the very idea of suffrage and diets—assemblies or parliaments—laid out explicitly in the Treaty of Westphalia. Hence, we must explore how monarchic power might be expanded both by conquest and by negotiation. That will help us work out the optimal path of action for rulers given specific, local conditions.

WAR AND ACCOUNTABILITY

As Geoffrey Chaucer wisely observed in "The Tale of Melibee":

> Since there is no man certain if he be worthy that God give him victory..., therefore every man should greatly dread to begin wars. And because in battles many perils befall, and happens another time that as soon is the great man slain as the little man..., therefore should a man flee and shun war, insomuch as a man may goodly (do so). For Solomon says, "He who loves peril shall fall in peril."[9]

Wars always have losers and only sometimes have winners in the sense that there is a net gain from fighting rather than a net loss compared to whatever deal might have been reached to avoid fighting in the first place.[10] Furthermore, war, being a costly business, required willing or coerced support from those who could provide the revenue to pay, feed, and maintain the soldiers who would wage it. Where coercion failed or was anticipated to fail, persuasion was necessary, and persuasion meant making concessions to secure support from those whose help was needed. That could mean concessions to knights for their service, concessions to lords for their provision of knights and money, concessions to merchants for their payment of taxes to offset the costs of war, and concessions to peasants and laboring classes, whose support might be demanded in the form of taxation or in the form—to be anachronistic—of being used as cannon fodder. We can see a powerful instance of this sort of horse-trading in England's King Edward I's war in Gascony from 1294 to 1303.[11]

Edward was not only king of England but also duke of Aquitaine. In the latter position, France's Philip IV was Edward's liege lord. Thus Edward was, in the peculiarities of the (waning) feudal world, Philip's equal as a monarch and his subordinate as a duke. Philip struck a deal with Edward in which Edward gave Gascony, then Edward's possession, as collateral to Philip as part of a marriage dowry. The agreement was that Philip would only hold Gascony for a moment as a symbolic gesture and would then return it to Edward. Of course Philip reneged. This precipitated a war between them.[12]

Like Philip, Edward was embroiled in wars of territorial expansion and was heavily in debt. He invaded Scotland and secured Wales for Britain, laying the foundations of the United Kingdom. Finding himself out of money, he was in desperate straits when the English lords refused to support his war in Gascony. He then tried to tax the clergy, prompting Boniface VIII's bull *Clericis laicos*, forbidding the clergy to pay a tax to Edward or to Philip. Edward, now truly desperate, with knights, archers, and other soldiers already fighting in Gascony, tried to tax the commoners, especially the wool merchants through a heavy tax on their wool (the *maltolt*, or "bad tax" in the French of the time), as well as attempting to seize some of their wool and profit directly from its sale. These efforts faced intense resistance and failed. The *maltolt* was rescinded on November 24, 1297.

Just how desperate Edward must have been is evident from Michael Prestwich's observation, "[Edward's] government led a hand-to-mouth existence. A shortage of ready funds could have drastic consequences. At the end of August 1301 a sum of £200 was sent to Berwick for the payment of wages. This arrived late and was less than had been expected. . . .

The result was mutiny, mostly among the crossbowmen and archers supported by a few men-at-arms and even by a household knight, Walter de Teye."[13] A mutinous army, unpaid and fighting a war that was not viewed as necessary under the feudal obligations of the time, and a nobility questioning whether they were obliged to provide support to the king for his war of choice, all meant that Edward was in deep trouble.

Edward, with his army already in Gascony and with insufficient funds to support them, found it necessary to make a deal with the lords and the commons as the price for their support of his campaign. In exchange for their willingness to pay taxes toward the present conflict and future wars, Edward agreed to a new form of government that was more accountable to his subjects. The deal may have been too little and too late for Edward's war, but it certainly was transformative for England's future political evolution. As the pathway to raise future funds, Edward signed the *Confirmatio cartarum*, the Confirmation of the Charter, on November 5, 1297, a date that should be celebrated every year.

The charter expanded upon the terms laid out in the Magna Carta eight decades earlier. In the confirmation of the charter, an act designed to get him some cash quickly, Edward created a parliament that included rights and representation for the commons as well as for the lords. As he stated:

> AND for so much as divers people of our realm are in fear that the aids and tasks [that is, taxes] which they have given to us beforetime towards our wars and other business, of their own grant and good will (howsoever they were made) might turn to a bondage to them and their heirs, because they might be at another time found in the rolls, and likewise for the prises [taxes] taken throughout the realm by our ministers: ... We have granted for us and our heirs, that we shall not draw such aids, tasks, nor prises into a custom, for any thing that hath been done heretofore, be it by roll or any other precedent that may be founden.... Moreover we have granted for us and our heirs, as well to archbishops, bishops, abbots, priors, and other folk of holy church, as also to earls, barons, and to all the communalty of the land, that for no business from henceforth we shall take such manner of aids, tasks, nor prises, but *by the common*

assent of the realm [emphasis added], and for the common profit thereof, saving the ancient aids, and prises due and accustomed.[14]

With the figurative stroke of a pen, Edward, his hands tied by the pope's threat to excommunicate any clergy who paid taxes without papal permission, by the reluctance of lords to provide and pay for knights, and by the reluctance of the wool merchants to pay the *maltolt*, now institutionalized the age of organized, regulated political competition not only among the elite but between the elite and the commons. That the king's world was being altered is evident from the fact that it took only three weeks from the signing of the charter to the revocation of the *maltolt*, a tax that indeed was not among the king's "ancient . . . prises."

A parliament had been born in England, and parliamentarianism was spreading in Europe. France was not far behind. Like Edward, Philip granted rights to the French estates in exchange for their support against the church. Just as Edward had done in England, Philip set a broader, more representative government in motion in France.[15] Many others would follow down this more accountable path in the decades and centuries to come, putting Europe on the path to representative, democratic government, which today dominates most of the continent.

The struggle with Edward resulted in the extraordinary idea that even the most ordinary folks, the commoners, have the sorts of rights that America's Founding Fathers five hundred years later enshrined in their Declaration of Independence—that is, the right to no taxation without representation. Horse-trading between kings and their subjects increasingly became a normal part of political intercourse. This compels us to address why any monarch would have agreed to such constraints.

The concordats suggest an answer grounded in each monarch's need either to coordinate with or defeat rival rulers. The choice to coordinate must have been related to the single most important consideration any ruler had then or has today: the desire to survive in power.[16] Therefore, after we see how the concordats stimulated the creation of parliaments, we will conclude by assessing how the granting of more accountable government shaped the prospects of political survival for the monarchs of Europe. But first, let's have a look at the role that war, as distinct from negotiation, played in shaping Europe's modern, exceptional, and accountable form of government.

War was an old, well-tested way for monarchs and aspiring rulers to expand their power, their territory, and their access to wealth by looting new lands and taxing new subjects. It had the great attraction that huge rewards were reaped when it was successful. But it also had the great downside that at most only one side could win, and life took a sour turn for the losers. As the earlier quotation from Chaucer points out, even kings might fall in battle. And that might not have been the worst that could happen to them. Perhaps worse in this time of chivalry, a king might be captured and ransomed for, as it turns out, a "king's ransom" that could bankrupt their family, their treasury, and their people. Still worse, they might not be ransomed at all and might remain the captor of their enemies. The pressures to win, as Edward and Philip both learned, sometimes necessitated bargaining with the very people who were supposed to be subject to the king's will.

War could be attractive to monarchs if they expected it to help them consolidate their power at home. It could be less appealing if, instead, they anticipated the costs and other exigencies of war to force them into some form of power-sharing arrangement with their subjects. If, for instance, the required support from subjects necessitated concessions such as the creation of a parliament in which subjects were granted a greater say in how they were governed, then the monarch's gains might be diminished, making war a less attractive choice. It seems evident that no ruler would have been keen to concede even the appearance of political rights to his subjects as the price of waging war. Indeed, the feudal system obliged subjects to defend their rulers against threats to his land and kingdom. Under the old rules and preconcordat incentives, the king would have commanded support, and the people would have had little choice but to obey. Under the incentives of the concordats, in contrast, it may have been more difficult to wage war until the sorts of rights granted by Edward came into being.

The experiences of Edward and Philip in bearing heavy economic burdens during times of war were far from unusual. Indeed, the economic and political demands of war provide an important explanation of the forces that helped transform Europe in the Middle Ages. Successful wars meant that rivals were defeated and that the emerging states and dynasties of Europe were consolidating their power. As was famously observed by the eminent polymath social scientist Charles Tilly, "War made the state and the state made war."[17] This is unquestionably true up to a point, although Tilly and others did not give much consideration to negotiations between a king and his own subjects, which was sometimes necessitated by war and sometimes by state building without war. Inadequate attention has been paid to the *kind* of state that war made and to how that sort of state might have differed from those that were created through the less dramatic, less well-remembered path of horse-trading, of negotiating with one's own subjects.

Although making deals naturally gets less attention than fighting wars, as long as there have been kings, a great many threats have been settled without resort to war. Consider, for instance, the circumstances behind the emergence of Sweden as a sovereign state with a government accountable to its people.

Engelbrekt Engelbrektsson's 1434 rebellion against Eric of Pomerania, king of Sweden, Denmark, and Norway, enjoyed a mixture of support from members of the lower nobility (like Engelbrekt himself), the peasantry, and laborers (especially miners).[18] As was so often the case, this particular rebellion was motivated by the heavy wartime taxes that the king imposed without consulting the various estates who were burdened by his war, echoing the problems of Edward I in England 150 years earlier. To rally support against the king, Engelbrekt, with no apparent authority other than local popular support, called a meeting of the Estates General in Sweden in 1434. Although he was assassinated and others took over, the Estates General session that he organized is often thought of today as the start of Swedish sovereignty and its parliament. The rebellion certainly ended with the deposition of the king and the weakening of the Kalmar Union of Denmark, Sweden, and Norway, placing these countries on their relatively peaceful, negotiated path to becoming modern, accountable states.

Sweden's experience with negotiations was not at all unique. Grievances sometimes arose over taxation and at other times revolved around feudal claims and religious rights. Efforts by leaders to extract money from the nobility, the church, and the commoners, as well as efforts to impose unwanted policies, was ubiquitous and often led to threats to the regime's survival and to the formation of national assemblies to mollify such threats. Movements to accept some increase in government accountability, such as establishing a parliament, did not require war in the Middle Ages any more than efforts to adopt more accountable governance practices today require the realization of war. Indeed, most such changes, as demonstrated in the contemporary empirical context, arise in response to the *belief* that a rebellion will occur if there are no concessions and reform rather than to the actual occurrence of a rebellion.

Credible threats to a monarch's survival in office surely captured his or her attention, and such conflicts were often settled without resort to warfare.[19] The realization or expectation of such threats would have prompted a response, and under the right conditions, that response would have included expanding accountability by, for instance, creating a parliament and granting a say in taxing and spending policies. But of course, sometimes war occurred. Now we want to ascertain what warfare meant for state building and especially for the creation of national assemblies.

WAR AND STATE BUILDING

Did war make the sort of consolidated, powerful monarchies that the state builders, the monarchs of the time, presumably had in mind? Or did the sort of state that emerged out of war advance Europe toward its modern, exceptional, accountable form of government in which a representative assembly, a parliament, came into being? Tilly contended that "the central, tragic fact is simple: coercion works; those who apply substantial force to their fellows get compliance, and from compliance draw the multiple advantages of money, goods, deference, access to pleasures denied to less powerful people."[20] Of course, war certainly made its victors more powerful and better able to extract compliance from the vanquished, at least until the next war. Unquestionably, victorious rulers enjoyed the "advantages of money, goods, deference, access to pleasures denied to less powerful people," making war an attractive way to enhance the already tremendous advantages of being a king. But did war sometimes come with a domestic political price tag? Did war sometimes also mean that the nobility, the merchants, and ordinary workers also enjoyed some great benefits from their participation in war, with those benefits coming directly at the expense of their ruler?

A look at the history of fighting wars and of constructing parliaments can help show whether war, when it made states, made the accountable states that helped lay the foundation of Western exceptionalism, or alternatively, whether the roots of representative states came from some source other than war. If wars fought before the creation of parliaments gave impetus to the rise of such assemblies, then we can say, at least in a correlational sense, that war seemed to be an essential element in building the sorts of states that began to make Europe exceptional in the Middle Ages. If, however, war did not give birth to more accountable government, then war might have made the state, but it did not make anything like the modern, representative governments of Europe.

To evaluate whether war contributed to the rise of more accountable government in Europe, I look at each of Europe's kingdoms every half century starting with the half century that began in 1100 and concluding with the half century that ended in 1699. I ask a few straightforward questions of the information that has been assembled about the incidence of war and the rise of parliaments.[21] To begin, I identify the half century in which a kingdom experienced the first meeting of its parliament, fully appreciating that some kingdoms never held a parliament in the time interval of interest. I ask for each kingdom whether it went to war in the fifty years before its first parliament. For instance, if a kingdom's first session of parliament was held in 1100, had the kingdom been at war at any time between 1050 and 1099? The idea is to see whether a larger or smaller proportion of periods with a first parliament were preceded by war than were periods when a first parliament had not met. While not definitive, this gives us a way to see whether the costs and demands of war more often than not necessitated concessions to some subjects by granting them subsequent rights in a newly formed national assembly.

The evidence suggests that war was not the impetus for accountable government. Of the forty-one kingdoms for which I have the necessary information, twenty-three held at least one meeting of a parliament. Of these twenty-three first-time meetings of parliament, one was preceded by an interval of war during the previous fifty years. War was not a meaningful stimulant to the creation of national assemblies. We can safely say that whatever sort of state war helped make, it did not help make for improved accountability.

Still, before rejecting the possibility that war contributed to the rise of accountable government, I switch our focus from the first-ever parliament benchmark to ask, instead, whether sessions of parliament were more likely following half-century interludes that included war or half-century interludes that were peaceful. Maybe war did not directly contribute to the creation of parliaments, but perhaps it did contribute to the likelihood that a national assembly would be called into session. It turns out that sessions of parliament were preceded by war 13 percent of the time, while peace preceded parliamentary sessions just 8 percent of the time. Flipped around, 42 percent of the time when there had been a war, it was followed by a parliamentary session within fifty years, and 29 percent of the time when there had been peace, a parliamentary session occurred in the subsequent fifty years. Although parliamentary sessions were more often preceded by war than by peace, the difference in frequency is not statistically meaningful. Wars happened and parliaments happened, and their incidences were statistically unrelated to one another. War may have made the state, but apparently it did not make parliaments. What, then, did make for more accountable states? Did whatever helped stimulate accountable governments have anything to do with the concordats?

THE CONCORDATS AND ACCOUNTABLE STATES

The part played by the concordats in forging accountable, sovereign states has barely been considered before. Certainly, as we have already observed, scholars like Tilly thought carefully about how war was used to concentrate control over territory. He, like so many others, however, fails to mention the Investiture Controversy or its resolution through the Concordat of Worms in his assessment of the rise of states. Indeed, it appears that little thought has been given to how the shifting bargaining leverage incentivized by the concordats may have given rulers and their subjects the reasons to begin the creation of modern, accountable states. It is odd that the concordat's role in the creation of accountable government has been downplayed or even overlooked when we recognize that one of the great controversies surrounding the impact of the concordats is whether, in their aftermath, they strengthened the church or the kingdoms subject to them. This controversy may be resolved by attending to the ties between economic growth and political leverage highlighted by the concordat game.

To be sure, there are well-crafted arguments for the concordats having strengthened the church or having strengthened states, but these perspectives all suffer from a common problem: either they speak of the impact as if it were uniform across Europe or, if they attend to geographic differences, their geographic divisions rely on knowing outcomes rather than being motivated by analytic logic. The logic of the concordats, however, uncovers where and why the strength of the church and of kingdoms varied geographically across Europe, and varied depending on the initial economic conditions highlighted by the concordat game.

The game has shown us logically and the evidence in the historical record has supported the contention that in those parts of Europe that were located relatively close to Rome and that were relatively poor when they became subject to the terms of a concordat, the resolution of the Investiture Controversy favored the church at the expense of secular rulers. Likewise, those monarchies that were not signatories to a concordat were deprived of the bargaining leverage with the church that translated into economic growth and greater political autonomy. Hence, those kingdoms, like the signatories that were close to Rome or were initially poor, were unlikely to emerge as strong, independent, economically sound states during the interlude of the concordats or its near-term aftermath. That meant little secularism and more limited economic growth in those parts of Europe. In wealthier territories, especially if they were far from Rome, however, the concordats strengthened states at the expense of the church, doing so by stimulating improved economic performance as the way to gain greater secular political power. The ability of the church or the king to secure a deferential bishop then translated into even greater distinctions between the outcomes for initially poorer places, especially if they were close to Rome, and farther-away places, especially if they enjoyed wealth.

Under the new conditions for choosing bishops, the leaders of signatory territories now had three prominent ways to improve their political power toward the church and toward rivals, whether their rivals were domestic or foreign. War, of course, was a natural, time-honored way to secure more territory and greater wealth that could translate into more bargaining leverage both with the church and with secular rivals. Marriage was another time-tested means of gaining wealth, territory, and power.[22] But the concordat promoted a different pathway, a newer, previously less prominent pathway to achieve enhanced bargaining leverage and political authority. Thanks to the incentive to stimulate economic growth that was an essential consequence of the concordats, negotiated agreements between kings and "their" nobles, merchants, and other influential subjects of the crown became a new way to consolidate territorial control and build a sense of national loyalty.

Local lords and merchants controlled wealth, land, some regalian sees, and, critically for economic expansion, the labor that could improve productivity, making the king wealthier and therefore placing him in a stronger bargaining position vis-à-vis the church. Coercing subjects to do what the king wanted could be a bloody, costly way for the king to secure control over peasants and their sources of influence. Negotiating with them was an alternative way to secure their support in exchange for lasting, tangible benefits for the king and for at least some of his subjects. With the possibility of negotiation in mind, let us work through the intuition behind a straightforward strategic setting in which coercion or negotiation are two of several ways for a ruler to settle political differences with his subjects over, for example, the efforts they will make on his behalf.

Assume the king moves first. This is just a convenience. We can just as readily identify conditions that result in negotiation—deal making—or in coercion by letting a potentially rebellious group of subjects (or their leader) be the first to move.[23] Either way, we can see the logic behind

deal making in the shadow of the threat of coercion as a viable alternative to violent conflict. Compromise, rather than coercion, always
had the potential to advance both a king's interests and those of at least
some subjects. Indeed, reaching compromise agreements in which dis-
putants exchange concessions proves to be a far easier and far more
likely means of resolving disputes than does any sort of coercive action.
In fact, although far more attention is paid to the history of violent disputes, many more disputes are resolved through diplomacy—civil or
uncivil—than by war.

Imagine the king is aware of rumblings among some of his subjects
who seem discontented with whatever the current status quo is. Perhaps the king is demanding too much in taxes; perhaps he is engaged in
costly fighting that is not considered necessary; perhaps the people are
being struck down by a disease that they see as God's punishment for
the ruler's offense. Lots of policies—real and imagined—might lead to
discontent with how people feel they are being governed. Those rumblings create the necessity for the king—or his inner circle—to think
about whether he must address the concerns of his subjects or whether
he can afford to ignore them. The king has an initial decision to make:
continue to behave as he generally has toward his subjects or propose a
policy change to them, such as asking them to work harder on his behalf. If he proposes a policy change, then he also has to decide whether
he intends to negotiate with his subjects over his proposal or whether he
is demanding their compliance with whatever new policy he wants.

In the particular context of the growth-inducing incentives of the concordat, let us suppose that the king specifically proposes—or demands—
that his subjects work harder to produce more so as to help improve his
bargaining position with the church. There is nothing essential about
this specific proposal, of course, but it is useful to demonstrate the main
point that negotiation is often preferable to coercion and always preferable to war. If the king ignores the rumblings among some of his subjects,
then life might just go on as it has in the past; the status quo prevails.
Or the grumbling subjects might rise up to rebel against existing policy, as was illustrated in the case of Engelbrekt Engelbrektsson, a development that the monarch surely would like to forestall. If the king, as

in our convenient example, asks the local lords or merchants or laborers or farmers to work harder to produce more or asks them to pay a larger share of their income to him, then they, or a small group of rebel leaders, have a decision of their own to make. Should they resist his demand for more effort on their part, should they agree to what he wants, or should they try to find a compromise in which he gets more effort from them and in exchange gives them some new benefit they really want?

What might the king's subjects, or at least some of them, want in return for paying higher taxes or in exchange for greater effort on their part to produce more wealth for the monarch? Whatever they might want, it would need to be pretty valuable to them, as their ruler is asking a lot from them. Perhaps they ask the king to reduce their tax rate in return for more effort on their part. Perhaps they ask him to reduce their tax burden even if they make no more effort on his behalf. Perhaps they ask the king to spend more money to assart potentially productive land to help them—and him—become more prosperous. Perhaps, thinking longer term, they agree to more effort on behalf of the king in exchange for a representative parliament in which they will have a say in how they are governed not only now but in the future too.[24]

We know that each of these ideas was exchanged between rulers and subjects. There are, of course, many other benefits subjects could have asked for, but among the many proposals that might have been made, demanding some say in policy making through an assembly would have been highly valuable and efficient. If the proposed assembly were meaningful, it would give at least some subjects a say in all-important policy arenas, including taxing and spending decisions. Creating a parliament with such rights for its members would mean that they would have a say in the outcome of whatever issues came up in the future. Such rights as a veto over new taxes, as in Edward's *Confirmatio cartarum*, and a veto over spending decisions, as in Philip's Estates General, would transfer real clout to the proposed parliament, not only for the situation of the moment but for all future time.

No king would have been eager to grant such concessions. He might respond by threatening or even implementing coercive action to punish his underlings, making it costly for them to resist his wishes. Coercive measures would have been painful for their targets, who might have been deterred from resisting or even questioning the ruler's wishes. The king's subjects might have avoided coercive pressures by going along with what he wanted in the first place or by making more modest demands in the hope of inducing him to compromise. But then too, they might have anticipated that coercive measures by the king could also mean heavy costs for the monarch. The local lords, the merchants, or even the peasants might refuse to work or might even rebel. Such resistance to the ruler's wishes were far from unknown. The king could end up provoking civil uprisings—many occurred—that deprived him of the very increase in wealth and bargaining leverage that he sought to use in his dealings with the church and with rival monarchs. If the monarch had anticipated such heavy costs to himself, he might even have made a more modest initial proposal so as to induce his subjects to make a deal with him, a deal that would improve their circumstances and his.

Sometimes, of course, rulers would look at the situation I just described and choose to fight. Sometimes they would try to resolve the tension by offering concessions; sometimes those concessions would be accepted, and other times they would prove inadequate. Rebellion might ensue. But to flesh out the implicit calculations a tad more: coercion, rebellion, and war were costly not only to their targets but to their initiators as well. Crops—money—might be destroyed in the process. Mills—money—might be destroyed. Farmers and laborers—money—might be killed or maimed. If these and other costs that result from imposing costs on one's subjects became too great, the king was liable to back down. If backing down could be foreseen by his potentially rebellious subjects, then it was far better for the king to seem magnanimous by granting the requested concessions up front, saving the costs of coercion, the costs of possibly capitulating, and the loss of leverage with his rivals. Thus, in fraught, tense circumstances, rulers might turn away from the use of force and choose diplomacy as the cheaper alternative. If they needed the cooperation of their subjects for bigger purposes, then granting concessions could be—and often was—a more attractive mode of engagement than mustering an army to crush internal opposition. Indeed, as each side has an incentive to think ahead—playing chess—they can *always* find proposals, at least in principle, that the other finds at least as attractive as using force, and at lower cost. Then, indeed, barring miscalculations due to uncertainty or some other fundamental inhibition to negotiating in good faith, a bargain can be struck!

This simple bargaining setting reminds us that coercion is often costlier than granting concessions. War is, in the jargon of political science, ex post inefficient—that is, however a war is resolved, it could in principle have been settled on the same terms beforehand, saving the costs in lost lives and property.[25] The difficulty, of course, is in figuring out beforehand who is likely to win and what the ultimate settlement will look like. Then too, threats to repress uprisings, to deter resistance to the king's wishes, could backfire on the ruler, weakening him even more than negotiating some deal—such as the creation of a national assembly, possibly with taxing and spending authority—would have. Unfortunately, we generally do not pay much attention to simmering crises that are settled before they break out into fighting. War is sexy; diplomacy is not. And so we are much more aware of the wars that monarchs fought than we are of the deals they made to avoid war. War may indeed have made some states, but diplomacy probably made many more.

Wars that were avoided make up a much larger portion of history and crisis resolution than do wars that were fought.[26] And wars are avoided by making exactly the sorts of deals that generally bore us and so are forgotten shortly after they are made. The concordats provided both a new incentive structure and a diplomatic model of how to resolve problems through bargaining and compromise. Yet the concordats are not part of the conversation about state formation, war avoidance, and deal making. They should be.

Indeed, paying attention to the rise of threats may be every ruler's principal job. As Italo Calvino noted in his fictional—but ever-so-accurate—account:

> In sum, the throne, once you have been crowned, is where you had best remain seated, without moving, day and night. All your previous life has been only a waiting to become king; now you are king; you have only to reign. And what is reigning if not this long wait? Waiting for the moment

when you will be deposed, when you will have to take leave of the throne, the scepter, the crown, and your head.[27]

The expectation of threats to one's rule should have prompted a response, and under the right conditions, that response would have included expanding accountability by, for instance, creating a parliament and granting one's subjects a say in taxing and spending policies. Whenever a threat is perceived, action is needed to neutralize it. As the evidence will show, the formation of parliaments was especially common among those rulers who pursued economic growth in keeping with the incentives instilled by the concordats.

Of course efforts at conquest continued, as did efforts to negotiate lucrative and power-enhancing marriage alliances, but now, following the incentives put into place by the concordats, there was also an economic incentive to induce subjects to improve economic productivity as the way for rulers to improve their bargaining power and secure bishops and policies more aligned with the king's interests than with those of the church. With rising productivity, wealth spread, and those who enjoyed newfound wealth recognized that the king needed their wealth and could be induced, as Edward had been, to compensate them for his share in it. Local lords and merchants, as in the bargaining game I outlined, began to demand a say in how the fruits of their labor were taxed and spent. These demands and the leverage gained with growing productivity could be expected to translate into a push from below for a greater say in governance. The growing mutual dependency between rulers and subjects meant a shift away from Quidort's meaning of tyranny and toward his meaning of monarchy as an accountable institution acting for the welfare of some of the monarch's subjects. The growing ideas about political accountability, then, created new tensions and new opportunities that had to be managed by lay rulers. What path a ruler took in dealing with issues of expanded accountability depended on where the leader stood with regard to the outcomes of the concordat game.

The logic that created economic growth incentives for rulers during the concordats followed the principle that good, responsive governance arises when rulers must depend on the cooperation of many, whereas poor governance is the consequence of reliance on only a small coalition of loyalists. Greater prosperity might have been understood as a boon only for the monarch and his inner circle, or the creation of greater prosperity might have been seen as a public good, a benefit to all, including the monarch. Generating economic growth, expanding the effort needed to fabricate new wealth, without the cooperation of one's subjects was a challenging task indeed. It was more readily accomplished by cutting a deal with subjects, expanding the government's winning coalition and forming a better, more accountable government.

Thus, the economic incentives fostered by the concordat meant that rulers seeking greater wealth had new reasons to reward peasants and laborers who gave the king improved productivity. These incentives may well be the source of the work ethic that helped convert northern Europe into a prosperous area, as seen in Figure 6.6, long before the rise of what Weber attributed to the Protestant work ethic. The incentives highlighted by the concordat game help explain not only the differential rise of prosperity far from Rome but also the work ethic that created both that prosperity and the opportunity for the Protestant rebellion in 1517 against the Catholic Church. It seems that Weber's well-known explanation for northern Europe's success may need rethinking and may need to be pushed back about four hundred years.

By providing a way for the monarch's subjects to improve their lot—as England's Henry II did through his writs and the broader body of the Constitutions of Clarendon, or as France's Philip IV did through the establishment of the Estates General—the king had a mechanism that could work directly in his interest. The incentives implanted in the terms of the concordats meant that leaders recognized that economic growth would give them more leverage with which to improve their lot, and with it, maybe even the national stature and security that could prove to be a benefit to one and all. The monarch's subjects could provide that wealth by working harder, by adopting the latest technologies and machines, and by becoming more productive. That meant, as in our bargaining game, that their rulers had to adopt policies that would either coerce or encourage (and reward) the productivity of their subjects.

Creating a more accountable government certainly could have served to encourage greater cooperation by granting to some subjects, at least, a say in how they were governed. Coercing subjects to do what the ruler wanted raised the risk of costly rebellion. We can be confident that coerced compliance would not have been accompanied by the creation of a parliament that made the monarch somewhat answerable to his subjects.

The upshot of the direct link between wealth and power for kings who were subject to the terms of a concordat was that the king needed support from many more people than had been true before the concordat if he was to fulfill the opportunity it gave him to become wealthier and more powerful through means other than conquest or even marriage and dynasticism. To get the help they needed, kings had to adopt better policies toward more of their subjects, expanding their winning coalition, granting more subjects a say in those policies that most directly shaped their welfare. So parliaments should have emerged and proven more consequential in kingdoms that were covered by the concordats and that relied on a large coalition. This should have been especially true, perhaps ironically, if those kingdoms initially possessed enough wealth to give the king a critical weapon in his arsenal for bargaining with the church and to be a critical weapon for the king's subjects in their bargaining with him.

We have no reason within the logic of the concordat game to believe that kings who were not subject to the terms of a concordat had the same incentives to expand their winning coalition, creating parliaments, as those who were subject to those terms. If, indeed, the evidence supports the inference that the concordats nudged monarchs in the direction of creating more accountable governments, that would be a big deal. After all, the incentives set in motion by the concordats have not only been overlooked in evaluating the shifting distribution of wealth, work ethics, and power in Europe; they have also been ignored by previous investigations into the rise of more accountable government. Indeed, as far as I know, no one has given more than passing attention to the incentive to negotiate domestic agreements as a vehicle that could lead to territorial consolidation in medieval Europe.[28]

To get a sense of how much, or how little, coalitions were being expanded in Europe's monarchies as a consequence of their wealth and of
whether they were, or were not, covered by a concordat, we need to find
a way to estimate how big the coalition was that was represented by the
parliament, if there was a parliament at all. Monarchies were, of course,
divided into dioceses. We can use the number of dioceses per monarchy
per half century as a very rough approximation of how many of a kingdom's regions and local interests were being represented if the king established a parliament. Bishoprics, as we have seen, often coincided with
local political power centers as well as with the interests of bishops.[29] So
I define the prospective coalition size as the number of dioceses within
each kingdom, and I identify whether the kingdom formed a parliament
and, if so, when the parliament was first called into session.

Before we examine the implications of coalition size, coverage under a concordat, and the interaction of these two factors on the chances
of forming a parliament, it is worth observing that coalition size—the
number of dioceses within a king's domain—differed dramatically
for those who did or did not form a parliament. In kingdoms without
a parliament, the average number of dioceses—a source of power and
economic control—was a modest seven. In monarchies that formed a
national assembly, in contrast, coalition size—dioceses—numbered on
average twenty-five, a significantly larger size.[30] And lest you think the
number of sees just reflects the geographic area of a kingdom, remember
that there were lots more sees packed into a smaller space close to Rome
than was true farther away from the seat of the Catholic Church.

Just as today we can have big countries, like China, with small coalitions and small countries, like the Netherlands or Switzerland, with
relatively large coalitions, so too was this possible in the Middle Ages.
Ireland and Hungary, for instance, were relatively equal in geographic
area, and yet the kingdom of Ireland had 2.5 times more dioceses than
Hungary between 1100 and 1500. This dynamic—the relationship of
coalition size to the form of government—is examined in Figure 7.1.

The gray bars in Figure 7.1 depict the probability that a kingdom had
a parliament between 1100 and 1517 when it was not a signatory to a
concordat, had a below average sized coalition, or had below average

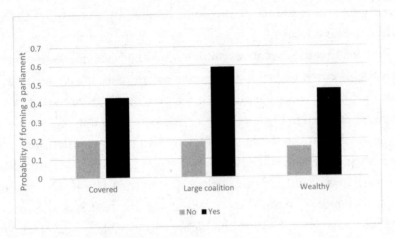

Figure 7.1: Did the concordats influence the creation of parliaments?

wealth (as measured by trade-route prevalence). The black bars, in contrast, assess the probability that a kingdom had a parliament when the kingdom was subject to a concordat, had a large coalition (many sees), or was above average in wealth.

The graph tells a story very much in keeping with the expectations we have inferred from combining the results of the concordat game and the bargaining approach we discussed. Being subject to a concordat meant a higher probability of forming a parliament; depending on a larger coalition—many power centers—tripled the probability that a kingdom had a national assembly; and being wealthy also tripled the odds of having a parliament. Apparently, when rulers were incentivized to bargain with their subjects to assure economic expansion, they also were incentivized to create a more accountable government.

Before leaving the broad, general impact of the concordats on the creation of parliaments, it is worth noting one more high-level general fact. Not all places were alike in their decision to form a national assembly. As we know, being subject to a concordat, being wealthy, and having a large coalition all created particular incentives that were absent in places without these features. In fact, the idea of forming parliaments generally came earlier in kingdoms subject to the terms of a concordat than in those that were not party to the trade-off between money, power, and secularism. Indeed, the first assemblies began an average of seventy-five years sooner in kingdoms covered by a concordat than in uncovered kingdoms.

It seems that the incentives brought into existence by the concordats were highly correlated with the creation and functioning of parliaments. If one is to believe the bargaining inferences drawn from the concordat game and laid out in the bargaining game I sketched out, the one played in the shadow of the threat of coercion, then the concordats may have been a cause behind the advent of early governmental accountability in those parts of Europe that were subject to their terms. The evidence so far certainly encourages us to look more closely at how the concordats may have given birth to the highly accountable governments that dominate Europe today and at the extent to which early wealth played a central part in the shift toward that accountability.

SECULARISM, WEALTH, AND PARLIAMENTS

Now that we have seen a strong association between whether a kingdom was subject to a concordat and whether it introduced parliamentary government, we should zoom in on the details. Did the wealth distribution across dioceses that the concordat game emphasizes contribute to shaping the onset of civil, competitive politics in parts of Europe? Other research into the origins of parliamentary government has already noted that "if we try to assess the role of economic development by looking within Europe itself, then there is a decent case to be made that the practices of representation and consent developed earlier and to a greater extent in richer regions."[31]

Before looking at the broad evidence in support of a tie between wealth and the creation of parliamentary governments, let's pause to delve into the details of cities of Flanders that illustrate the rebellious pressures instigated in wealthy territories that resulted in accountable government.

In the cities of Flanders, especially Bruges, Ghent, and Ypres, the populace revolted against the taxation and pro-French policies imposed on them by successive French and Burgundian dukes throughout the 1300s and 1400s. The cities had already secured the right to choose their own town leaders, but they lacked authority over their own taxation. In each of these key wealthy cities of Flanders, popular uprisings, frequently supported by rich farmers, merchants, and guilds, fought back against the policies and taxes imposed on them first by French and Burgundian dukes and later by the Austrian crown. Their interest was in protecting their wealth, controlling their taxation, and securing greater rights of self-government, at least for the wealthy citizens of the cities.

For instance, in 1449–1453 the city of Ghent (in modern-day Belgium) mobilized a deadly revolt—costing thousands of lives—against Burgundy's Duke Philip the Good. The revolt was mobilized by successful, prosperous guild and town leaders who objected to Philip's efforts to levy new taxes on salt and flour, two essential commodities. Philip quite sensibly attempted to negotiate a compromise settlement, but he was not prepared to concede enough to mollify the demands of Ghent's merchants and guildsmen. Having failed to strike an agreement with the rebels, Philip mobilized an army to crush their resistance. He succeeded at the moment, but the longer-term impact was the rise of parliamentary government.

In hindsight, despite the defeat of the rebels, the Ghent revolt, along with rebellions in Bruges and elsewhere in Flanders, culminated in the creation of representative, accountable government in what became today's Belgium and Netherlands. Indeed, the pressure from merchants and guildsmen resulted in the first-ever meeting of the States-General in Bruges in 1463–1464. The States-General continues to this day as the parliament of the Netherlands.

Despite the emergence of national assemblies at least in partial response to rebellions by wealthy, secular merchants and guildsmen who sought greater control over their local economic and political policies, some otherwise-thoughtful studies of the emergence of sovereign states deny that there was any connection between secularism's rise and European economic development as joint products of the concordats.[32] Instead, the accounts that draw a link between the rise of wealth or secularism and of more accountable government view these developments as having been more or less the luck of the draw, unrelated to each other and unrelated to the incentives set in motion by the concordats. Yet as the evidence we have seen so far shows us, we do much better at tracing the origin of parliaments by taking into account which monarchies were subject to the terms of the concordats than by ignoring who signed on to these treaties. Furthermore, we have seen the logic and the evidence for the contention that greater wealth arose in those parts of Europe that were subject to the concordats, especially when they were remote from Rome, compared to those that were not.

It is a small inferential step from the concordat game to the contention that, because of the political bargaining power the concordats created and because of the incentives they fostered to stimulate economic growth, the agreements paved the way for the formation of accountable governments. Given the new institutions and incentives engendered by the concordat, the king and such classes of people as wealthy merchants and the local aristocracy now found it advantageous to strike agreements. These agreements had to balance the shared interests of monarchs in increased economic productivity and in secular rule against the competing interests of local lords and merchants. Local lords would surely not give up their privileges without sufficient compensation. Merchants would surely not pay heavy taxes to their king—or their local lord—without sufficient compensation. These competing demands and interests inevitably led to friction between the various segments of any monarchy's population, as the experiences in Flanders illustrate. How these rising tensions over economic and political control were resolved depended on the relative strength or weakness and compactness or extensiveness of the competing groups.

From one perspective, parliaments provided a means to resolve these tensions when nascent states were small and weak. According to this perspective, locals would have been at a great disadvantage in a kingdom covering an extensive territory because of the difficulties of communicating over large distances. Small, compact territories simply made it easier for people to assemble and come to agreement on important matters of the day.[33] But other scholars have argued the opposite. From an alternative point of view, attendance at representative bodies, such as parliaments, was not a matter of choice but, rather, was compelled by powerful rulers who imposed their will on lesser lords, merchants, and others.[34] In this account, the costs of communication and transportation played an insignificant role. Rather, leaders picked those who sat as representatives and, therefore, were likely to do the king's bidding.

These two points of view need not be mutually exclusive. They speak to differences in the accountability and functioning of parliaments and not to their formation, which, in either case, represented some degree of concession by the monarch to some portion of his subjects. How large the concession might have been, of course, could have depended on whether the kingdom was rich or poor, close to or far from Rome, and, critically, subject to or not subject to a concordat, all of which we can examine through the record of history. What may separate these arguments from one another is the extent to which different kingdoms, with different conditions of wealth and with differences in whether or not they signed a concordat, created rubber-stamp parliaments or meaningful assemblies. We know that the concordats were intended to regularize the appointment of bishops by recognizing church authority where rulers were weak and by introducing a cost rulers could inflict on the church to gain greater influence, provided the rulers' lands were wealthy enough to make the prospective cost painful. We also know that the rise of secular control could only be sustained and expanded through economic growth. Thus, the bargaining leverage of local lords, merchants, and even laborers and peasants is expected to have been elevated where greater secularism or greater wealth arose following the concordats, just as was the case in the cities of Flanders. We can see evidence that this logic was working by examining Figure 7.2.

Figure 7.2 divides kingdoms into three main groupings: those whose dioceses were below average both on secularism and on wealth in the half century prior to the kingdom's first parliament, those that were above average on secularism in the half century prior to the kingdom's first parliament, and those that were above average on wealth in the fifty years before the kingdom's first parliament. For convenience, I have also divided the information into gray bars that capture all kingdoms not subject to a concordat and black bars that show the effects only for those kingdoms subject to a concordat. Thus, each bar addresses the proportion of the opportunities to hold a first parliament that were taken under the conditions specified by the bar.

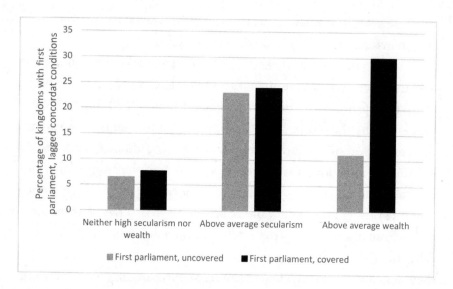

Figure 7.2: First parliaments, secularism, wealth, and the concordats

As is evident in Figure 7.2, there was little chance of an initial meeting of parliament in monarchies whether covered by a concordat or not if the kingdom was both poor and dominated by religiously aligned bishops in the preceding half century. Naturally, under the terms of the concordats, these monarchies would not have had strong incentives to grant a say in governance to their subjects in exchange for their efforts to improve wealth so as to make the king more competitive with the church. These monarchies were made up of dioceses that were following the interests of the church rather than their king, so they were less inclined to promote economic growth. We will have to see whether these parliaments or any uncovered parliaments were just rubber-stamp bodies. We will learn more about that shortly.

In contrast to poor, religious kingdoms, we see that there is a higher probability of a parliament in kingdoms when they have wealth or secularism, especially if they were covered by a concordat. The difference is small and insignificant between covered and uncovered secularly leaning kingdoms but is significant for wealthy ones. This is as we should expect, since wealth and secularism went hand in hand and both attainment and expansion of either may have depended on making concessions to subjects in exchange for their support. Thus, Figure 7.2, in conjunction with our earlier analysis, shows us that uncovered kingdoms were less likely to have the precursors for accountability that we have inferred from the concordat game—that is, significant secularism and wealth—and that even among those that met these preconditions, fewer held a parliament. In contrast, for those subject to the incentives set out in the concordats, especially for those with substantial wealth in the half century before we assess whether there was a parliament, we see that decisions were made to hold a parliament. By looking fifty years ahead, we begin to get a stronger picture of the incentives at work, maybe even encouraging us to conclude that more than correlation is being seen here and in Figure 7.1.

The rise of parliaments highlights the two edges of the sword of political power in the age of the concordats: wealth encouraged secularism, and secularism encouraged wealth. Ultimately, wealth was the key mechanism by which lay leaders could gain increased power in their dealings with the church. But where there was greater pursuit of wealth, kings had diminished power in dealing with their subjects. Wealth, especially in conjunction with the concordats, made the establishment and holding of parliaments much more likely. For instance, looking at all kingdoms, those that were covered by a concordat and enjoyed above average wealth apparently had a three times higher probability of also having to hold parliaments on behalf of at least some of their subjects than wealthy, uncovered kingdoms. Furthermore, the situation in kingdoms that were below average on the wealth dimension looked entirely different. They experienced parliaments far less often than covered, wealthy monarchies.

RUBBER STAMPS OR REAL PARLIAMENTS

Knowing that having a high percentage of secularly aligned bishops and/or having significant diocesan wealth substantially increased the odds that a kingdom had a national assembly does not tell us whether these assemblies were decorative rubber stamps doing whatever the king wanted or, instead, acted as a real constraint on the king's future actions. Remember, there are two perspectives regarding state size and the function of parliaments: small, compact states are more likely to have representative assemblies, and large states are more likely to have rubber-stamp assemblies. From the point of view here, big or small, if the king had to strike a bargain with local lords and other subjects in order to implement crucial policies, then his actions were genuinely limited by the decision-making authority granted to his subjects. We can burrow down into the evidence to ascertain whether the parliaments of the twelfth to seventeenth centuries were rubber stamps or really did begin to nudge, if not compel, kings to act in an accountable way. To do so, we first assess whether the existence of a parliament altered the ability of kings to wage war. If parliaments were able to have that really big effect, then we will want to know how war-making decisions were affected, if at all, by any taxing and spending authority that was granted to the members of the national assembly.

Waging war was surely among the costliest policy choices a king could make. As such, even in a chivalrous time, war was relatively infrequent. Was its frequency influenced by the existence of a parliament? If the frequency of war was dampened by a parliament's right to agree to or reject support for war, that would then have been one of their most important means of shaping the king's policies. Monarchs, of course, stood to be big winners (or big losers) in war. Sharing the bounty that came with a successful war was one way to reward the people whose support was needed. The king could promise to share the fruits of victory, but could the lords, the clergy, and the merchants really count on the monarch to fulfill his promise once the war was over? Could the monarch make, in game theoretic speak, a credible commitment?

Some representatives in parliament may have trusted their king to carry out such a promise, and others may have doubted that the king would share the wealth after the fighting was over. We cannot know who was trusted and who was not. Nor can we even know what promises were made and what promises were not made. We just have no way to know which wars assemblymen—they were nearly always men in this period—favored and which they opposed, but it is a pretty safe bet that they would have been more reluctant to engage in costly wars than their monarch was. He, after all, would surely have been paying most of the cost of war out of the pockets of his lesser lords, merchants, clergy, and everyday people, and there was no assurance, no credible commitment, that he would share the bounty of victory unless everyone knew the king needed their continued support in the near term. Still, the incidence of war when there was a parliament compared to when there was not can give us some hints into whether the newly created national assemblies were doing important work.

It turns out that kingdoms without a parliament in the previous half century found themselves at war about 8.5 percent of the time per half century. Monarchies with parliaments, in contrast, found themselves at war more frequently, at about 19.8 percent of the time, significantly more frequently than those that had no national assembly.[35] If, however, the two decisions—to hold a session of parliament and to fight a war— are looked at within the same half century, making the events both more proximate in time and harder to discern as to sequence, then the frequency of war for kingdoms without a parliament and for those with one is 7.9 percent and 1.2 percent, respectively. Looked at this way, the odds that the difference happened by chance is only 3 percent, but this time suggesting that parliaments might have been pacifying rather than acting as stimulants for war. It seems that parliaments exerted some pacifying influence and some bellicose influence. Either way, parliaments probably were more than mere rubber stamps, at least on the big war-or-peace decision. That leaves us with the question, What was it about the rights of assembly members that dampened or stirred enthusiasm for war?

Not all parliaments were created equal. Some, indeed, were rubber stamps. Still others were granted potentially important rights that could constrain what a monarch did, making his government more accountable than had been true before the creation of the new incentives put into play by the concordats. Just about 80 percent of parliaments were held with the assembly having the right to veto new taxes, and more than 50 percent of parliaments obtained the right to veto spending decisions; two-thirds if they already had a veto on taxes. These two powers translated into a significantly diminished risk that the kingdom would wage war.

Parliaments with a veto on taxes waged war per half century less than half as often as kingdoms with a parliament but without a veto on taxes. That difference is unlikely to be due to chance, although we must interpret it cautiously as we are necessarily dealing with a small number of cases.[36] The picture, although again based on few cases, is stronger when we examine parliaments with a veto over spending. War happened five times more frequently in parliaments without a spending veto as in parliaments with it.[37]

Apparently, kings who formed parliaments, especially if the parliament had a veto over taxing and spending decisions, actually traded away an important portion of their power to the representatives of their subjects. We know that kingdoms committed to a concordat were substantially more likely to have formed a parliament. Putting these facts together, we can conclude that the concordats do seem to have created bargaining leverage that, at least correlationally, translated into real influence on the part of the nobility, the clergy, and the commons in shaping the policies of their ruler. The power of the purse, then as today, was the means to avoid or at least diminish the extreme costs of war.

DID PARLIAMENTS HELP OR HURT MONARCHS?

The aftermath of the actions incentivized by the concordats provides an ample supply of examples in which pressure on kings to concede representative authority to lesser lords (and, in extremis, even to their commoner subjects) changed fundamental political decisions. The right to veto taxing and spending decisions imposed a dramatic limit on war fighting compared to the absence of that right. But did these and other factors that contributed to more accountable government ultimately benefit or harm the monarch's interests?

The creation of parliaments, especially if they controlled revenue, limited rulers' opportunities to expand and consolidate their power through warfare. Surely no monarch voluntarily accepted such constraints, yet assemblies were created. Putting ourselves in the shoes of such monarchs we must ask three questions: (1) What were the conditions, beyond the necessities during times of war, that led monarchs to agree to have a parliament? (2) How did the agreement at Worms influence those conditions? (3) What benefit, if any, did monarchs gain as a result of agreeing to the creation of a parliament? These questions are prompted by the belief that no secular ruler would have tied his or her fate to the will of a parliament unless doing so served the ruler's interest.

The bargaining leverage conferred as a consequence of the concordats enhanced the power of local interests. Indeed, this conclusion, although generally not linked to the concordats, is supported by numerous historical accounts of the period. For instance, Joseph Huffman, reporting on the diplomacy of the period and its ties to political struggle, observes, "Royal grants to cities during the Investiture Controversy ultimately strengthened them. Though serving as royal fortifications, in time they enabled the citizens to resist both royal and episcopal authority and achieve a larger measure of independence."[38] It would seem that there was an inherent contradiction between strengthening "the citizens" and improving the lot of the monarch, yet contemporary experience with accountable monarchies points the way to synergy between accountable government and monarchical longevity. Perhaps parliaments were good both for the people and for the king.

The interdependent incentives to make deals at various levels of government and between government and the church indicates that diplomacy, maybe even more than war, was stimulated initially by the rift between church and state. Diplomacy then contributed to a new political landscape characterized by shifting leverage and competition for authority in Europe following the change in institutions and in incentives wrought by the concordats. It was diplomacy, as Huffman has argued, that integrated Germany into western Europe and that solidified England's and France's places in the emerging state system of Europe. Diplomacy, as argued by Huffman without appeal to the concordats (signed by England, France, and Germany), also contributed to reshaping the standing of the Catholic Church.[39] But how did this diplomacy with the church and with subjects work out for kings?

We can be confident that political leaders, either today or in the Middle Ages, do not volunteer to diminish their power unless they expect that not doing so will bring them harm. Naturally, any governmental concession—such as the creation of a meaningful parliament—must have been expected to provide a benefit that a ruler would be denied in its absence. The biggest benefit a king could hope for, as Italo Calvino reminds us, is to keep his throne, his crown, and his head. Hence we should expect that parliaments with actual authority would have had a direct, positive influence on the prospects that monarchs survived in office. The privileges and power of office, after all, cannot be enjoyed from beyond the grave.

To evaluate the degree of support for this contention, let's analyze monarchical tenure in office and how it relates to whether the kingdom was subject to a concordat, meaning the king had to make deals with his subjects, deals that provided mutual benefits or else would not have been made. I also want to assess how the length of a ruler's reign related to his or her reliance on a parliament, the degree to which the kingdom had successfully secularized bishops, the extent to which the kingdom was rich or poor, and whether the monarchy had granted authority to parliament to influence big decisions, including taxation, spending, and waging war. Doing so will close the historical loop—we have, I believe, closed the analytic loop—from the concordats to secularism, to differentiated economic growth across Europe, to rifts in the church's political say in secular affairs, to the urge to strike bargains with subjects in order for kings to improve their political standing, incentivizing an improved work ethic in the process, to the formation of parliaments with real teeth, and to the creation of Western exceptionalism.

The puzzle we face is to see how the factors we have focused on shaped political survival for monarchs, while relying on the tenure of bishops as a control group to check against general trends.[40] Kings and bishops survived for highly variable lengths of time, ranging from practically no time in office to seven decades or more. One might look at the highly varied tenure of kings (or bishops) and be tempted—mistakenly—to think that how long a king survived in office depended only on luck. Luck, particularly in the form of good health, certainly played a part in how long rulers or anyone else lasted. But there were also systematic factors at work, especially in the case of powerful people like kings and bishops, that did not apply to most folks.

Being a king, in particular, usually meant great wealth, an ample supply of the best food and drink, the best horses, and the best soldiers to protect him. But those same trusted soldiers were well armed and might just as readily have turned on the king as defend him. Medicine was pretty useless. Enemies were everywhere. There was no shortage of people, as described by Italo Calvino, waiting for the right moment to take the king's head. The same was true for bishops, a surprisingly large number of whom died on their way to or from their consecration or even during their celebratory installation dinner. If the thesis set out here is a decent approximation of the truth, political survival would not have depended just on luck. A few key considerations that we now know drove the rise or decline of political power should have also influenced longevity in office. A comparison of Figures 7.3 and Figure 7.4 gives us a first look at the longevity of kings (and bishops) as a function of the factors that concern us here.

The first pane in Figure 7.3 looks at what we might think of as the reigns of "traditional," "nonexceptional," or "preexceptional" monarchs, and the second pane repeats the analysis for bishops. (In all the graphs in Figures 7.3, 7.4, and 7.5, the vertical axes begin at twelve years. That is close to the baseline, average number of years for bishops' tenures, and we want the graphs to be as comparably drawn as possible. Setting the bishop's tenure origin of the graph at twelve years instead of zero years makes it easier to see and compare the marginal gain or loss in survival time as we add the conditions that affect time in power.)

The first pane of Figure 7.3 compares the average, baseline term in office of all kings to the reigns of those kings who did not sign a concordat, those who were not beholden to a parliament (which, as we have learned, also meant that they tended not to be a signatory to a concordat), those whose bishops more faithfully represented the interests of the church than the monarch, and those whose kingdoms were relatively poor.

Being poor meant, of course, that even if some of these rulers had signed on to a concordat, they had little bargaining leverage with the church. It also meant that the church had little incentive to support efforts to stimulate the king's economy, as that would have given him more bargaining leverage. And that in turn meant that as long as the

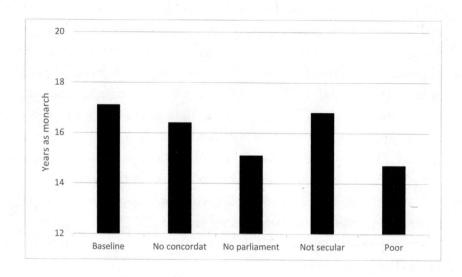

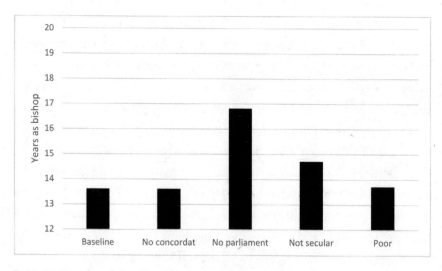

Figure 7.3: How long did traditional kings and bishops reign?

kingdom remained poor, the monarch had little reason to strike deals with his subjects—deals such as giving them a parliament in exchange for their help in his power struggle with the church. After all, what reason would he have to grant concessions to them when there was, within the logic of the concordats, precious little they could do to help him? The second pane controls for exactly the same information but at the bishop's diocese level.

It turns out that kings who remained outside the constraints of a concordat fared a little more poorly than those who were part of a concordat. Failing to sign a concordat is associated with the length of their reign being down by several months on average when compared to the tenure of all kings, signatories and nonsignatories alike. Being the ruler of a poor kingdom appears to have hurt survival prospects by about a year. Those whose monarchies were relatively poor survived less than the baseline for monarchs in general, whereas poverty had no bearing on the survival of bishops relative to their baseline. The absence of a parliament seems to have shortened the tenure of kings on average by about two years, whereas the absence of a parliament was quite good for the tenure of bishops. Bishops in sees dominated by religiously leaning bishops enjoyed a small boost in their survival time, while that made almost no difference for kings. Most of these differences in survival time are small enough that they may well be explained by random good or bad luck.

The sorts of monarchs who were unlikely to benefit from the leverage a concordat could render in fact had diminished time as king. They were worse off than the average if they were poor, outside of a concordat, and had no parliament. That helps warn us that there is a good chance that kings who followed through on the direct, positive incentives provided by a concordat—the pursuits of wealth—may indeed have benefited personally from making concessions to their subjects by creating a parliament. Generally, these factors that were absent for "traditional" kings just worked to shorten the time they would wear the crown.

Figure 7.4 shows how life looked for monarchs who either signed on to a concordat (and therefore were likely to form a parliament, promote wealth, and achieve secular control) or who, seeing the benefits those rulers enjoyed, emulated them by forming a parliament and becoming

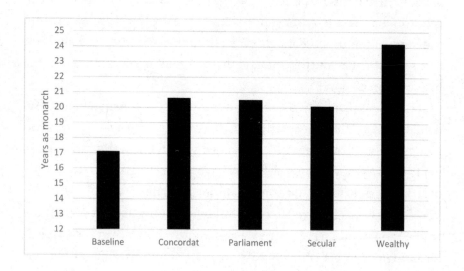

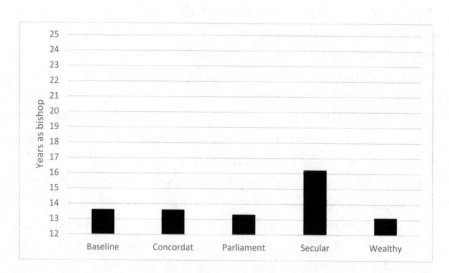

Figure 7.4: What factors influenced a king's or bishop's political survival?

rich enough to shape their destiny and maybe even gain secular control over the church's princes in the monarch's realm.

The signatories to the Concordat of Worms or its precursors in England and France enjoyed a significant boost in the length of their reign. While the average king remained in power for about seventeen years, those who were party to a concordat served for nearly twenty-one years. The kings who agreed to be at least somewhat accountable to a parliament reigned for just over two decades, well above the time for those "traditional" kings who eschewed accountability. Secular kingdoms had monarchs who did well, averaging twenty years as king, and those kings who ruled over a rich kingdom enjoyed an ample reward: they reigned for an average of twenty-four years. Doing the things that were fostered by the concordats in places where there was an opportunity to enhance one's power at the church's expense seems mostly to have worked to significantly prolong political survival for kings despite the many random shocks and other exigencies of the times.

Did these same factors have similar benefits for bishops? Were they just signs of the times rather than the distinctive benefits to be obtained by monarchs who gained independence from the church and consolidated their power at home? The second pane in Figure 7.4 answers these questions quite starkly. The two graphs use the same vertical axis so that the two panes are visually comparable; we see immediately that bishops did not do nearly as well as kings in terms of political longevity. Maybe they were just older when they first became bishops than kings were when they first wore the crown. But they were not so old that they did not live on for many years. Many bishops had careers that lasted for several decades. Yet none of the conditions that seemed to boost a king's average survival time—being party to a concordat, having a parliament, or having wealthy territory—made any meaningful difference in the total years in office for bishops. Only greater secularism proved to be accompanied by a boost to their tenure.

The boost in the longevity of kings seems not just to have been a sign of the times or a broad-based impact of choices that might only coincidentally have had anything to do with signing a concordat. The benefits were substantial, and they redounded to secular leaders, whether they were monarchs in the secular world or royalist bishops in the religious world, but not to men chosen for their religious alignment with the church. Indeed, when we look at personal characteristics rather than diocesan circumstances, we see that the benefits implied by the concordats carried over to a select group of individual bishops. For instance, secularly aligned bishops survived 2.5 years longer, on average, than did religiously leaning bishops, a difference that would happen by chance less than once in ten thousand tries. It seems that when monarchs got to pick their bishops, they chose men who would last a long time to help formulate and enforce the policies the king wanted, much as presidents of the United States try to pick Supreme Court justices who will outlast them to carry on their vision of the law.

The conditions engendered by the concordats, including the pressure to negotiate with their subjects over wealth and power, paid off for lay leaders. They kept the crown longer than their less responsive, less accountable counterparts. The initial condition that, according to the concordat game, made the concordats a potential source of leverage—wealth—translated into more power, as expected, and also into bigger political concessions once parliaments were formed. Some parliaments appear to have been rubber stamps, but others gained authority over the big taxing and spending decisions that,

Figure 7.5: How was a monarch's tenure altered by granting authority over big decisions?

as we have seen, also influenced the prospects of the big decision to wage war or pursue peace. What did these by-products of parliaments do to the chances that the monarch would have staying power or would be out of office more quickly? Figure 7.5 helps us answer this question.

As we know, many scholars have argued that war was the central factor bolstering the success of kings in building their states. Yet Figure 7.5 shows that state stability, as manifested through the longevity of its kings, was at best only very modestly bolstered by war. The typical monarch reigned for around seventeen years, and those kings (or queens) who waged war seem to have reigned only a couple of years longer. They gained little extra time that might have benefited a king trying to consolidate his sovereign authority within his kingdom and trying to establish control over succession.

War may have helped build the state, but it was not the best way, or even all that good a way, to construct a stable state. Figure 7.5 shows us that a regime's stability and its consolidation of sovereignty, as indicated by the longevity of the monarch, was *much* more enhanced by the recognition of rights for members of parliament, rights that shaped pretty much all of the kingdom's policies. Monarchs who faced a parliament that had a veto over tax decisions averaged nearly thirty-two years in office, hugely outstripping the time for state consolidation that seemingly was associated with warfare. And enormous though the effect of taxing authority was, it apparently did less for a king's longevity than spending authority. Kings who had a parliament with a veto over spending decisions (so that parliament could be blamed for programs that turned out poorly) reigned for an average of thirty-five years.

Of course, we must be careful. Some kings will have granted a veto over taxes or over spending late in their term, after they had already enjoyed a long time wearing the crown, and likewise, some kings will have created a parliament very late in their term. They might have done any of these things to curry favor with powerful cliques, keeping them within the monarchical coalition by giving them new concessions rather than giving them an excuse to depose the monarch. But something more was happening too. We can check by restricting our examination to kings who came to power after the first parliament met compared to those who became king earlier. The creation of a parliament seems to have added several years to the monarch's expected reign. Add a veto on taxation, and the king gains an additional six years as compared to those who came to wear the crown before a first parliament was assembled. The extension of a veto over spending adds another four years to the king's expected post–first parliament tenure. All these concessions that monarchs gave to some of their subjects apparently worked to the advantage of the ruler as well as many of his subjects.

War may have helped to make the state, but the diplomacy that produced parliaments with real power did vastly more! Bishops, in contrast, enjoyed no meaningful deviation from their average longevity in power if they presided over sees in kingdoms that waged war, granted a tax veto to its parliament, or conceded a veto on spending to its assembly. All the action in terms of political survival—and it was substantial action—fell to monarchs as a function of the sorts of choices they made in subscribing to a concordat or not, in building on secularism or not, in building wealth or not, in agreeing to a parliament or not, in accepting a veto over taxation or not, and in agreeing to a spending veto or not. War was sexy, war was honored, but war did not provide nearly as big a boost to a monarch's survival as these other choices did.

Naturally, many factors contributed to the rise of national assemblies, to war, and to Europe's secularization besides the institutional innovations and changed incentives put into motion by the Concordats of London, Paris, and Worms. But well before the Treaty of Westphalia was signed in 1648, and indeed, before Martin Luther nailed his theses to the church door in 1517, the fierce competition between the secular and the spiritual swords had begun to resolve in favor of the temporal world. Lay leaders had invented new powers for themselves. They had defeated the pope and church on the political front, and through their support of the Avignon papacy and the Protestant Reformation, they had weakened both the papacy and the church on the religious front as well. The policies that the temporal elite adopted to achieve these outcomes came, however, at a steep price for the institutions of government with which they had entered into this competition in the eleventh and twelfth centuries.

The incentives created by the concordats meant that for rulers to gain leverage, they needed more wealth at the local, diocesan level. To secure that wealth, they needed new tools beyond the old methods of conquest and marriage. By encouraging economic development in their defined diocesan territories, they gained greater political leverage over the Catholic Church and its leadership. In pursuit of that political leverage, wherever they could, lay leaders apparently adopted policies to stimulate growth by rewarding labor's productivity.

The evidence has shown us that where the costs of punishments inflicted on secular rulers by the church could be minimized, secularism grew. Where there was wealth, secularism grew. With the growth of secularism, wealth grew. With greater wealth, rebellion against the church's political power grew. And with the loss of the church's political clout, sovereign states rose.

Because punishment was more easily inflicted close to Rome than far from it, all these effects were magnified as a ruler's distance from Rome increased. This meant that northern Europe became wealthier, less dependent on the church, and more likely to create sovereign states, while southern Europe stagnated economically, sustained its loyalty to the church, and was slower to adopt political accountability.

The policies that successful leaders adopted to escape the political clutches of the church did not come without their own, longer-term costs for monarchy, even if not for the monarchs of the moment who adopted those policies. To achieve independence from the church by promoting economic expansion and secularism, monarchs found they needed to trade money for political control over diocesan policy. These trades were made with local lords and even with commoners. Many local lords directly influenced diocesan policies within their territorial domain, including influencing the selection of bishops, the central political figures who intersected between the policies of the church and of the state.

Either princes, dukes, and other local elites, and even merchants, guildsmen, and other influential commoners, could expand their own power by making deals with other local centers of power, or they could make deals with their nominal superiors—that is, the monarchs who sought to control local actions and policies. What they worked out at the dawn of Europe's exceptionalism was much like dividing up shares in a modern company. By finding ways to cooperate with one another, the greatest lords and the meanest laborers also found ways to secure more money and better connections for themselves. They learned that the moments of economic growth are also the key moments for ensuring accountability in the long term. Competition punctuated by cooperation did not make laborers and kings remotely equal, but it did provide them with similar incentives that enhanced the economic, political, and social well-being of many more people than was true where the concordats had not taken hold.

To be sure, the horse-trading induced by the concordats was sometimes resolved through war, sometimes through local rebellions, and sometimes, in anticipation of these costly events, through compromise. Those compromises created the beginnings of representative, parliamentary government that introduced a new balance between the authority of monarchs and the demands of some of their subjects. War had limited prospects for enhancing a monarch's tenure in power, but accepting a parliament that in some ways tied the king's hands improved his political survival and became an attractive means by which power could be consolidated. Thus, the political leverage that monarchs gained at the expense of the church transformed the arena of competition; it no longer lay between popes and kings but was now within the territorial borders of kings, lesser nobles, and their subjects. And that transformative process made Europe succeed in moving toward representative, democratic governance and toward innovation and prosperity at a faster and surer pace than anywhere else in the world between the signing of the Concordat of Worms and now.

All the conclusions we have reached so far have followed logically from the conditions established by the Concordat of Worms. The evidence has overwhelmingly supported these logical conclusions. We did not need any appeal to cultural, racial, religious, or ethnic superiority, as has so often been claimed, to explain Europe's exceptionalism. Simply looking at who signed on to a concordat and who did not, combined with an examination of which bishoprics were wealthier and which poorer, turns out to be sufficient to explain the nuanced variations in the evolution of secularism, wealth, religious diversity, and governmental accountability across Europe that gave birth to what we, today, call the West.

8

TODAY

THE INTERLUDE FROM THE CONCORDATS TO THE START OF THE AVI-
gnon papacy seems so far removed from our own time that we may
think those long-ago years are obscure and irrelevant. Yet it is a period
so deeply pertinent to our own that even now we turn to these very
years both for entertainment and for enlightenment as to the right way
of living. Every English-speaking child knows that Robin Hood roamed
Sherwood Forest in the time when King Richard the Lionhearted was
off on crusade and that his brother, Prince John, ruled in his place.
Robin famously—and belovedly—stole from the rich, gave to the poor,
and bedeviled the shire-reeve of Nottinghamshire, remembered today
as the evil sheriff of Nottingham. Robin taught the charitableness that
was sorely missing in that time, and maybe still is in ours.

Brother Cadfael, a modern invention, is a Benedictine monk situated
in England in the 1130s and 1140s. He also instructs us on proper living.[1] Cadfael reminds us of what justice is and how it can be muddled by

entrenched authority and especially by such authority when it is wielded by the hands of the church and the state, a lesson still pertinent today.

And who does not know of Merlin the magician, first created in 1136 as a great wizard with a hatred of war, a hatred that may be missing even now from our leaders but certainly is shared by many—perhaps most— of us.

Far removed though we are from the twelfth century, many of us nevertheless recall and take lessons from the years of which I have written. My purpose in this final chapter, however, is not so much to remember how alive those years still are but, rather, to explore the ways the developments of those years continue to contribute to variations in exceptionalism in our time and the ways lessons from those developments, rather than unwarranted, illogical, destructive accounts of superiority, might be used to make more lives more exceptional today. In applying the lessons I take from the concordats, I may commit the sin of misjudging what others think a good life ought to be like, so let me lay my cards on the table now, mindful that some will disagree—which, of course, is fine. My opinion is just that, my opinion, not more and not less.

I believe everyone seeks a life without hunger and in good health, filled with the opportunity to create and do what we each want, filled with happiness and free to think and believe what we want but not free to act against the same rights and opportunities for others, an accountable life filled with chances to make society better or to choose not to make such an effort. Others, of course, will have different ideas about what makes life and society exceptional. I believe the view of exceptionalism I just set out, however, is unexceptional. It is the ideas and conditions, still imperfectly fulfilled, of the world the concordats created, slowly, painstakingly, incompletely, for Europe and for its Western offshoots, and these same ideas can and, I believe, should be spread everywhere.

Europe's settler offshoots, in particular, illustrate how the ideas and practices inculcated in different parts of Europe during the time of the concordats can and have been exported elsewhere. In contrast, many of Europe's nonsettler colonies illustrate the difficulties in transmitting the institutionalized incentives promulgated by the concordats. Although the subject of colonization, whether by settlers or by soldiers and civil servants, is too complex to treat thoroughly here, it is thought provoking to consider the different experiences of lands that were colonized hundreds of years after the concordats by the descendants of signatories and nonsignatories. I do so without in any way excusing the inhuman treatment endured by those people who already lived in the lands that were subjected to colonization, whether by settlers or not. What is crucial for success today is not the fact of settlement; it is the extent to which competitive institutions are adopted.

Few of today's wealthiest countries, on a per capita income basis, are former colonies of Spain, England, France, Portugal, the Netherlands, Germany, or Belgium. But there are notable exceptions: England's former American, Australian, and New Zealand colonies are among the world's most prosperous places. France's former Louisiana Territory, though poorer than much of the United States, still would be among the world's wealthier countries, as would the territory that once constituted the New Netherlands and that today makes up New York State, Delaware, and parts of Maryland. What made the difference between the poorer ex-colonies and the wealthier ones?

Of course a great many factors distinguish the levels of economic success of the world's former colonies. Hence we do not want to make too much of what nevertheless is a tantalizing fact. The wealthiest former colonies were populated by people who left England, France, or the Netherlands, all signatories to a concordat. Some departed in pursuit of freedoms denied them in their home country—for instance, the Pilgrim settlers in New England. Others had no choice—such as the English prisoners first shipped off to North America and, following the American Revolution, then transported to Australia. Still others left their homelands in pursuit of economic opportunities—for example, many Dutch settlers. Even those fleeing persecution nevertheless erected government and economic institutions and a work ethic similar to the ones they had experienced at home. English settlers, for instance, brought the ideas of accountable government with them to the American colonies. The descendants of these settlers were later to insist, just as *Confirmatio cartarum* had stipulated five hundred years earlier, that there should be no taxation without representation. Similarly, the Dutch settlers brought the ideas of a free society with them. Indeed, even today, much of New York City's charter is the remnant of the New Amsterdam charter written by Adriaen van der Donck (1618–1655). That charter guaranteed extensive freedoms that foreshadowed, for instance, the Bill of Rights in the US Constitution.[2] Likewise, we should note that Louisiana today still adheres to France's Napoleonic Code as the foundation of its legal system, and the former English settler outposts all adhere to variants of English common law, as do some, but certainly not all, former British nonsettler colonies.

Where colonial powers did not rely on relatively large settler populations but, instead, governed with a small military force accompanied by government bureaucrats, they still brought their institutions of governance with them. But whereas the settler colonies, like the nonsettler ones, ultimately ousted their colonizers, the colonizers' institutions rarely stuck once the indigenous population took charge. And as it happens—maybe by coincidence, maybe not—the settler ex-colonies were *all* the product of concordat signatory states. A great many of the nonsettler colonies, such as most of Spain's and Portugal's colonies in Latin America, were not signatories.

Whether by chance or not, the settler colonies had the competitive advantage of relatively secularized, wealthy, concordat-based home societies that had inculcated competitive, nascent market-oriented economies and accountable, representative government. Hardly anyplace without settler colonization, including colonies controlled but not settled by concordat signatories, internalized these concordat-based institutions. In that sense, the settler colonies may provide examples of the transportability of the ideas and incentives inculcated by the competitive but regulated environment created by the concordats. Perhaps the lesson of such competitive, regulated societies can also be inculcated elsewhere without the accompanying miseries and oppression of colonization, settlement, or occupation.

Before exploring further what specifically might be done to improve quality of life through regulated, competitive institutions—the actions I said I would bet on—I first should demonstrate how alive the impact of the concordats is in Europe's daily realities today, especially where the concordats promoted wealth and secularism nine hundred years ago.

I hope you are persuaded, or at least intrigued, by the extent to which the concordats of the early twelfth century helped shape Europe for the next several centuries. I hope you have looked at the evidence and agree that the concordats helped create what today some think of as European or Western exceptionalism. The concordats seem to have done so by fostering, regulating, and managing intense competition between powerful institutions. In the case of the concordats, that meant managing the competition between the Catholic Church and Europe's then-nascent states.

Our world is certainly, but perhaps superficially, very far removed from the world of the concordats. The circumstances of life have changed vastly from that time, yet as we are about to see, much of the variation that exists today across Europe fits neatly within the confines of the incentives and actions set in motion by the concordats of 1107 and 1122.

Science has come to be a competitor with religion as a means of explaining what happens in the heavens and on earth. It seems to have taken on the role that rebellions against the Catholic Church took on first in 1309 and then again in 1517, and it seems to be the ultimate rebellion. Neither the Avignon nor the Protestant rebellions questioned the fundamental scriptural texts of Christianity, but science did and does. Machines, like science, play a radically different part today than their predecessors did in the twelfth and thirteenth centuries. Machines are now a ubiquitous part of everyone's life, even as automation is feared as much today—when more people are employed than ever in human history—as idle hands were feared in the twelfth century. Life expectancy at birth and the quality of life during the many more years we have has greatly improved. Literacy in Europe is nearly universal and expected, whereas it was frowned upon in Catholic Europe before the Reformation. Workers now enjoy more leisure time and greater resources with which to enjoy and understand their world than was true even for the wisest, smartest, or best-educated eight hundred years ago. Life, indeed, seems very different today—so different that surely few of us would gladly be transported back in time to the twelfth century.

Yet much about the variation in the quality of life, in innovation, in decency and humanity across Europe today appears to remain tied to the changed incentives that we investigated. At least in a correlational sense, whether or not the clusters of dioceses that delineate today's countries were subject to the new rules created by the concordats, whether or not these places prospered in the twelfth and thirteenth centuries, is indicative of current conditions. Those parts of Europe that were not subject to a concordat, regardless of their wealth then, are faring far worse now than are those places that were wealthier in the early twelfth century and were subject to a concordat. The evidence suggests that the rules and incentives embedded in the concordats continue to matter to outcomes today, these many, many centuries later.

Of course, an enormous number of events, big and small, planned and random, have happened in the hundreds of years since the concordats were agreed to by some and not by others. This makes any suggestion of causality a fool's errand. Yet the correlations to be found are tantalizingly suggestive. It may be too bold to claim that the concordats *caused* Europe's exceptionalism, but a great many important outcomes today are consistent with this theory. We should keep open minds about the possibility, not minds closed either by conviction or by prior doubt. We are now ready to complete our journey into European exceptionalism by looking at the relationship between the factors that the concordats have taught us were important and their connection to the outcomes across Europe today.

THE ALTERED TIDES OF POWER

The unique competition for political power between the Catholic Church and Europe's secular rulers provided a central theme through which to understand Europe's political and economic development. At the outset I claimed that in the rest of the world, for most of history, either the head of government and the head of religion were the same person, or one was clearly subservient to the other. In Europe, however, once the Holy Roman Empire was created by the pope in 800 to protect him, his Papal States, and the church, fierce competition for political preeminence between the pope and Europe's secular rulers was inevitable. That competition—governed by the agreed-upon terms of the concordats—was central to Europe's development because it set organized, structured competition into motion. The fostering of such regulated competition is, I believe, one of the central lessons to be taken from Europe's medieval experience.

We have viewed the ebb and flow of the political competition for influence between kings and popes, between the secular sword and the spiritual sword, in three distinct ways. We watched the progression in artwork, sometimes toward religious subjects and sometimes toward secular ones, tying the shift in emphasis to specific events in the unfolding struggle between the church and the emerging states in Europe. Likewise, we looked at the shifting levels of papal nepotism and tied it to critical events in the competition for power between the secular and the spiritual swords, noting that the spiritual sword was often in the hands of venal religious leaders. And I have depicted the altered size of the essential coalition of supporters needed to (s)elect popes, again tying shifts in the size of that coalition to critical events.

These three ways of thinking about who was winning and who was losing the competition for political power and control over money captures three distinct points of view. The battle over artwork was something of a symmetrical struggle. The church strove to elevate religious themes and suppress secular themes. Lay rulers did the opposite, trying to promote their images and their power against that of the pope and church. Nepotism and the papal (s)electoral coalition were more directly in the hands of the pope and church than was the distribution of inspirations for artworks, but nevertheless both nepotism and the number of papal (s)electors served as indicators of the church's perceived need to grant or deny concessions in the sustained competition for power and money.

The battle over artwork ended long ago. Religious art continues to enjoy a niche today, but only a niche. At least since the end of the Thirty Years' War, religious art has been in retreat. Indeed, it is worthwhile to go back even earlier, to where we began in the eighth century with the birth of the Iconoclast Movement, and reflect a bit on the ups and downs in the use of imagery to project power.

Nine of the fourteen quarter-century-long observations of secular and religious artwork between 752 and 1100, as seen in Figure 2.4 (p. 56), had no secular art, only religious art. This domination of imagery by the Catholic Church is too easily forgotten or ignored from today's more secular perspective. It is also too easily forgotten that this domination of Christian art arose during a battle over Christianity's very existence, a battle carried on both by the leaders of a rival religion, Islam, and by a rival secular power, the Byzantine emperor. The preeminence of religious art illustrates the extraordinary dominance of the church in the European world of ideas and inspiration during those many centuries.

In contrast to the church's domination of imagery before the concordats, from the time of the Concordat of Worms until the Treaty of Westphalia, as Figure 6.8 (p. 196) makes abundantly clear, there was just one quarter century, just before the French king Philip IV rebelled against the church, that was devoid of secular art. The postconcordat centuries saw a dramatic revival of secular images that accompanied the rise in secular power in the European world.

Today, in the West, neither religious nor secular art is widely promoted by government or by religious institutions as a significant instrument in the struggle between church and state. Today, artists create whatever inspires them or their clients (for the lucky ones who have clients). The church lost the battle to control imagery hundreds of years ago. But so too did secular rulers. By the time of the Renaissance, art was shifting away from representations of the high and mighty, whether religious or secular, and was, instead, depicting everyday people. And by the late nineteenth century, taste had moved again, this time toward the depiction of light and color, shapes and motion. The people of the Western world had won their right to depict the world and its abstractions however they wanted. If there is a battle over power through the use of art today, it is a battle between corporate, commercial interests and individual desires and tastes. That is surely an important struggle in its own right, but it is not the struggle that made Europe exceptional, although it may well be a latter-day manifestation of the outcomes of that battle.

The contests over nepotism or religiosity also seem to be resolved today, although their details are probably less familiar to most than is the outcome of the battle for power through control over imagery. Hence, we should now reprise our assessments of nepotism and also of the shifting size of the papal winning coalition. I will review these imperfect measures of power to see the big picture of how they shifted over the long time period from where we began, with the Iconoclast Movement in 726, and where we are ending, in the third decade of the twenty-first century.

Papal nepotism tells much the same story as was told with artwork, albeit less starkly. When we first looked at nepotism in the papacy, in Figure 2.1 (p. 34), we saw that the office of the bishop of Rome was overwhelmingly filled by religious men before Pope Stephen II severed papal ties with the Byzantine emperor and secured control over the lucrative Papal States. Then nepotism rose steadily, giving us the *saeculum obscurum*, peaking as the Investiture Controversy got under way. We can see this quite clearly in Figure 8.1. The Concordats of London, Paris, and Worms began to resolve that struggle, doing so in a way that was advantageous for temporal interests at the expense of the pope. Nepotism went into a deep decline during the years of the concordat interlude and

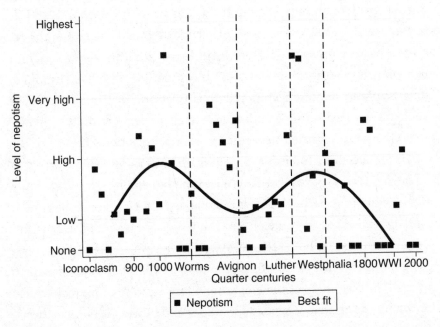

Figure 8.1: Nepotism in the papacy, iconoclasm to today

continued downward through the early years of the Avignon papacy. Nepotism was down but, as the coming centuries revealed, it was not out! The papacy was just too lucrative a post to be left to men of religious calling rather than to men from influential, rich, and ambitious families.

Nepotism began to be prominent again at around the time of the Council of Constance, continuing until Martin Luther's Reformation shook the foundations of the Roman Catholic world. Then a long struggle began in which nepotism in the selection of popes gradually became a failing business. Though nepotism still occurred, the trend was against it; religious calling was supplanting family loyalty among the church's leaders.

After the church's further setback in the resolution of the Thirty Years' War, nepotism declined markedly, and there were a great many extended periods up to the present without any sign of papal nepotism at all. Nepotism in the church and papacy of the twentieth and twenty-first centuries seems, indeed, to look much as it did before Emperor Justinian ruled in the mid-sixth century. The papacy once again looks like a religious office at the head of a religious organization struggling to advance its religious agenda, rather than a venal or power-seeking one. That seems like an important shift for the good of the church and its adherents. But the church's institutional structure—the size of the required papal winning coalition—still leaves it vulnerable to corrupt behavior. Its institutional design is incompatible with the sustained, uncorrupted promotion of its religious mission. That incompatibility could be changed, although doing so is likely to be profoundly difficult.

As the papacy battled to secure its political position, the size of the coalition necessary to elect a pope remained as an additional arrow in its quiver. It was, and may still be, a weapon beyond imagery and family ties by which the papacy's power is enhanced. The leaders of the church already realized at the time of the Council of Nicaea that their institutional strength could be secured by wresting control over the appointment of bishops away from the community of Christians and placing it, instead, in the hands of the emerging church and the political leaders on whom the church depended for money and power. At Nicaea, the assembled bishops elevated the role of each metropolitan bishop and each community's nearby bishops in choosing candidates pleasing to their own interests, whether or not they were also pleasing to the local community. Thus they shrank the number of people needed, for instance, to pick the bishop of Rome from potentially thousands to a few hundred or even less. As we have seen, this gradually led to an expansion in nepotism and a consolidation of church power in the papacy.

The logic driving the past bad behavior of the church during the medieval period has not changed. What has changed is the political power of the church vis-à-vis secular rulers. The decline in Catholic political power means that its institutional structure is now more likely to lead to internecine corruption than to corrupt dealings between the secular and the sacred swords. Europe's contemporary Caesars have so worn down the church's temporal power that they need no longer take that political dimension significantly into account.

Figure 8.2 depicts the evolution of the papal winning coalition—the number of supporters needed to pick the pope, the bishop of Rome—over the 1,300 years from the time in which we began, in 726, to the start of the twenty-first century. As is evident, while nepotism was in retreat and secular art was resurgent during the interlude from the

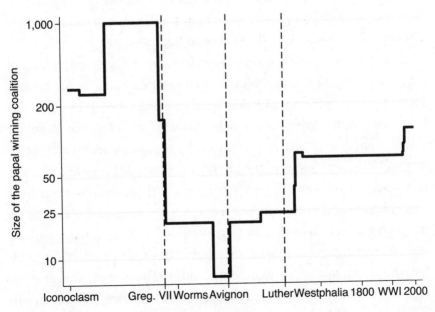

Figure 8.2: Papal winning coalition, iconoclasm to today

concordats to the capture of the papacy by the king of France, the papacy was fighting back, trying to preserve its political clout by shrinking
the number of people to whom the pope was answerable. The pope's required coalition shrank notably during the papacy of Gregory VII, and
then, midway through the concordats-to-Avignon period, it plummeted
to the point that the pope needed fewer than ten essential supporters to
be elected and sustained in his office. These few supporters were often
the cardinal-nephews of the pope himself, tying the size of the coalition
to the maintenance of nepotistic, family interests.

The coalition, shown on a logarithmic scale to make it easier to
see changes, barely increased for two hundred years, until shortly after Martin Luther began the Reformation. These centuries, especially
from Gregory VII to Luther, should have—and did—shake the foundations of popular support for the church as it increasingly became a
self-serving institution in which, during the period when the papacy depended on its smallest-ever coalition, many popes lived sumptuously
and even condemned the poverty avowed by the early church leaders.
Then, following Luther, the papal winning coalition was expanded from
around twenty-five to around one hundred, still quite small, and then to
a bit more in the twentieth century. Even after these expansions, however, the papal winning coalition remains much smaller today than it
was before the Council of Nicaea or even right after it.

Thus today's papacy remains dependent on a rather modest level of
support, a level that remains consistent with its being an autocratic,
corruptible institution that would surely benefit its flock by returning
to the pre-Nicaea approach, in which bishops, including the bishop of
Rome, were chosen *a clero et populo*—by the clergy and the community of Catholics. Some of the church's greatest figures, men like the
third-century martyr Bishop Cyprian of Carthage, rose to their high
offices by the will of the Christian community and against the will of
the higher clergy. Selection by those earliest practices, or at least by a
representative, accountable resurrection of the ideas behind the conciliar movement, might reinvigorate the church, its community, and the
regard in which it is held. In the absence of such reforms, the church will
remain vulnerable to corrupt practices—such as the child molestation

scandals—that sustain loyalty by granting the inner circle and the inner circle's inner circles the reward of remaining in their offices almost without regard to behavior the church deems sinful.

While the church was working hard to limit the size of the papal winning coalition and sustain the church's secular as well as sacred influence, so too were kings. Thanks to the incentives put into play by the concordats, secular rulers, especially in wealthier places that were far from Rome, emerged victorious in their competition to place the earthly ahead of the sacred, at least in day-to-day affairs. The most successful among lay leaders generated economic growth, expanded secularism, entertained alternative views of church-state relations, and accepted accountable parliamentary government in return for political loyalty that significantly improved their chances for political survival. The question that remains, then, is whether their efforts to secure their power provide guidance in our effort to understand variations in economic, social, and political performance across Europe today. The logic of the concordat game, its extensions, and reasonable inferences from it all say that the way the competition unfolded hundreds of years ago mattered then and should still matter today. The incentives instituted in the twelfth century should have left a legacy of advantage for those parts of Europe that benefited from the concordats in the Middle Ages. Let's see whether the evidence is consistent with that contention.

THE CONCORDATS AND TODAY'S QUALITY OF LIFE

The quality of life for the average citizen in each of Europe's countries today could be assessed in myriad ways. I examine the following important indicators of quality of life for each modern European country:[3]

1. Average per capita income from 1960 to 2018.[4]
2. Average level of democracy between 1918 and 2018, thus including the challenging years right after World War I, the years of World War II, and the Cold War and its aftermath. Higher values reflect greater democracy and lower values less democracy.[5] I summarize parallel results for the average level of democracy from 1968 to 2018.[6]

3. Life expectancy at birth as of 2018.[7]
4. The average estimated perception of corruption from 2015 to 2018. Lower values mean more corruption and larger values mean more honesty.[8]

One could readily imagine using other indicators of quality of life, but these cover a broad range of topics. They capture important indications of prosperity, freedom, health, and rule of law, and the findings based on these indicators are readily replicated with alternative measures of people's quality of life.

Once we finish assessing differences in the quality of life across Europe, I then evaluate other aspects of Western exceptionalism, such as inventiveness and creativity. We will look at the distribution of patents, Nobel prizes in the sciences, and Nobel prizes in the humanities as a further probe into just how long-lasting and important the effects of the concordats are. I believe we will all be amazed by just how evident a legacy Holy Roman Emperor Henry V and Pope Calixtus II left when they signed their names to the concordat of Worms on September 23, 1122!

As we know, the concordat game tells us directly that relatively wealthier dioceses that signed on to a concordat back in the twelfth century should have, by turns, grown more secular, wealthier, and more democratically governed. We saw that the record of European history supports these expectations. The question now is whether those effects were so large, so dramatic, and so long-lasting that we can still see them at work across Europe today.

Is it true today that Europe's wealthier, more democratic, healthier, and more lawful countries are those that were covered by the concordats and that achieved greater economic prosperity during the interlude of the agreements? Is it true today that those countries that were not covered by the agreements in 1107 and 1122, even if they were prosperous then, are not as prosperous, democratic, healthy, and law-abiding today? Is it also true that those that did not do well economically then—and therefore were likely to be more under the control of the church—did not become so prosperous today and did not experience the same pressures to become more democratic and more focused on improving the health and lawfulness under which citizens live even today?

To answer these questions, I focus our attention on the average percentage of years that the dioceses in each modern European country were on major trade routes—and therefore presumably relatively prosperous—between 1122 (or 1107 for France and England) and 1309. I ask whether there is a difference in their record on per capita income, level of democracy over the past century or half century, recent life expectancy, and recent degree of corruption, holding approximate wealth during the Worms interlude constant by looking across countries in terms of whether they were or were not covered by a concordat. To hold twelfth- and thirteenth-century wealth at comparable levels, I aggregate all the then dioceses into their modern countries and divide them into four groups. The groupings are based on whether these aggregated dioceses per modern country were above or below the median percentage of accumulated years on major trade routes, on average, during the concordats interlude and whether they were or were not subject to the terms of a concordat. Remember, if the concordats have had a lasting effect, then we should see, in particular, a meaningful difference in current performance on every modern factor we look at for those countries whose dioceses in the twelfth century were subject to a concordat and started out wealthy back then when compared to any of the other three groups, for those that were covered but poor, for those that were wealthy but not covered, and for those that were poor and not covered. Here is what we discover.

The first frame in Figure 8.3 examines contemporary per capita incomes and contrasts those countries that were wealthy and subject to the concordats in 1122–1309 with those countries that were wealthy but not subject to the concordats. The second frame repeats the exercise but for countries that were not wealthy in the interlude between the signing of the concordats and the start of the Avignon papacy. The differences are substantial.

Those dioceses that were wealthy during the time of Robin Hood and that now make up today's modern countries are substantially and significantly more prosperous if they were subject to a concordat than if

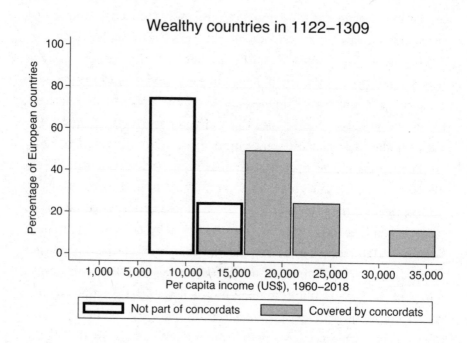

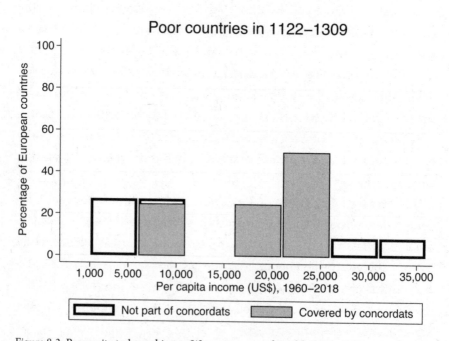

Figure 8.3: Prosperity today, subject to Worms or not, and wealth, 1122–1309

they were not. Those wealthy places in 1122–1309 that were not covered by the concordats enjoyed an average per capita income, stated in inflation-adjusted dollars, from 1960 to 2018 of $10,684. This compares unfavorably to the mean income for the same years of $21,521 among the equivalently wealthy places during the Worms interlude that were subject to the concordat.[9] And lest there is concern about smoothing out differences over a fifty-year time span, per capita income as of 2020 is $49,692 for countries that were wealthy during the time of the concordats and that signed on to one of the treaties. In contrast, per capita income in 2020 was $33,440 for those countries that were wealthy then but did not participate in a concordat. That is a difference of 48 percent, even though all the countries in this comparison were wealthy in the twelfth and thirteenth centuries. As the concordat game instructs us, coverage for the wealthy created a bargaining advantage that should have—and apparently did—set those kingdoms on a path to economic success.

Having been wealthy during the time of the concordats does not predict that countries are doing so well in the recent past up to today if they were not subject to the incentives put into motion by the deals signed in 1107 and 1122. In addition, having been a signatory does not matter for today's prosperity for those who were poor then and who therefore were more likely to remain under the then-growth-limiting incentives of the Catholic Church rather than the growth-oriented interests of secular rulers who were subject to the concordat. The average per capita income from 1960 to 2018 in inflation-adjusted dollars was $17,592 among those covered by a concordat but poor in the years between 1107 and 1309. For the poor not covered by a concordat, the equivalent per capita income averages $16,020, a statistically meaningless difference. Both, of course, are substantially below the average per capita income for those places that were wealthy and subject to a concordat starting back in the twelfth century, exactly as we should expect if the incentives for or against prosperity incorporated within the terms of the concordats had the anticipated effect.

Figure 8.3 has shown us that having been rich during the interlude of the concordats by itself does not help us anticipate contemporary prosperity. Wealth today follows, at least in a correlational sense, from having been rich then *and* having been part of the deals that ended the Investiture Controversy. The evidence on contemporary prosperity goes even deeper. Recall that in Chapter 4 we looked at an alternative way to evaluate wealth. Using the UN Food and Agriculture Organization's estimate of the caloric potential of each diocese based on pre-Columbian crops, we saw that secularism went hand in hand both with the trade-route indicator of wealth and also with the caloric potential indicator. Subsequent wealth will surely have been helped if the land had a high productivity potential. That potential's existence was unaffected by the concordats; the concordats cannot have produced the land quality that enhanced the opportunity for wealth. It was simply an inherent characteristic of the soil and local climate. And indeed, land that had high potential then still has high agricultural potential today. Today's European countries whose average dioceses were above average in caloric potential at the time of the concordats in fact enjoy higher per capita incomes today. Still, knowledge of both caloric potential and trade-route prevalence gives us a way to probe the proposition that the concordats incentivized economic expansion and that it was the incentives created by the concordats, and not inherent land conditions, that distinguished those places in Europe that are doing exceptionally today from those that are not.

Figure 8.4 offers us a demanding way to use the two distinct indicators we have for measuring wealth at the time of the concordats. For this analysis, I pit caloric potential of land in *opposition* to trade-route placement, examining only those countries that have one but not the other.

With that in mind, let's divide today's countries into four groups: (1) those that scored above average on caloric potential but below average on trade-route persistence and were not covered by a concordat; (2) those that scored above average on caloric potential but below average on trade-route persistence and were covered by a concordat; (3) those that scored below average on caloric potential but above average on trade-route persistence and were not covered by a concordat; (4) those that scored below average on caloric potential

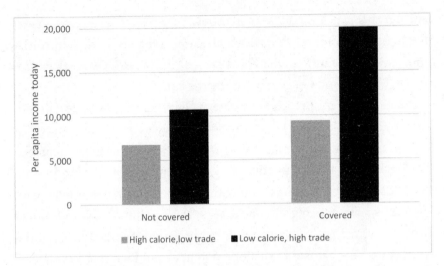

Figure 8.4: Prosperity today, caloric potential, or wealth creation and the concordats

but above average on trade-route persistence and were covered by a concordat. This fourfold division sets up what we might call a critical test, a test that separates the impact of the land's caloric potential from economic outcomes that are consistent with the incentives induced by the concordat game. The test is critical because the two indicators of wealth—caloric potential and trade-route prevalence—are pulling against each other. By making them work against each other, we can work out whether the inherent agricultural quality of the land (its caloric potential) or the diocesan policies that helped promote trade better explains which countries in Europe are relatively rich or relatively poor today, excluding those that were high on both caloric potential and trade-route prevalence or low on both.

If, on the one hand, the land's potential was driving wealth then and its benefits are still contributing to wealth today, and if, on the other hand, the strategically shaped source of wealth—trade routes—either depended on caloric potential or was and is irrelevant as a source of wealth, then what Figure 8.4 would show us is that, regardless of coverage under a concordat and regardless of differences in trade-route prevalence, where caloric potential was high, incomes should be high today, and where caloric potential was low, incomes today ought to be low. But this is not what the graph shows. On the contrary, it suggests that historical trade routes, which could be affected by the concordat game, are much more predictive of present-day wealth than caloric potential, which could not be affected by the concordat.

Per capita income in today's European countries over the past half century averaged only $6,734 for those places that had high caloric potential but low trade-route coverage if they were not subject to the concordats. The high calorie, low trade, covered countries over the half century from 1960 to 2018 had per capita incomes that averaged $9,324. For those with low caloric potential, high trade-route persistence but no coverage under a concordat, the per capita incomes in the period averaged $10,684. Finally, countries that had low caloric potential and high trade-route coverage and were signatories to a concordat—the set of countries we most care about—enjoyed per capita incomes that averaged $19,887.[10]

Although the number of countries in each of these four categories is necessarily small, the graph looks tantalizingly, but cautiously, like evidence that the concordat game is telling us the right story both about Europe's economic development hundreds of years ago and about differences in that development to this day. Naturally, agriculture is a much less important economic sector today than it was in the time of the concordats, and that might distort what we find. But also, the sorts of trade that went on before 1309 were very different from trade today, and there was then no trade with the Western Hemisphere and relatively limited trade—compared to today—with Asia. Agricultural production and trade-route considerations have both changed markedly since the time of the concordats. In either case, however, successful enterprise—whether trade or agricultural—was a source of growing wealth that could have carried forward to the present time. That the element that could be influenced strategically, trade, had the bigger lasting impact than the element that was inherent to the land, caloric potential, certainly encourages confidence in the strategic effects of the concordats in fostering exceptional economic growth in some parts of Europe and not in others.

Prosperity is important, but it is neither the only nor even the most important thing that matters for quality of life. We can ask the same question about wealth and participation in the concordats with regard to having become more democratic and thus more responsive to the interests of the citizens. I do so across two time spans: the one hundred years from World War I to 2018, and the fifty years from 1968 to 2018. Just picking a moment in time could mislead us. Almost all of western Europe today, for instance, is democratic. This is especially true among those countries that were subject to the deals back in 1107 and 1122, countries like Germany, Austria, France, Britain, Italy, the Netherlands, and Belgium. But many of these countries have had their ups and downs, as have those that did not fall within the rules put in motion by the concordats. Did the dioceses that today make up these countries do differently than the countries that were not covered by a concordat or than each other depending on how well they built up their wealth during the interlude of the concordats? Let's have a look.

Although just about every part of the world has faced government by monarchy, military rule, or authoritarianism at some point in history, western Europe's monarchs, especially among those whose kingdoms were covered by a concordat, began a concerted departure from absolutism and toward accountable government during the Middle Ages. In Chapter 7 we saw the evidence for that gradual shift toward accountability among concordat signatories. The acquiescence to parliamentary government that started during the centuries between the concordats and Luther's rebellion against the Catholic Church continued to gradually shift more say in government to more and more people. Of course, there were enormous challenges to this progression. Adolf Hitler's Germany and Benito Mussolini's Italy remind us that being party to a concordat did not assure a one-way linear progression to good government. Still, everything I have argued points the way to translating the incentives instigated by the concordats into conditions in the modern western European world.

The logic of the concordats, coupled with the logic of the negotiation process and the evidence we have already seen, tells us that where monarchs faced greater bargaining pressure from below, they tended to acquiesce in the creation of more accountable government. Figure 8.5 allows us to see how that pressure may have helped shape today's

Europe. Mindful of the anomalies of the 1930s and 1940s and beyond in the cases of Germany, Italy, Spain, Portugal, and much of eastern Europe, the figure assesses the average level of democracy or authoritarianism in each of Europe's countries from the end of World War I to 2018.[11] The two frames in the figure display the degree to which governments across Europe are rated as democratic or autocratic on average over the past century, tying those ratings to their membership in a concordat and their wealth or poverty in the Worms-to-Avignon interlude. The concordat game, our bargaining logic, and the evidence from the Middle Ages tell us that those lands that were covered by a concordat and were wealthy should have more accountable government today than those that were not covered by a concordat or those that were but were relatively poor, on average, in the twelfth to fourteenth centuries. That is just what we see in Figure 8.5.

The average level of democracy, as assessed on a 100-point scale where 100 is most democratic and 0 is least, over the hundred years from 1918 to 2018, is 84 among those dioceses that were covered by a concordat and were relatively wealthy during the concordat interlude. As we can see in the graph, the dark bars in the first panel are distributed around very high democracy scores. In comparison, those dioceses that were wealthy but not covered by a concordat (the white bars) averaged a democracy score of 70 during the past century, a difference that is not likely to be due to chance.[12] Shifting our attention to the second panel, four implications are evident. (1) A large batch of relatively poor places that were subject to a concordat—nearly two-thirds of such countries—have been highly democratic over the years from 1918 to 2018. (2) There is a consequential bloc of poor, covered countries that were not particularly democratic during the graph's time span. (3) Those poorer medieval places that were not covered by a concordat have been all over the map in terms of their recent governance, with some being pretty democratic and some leaning toward autocracy. (4) There is not a statistically meaningful difference in the contemporary governance scores for covered and uncovered poor countries.

The story is much the same if we repeat the above accountability/democracy exercise for Europe over the years from 1968 to 2018. The

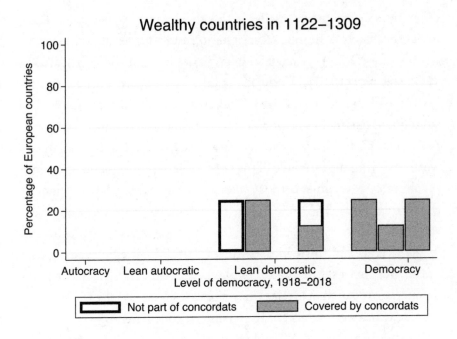

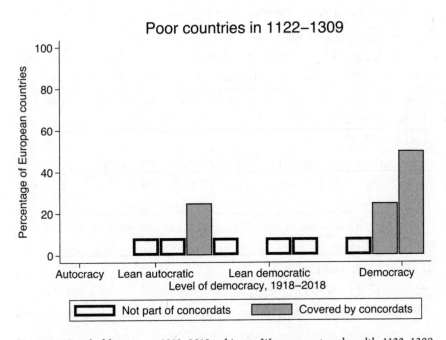

Figure 8.5: Level of democracy, 1918–2018, subject to Worms or not, and wealth, 1122–1309

differences in groups are smaller in this shorter interval because it elim-
inates the effects of Europe's fascist period and concentrates on a period
when western Europe, except for a few years in Spain and Portugal after
1968, was essentially entirely democratic and eastern Europe, following the collapse of the Soviet Union, saw a significant rise (and, alas,
subsequent decline) in democratic governance. As we have come to expect, those places that were subject to a concordat and became relatively
wealthy during the interlude of the treaties have more democratic, more
accountable governments today than those that were relatively poor in
the Middle Ages. The same holds true when we restrict our comparison to the relatively well-off in the Middle Ages. Those wealthy locales
in the twelfth and thirteenth centuries that did not enjoy the benefits
of the incentives set in motion by the concordats are significantly less
democratic today than locales whose dioceses were equally well-off economically but were subject to the terms of a concordat.

Prosperity and political freedom are two big prongs in any evaluation
of quality of life. A third prong is the opportunity to live a full, long,
healthy life, able to enjoy the benefits of freedom and prosperity. Finally, a fourth prong relates to the extent that one lives in a society that
minimizes corruption, instead valuing honesty and transparency. Have
the concordats, coupled with their favoring of secularism in wealthier
places, materially influenced personal longevity and government transparency today?

To capture a picture of how the opportunity for a long life in modern
Europe relates to the concordats and the incentives they generated—
depending on initial conditions and on church or monarchical dominance—we now take a look at life expectancy at birth. As before, we
gain a snapshot of the relevant comparison by examining the two graphs
in Figure 8.6. The first frame shows us the distribution of life expectancy among today's countries that were relatively rich in the Worms-
to-Avignon interlude depending on whether they were obliged to abide
by the terms of a concordat or not. The second frame repeats the process
but for today's countries whose dioceses in the Middle Ages were relatively poor and so more likely to be dominated by the church than by
their secular rulers.

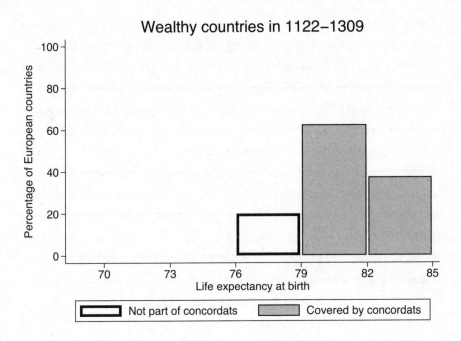

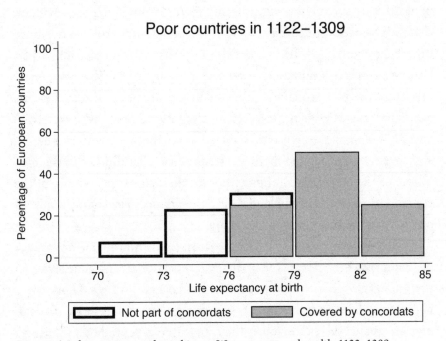

Figure 8.6: Life expectancy today, subject to Worms or not, and wealth, 1122–1309

Once again the evidence points in favor of the contention that having signed on to a concordat and having become wealthy and secular in the concordats interlude translates into longer life today. That conditions in the time of the concordats are predictive of contemporary longevity is particularly strong evidence for the lasting impact of those long-ago, obscure agreements.

The test against today's life expectancy at birth is a particularly tough test. Two factors, at least, make it so. The developments in medical technology are so enormous as to make the gulf between the twelfth century and today almost unfathomable. And the technology for saving and extending life, from basic improvements in sanitation and in sterilization to the introduction of vaccines, effective anesthetics, antibiotics, transplants, and genetic treatments, all spread rapidly. They become available to much of the world, at least to much of the well-to-do world, almost as soon as they are deemed safe and effective. Certainly in Europe, where even poorer places are relatively prosperous, life-saving improvements in health care spread like wildfire. And yet, as Figure 8.6 makes evident, there are meaningful differences in life expectancy today, and those differences coincide with medieval prosperity and the placement of a king's or emperor's signature on one of the concordats. The average life expectancy at birth today for then-wealthy countries that were concordat signatories is eighty-two years. It is eighty for those who were rich and did not sign a concordat, eighty-one for the poor who signed on, and seventy-eight for the medieval poor places that did not participate in one of the concordats. Those who put their signature on one of the concordats seem to have helped their descendants these many hundreds of years later to live a longer, better life.

Finally, in terms of life's quality, we turn to the prevalence or absence of corruption in society. Transparency International ranks countries on their honesty or corruption in business and other dealings. High scores here mean that the government is transparent and that business dealings are aboveboard. The lower the transparency score here, the worse the society's performance when it comes to transparency and honesty. Figure 8.7 tells us what we need to know.

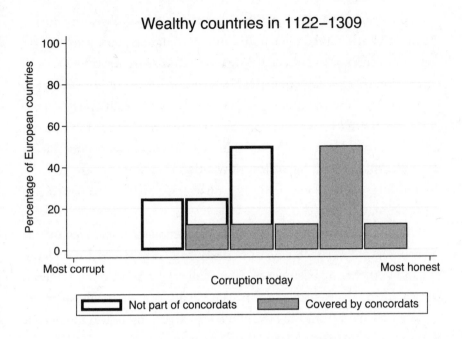

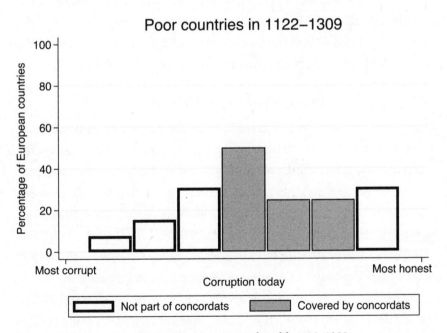

Figure 8.7: How corrupt, subject to Worms or not, and wealth, 1122–1309

Countries that were subject to a concordat and were wealthy during the period between the concordats and the Avignon papacy are significantly less corrupt today, according to the Transparency International corruption index, than countries that were wealthy but not subject to a concordat.[13] The wealthy signatory countries enjoy an average score of 72, compared to only 51 for those that were well-to-do then but were not covered by a concordat. Those countries that were poor during the concordat period, regardless of whether they were covered or not, do not differ much from each other, on average, when it comes to corruption today.

Better performance today, whether on per capita income, accountable government, life expectancy, or honesty and transparency, goes hand in hand with having been covered by a concordat and having achieved wealth during the twelfth and thirteenth centuries. Those whose predecessors benefited from the advantageous bargaining power created by the concordats continue to reap rewards to this day. Those whose predecessors did not, either because they were not signatories or because they were too poor to secure the bargaining leverage to control the policies within their domain, continue to lag behind on quality of life to our time!

INNOVATION AND DISCOVERY

Prosperity, democracy, and transparency are hallmarks of Western exceptionalism that seem to have been advanced thanks to the concordats. Each of these benchmarks of social success is also a potential source of inventiveness and creativity. They are not, of course, the sole province of Western societies. Many parts of the globe have joined Europe on several of these dimensions, to their benefit and the benefit of all of us. Parts of Asia, in particular, have begun to embrace the competitive spirit implied by the pursuit of prosperity, democracy, and transparency.

Although Europe's economic growth has been on an almost ineluctable upward trajectory for a thousand years, recall that we saw in Chapter 1, from the Maddison Project data, that western Europe was in economic decline for substantial portions of the first thousand years of the Common Era. That should serve as a reminder that nothing is inevitable in politics or economics. Fortunes may reverse, and we would do well to consider that when we reflect on what western Europe did "right" and on how what it did might be adopted and adapted to the rest of the planet. The recent record of patent filings, for instance, may give one pause in being overly celebratory regarding Europe's trajectory, still impressive though it is.

Looking at patent applications per million population tells both an encouraging story and a cautionary tale for those who celebrate Western culture.[14] On the plus side for exceptionalists, western Europe and its settler offshoot the United States include seven of the ten most inventive countries in the world. Indeed, if we were to expand our count to the top twenty countries, then the West occupies thirteen of those spots. And it is worth observing that while signatories to the concordats cover, in whole or in part, 30 percent of the countries in today's Europe, twice that, 62 percent of the thirteen top European innovating countries, were subject to the rules put in place in 1122. Coincidence? Maybe, but the evidence we have explored makes it hard to sustain the view that the outstanding record of those places that were covered by the concordats is just due to chance.

Clearly, the West continues to be remarkably innovative and inventive compared to most of the world. But it is not alone at the top any more. Korea, Japan, and China hold three of the four lead positions, with Switzerland also in the top four. If we look at a longer period, we see that the Republic of Korea and China have both shot up in patent filings in the past decade or so (although we must be cautious as the methodology behind China's reporting was different from that of the rest of the world before 2017). However sliced, there seems to be no doubt that while the Western world continues to be highly innovative, those parts of Asia that have adopted Western economic models of relatively competitive markets are outshining the "exceptional" Western inventors, with those that have chosen to implement both European-style regulated, competitive markets and competitive, accountable politics—Korea and Japan—leading the list. Maybe the great benefits of competition for money and for power are now helping propel other parts of the globe forward, just as they did for parts of Europe in the two hundred years between the signing of the first concordat and the start of the Avignon papacy.

Whatever the future may hold, we have seen that the past's regulation of competition for political power and policy control proved beneficial for those in the 1100s who were well positioned to exploit that regulated, structured competition. And, as we have learned, by encouraging secularism and economic growth, the concordats helped defeat the church as a political power. In doing so, the concordats also weakened the church's ability to restrict, for instance, the pursuit of knowledge and science. That tremendous benefit of the concordats can be readily seen by taking a look at the distribution of Nobel Prizes in physics, chemistry, physiology or medicine, and economics. It would be perfectly reasonable to believe that the extraordinary creativity and innovativeness required to win a Nobel in one of the sciences has to do with the presumably random distribution of extremely smart people. But the evidence tells us otherwise.

Figure 8.8 repeats the analytic process we have been following. The graph's two frames display the number of Nobel Prizes in the sciences per million population based on two considerations: Was the country where the recipient did her or his Nobel research covered by a concordat? And was it relatively wealthy or relatively poor in the Worms-to-Avignon interlude? It seems incredibly surprising to contemplate that the highest quality of research, research worthy of a Nobel, has been in any way influenced by decisions made by popes and kings nine hundred years ago. Yet the figures could not tell a clearer story. As we have come to expect, countries that were relatively wealthy between 1122 and 1309 and were subject to a concordat outperform all other types of countries in winning Nobel's for science subjects. These top-performing countries win 1.07 Nobels in a science field per million population on average (with a high of 2.32 and a low of 0.25). In comparison, wealthy nonsignatories have only averaged 0.035 such Nobel prizes. Remember, this analysis is per million population, so every country's scientists have, in that sense, an equal chance. The difference is so large that it is very unlikely to be random.[15] The average number of science Nobel's in countries that were relatively poor during the concordat interlude but had signed on to a concordat is 0.67 per million. For those that had not

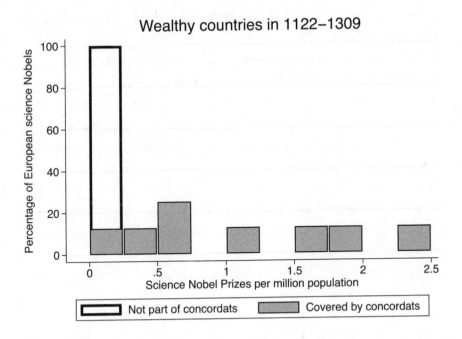

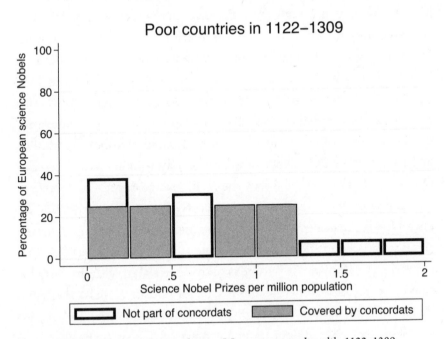

Figure 8.8: Nobel Prizes in science, subject to Worms or not, and wealth, 1122–1309

signed on to a concordat but were poor, the average number of science Nobel's is 0.68 per million.

We should look at the evidence on science Nobels both as encouraging for the thesis proposed by the concordat game and as a cautiously interpreted set of results. While the intellectual ability and creativity needed to win a science Nobel may be randomly distributed across Europe, a country's contemporary wealth is a powerful predictor of its odds of hosting the winner of such a prestigious award. Especially in the experimental sciences, laboratories are extremely expensive and so are dependent on contemporary wealth. Thus, the distribution of today's national GDPs per capita is a powerful indicator of a country's chances of being home to a science Nobel winner. But as we have seen, variation in contemporary per capita incomes is readily tied back to variations in the strategic setting created by the concordats in the twelfth century.

The picture for Nobel Prizes per million population in the humanities is different, although the differences across contemporary country categories are less stark. The distribution of winners for literature or for peace skew in favor of those whose work was done in countries that were not above average in trade-route prevalence between 1122 (or 1107 for England and France) and 1309 without regard to whether those countries signed a concordat. There are no statistically meaningful differences in the average number of humanity Nobels per million population as a consequence of wealth or commitment to a concordat. One explanation might be that the facilities and resources needed to win a humanities Nobel are just less costly than those needed for science Nobels, making the sources of contemporary wealth irrelevant. Against this proposition, however, is the fact that today's per capita income distribution across Europe is highly correlated with the distribution of humanities Nobels just as is true for science Nobels. There may be lots of explanations for the distribution of humanities Nobels. We simply cannot be confident about any one explanation for the variation in the distribution of these prizes.

I could, of course, go on with many other indicators of high performance today tied to bargaining leverage in the time of the concordats.

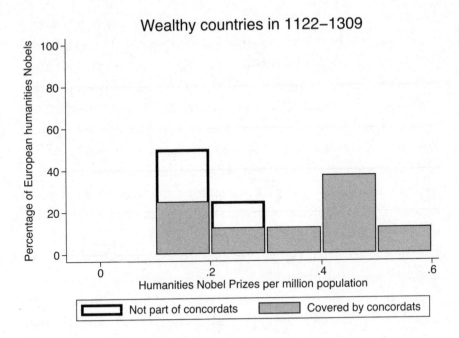

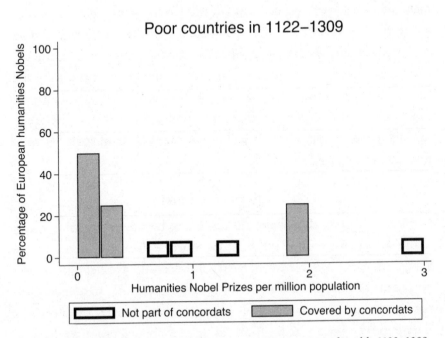

Figure 8.9: Nobel prizes in the humanities, subject to Worms or not, and wealth, 1122–1309

As I illustrated in Chapter 1, we see the same general pattern when we examine contemporary labor policy decisions, such as the average number of weeks per year that people work. This too is strongly associated with having been wealthy and covered by a concordat those many centuries ago. Why are these patterns so persistent? What is it about these more exceptional parts of Europe today that has made them stand out? What about these successful countries has led many to point to them as proof of Western exceptionalism? Why have these countries been especially good at creating prosperity, democracy and freedom, good health and longevity, tolerance, inventiveness, and just about any other indicator of a high quality of life?

I argued that a root element behind their exceptionalism is the fact that they were parties to an obscure agreement signed on September 23, 1122.[16] The evidence we have seen that the conditions of the concordat should have predicted—and apparently did predict—Europe's differentiation along the dimensions of prosperity, free and accountable government, good health, tolerance, and inventiveness encourages me now to probe what it was specifically about the Concordat of Worms and its two predecessors that created the legacy that the evidence has uncovered. Answering that probe, we can then conclude by evaluating the lessons that all of us, whatever part of the world we live in, can take away from the concordats in thinking about how to realize the benefits and avoid the pitfalls that lie behind the success of some parts of Europe as compared to others.

INSIGHTS FOR TODAY

Nothing was inevitable about the success of Europe or any of its parts at the start of the second millennium. Europe then was economically a laggard. Any observer in the year 1000 would have bet against the kingdoms of Europe so transforming themselves that people a thousand years later, in our time, would speak of those parts of Europe as "exceptional." There was just nothing special about Europe or Europeans. Nothing impressive stood out in the quality of their monarchies, the quality of their health, their inventiveness, or anything else. Europe's economic performance stood out, but not in a desirable way. The average European's income had been falling for centuries, and no reversal in their misery was in sight.

True, the Commercial Revolution was just beginning, but as we saw, its effects were not uniformly distributed across Europe. As with incomes, working hours, life expectancy at birth today, and so much more, the impact of the Commercial Revolution that began around 950, long before the concordats, was most keenly realized in those parts of Europe that were subject to the terms of the agreements in 1107 and 1122. The kingdoms that the concordats put in a more competitive setting in their struggle to gain political leverage against the interests of the church enjoyed a much more rapid and dramatic expansion of secularism-induced trade or trade-induced secularism than did the rest of Europe. Those kingdoms that secured a competitive advantage against the church in promoting secularly driven policy control grew economically more than the rest of Europe. Indeed, the advantages to growth conveyed by the concordats could be seen even when we broke kingdoms down to the level of the individual dioceses in Europe. Secular rulers secured greater political leverage directly from the change in policy over the allocation of regalian revenue thanks to the new ideas promulgated by the concordats.

Before the concordats, the great battle that raged across a large part of Europe involved unfettered, disorderly, sometimes murderous competition between popes and kings. That unruly competition between the secular and the sacred swords had little to do with religious faith. By the time of the Investiture Controversy, just about every kingdom in every corner of Europe had embraced Catholicism as the one true path to eternal salvation. The battle was not about religion; it was about political power and political control through the sacred and secular levers available to the Catholic Church and lay leaders. The struggle was settled by working out a way to trade power for money and money for power. Power on earth was to be rendered unto Caesar, and money on earth was to be rendered unto God's vicars in exchange for a portion, at least, of their secular power.

Bishops were central to the church's political reach beyond its religious mission. Bishops could be the policy agents of the pope and his church, they could be the agents of the local Catholic community, or they could be the agents of the local lord or king. Which role they played mattered a great deal. Each bishop "was a focal point for the flock, the local ecclesiastics and the pope, the aristocracy and the ruler; his election was of great interest to many people."[17] Yet no orderly process had been agreed to for the selection of these incredibly important people. The concordats signed in England and France and in the city of Worms resolved that problem. They established an orderly process that kings and popes could and did accept, albeit with much coercion and subterfuge.

The deal that was struck acknowledged, however unconsciously, a feature of European politics that made Europe different from much of the rest of the world. The concordats admitted that power was more or less equally divided between the secular sword wielded by kings and the sacred sword wielded by popes and the church. The haphazard, highly variable procedures for electing bishops—even the bishop of bishops, the pope in Rome—had produced disastrous consequences for everyone. Popes were vulnerable to being deposed by emperors. Emperors were vulnerable to being condemned and excommunicated by popes. Ordinary people did not know where to turn to assure their pathway to heaven. Were they to do the bidding of their local bishop, who might have been the choice of the pope or who might have bought his post, either from the local metropolitan bishop or from a secular lord? Were they to listen to the pope, who might have been elected by church leaders, might have been imposed by the Holy Roman emperor, might be an antipope, or might have secured the position through the pressure and nepotistic power of his family? These and other critical elements in managing the sacred and the secular were at loggerheads and needed to be resolved.

Following decades of struggle, the church and the leading secular rulers in Europe came to terms over how to manage their power struggle and its manifestation through the appointment of bishops. They settled the selection of bishops by constructing a balancing act between the authority of kings and the authority of the church. That balancing act gave advantages to rulers in wealthy places and to the church in poor places. Popes quickly grasped that their power could be better secured by keeping as many dioceses as possible relatively poor. Kings just as quickly realized that their power could be better secured and expanded by making more of the dioceses within their realm wealthier. With these realizations moved front and center by the terms of the concordats, the struggle to make parts of Europe more secular, richer, and more innovative was underway. Modern Europe was the result.

What lessons can the rest of the world take from the seemingly unique struggle between church and state in the twelfth century? Several lessons remain pertinent and instructive today. Of course, the specifics of the Investiture Controversy and the concordats will never be repeated, but the general thrust behind their particulars are everywhere to be seen and grappled with.

Europe's "exceptionalism" was launched by the recognition that there was competition between the secular and the sacred and that competition needed to be orderly, institutionalized, and managed by creating a space for bargaining rather than waging a winner-take-all fight. Today, there are parts of the world that are dominated by secular governance, and there are others under religious rule, each with little regard for the relevance of the other. Marxist societies, such as the old Soviet Union, fall into the antireligious camp. Many Islamic countries today fall into the antisecular camp. None perform well on behalf of their people when it comes to the series of indicators of a good life that we just reviewed. Each stifles ideas and innovations that question or try to compete with the ruling authorities. These winner-take-all societies follow a recipe for rule that limits innovation in ideas and institutions. It is great for the rulers, whether they be religious or secular, but it is generally miserable for the citizenry.

When the sacred and the secular levers of influence are mixed and coexist, each competing with the other for priority in shaping the institutions that regulate their competition, then the exceptional benefits that parts of Europe most enjoy today and that arose thanks to the rules and pressures of the concordats will probably be realized elsewhere as well. All societies seem to do well that respect Friedrich Hayek's advice in the epigraph to Chapter 6: "The spiritual and the temporal are different spheres which ought not to be confused."[18] Indeed, if we look at religiosity indicators around the world and their correlation with per capita incomes, we see what happens when they are confused. The most religious societies, the ones that most allow religious precepts to dictate secular choices and governance, tend to do poorly on critical indicators of prosperity, longevity, education, or innovation, especially if we take into account whether they have artificial access to wealth through the luck of oil or diamonds or gold in the ground.

Secular governments that respect and tolerate competing religious precepts seem to avoid doctrinaire views getting in the way of producing an exceptional quality of life for their citizens. Such societies thrive on competition, whether over religious beliefs, scientific inquiry, artistic endeavors, economic practices, or governance. Indeed, those contemporary European countries that lean least in support of a large role for religion in the secular side of society while respecting religious institutions as sources of judgment about good, ethical behavior are the very ones that were signatories to a concordat and were wealthy and so headed toward greater secularism in the Middle Ages.[19] And, as we have seen, these are the countries that are doing best today and that most closely follow Hayek's advice, recognizing, tolerating, and respecting diverse religions in their sacred function and doing the same for government in its secular role. Each competes with the other in a setting that carefully defines and draws lines between their respective spheres.

Europe's long-term benefits from the deal signed in Worms depended to a significant degree on the incentives the concordats created to generate prosperity by rewarding people for their hard work and productivity. Economic growth had not been the pathway by which rulers became rich before the time of the concordats. Neither had economic growth been the pathway through which many people, whether farmers, laborers, or lords, had begun to become rich. The world before the concordats was a predatory, confiscatory world. Conquest, mayhem, looting, pillaging, ransoming, and marrying for money were the pathways to personal economic success. Improved economic productivity was on almost no one's radar. While war and marriage made some well-off, they were not routes to success for society as a whole. Instead, economic competition, regulated capitalism, fettered by the need for political compromise between rulers and their productive subjects, inspired an intense work ethic, expanded economies, and improved life slowly, in fits and starts, for those people lucky enough to be in the parts of Europe best positioned to exploit the new incentives engendered by the concordats.

Economic competition, constrained by concern for social coherence, a constraint brought on by reliance on an expanded winning coalition, is no less important today than it was in the interlude of the concordats. Personalist governments, ruled by cultish dictators or by monarchs, almost always fail today to produce successful societies that people want to live in, stay in, or move to. Those governments that emulate the economic lessons of the concordats, the lessons of regulated, competitive capitalism and a politically empowered public, are the places that are doing and will do best. No one was really eager to make political bargains in the Middle Ages, and no one is eager to do so today. Rather, we are all interested in doing what is best for us. But the concordats compelled bargaining as the way to manage the fierce competition that Europe endured before the agreements of the twelfth century. Government policy can help sustain the same sort of healthy, regulated competition today by not favoring one party over another, not predetermining winners and losers, just as the concordats were intended to balance, not favor, the interests of kings or of popes. Reliance on a large governing coalition is *the* path to government that works as an agent for sustained, healthy competition.

The economic competition that generated prosperity across societies was structured in particular by the creation of accountable government. Europe's monarchs did not choose to be accountable; they did not crave the opinions or the constraints imposed on them by laborers, farmers, merchants, clerics, or the lesser nobility. Rather, they understood that their own ability to survive in power depended on making deals with all those groups of interests. Those who failed to do so, as we have now seen, were more quickly ousted from office. Political survival in the age of the concordats demanded that every aspect of governance be limited so that no one group could rule just for its own interests. This lesson is no less critical today. The wealthiest places in the world, almost without exception, rely on a government that is dependent on a large, democratically chosen winning coalition; the poorest places on earth almost never rely on accountable government. And as we have seen, accountable government encourages not only productivity and good health but also innovation and creativity. Take a look at a list of the one hundred or two hundred or four hundred best universities in the world. Where are they? Overwhelmingly in places that have followed the incentives set into motion by the concordats. They are in democratic, competitive, prosperous societies, especially those that in fact were subject to one of the concordats or, in the case of settler outposts, transported the concordat-inspired institutions to their territory.

The road to a better world is not terribly complicated. It is not mysterious. It is not unknown. Democracy—dependence on a large winning coalition—combined with regulated, constrained economic competition, institutionalized distinctions between the secular and the sacred, each powerful in its own domain and each open to competition by the other, makes for tolerant, innovative, prosperous, healthy, free societies. That is what the concordats produced; that is what made Western exceptionalism; and that is what can be and, by my lights, should be repeated everywhere, in all times. That is the way to make everyone's opportunity for a great life, exceptional. That is the great, enduring lesson of and contribution to modern exceptionalism made by the Concordats of London, Paris, and Worms.

ACKNOWLEDGMENTS

This has been a project a great many years in the making. I have accumulated debts to so many colleagues, friends, students, and family members that I must begin by apologizing for anyone I have neglected to thank. Everyone who listened to, complained about, or offered suggestions to me has my unending appreciation. I particularly want to single out those people whose assistance and comments have been especially important.

My literary agent, Eric Lupfer, has believed in this project even longer than I have! As always, he has been great. I am very appreciative as well of the support and encouragement given to me by Ben Adams, Clive Priddle, and all the team at PublicAffairs Press. Ben, in particular, provided enormously helpful feedback as the manuscript developed. He made it a better book! Michelle Welsh-Horst did an exceptional job overseeing the editorial production, and Kathy Delfosse did a superb job as copyeditor, greatly clarifying and tightening my writing. Thank you all!

I am most grateful to Nathaniel Beck, Ethan Bueno de Mesquita, Sanford Gordon, Jonathan Grady, Eleanor and Sam Gubins, Rose McDermott, Cary Nederman, Adam Przeworski, Shanker Satyanath, Randolph Siverson, Alastair Smith, David Stasavage, and Thomas Zeitzoff for their willingness to listen to me go on endlessly about the Concordat of Worms and, more important, to provide valuable feedback that made the project better. Parts of Chapters 3 and 4 are the offshoots of collaborative work on a part of this project with my son, Ethan Bueno de Mesquita. We both took advantage of the useful feedback provided to us on that portion of the project by Scott Ashworth, Chris Berry, Wioletta Dziuda, Mark Fey, Alexander Fouirnaies, Anthony Fowler, James Robinson, Nico Voigtlaender, Austin Wright, and seminar participants at the University of Chicago, the American Political Science Association annual meetings, the Political Institutions and Economic Policy conference at Harvard University, and the participants at the Duke University Hayek Lecture series and from discussion with Professor Alex Rosenberg—my friend since fifth grade—who arranged for my presentation at Duke. I have also been helped by expert guidance provided by Archbishop Roland Minnerath.

I received extraordinary research assistance from Tristan Baylor, Dan Chambers, Sasha Daich, Katie Jagel, Caleb Lewis, Matt Osubor, Boris Paunovic, Andrew Peterson, Yada Pruksachatkun, Isabella Schumann, Orion Junius Tayler, Marija Vujic, Winnie Wang, and Ga Young You.

Everyone in the Department of Politics at NYU has been a source of support and encouragement throughout this project. I do not think it is possible to be part of a more congenial department. I additionally received generous support, encouragement, and insights from members of NYU's Art History Department. I am especially grateful to Professors Miriam M. Basilio, Carol Krinsky, and Kathryn A. Smith for providing excellent guidance and criticism on the art history aspects of this project. I benefited as well from comments on a presentation I made to the NYU Art History Department.

Additionally, I want to remember my late, beloved mentor, Abramo Fimo Kenneth Organski, and his wonderful brother, Guido. I began to discuss the ideas for this book with them in the late 1990s. I believe the book has benefited greatly from their vigorous arguments with each other over the ideas that were then just starting to develop for *The Invention of Power*.

Of course, none of these good people are responsible for any factual or analytic errors I have committed. Additionally, many colleagues have encouraged me and provided me with additional data. Alas, I have not been able to use all of it, but all of it was greatly appreciated. I am especially grateful to Leandro De Magalhaes, David Stasavage, Fabian Wahl, and Yuhua Wang for their encouragement and help on this front.

Throughout this very long project I benefited from the support of my family, especially my wife Arlene, to whom this book is most gratefully and lovingly dedicated; our children Erin, Ethan, and Gwen and their patient and tolerant spouses, Jason Wright, Rebecca Milder, and Adam Edgell-Bush; my sisters, Mireille Bany and Judy Berton, and my brother-in-law, Steven Steiner; and all of their extended families. I truly missed no opportunity to talk to captive audiences about this project. My grandchildren listened with varying degrees of interest, patience, tolerance, and bemusement. I thank Nathan, Clara, Abraham, Hannah, Isidore, and Otis for bringing me so much joy.

NOTES

Chapter 1: Exceptionalism

1. Quotations from the New Testament are from the King James Version. Quotations from the Old Testament are from *The Holy Scriptures According to the Masorertic Text* (Philadelphia: Jewish Publication Society of America, 1917; forty-first impression, September 1958). I include Western Europe and its settler offshoots in the term "West." The claims for exceptionalism are readily supported by the ranking of nations on, for instance, the World Bank's Development Indicators, the World Happiness Report, Freedom House's country scores, Polity country scores, and many other widely respected sources.

2. Henrich, *The WEIRDest People in the World.*

3. Rubin, *Rulers, Religion and Riches.*

4. Weber, *The Protestant Ethic.*

5. A comparable agreement was reached by Pope Paschal II in 1107 with the kings of England and France. Those earlier deals differed from the Concordat of Worms in ways that are not important for the investigation conducted here. See, for instance, Sweeney and Chodorow, *Popes, Teachers, and Canon Law,* 14.

6. The per capita income values are from the World Bank Development Indicators, 2019, the most current year as of this writing. "GDP Per Capita (Current US$)," World Bank Group, https://data.worldbank.org/indicator/NY.GDP.PCAP.CD. Data for labor/leisure time are from the Organization for Economic Cooperation and Development (OECD) for 2018/2019. "Average Annual Hours Actually Worked per Worker," OECD.Stat, https://stats.oecd.org/Index.aspx?DataSetCode=ANHRS.

7. See Henrich, *The WEIRDest People in the World,* for a more psychological, less strategic view.

8. Lopez, *The Birth of Europe;* Lopez, *Commercial Revolution;* Cantoni, Dittmar, and Yuchtman, "Religious Competition and Reallocation"; Weber *The Protestant Ethic.*

9. See Nick Pisa, "Oldest Image of St Paul Discovered," *Telegraph,* June 28, 2009, www.telegraph.co.uk/news/worldnews/europe/vaticancityandholysee/5675461/Oldest-image-of-St-Paul-discovered.html, and Wikipedia, s.v. "Catacomb of St. Theresa," accessed June 8, 2021, https://en.wikipedia.org/wiki/Catacomb_of_Saint_Thecla, for reports of the

discovery of the fourth-century frescoes of Saint Peter and Saint Paul in the Catacomb of Saint Thecla.

10. See Wikipedia, s.v. "Colossus of Constantine," accessed June 8, 2021, https://en .wikipedia.org/wiki/Colossus_of_Constantine.

11. For a sample of investigations into global historical developments, see, for instance, Toynbee, *A Study of History*; William McNeill, *The Rise of the West*; William McNeill, *The Global Condition*; Levi, *Of Rule and Revenue*; Diamond, *Guns, Germs and Steel*; Dincecco and Wang, "Violent Conflict and Political Development"; Stasavage, *The Decline and Rise of Democracy*.

12. Bolt and van Zanden, "The Maddison Project."

13. See the Maddison Project, Maddison Project Database, releases of 2010, 2013, and 2018, Jutta Bolt, Robert Inklaar, Herman de Jong, and Jan Luiten van Zanden, available for download at www.rug.nl/ggdc/historicaldevelopment/maddison/releases. Income estimates are in inflation-adjusted, constant dollars, also often referred to as real dollars.

14. All of Maddison's 2010 data series on per capita income are adjusted for inflation and estimated based on 2005 dollars.

15. Hobbes, *Leviathan*, 89.

16. The difficulties that Europe experienced between the collapse of Rome in 476 and the start of the second millennium challenge many of the ideas in works by people like Stark, *How the West Won*, or Henrich, *The WEIRDest People in the World*.

17. Henrich, *The WEIRDest People in the World*; Nixey, *The Darkening Age*.

18. For a clever attempt at working through terms of marriage as a critical social and organizational factor across at least some parts of the medieval world outside of Christian Europe, see Henrich, *The WEIRDest People in the World*.

19. McLynn, *Genghis Khan*, 111.

CHAPTER 2: TWO SWORDS, ONE CHURCH

1. Norwich, *Byzantium*, 356.

2. Mann, *The Lives of the Popes*, vol. 1, 191–192.

3. Lord Acton to Bishop Mandell Creighton, April 5, 1887, in Dalberg-Acton, *Historical Essays and Studies*.

4. See Eugenius Vulgarius, *De Causa Formosiana*, as discussed in Wikipedia, s.v. "Eugenius Vulgarius," accessed June 8, 2021, https://en.wikipedia.org/wiki/Eugenius_Vulgarius.

5. Mann, *The Lives of the Popes*, vol. 4, *The Popes in the Days of Feudal Anarchy*, 163–164.

6. Mann, *The Lives of the Popes*, vol. 4, *The Popes in the Days of Feudal Anarchy*, 119.

7. The graph is based on a statistical model that explains the variation in the observed degrees of nepotism based on the quarter century, the quarter century squared, and cubed. The details are reported in the online appendix at https://wp.nyu.edu/brucebuenodemesquita /books/.

8. Rouche, "The Early Middle Ages," 529.

9. For a technical account, including formal proofs, see Bueno de Mesquita, Smith, Siverson, and Morrow, *The Logic of Political Survival*. For a nontechnical account see Bueno de Mesquita and Smith, *The Dictator's Handbook*.

10. Peltzer, *Canon Law, Careers and Conquest*, 1.

11. Hallam, *View of the State of Europe*, 279; Costigan, "State Appointment of Bishops."

12. Melve, *Inventing the Public Sphere*.

13. Lynch and Adamo, *The Medieval Church*, 156.

14. Poole, *Benedict IX and Gregory VI*.

15. Poole, *Benedict IX and Gregory VI*, 10.

16. See Specht and Fischer, "Vergiftungsnachweis an den Resten einer 900 Jahre alten Leiche," and Emsley, *The Elements of Murder*, 317.

17. Epistle of Ignatius to the Magnesians, quoted in Wikipedia, s.v. "Vicar of Christ," accessed June 8, 2021, https://en.wikipedia.org/wiki/Vicar_of_Christ.

18. Quoted in Melve, *Inventing the Public Sphere*, 151.

19. Quoted in Melve, *Inventing the Public Sphere*, 158.

20. Quoted in Melve, *Inventing the Public Sphere*, 164.

21. Schimmelpfennig, *The Papacy*, 133.

22. Colomer and McLean, "Electing Popes"; Schwartzberg, *Counting the Many*.

23. Quoted in Melve, *Inventing the Public Sphere*, 143n117. For the influential life of Abbot Abbo of Fleury, see Lutz, *Schoolmasters of the Tenth Century*; Maitland, *Constitutional History of England*, 43–50.

24. Nixey, *The Darkening Age*.

25. Schimmelpfennig, *The Papacy*, 138.

26. Poole, "Names and Numbers."

27. See Maureen Miller, quoted in Körntgen and Waenhoven, *Religion and Politics*; Leyser, "Crisis of Medieval Germany."

28. Schimmelpfennig, *The Papacy*, 135.

29. Quoted in Morris, *The Papal Monarchy*, 127.

30. Prutz and Wright, *Age of Feudalism and Theocracy*; Melve, *Inventing the Public Sphere*.

31. Guido of Ferrara, *On Hildebrand's Schism: For and Against Him*, in "The Age of Gregory VII, 1073–85: Extracts from Two Anti-Gregorian Tracts," translated by Peter Llewellyn, introduction and abridgement by G. A. Lord, accessed June 8, 2021, http://legalhistorysources.com/Canon%20Law/GregorianReform/PeterCrassusTreatise.html. Guido's tract was written circa 1086 or possibly earlier while Gregory was still alive.

32. Kantorowicz, *The King's Two Bodies*; Schimmelpfennig, *The Papacy*; Melve, *Inventing the Public Sphere*.

33. Eusebius, *Life of Constantine*, 70.

34. Nixey, *The Darkening Age*.

35. Kleiner, *Gardner's Art Through the Ages*; Honour and Fleming, *The Visual Arts*; Janson and Janson, *History of Art*, rev. 5th ed. and 6th ed.

36. To estimate the relative prevalence of secular versus Christian art, I asked art history students to code the images of European art based on whether their primary subject matter was Christian (including, for instance, images of popes, bishops, angels, saints, Jesus, apostles, Bible stories, or other clearly Christian subjects) or non-Christian (such as representations of kings, princes, other secular leaders, landscapes, castles, folk characters, or Greek or Roman mythological characters). They did so for the period from 300 to 1700 CE. I am grateful to Professor Carol Krinsky in New York University's Art History Department for several interesting and important arguments about the differential survival of religious and secular art. In particular, one might reasonably object to the indicator I am using to estimate changes in church power by arguing, for instance, that secular art was less likely to survive in the long interlude following the Council of Nicaea and the rise of the Holy Roman Empire (and beyond) simply because churches were less likely to be destroyed by war or even fire than secular repositories

of art. This argument, however, is problematic. Of course, we must acknowledge that Christians openly, explicitly, and mostly without retribution set out to destroy non-Christian images as a matter of policy as soon as they were a recognized religion in the Roman Empire. They could not have done so without at least tacit political approval and without the power to cow secular rulers into granting that approval. However, if the proliferation of churches enhanced the survival of religious art but not secular or non-Christian art, then we must provide an explanation for the survival of a significant amount of secular art from the fourth and fifth centuries and from much earlier than that but not, for example, from the ninth or tenth. Even a brief excursion through any major art museum, say the Metropolitan Museum of Art in New York, will reveal room after room of magnificent artwork from pharaonic Egypt, ancient Greece, and other early civilizations from all around the globe. Yet the post–Roman Empire collections will almost always be filled with religious art and only very limited quantities of secular art for those regions in which the Catholic Church was the monopoly provider of salvation. It defies reason to believe, for instance, that sculptures from 5000 BCE survived more readily than sculptures of kings in the early Middle Ages by chance, as distinct from by political design. And we must also explain why secular art began to become more prominent or simply to survive better following the eleventh century, even though there were no technological improvements that favored secular artwork over religious artwork. It is true that castle construction, for example, turned away from wood and toward stone around the twelfth century, but so too did church construction. Additionally, we cannot argue that religious art was better protected simply because it was thought of as more important than secular art without then also conceding that the relative frequency of such art is a reasonable indicator of the relative clout of the Roman church and the secular world of Catholic Europe. And we must acknowledge that the eighth-century Iconoclast Movement lasted a few decades and aimed its efforts explicitly at destroying Christian images. Later iconoclast movements, such as during the French Revolution, were aimed at destroying images of France's monarchs, but also at suppressing the church and its imagery. Thus, the deck seems not to have been stacked in favor of the survival of religious imagery over the time span seen in Figure 2.4 or, indeed, even earlier.

37. Robinson, "The Church and the Order Clericorum," 253.

38. See "Medieval Sourcebook: Henry IV: Letter to Gregory VII, Jan 24 1076," Internet History Sourcebooks Project, Fordham University Center for Medieval Studies, https://sourcebooks.fordham.edu/source/henry4-to-g7a.asp. For an excellent dissection and analysis of the letter, see Melve, *Inventing the Public Sphere*, 202–207.

39. Melve, *Inventing the Public Sphere*; Browne, "The Pactum Callixtinum"; Leyser, "England and the Empire"; Leyser, "Crisis of Medieval Germany."

CHAPTER 3: THE CONCORDAT GAME

1. Sweeney and Chodorow, *Popes, Teachers, and Canon Law*, 14.

2. Portions of this chapter are derived from my paper, coauthored with Ethan Bueno de Mesquita, "From Investiture to Worms." Other, significant, portions of this chapter represent new analysis.

3. Sweeney and Chodorow, *Popes, Teachers, and Canon Law*; Baldwin, *Government of Philip Augustus*, 62–66; Abbot Suger, *Life of King Louis the Fat*, Internet History Sourcebooks Project, Fordham University Center for Medieval Studies, https://sourcebooks.fordham.edu/basis/suger-louisthefat.asp. All quotations from Abbot Suger are from this source.

4. Huffman, *Social Politics of Medieval Diplomacy*, 40.

5. For the full account of the meeting and much more, see Suger, *Life of King Louis the Fat*, esp. chap. 10.

6. Browne, "The Pactum Calixtum," 184; Sweeney and Chodorow, *Popes, Teachers, and Canon Law*, 3–25.

7. Browne, "The Pactum Calixtum," 184; Sweeney and Chodorow, *Popes, Teachers, and Canon Law*, 3–25.

8. Benson, *Bishop-Elect*, "The Church and the Regalia," 303–334.

9. "Documents Relating to the War of the Investitures: Concordat of Worms; September 23, 1122," Avalon Project, Yale Law School, https://avalon.law.yale.edu/medieval/inv16 .asp. A translation of the concordat also appears in Henderson, *Select Historical Documents*, 408–409.

10. Chodorow, "Paschal II, Henry V, and the Crisis of 1111," 14.

11. Council of Chalcedon, canon 3, Early Church Texts, https://earlychurchtexts.com /public/chalcedon_canons.htm.

12. Kantorowicz, *The King's Two Bodies*.

13. Benson, *Bishop-Elect*, 305.

14. Browne, "The Pactum Calixtinum," 186.

15. Sweeney and Chodorow, *Popes, Teachers, and Canon Law*, 14.

16. Quoted in Benson, *Bishop-Elect*, 305.

17. Carlyle and Carlyle, *History of Medieval Political Theory*, esp. 165–210.

18. Quoted in Benson, *Bishop-Elect*, 314.

19. Benson, *Bishop-Elect*, 282, 309.

20. Benson, *Bishop-Elect*, 312.

21. Benson, *Bishop-Elect*, 304.

22. Council of Chalcedon, canon 25, Early Church Texts, https://earlychurchtexts.com /public/chalcedon_canons.htm.

23. Brown, "Economic Life."

24. Barraclough, "Making of a Bishop in the Middle Ages."

25. Although the title of archbishop evolved out of the office of metropolitan, then for a while became equivalent and then, again the two titles were and are used to make a hierarchical distinction, for the purposes here they may, with minimal affront to the argument or to Church titles, be used interchangeably.

26. For a useful discussion of public versus private goods and their distribution as a function of group size, see Bueno de Mesquita et al., *Logic of Political Survival*; Lake and Baum, "Invisible Hand of Democracy."

27. I say "generally" to remind us that occasionally children as young as three years old were chosen as bishops or archbishops. Child-bishops certainly did not have a prior history from which to evaluate their loyalties in the future, although, of course, their regents did have such histories.

28. Janssen, *Das Erzbistum Köln im Späten Mittelalter 1191–1515*.

29. Attwater and John, *Penguin Dictionary of Saints*.

30. The more precise, technical development of the implications of the concordat game can be seen in Bueno de Mesquita and Bueno de Mesquita, "From Investiture to Worms."

31. In simplifying here, I ignore the effects of uncertainty that could lead a pope to nominate someone too closely aligned with himself, thus leading the ruler to reject the nominee

and creating an interregnum. Of course, popes and rulers might mistakenly anticipate support from nominees who turn out not to favor them. In the technical game, players are assumed to be Bayesians, meaning that they modify their expectations—or beliefs—and their subsequent choices whenever previous results prove to be sufficiently inconsistent with what they expected to happen. That is, they learn by following Bayes's Rule for evaluating conditional probabilities (the probability, for instance, of rejection of a bishop nominee given that we observed the nominee's expected alignment with the king). Hence, by repeating the nominating and approval or rejection process, either both popes and kings would gradually learn the error of their choices and would eventually converge on the right choice of alignment so that they would agree on who should be the next bishop, or their link would be broken if the see became sufficiently wealthy that the king chose the outside option.

CHAPTER 4: SECULARISM SURGES

1. To be clear, accurate, and precise, Clement V, the first pope of the Avignon papacy, was not strictly French. He was born in Aquitaine, English territory embedded within France.

2. Stephen, *Lectures on the History of France*, 240.

3. Gilchrist, *Church and Economic Activity*.

4. Baldwin, *Government of Philip Augustus*, 178.

5. For the data, see Wikipedia, s.v. "List of People Excommunicated by the Catholic Church," accessed June 9, 2021, https://en.wikipedia.org/wiki/List_of_people _excommunicated_by_the_Roman_Catholic_Church.

6. Details about the data are found in Bueno de Mesquita and Bueno de Mesquita, "From Investiture to Worms." Dioceses are recorded as long as they had their own bishop. We should be mindful that over the centuries, some dioceses merged, some split, some ceased to exist, and new ones were created.

7. Of the dioceses for which alignment is known, approximately 52 percent were from dioceses covered by the concordats.

8. Weber, *The Protestant Ethic*.

9. The information about the alignment of bishops and their consecration and departure dates were derived by scraping Catholic Church websites and Wikipedia sites in English, German, and in a few cases, French, Spanish, or Swedish for the biographies of bishops. I classify nominees into two categories: religiously leaning or secularly leaning. Bishops are classified as religious (i.e., aligned with the pope and church) if their job prior to becoming bishop for the first time was a religious post, such as abbot, monk, hermit, deacon, archdeacon, or priest. Bishops are classified as secular if their prior post was as an agent of the secular authorities, such as court ambassador, chancellor, tutor to a monarch or his children, and the like, or if their biographical information indicates that they were specifically linked to or were suggested as a candidate by the secular ruler over the diocese to which they were appointed.

10. Among these bishops between Nicaea and Martin Luther for whom it was possible to evaluate their expected alignment, 2,034 were covered by the terms of the concordats and 675 were from dioceses that were not subject to the agreement; that is, they were uncovered.

11. See Bueno de Mesquita and Bueno de Mesquita, "From Investiture to Worms," for an analysis of missing information.

12. T. Matthew Ciolek, Old World Trade Routes (OWTR) Project, accessed June 10, 2021, www.ciolek.com/owtrad.html.

13. See Bueno de Mesquita and Bueno de Mesquita, "From Investiture to Worms," for several additional trade-based variables used to estimate wealth. The authors test the robustness of the results they investigate against alternative specifications and find that all the results on secularization are robust to different specifications.

14. The UN Food and Agriculture Organization (FAO) estimates the potential of small areas of land all over the world to produce calories based on crops that were available before Columbus brought crops back to Europe from the Americas. The FAO's estimates for Europe have been reassembled to compute the caloric potential productivity of the land in each diocese in Europe. Presumably those places whose land had higher caloric potential would, on average, have produced more or better and more marketable crops that would have rendered them wealthier than other places. My thanks to Professor Michael Austin of the Harris School at the University of Chicago for helping my son and me convert the FAO data to match diocese boundaries. For other uses of these data to study historical political economy puzzles, see Galor and Özak, "Agricultural Origins of Time Preference."

15. $P \leq .004$ for high- and low-calorie sees during the concordat interlude, and $p \leq .003$ for high-calorie bishoprics during the concordat period compared to high-calorie dioceses before the concordats were signed.

16. Boulding, *Conflict and Defense*; Bueno de Mesquita, *The War Trap*; Lemke, *Regions of War and Peace*.

17. Weinstein, *Savonarola*; Martines, *Lawyers and Statecraft*.

18. "John Huss, Pre-Reformation Reformer," *Christianity Today* 65, no. 4 (May/June 2021), www.Christianitytoday.com/history/people/martyrs/john-huss.html.

19. Biller, "Goodbye to Waldensianism?"

20. Statistical analyses that control for any characteristics of each diocese that did not change over time (known as fixed effects) and also control for anything generally going on in specific centuries, half centuries, or quarter centuries (known as temporal fixed effects) demonstrate that the results are highly robust.

21. Here I report "far away" as more than 1,115 kilometers from Rome, the mean distance in the data, but in the full analysis, I also take into account the continuous impact of the log of the distance from Rome on the proclivity to select secular bishops, and I get equivalent results.

22. Twenty-three percent of covered bishops in dioceses more than 1,115 kilometers from Rome, regardless of wealth, were secular during the concordat interlude, whereas 6.67 percent were secularly leaning within 500 kilometers of Rome.

23. For a demanding statistical assessment of the differences between covered and uncovered dioceses, with fixed-effect controls for each diocese's characteristics and for each half century to correct for trends over time, see the tests of robustness in Bueno de Mesquita and Bueno de Mesquita, "From Investiture to Worms."

24. Bueno de Mesquita and Bueno de Mesquita, "From Investiture to Worms" shows similar placebo tests—the period of the concordat is the true treatment and all other concordat-length interludes are tested to see if they boosted secularism too, serving as placebo treatments—but vary their length for covered bishoprics depending on whether their concordat took effect in, for instance, 1107 instead of 1122. The results are essentially the same. I also duplicated these tests, but only for those dioceses that were not covered by a concordat. That analysis further reinforces the conclusion that the concordat was fundamental to the rise of secularism in those parts of Europe that signed on to it and that were wealthy.

Chapter 5: The Road to Prosperity

1. White, *Medieval Technology and Social Change*; Astill and Langdon, *Medieval Farming and Technology*; Lopez, *Commercial Revolution*; Spruyt, *The Sovereign State*; Andersen, Jensen, and Skovsgaard, "The Heavy Plough and the Agricultural Revolution"; Hunt and Murray, *History of Business*.

2. Spruyt, *The Sovereign State*, for instance, argues that economic development in Europe was exogenously determined and unrelated to secularization or to the resolution of the Investiture Controversy.

3. Kantorowicz, *The King's Two Bodies*; Spruyt, *The Sovereign State*.

4. Ladurie, *Times of Feast*.

5. Andersen, Jensen, and Skovsgaard, "The Heavy Plough and the Agricultural Revolution."

6. Lopez, *Commercial Revolution*; Hunt and Murray, *History of Business*; Greif, "Institutions and International Trade."

7. See, for instance, Tilly, *Coercion, Capital, and European States*, "How War Made States, and Vice Versa"; and Sharma, "Kinship, Property, and Authority."

8. Lopez, *Commercial Revolution*; Hunt and Murray, *History of Business*.

9. I use 150 years because the first post-signing bishop of known type came in, on average, in 1164, 42 years after the Concordat of Worms and 57 years after the concordats in England and France.

10. The calculation is $(1+(0.100-0.0383))^6$.

11. $X^2 = 24.89$, $p \leq .00001$. The number of dioceses by time period (N) with Cistercian monasteries was 103; the number of dioceses without Cistercian monasteries was 1,371.

12. Le Goff, *Time, Work, and Culture*, 110.

13. Quoted in Luscombe and Evans, "The Twelfth-Century Renaissance," 307.

14. Le Goff, *Time, Work, and Culture*, 82; Stark, *How the West Won*; Carus-Wilson, "An Industrial Revolution."

15. Carus-Wilson, "An Industrial Revolution," 56.

16. Luscombe and Evans, "The Twelfth-Century Renaissance," 308; see also Lopez, *The Commercial Revolution*; de Roover, *Business, Banking, and Economic Thought*; and de Roover, *The Rise and Decline of the Medici Bank* on early banking and trade.

17. Le Goff, *Time, Work, and Culture*, 111.

18. Le Goff, *Time, Work, and Culture*, 114–115.

19. Bartlett, *The Making of Europe*, 140.

20. Bernard of Clairvaux, *Military Orders: In Praise of the New Knighthood (Liber ad milites Templi: De laude novae militiae)* (early twelfth century), trans. Conrad Greenia, *ORB Online Encyclopedia*, https://history.hanover.edu/courses/excerpts/344bern2.html; see also Bernard of Clairvaux, *In Praise of the New Knighthood*, prologue–chap. 5, trans. Conrad Greenia, in *Bernard of Clairvaux: Treatises Three*, Cistercian Fathers Series no. 19, 127–145 (Collegeville, MN: Cistercian Publications, 2000).

21. Erlande-Brandenburg, *Cathedral Builders*.

22. All translation of the canons of Lateran I are from "Medieval Sourcebook: Ninth Ecumenical Council: Lateran I 1123," from H. J. Schroeder, *Disciplinary Decrees of the General Councils: Text, Translation and Commentary* (St. Louis: B. Herder, 1937), available at Internet History Sourcebooks Project, Fordham University Center for Medieval Studies, https://sourcebooks.fordham.edu/basis/lateran1.asp.

23. Although the scholar Jack Goody does not tie the celibacy ruling to the power struggle set in motion by the Concordat of Worms, he notes the linkage between inheritance and the effort to preserve church power; see Goody, *Development of the Family and Marriage*, 123.

24. All quotations from the canons of Lateran II are from Council Fathers, *Second Lateran Council—1139 A.D.*, Papal Encyclicals Online, www.papalencyclicals.net/Councils /ecum10.htm.

25. All quotations from the canons of Lateran III are from Council Fathers, *Third Lateran Council—1179 A.D.*, Papal Encyclicals Online, www.papalencyclicals.net/councils /ecum11.htm.

26. Quoted in Lapidus, "Information and Risk," 18.

27. All quotations from the canons of Lateran IV are from "Medieval Sourcebook: Twelfth Ecumenical Council: Lateran IV 1215," from H. J. Schroeder, *Disciplinary Decrees of the General Councils: Text, Translation and Commentary* (St. Louis: B. Herder, 1937), available at Internet History Sourcebooks Project, Fordham University Center for Medieval Studies, https://sourcebooks.fordham.edu/basis/lateran4.asp.

28. Le Goff, *Time, Work, and Culture*, 112.

29. de Roover, *Rise and Decline of the Medici Bank*; de Roover, *Business, Banking, and Economic Thought*; Greif, "Contract Enforceability and Economic Institutions."

30. Ekelund, Hébert, and Tollison, "Economic Model of the Medieval Church."

31. Gimpel, *The Cathedral Builders*; Swanson, *Promissory Notes*.

32. Swanson, *Promissory Notes*, 72.

33. Stark, *How the West Won*, Kindle location 2625.

34. Stark, *How the West Won*.

35. Stark, *How the West Won*, Kindle location 2629.

36. Ekelund, Hébert, and Tollison, "Economic Model of the Medieval Church."

37. Buringh et al., "Church Building and the Economy."

38. Quoted in McNeil, *English Heritage Book of Castles*, 43.

39. Hunt and Murray, *History of Business*, 21.

40. Hunt and Murray, *History of Business*, 84.

41. Taylor, *Origin and Growth of the English Constitution*; Van Caenegem, *Birth of the English Common Law*; Barzel, *Economic Analysis of Property Rights*.

42. Van Caenegem, *Birth of the English Common Law*, 63.

43. Leeson, "Ordeals."

44. Van Caenegem, *Birth of the English Common Law*, 64.

45. Guizot, *Popular History of France*.

46. I focus on the first four Crusades because the subsequent ones had different purposes, and the word "crusade," like "war" in modern usage, came to refer to every campaign against foes real and imagined.

47. By "lasting impact" I mean that I create a binary variable for each of the four Crusades, coding it as 0 before the Crusade and as 1 for all years from the start of that Crusade through 1700, which is when my data on secularism and trade routes ends. I am grateful to the librarian at the University of Chicago specializing in geographic information systems (GIS) data and to Ethan Bueno de Mesquita for assisting in coding the crusader route dioceses. For additional analysis of the impact of the Crusades, see Bueno de Mesquita and Bueno de Mesquita, "From Investiture to Worms."

48. Greif, "Institutions and International Trade"; Lopez, *Commercial Revolution*; Polanyi, *The Great Transformation*.

49. Lopez, *Commercial Revolution*.

50. Rubin, *Rulers, Religion and Riches*; Weber, *The Protestant Ethic*.

51. Stark, *How the West Won*; Mead, *Burdens of Freedom*.

52. Henrich, *The WEIRDest People in the World*.

53. North and Thomas, *Rise of the Western World*; De Long and Shleifer, "Princes and Merchants"; Acemoglu, Johnson, and Robinson, "The Rise of Europe."

54. "Near" is defined as less than the median 1,115 kilometers from Rome; "far" means more than 1,115 kilometers.

CHAPTER 6: THE ROAD TO PAPAL SERFDOM AND LIBERATION

1. The data contain some instances that appear as negative interregnums (i.e., one bishop coming in before the previous one leaves). Many of these are cases of very short duration (one to two years), probably reflecting a case where a bishop was put in place when the previous bishop was no longer able to serve (e.g., for health reasons) but had not yet left office. These cases are coded as zeros. There are also cases of longer negative interregnums, most of which result from papal schisms leading to a single diocese having more than one (contested) bishop at the same time. I drop these cases when evaluating interregnums but then make use of them to examine irregular bishop transitions, meaning interregnums of more than a year or the presence of dual occupants in the bishop's seat. Such analyses expand beyond the model, since it does not consider the possibility of antibishops as well as bishops.

2. Today's France, of course, includes the then Kingdom of Burgundy, which was part of the Holy Roman Empire.

3. The tests done here are of the type known as placebo tests. Each quarter century, we try to predict Avignon by seeing statistically whether trade-route prevalence in the chosen quarter century—the treatment period—sorts out French dioceses from all others. It is called a placebo test because there is one true treatment (when the Avignon papacy actually began) and many sugar pill–placebo treatments (across all other quarter-century time periods).

4. Quidort, *On Royal and Papal Power*, 23.

5. Quidort, *On Royal and Papal Power*, 23–24. The term "collation" refers to the granting of a church benefice such as promoting or granting an office; Philip claimed this right for himself, but the pope considered it to belong exclusively to the church.

6. Quidort, *On Royal and Papal Power*, 23. The original, complete text of *Ausculta fili* no longer exists. The content is only known through sources such as Jean Quidort and Pierre Flotte, both of whom are thought to have toned down the pope's original language.

7. Andersen, Jensen, and Skovsgaard, "The Heavy Plough and the Agricultural Revolution"; Hunt and Murray, *History of Business*.

8. For population data by country, see Wikipedia, s.v. "List of Countries by Population in 1500," accessed July 11, 2021, https://en.wikipedia.org/wiki/List_of_countries_by_population_in_1500.

CHAPTER 7: THE BIRTH OF STATES, THE BIRTHING OF REPRESENTATIVE DEMOCRACY

1. Quidort, *On Royal and Papal Power*, 76.

2. Canning, "Introduction: Politics, Institutions and Ideas," 347.

3. Spruyt, *The Sovereign State*.

4. The full text of the Treaty of Westphalia can be found at Multilaterals Project, Fletcher School, Tufts University, https://wayback.archive-it.org/1646/20091102214822 /http://fletcher.tufts.edu/multi/texts/historical/westphalia.txt.

5. Siverson and Starr, "Opportunity, Willingness and the Diffusion of War"; Vasquez, *The War Puzzle*; Huth, *Standing Your Ground*.

6. Spruyt, *The Sovereign State*; Krasner, *Sovereignty*.

7. Kantorowicz, *The King's Two Bodies*; Weber, *The Protestant Ethic*; Weber, *Economy and Society*; Wesson, *State Systems*; Tuchman, *The March of Folly*; Baldwin, *Government of Philip Augustus*; Rosenberg and Birdzell, *How the West Grew Rich*; Greif, "Historical and Comparative Institutional Analysis."

8. Kantorowicz, *The King's Two Bodies*.

9. Geoffrey Chaucer, *Canterbury Tales*, "The Tale of Melibee," lines 1664–1671, Harvard's Geoffrey Chaucer Website, https://chaucer.fas.harvard.edu/pages/tale-melibee-0.

10. Fearon, "Rationalist Explanations for War"; Slantchev and Tarar, "Mutual Optimism"; Powell, "War as a Commitment Problem."

11. Prestwich, *War, Politics and Finance*.

12. Prestwich, *War, Politics and Finance*, 31.

13. Prestwich, *War, Politics and Finance*, 166.

14. The full text can be found at "Confirmatio Cartarum [26]," Nitty Gritty Law Library, https://www.1215.org/lawnotes/lawnotes/cartarum.htm.

15. Guizot, *Popular History of France*.

16. Bueno de Mesquita et al., *Logic of Political Survival*.

17. Tilly, "Reflections on the History of European State Making," 42.

18. Wikipedia, s.v. "Engelbrekt Engelbrektsson," accessed June 11, 2021, https://en .wikipedia.org/wiki/Engelbrekt_Engelbrektsson.

19. Svolik, *The Politics of Authoritarian Rule*, shows this effect in modern autocracies.

20. Tilly, *Coercion, Capital, and European States*, 70.

21. The data on parliaments are an amalgamation of data sets by Stasavage, *The Decline and Rise of Democracy*, and by Wang, "Sons and Lovers."

22. Sharma, "Kinship, Property, and Authority."

23. See Bueno de Mesquita and Lalman, *War and Reason*, especially the crisis subgame of their international interaction game's domestic variant.

24. Wahl, "Political Participation and Economic Development"; Stasavage, "Was Weber Right?"

25. Fearon, "Rationalist Explanations for War."

26. Alastair Smith, "Alliance Formation and War."

27. Calvino, *The Jaguar Sun*, 36.

28. Hints at these ideas are found in Greif, Milgrom, and Weingast, "Coordination, Commitment, and Enforcement"; North, Wallis, and Weingast, *Violence and Social Orders*; and, more explicitly, in Belloc, Drago, and Galbiati, "Earthquakes, Religion, and Transition to Self-Government."

29. Belloc, Drago, and Galbiati, "Earthquakes, Religion, and Transition to Self-Government."

30. $P \leq .000$ that this difference in the number of dioceses per kingdom arose by chance.

31. Stasavage, "When Distance Mattered," 152; but see de Magalhaes and Giovanoni, "War and the Rise of Parliaments," for evidence that parliaments met more often during periods of economic stress.

32. See Spruyt, *The Sovereign State*, 50. For an excellent review of the literature, see Stasavage, "Representation and Consent."

33. Stasavage, "When Distance Mattered"; Stasavage, "Representation and Consent."

34. Boucoyannis, "No Representation Without Taxation."

35. $P \le .003$.

36. $P \le .100$ that the incidence of war is the same in parliaments with a tax veto and in parliaments without that authority.

37. $P \le .005$ that the incidence of war is the same in parliaments with a spending veto and in parliaments without that authority.

38. Huffman, *Social Politics of Medieval Diplomacy*, 35.

39. Huffman, *Social Politics of Medieval Diplomacy*, 25–56.

40. The data on European monarchs between 1100 and 1700 are drawn from Morby, *Dynasties of the World*; Blaydes and Chaney, "The Feudal Revolution and Europe's Rise"; Kokkonen and Sundell, "Delivering Stability"; and Bueno de Mesquita and Bueno de Mesquita, "From Investiture to Worms"; along with variables kindly provided by David Stasavage and by Yuhua Wang, for which I thank them both.

Chapter 8: Today

1. The stories of Brother Cadfael make up a series of mystery novels written by Edith Pargeter under the pen name Ellis Peters.

2. Shorto, *Island at the Center of the World*; van der Donck, *Description of New Netherland*.

3. Italy is the only major country whose current territory I divide, between the northern regions that were part of the Concordat of Worms and the southern regions that made up the Kingdom of Sicily, later the Kingdom of Naples, and were not parties to the concordat. Regional data on per capita income and life expectancy at birth are available for Italy, and the uncovered southern portions of Italy are substantial enough to be treated as if they were collectively a country for purposes of comparing how they are doing today with their circumstances during the interlude of the concordats. Unfortunately, it is much more difficult to make such distinctions for the small sections of such modern countries as Switzerland, Poland, or the Czech Republic that were covered by the Concordat of Worms because the covered areas are too small a portion of their modern whole to be thought of as countries either in the past or now. Limitations in regional per capita income data and in the imbalance in only separating one or two dioceses from a country prohibit a more refined look at income on a local basis. Per capita income is generally not available at the diocese level.

4. These data are taken from the World Bank Development Indicators and are the most current as of this writing on June 12, 2021.

5. The level of democracy is assessed using the widely employed Polity2 score that measures how autocratic or democratic each government is each year. Polity grades this variable from −10 to +10. For ease of interpretation, I normalize it to the range 0 to 100 by adding 10 to the score, dividing the result by 20 and then multiplying by 100.

6. I do not include a comparison for the current year by itself as there is now hardly any remaining variation on this dimension in most of Europe except for a very small set of outliers.

7. These data are derived from World Bank Development Indicators.

8. I used Transparency International's Corruption Index (2019 and 2020). This index is a widely employed judgment-based indicator of government corruption in, for instance, business dealings and government contracting.

9. The probability that this difference arose by chance is $p \leq .004$.

10. The probability that this income difference today is due to chance is $p \leq .001$.

11. Data on the level of democracy are taken from the widely used Polity IV data at www.systemicpeace.org/polity/polity4.htm. For explanations of the data and its variables, see Marshall, Gurr, and Jaggers, "Polity IV Project." Countries are divided by Polity into 21 degrees of governance, with −10 being the most autocratic and +10 being the most democratic. For ease of interpretation, I rescale these data to fall between 0 and 100 by adding 10 to the Polity score and dividing the result by 20 and then multiplying by 100. The most current data available as of this writing covers through 2020.

12. $P < .10$.

13. $P < .012$.

14. See *World Intellectual Property Indicators 2019*.

15. $P \leq .012$.

16. Or, of course, as we all know by now, in 1107 in the cases of England and France.

17. Peltzer, *Canon Law, Careers and Conquest*, 1.

18. Hayek, *The Constitution of Liberty*.

19. Using the World Bank's freedom of religion indicators at "GovData360: Freedom of Religion," World Bank, https://govdata360.worldbank.org/indicators/hd6a18526 ?country=BRA&indicator=41930&viz=line_chart&years=1975,2018, we see that among wealthy medieval societies, those that signed a concordat are significantly more likely to support religious freedom and to keep religion out of government, $p \leq .002$. Among those that were poor in the Worms-to-Avignon interlude, there is no significant difference today.

BIBLIOGRAPHY

Acemoglu, Daron, Simon Johnson, and James A. Robinson. "The Rise of Europe: Atlantic Trade, Institutional Change and Economic Growth." *American Economic Review* 95, no. 3 (2005): 546–579.

Alzog, John. *Manual of Universal Church History.* Vol 2. Translated by F. J. Parisch and Thomas S. Byrne. Cincinnati: Robert Clarke, 1902.

Andersen, Thomas Barnebeck, Peter Sandholt Jensen, and Christian Stejner Skovsgaard. "The Heavy Plough and the Agricultural Revolution in Medieval Europe." Discussion Papers on Business and Economics no. 6/2013. University of Southern Denmark, 2013.

Astill, Grenville, and John Langdon, eds. *Medieval Farming and Technology: The Impact of Agricultural Change in Northwest Europe.* Leiden: Brill, 2007.

Attwater, Donald, and Catherine Rachel John. *The Penguin Dictionary of Saints.* 3rd ed. New York: Penguin Books, 1993.

Bairoch, Paul. *Cities and Economic Development: From the Dawn of History to the Present.* Chicago: University of Chicago Press, 1991.

Baldwin, John. *The Government of Philip Augustus.* Berkeley: University of California Press, 1986.

Barraclough, Geoffrey. "The Making of a Bishop in the Middle Ages: The Part of the Pope in Law and Fact." *Catholic Historical Review* 19, no. 3 (October 1933): 275–319.

Bartlett, Robert. *The Making of Europe.* Princeton: Princeton University Press, 1993.

Barzel, Yorem. *The Economic Analysis of Property Rights.* New York: Cambridge University Press, 1989.

Barzel, Yoram, and Edgar Kiser. "The Development and Decline of Medieval Voting Institutions: A Comparison of England and France." *Economic Inquiry* 35, no. 2 (1997): 244–260.

Bates, Robert, and Da-Hsiang Lien. "A Note on Taxation, Development, and Representative Government." *Politics and Society* 14, no. 1 (1985): 53–70.

Belloc, Marianna, Francesco Drago, and Roberto Galbiati. "Earthquakes, Religion, and Transition to Self-Government in Italian Cities." *Quarterly Journal of Economics* 131, no. 4 (November 2016): 1875–1926.

Benson, Robert. *Bishop-Elect: A Study in Medieval Ecclesiastical Office.* Princeton: Princeton University Press, 1968.

Biller, Peter. "Goodbye to Waldensianism?" *Past and Present* 192 (August 2006): 3–33.

Blaydes, Lisa, and Eric Chaney. "The Feudal Revolution and Europe's Rise: Political Divergence of the Christian West and the Muslim World Before 1500 CE." *American Political Science Review* 107, no. 1 (2013): 16–34.

Bolt, Jutta, and J. L. van Zanden. "The Maddison Project: Collaborative Research on Historical National Accounts." *Economic History Review* 67, no. 3 (March 2014): 627–651.

Boucoyannis, Deborah. "No Representation Without Taxation: The Coercive Origins of Consent and Constitutionalism." *Politics and Society* 43, no. 3 (2015): 303–332.

Boulding, Kenneth. *Conflict and Defense: A General Theory.* New York: Harper, 1962.

Brown, A. T. "Economic Life." In *The Routledge Handbook of Medieval Christianity, 1050–1500*, edited by R. N. Swanson, 295–308. New York: Routledge, 2015.

Browne, P. W. "The Pactum Callixtinum: An Innovation in Papal Diplomacy." *Catholic Historical Review* 8, no. 2 (July 1922): 180–190.

Bueno de Mesquita, Bruce. "Popes, Kings, and Endogenous Institutions: The Concordat of Worms and the Origins of Sovereignty." *International Studies Review* 2, no. 2 (2000): 93–118.

———. *The War Trap.* New Haven: Yale University Press, 1981.

Bueno de Mesquita, Bruce, and Ethan Bueno de Mesquita. "From Investiture to Worms: A Political Economy of European Development and the Rise of Secular Authority." Working paper, Harris School of Public Policy, University of Chicago, 2020.

Bueno de Mesquita, Bruce, and David Lalman. *War and Reason.* New Haven: Yale University Press, 1992.

Bueno de Mesquita, Bruce, and Alastair Smith. *The Dictator's Handbook.* New York: Public Affairs Press, 2011.

Bueno de Mesquita, Bruce, Alastair Smith, Randolph M. Siverson, and James D. Morrow. *The Logic of Political Survival.* Cambridge: MIT Press, 2003.

Bueno de Mesquita, Daniel Meredith. *Giangaleazzo Visconti, Duke of Milan (1351–1402): A Study in the Political Career of an Italian Despot.* Cambridge: Cambridge University Press, 1941.

Buringh, Eltjo, Bruce M. S. Campbell, Auke Rijpma, and Jan Luiten van Zanden. "Church Building and the Economy During Europe's 'Age of the Cathedrals,' 700–1500 CE." *Explorations in Economic History* 76 (2020): 101316.

Burns, J. H., ed. *The Cambridge History of Medieval Political Thought c. 350–c. 1450.* Cambridge: Cambridge University Press, 1988.

Calvino, Italo. *The Jaguar Sun.* New York: Houghton Mifflin Harcourt, 1983.

Canning, J. P. "Introduction: Politics, Institutions and Ideas." In *The Cambridge History of Medieval Political Thought c. 350–c. 1450*, edited by J. H. Burns, 341–366. Cambridge: Cambridge University Press, 1988.

Cantoni, Davide. "Adopting a New Religion: The Case of Protestantism in 16th Century Germany." *Economic Journal* 122, no. 560 (2012): 502–531.

———. "The Economic Effects of the Protestant Reformation: Testing the Weber Hypothesis in the German Lands." *Journal of the European Economic Association* 13, no. 4 (2015): 561–598.

Cantoni, Davide, Jeremiah Dittmar, and Noam Yuchtman. "Religious Competition and Reallocation: The Political Economy of Secularization in the Protestant Reformation." *Quarterly Journal of Economics* 133, no. 4 (November 2018): 2037–2096.

Carlyle, R. W., and A. J. Carlyle. *A History of Medieval Political Theory in the West*. 2nd ed. London: W. Blackwell and Sons, 1938.

Carus-Wilson, E. M. "An Industrial Revolution of the Thirteenth Century." *Economic History Review* 11, no. 1 (October 1941): 39–60.

Chandler, Tertius. *Four Thousand Years of Urban Growth: An Historical Census*. Lewiston, NY: Edwin Mellen Press, 1987.

Chodorow, Stanley. "Paschal II, Henry V, and the Crisis of 1111." In *Popes, Teachers, and Canon Law in the Middle Ages*, edited by James Ross Sweeney and Stanley Chodorow, 3–25. Ithaca, NY: Cornell University Press, 1989.

Colomer, Josep M., and Iain McLean. "Electing Popes: Approval Balloting and Qualified-Majority Rule." *Journal of Interdisciplinary History* 29 (Summer 1998): 1–22.

Costigan, Richard. "State Appointment of Bishops." *Journal of Church and State* 8 (1966): 82–96.

Cushing, Kathleen G. *Reform and the Papacy in the Eleventh Century: Spirituality and Social Change*. Manchester: Manchester University Press, 2005.

Dalberg-Acton, John. *Historical Essays and Studies*. Edited by J. N. Figgis and R. V. Laurence, London: Macmillan, 1907.

de La Haye, Louis Marie, and James L. Gihon. *A Complete History of the Popes of Rome, from Saint Peter, the First Bishop, to Pius the Ninth*. Open Access: Rare Books Club, 1857. Available through Google Books at www.google.com/books/edition/A_Complete_History_of _the_Popes_of_Rome/aQMQAAAAIAAJ?hl=en.

De Long, J. Bradford, and Andrei Shleifer. "Princes and Merchants: European City Growth Before the Industrial Revolution." *Journal of Law and Economics* 36, no. 2 (1993): 671–702.

de Magalhaes, Leandro, and Francesco Giovanoni. "War and the Rise of Parliaments." Bristol Economics Discussion Papers 19/709, Department of Economics, University of Bristol, UK, 2019.

de Roover, Raymond. *Business, Banking, and Economic Thought in Late Medieval and Early Modern Europe*. Chicago: University of Chicago Press, 1974.

———. *The Rise and Decline of the Medici Bank*. Cambridge, MA: Harvard University Press, 1963.

Diamond, Jared. *Guns, Germs and Steel*. New York: W. W. Norton, 1997.

Dimont, Max I. *Jews, God, and History*. London: Penguin Books, 2004.

Dincecco, Mark, and Yuhua Wang. "Violent Conflict and Political Development over the Long Run: China Versus Europe." *Annual Review of Political Science* 21 (2018): 341–358.

Ekelund, Robert B., Robert F. Hébert, and Robert D. Tollison. "An Economic Model of the Medieval Church: Usury as a Form of Rent Seeking." *Journal of Law, Economics, and Organization* 5, no. 2 (1989): 307–331.

Emsley, John. *The Elements of Murder: A History of Poison*. Oxford: Oxford University Press, 2005.

Erlande-Brandenburg, Alain. *The Cathedral Builders of the Middle Ages*. New York: Thames and Hudson, 1995.

Ertman, Thomas. *Birth of the Leviathan*. Cambridge: Cambridge University Press, 1997.

Eusebius, *Life of Constantine*. Translated by Averil Cameron and Stuart G. Hall. Oxford: Oxford University Press, 1999.

Fearon, James. "Rationalist Explanations for War." *International Organization* 49, no. 3 (1995): 379–414.

Galor, Oded, and Ö. Özak. "The Agricultural Origins of Time Preference." *American Economic Review* 106, no. 10 (2016): 3064–3103.

Gilchrist, John. *The Church and Economic Activity in the Middle Ages.* New York: Macmillan, 1969.

Gimpel, Jean. *The Cathedral Builders.* New York: Grove Press, 1983.

Goody, Jack. *The Development of the Family and Marriage in Europe.* Cambridge: Cambridge University Press, 1983.

Gregorovius, Ferdinand. *The History of the City of Rome in the Middle Ages* (1894). Vol. 2. Translated by Annie Hamilton. New York: Italica Press, 2016.

Greif, Avner. "Contract Enforceability and Economic Institutions in Early Trade: The Maghribi Traders' Coalition." *American Economic Review* 83, no. 3 (1993): 525–548.

———. "Historical and Comparative Institutional Analysis." *American Economic Review* 88, no. 2 (1998): 80–84.

———. "Institutions and International Trade: Lessons from the Commercial Revolution." *American Economic Review* 82, no. 2 (1992): 128–133.

Greif, Avner, Paul Milgrom, and Barry Weingast. "Coordination, Commitment, and Enforcement: The Case of the Merchant Guild." *Journal of Political Economy* 102 (1994): 745–766.

Guizot, François. *A Popular History of France from the Earliest Times* (1874). Midland Park, NJ: Pinnacle Press, 2017.

Hallam, Henry. *View of the State of Europe During the Middle Ages.* Vol. 1. London: John Murray, 1860.

Hanfmann, George M. A. "Personality and Portraiture in Ancient Art." *Proceedings of the American Philosophical Society* 117, no. 4 (1973): 259–285.

Harrower, Michael J., and Ioana A. Dumitru. "Archaeology: Digital Maps Illuminate Ancient Trade Routes." *Nature* 543 (2017): 188–189.

Hayek, Friedrich A. *The Constitution of Liberty.* Chicago: University of Chicago Press, 1978.

Henderson, Ernest F. *Select Historical Documents of the Middle Ages.* London: George Bell and Sons, 1910.

Henrich, Joseph. *The WEIRDest People in the World: How the West Became Psychologically Peculiar and Particularly Prosperous.* New York: Farrar, Straus and Giroux, 2020.

Hobbes, Thomas. *Leviathan* (1651). Edited by Richard Tuck. New York: Cambridge University Press, 1996.

Honour, Hugh, and John Fleming. *The Visual Arts: A History.* 4th ed. Englewood Cliffs, NJ: Prentice Hall, 1995.

Huffman, Joseph P. *The Social Politics of Medieval Diplomacy: Anglo-German Relations (1066–1307).* Ann Arbor: University of Michigan Press, 2000.

Hull, Eleanor. *A History of Ireland and Her People.* Oxford: Phoenix Publishing, 1926.

Hunt, Edwin, and James Murray. *A History of Business in Medieval Europe, 1200–1550.* Cambridge: Cambridge University Press, 1999.

Huth, Paul. *Standing Your Ground: Territorial Disputes and International Conflict.* Ann Arbor: University of Michigan Press, 1996.

Janson, H. W., and Anthony F. Janson. *History of Art.* Rev. 5th ed. Englewood Cliffs, NJ: Prentice Hall, 1997.

———. *History of Art.* 6th ed. Englewood Cliffs, NJ: Prentice Hall, 2003.

Janssen, Wilhelm. *Das Erzbistum Köln im Späten Mittelalter 1191–1515.* Part 1. Geschichte des Erzbistums Köln, no. 2. Cologne: Bachem, 1995.

Johnson, Philip D. *Arnold of Brescia: Apostle of Liberty in Twelfth Century Europe*. Eugene, OR: Wipf and Stock, 2016.

Justi, Ferdinand, Sara Yorke Stevenson, and Morris Jastrow Jr. *A History of All Nations*. Vol. 7. Philadelphia: Lea Brothers, 1905.

Kantorowicz, Ernst H. *The King's Two Bodies: A Study in Medieval Political Theology*. Princeton: Princeton University Press, 1957.

Kelly, J. N. D. *The Oxford Dictionary of Popes*. New York: Oxford University Press, 1989.

Kleiner, Fred. *Gardner's Art Through the Ages*. 3rd ed. New York: Cengage Learning, 2013. First published 1948.

Kokkonen, Andrej, and Anders Sundell. "Delivering Stability—Primogeniture and Autocratic Survival in European Monarchies 1000–1800." *American Political Science Review* 108, no. 2 (2014): 438–453.

Körntgen, Ludger, and Dominik Waenhoven. *Religion and Politics in the Middle Ages: Germany and England by Comparison*. Berlin: De Gruyter, 2013.

Krasner, Stephen. *Sovereignty: Organized Hypocrisy*. Princeton: Princeton University Press, 1999.

Ladurie, Emmanuel Le Roy. *Times of Feast, Times of Famine: A History of Climate Since the Year 1000*. Translated by Barbara Bray. New York: Farrar, Straus and Giroux, 1988.

Lake, David, and Matthew A. Baum. "The Invisible Hand of Democracy: Political Control and the Provision of Public Services." *Comparative Political Studies* 25 (2001): 73–108.

Lapidus, André. "Information and Risk in the Medieval Doctrine of Usury During the Thirteenth Century." In *Perspectives on the History of Economic Thought*, vol. 5, edited by William Barber, 23–38. London: Edward Elgar, 1991.

Leeson, Peter. "Ordeals." *Journal of Law and Economics* 55, no. 3 (2012): 691–714.

Le Goff, J. *Time, Work, and Culture in the Middle Ages*. Translated by Arthur Goldhammer. Chicago: University of Chicago Press, 1980.

Lemke, Douglas. *Regions of War and Peace*. New York: Cambridge University Press, 2002.

Levi, Margaret. *Of Rule and Revenue*. Berkeley: University of California Press, 1988.

Leyser, Karl. "The Crisis of Medieval Germany." *Proceedings of the British Academy* 69 (1983): 409–443.

———. "England and the Empire in the Early Twelfth Century" in *Medieval Germany and Its Neighbours (900–1250)*. London: A and C Black, 1982.

Lopez, Robert. *The Birth of Europe*. London: J. M. Dent and Sons, 1966.

———. *The Commercial Revolution of the Middle Ages, 950–1350*. Cambridge: Cambridge University Press, 1976.

Luscombe, D. E., and G. R. Evans. "The Twelfth-Century Renaissance." In *The Cambridge History of Medieval Political Thought c. 350–c. 1450*, edited by J. H. Burns, 306–340. Cambridge: Cambridge University Press, 1988.

Lutz, Cora E. *Schoolmasters of the Tenth Century*. New York: Shoestring Press, 1977.

Lynch, Joseph H., and Phillip C. Adamo. *The Medieval Church*. Abingdon-on-Thames: Routledge, 2013.

Maitland, F. W. *The Constitutional History of England*. Cambridge: Cambridge University Press, 1961. First published 1908.

Manin, Bernard. *The Principles of Representative Government*. Cambridge: Cambridge University Press, 1997.

Mann, Horace K. *The Lives of the Popes in the Early Middle Ages.* Vol. 1, *The Popes Under the Lombard Rule.* London: Kegan, Paul, Trench, Trübner, 1903.

———. *The Lives of the Popes in the Early Middle Ages.* Vol. 4, *The Popes in the Days of Feudal Anarchy.* London: Forgotten Books, 2012. First published 1910.

Marshall, Monty G., Ted Robert Gurr, and Keith Jaggers. "Polity IV Project: Political Regime Characteristics and Transitions, 1800–2018." Center for Systemic Peace, 2019. Available at www.systemicpeace.org/inscr/p4manualv2018.pdf.

Martines, Lauro. *Lawyers and Statecraft in Renaissance Florence.* Princeton: Princeton University Press, 1968.

McLynn, Frank. *Genghis Khan: His Conquests, His Empire, His Legacy.* Boston: Da Capo Press, 2015.

McNeil, Tom. *English Heritage Book of Castles.* London: English Heritage and B. T. Batsford, 1992.

McNeill, William. *The Global Condition.* Princeton: Princeton University Press, 1992.

———. *The Rise of the West.* Chicago: University of Chicago Press, 1963.

Mead, Lawrence. *Burdens of Freedom.* New York: Encounter Books, 2019.

Melve, Leidulf. *Inventing the Public Sphere: The Public Debate During the Investiture Contest (c. 1030–1122).* Leiden: Brill, 2007.

Morby, John. *Dynasties of the World: A Chronological and Genealogical Handbook.* Oxford: Oxford University Press, 1989.

Morris, Colin. *The Papal Monarchy: The Western Church from 1050 to 1250.* Oxford: Oxford University Press, 1991.

Nixey, Catherine. *The Darkening Age.* New York: Houghton Mifflin Harcourt, 2017.

North, Douglass, and R. P. Thomas. *The Rise of the Western World: A New Economic History.* Cambridge: Cambridge University Press, 1973.

North, Douglass, John Wallis, and Barry Weingast. *Violence and Social Orders.* New York: Cambridge University Press, 2009.

Norwich, John Julius. *Byzantium.* New York: Alfred A. Knopf, 1989.

Olson, Mancur. "Dictatorship, Democracy, and Development." *American Political Science Review* 87, no. 3 (1993): 567–576.

Organski, A. F. K. *World Politics.* New York: Alfred A. Knopf, 1958.

Pella, John Anthony, Jr. "Expanding the Expansion of International Society: A New Approach with Empirical Illustrations from West African and European Interaction, 1400–1883," *Journal of International Relations and Development* 17, no. 1 (2014): 89–111.

Peltzer, Jörg. *Canon Law, Careers and Conquest: Episcopal Elections in Normandy and Greater Anjou, c. 1140–c. 1230.* Cambridge: Cambridge University Press, 2007.

Pitkin, Hanna. *The Concept of Representation.* Berkeley: University of California Press, 1967.

Pocock, J. G. A. *The Machiavellian Moment: Florentine Political Thought and the Atlantic Republican Tradition.* Princeton: Princeton University Press, 1975.

Polanyi, Karl. *The Great Transformation.* New York: Farrar and Rinehart, 1944.

Poole, Reginald L. *Benedict IX and Gregory VI.* From the *Proceedings of the British Academy* 8 (London: Published for the British Academy by Oxford University Press, 1917).

———. "The Names and Numbers of Medieval Popes." *English Historical Review* 32 (October 1917): 470–492.

"Pope Benedict XI." In *Catholic Encyclopedia,* edited by Charles Herbermann. New York: Robert Appleton, 1913.

Powell, Robert. "War as a Commitment Problem." *International Organization* 60, no. 1 (2006): 169–203.

Prestwich, Michael. *War, Politics and Finance Under Edward I.* Totowa, NJ: Rowman and Littlefield, 1972.

Prutz, Hans, and John Henry Wright. *The Age of Feudalism and Theocracy.* Philadelphia: Lea Brothers, 1905.

Quidort, Jean (John of Paris). *On Royal and Papal Power* (1302). Translated and edited by John Watt. Toronto: Pontifical Institute of Mediaeval Studies, 1971.

Reba, Meredith, Femke Reitsma, and Karen C. Seto. "Data Descriptor: Spatializing 6,000 Years of Global Urbanization from 3700 BC to AD 2000." *Scientific Data* 34, no. 1 (2016): 1–16.

Robinson, I. S. "The Church and the Order Clericorum." In *Church and Papacy*, edited by J. H. Burns, 252–305. Cambridge: Cambridge University Press, 1988.

Rosenberg N., and L. E. Birdzell Jr. *How the West Grew Rich: The Economic Transformation of the Industrial World.* New York: Basic Books, 1986.

Rouche, Michel. "The Early Middle Ages in the West: Sacred and Secret." In *A History of Private Life 1: From Pagan Rome to Byzantium*, edited by Paul Veyne. Cambridge, MA: Harvard University Press, 1987.

Rubin, Jared. *Rulers, Religion and Riches.* New York: Cambridge University Press, 2017.

Schimmelpfennig, Bernhard. *The Papacy.* New York: Columbia University Press, 1992.

Schwartzberg, Melissa. *Counting the Many: The Origins and Limits of Supermajority Rule.* New York: Cambridge University Press, 2014.

Sharma, Vivek. "Kinship, Property, and Authority: European Territorial Consolidation Reconsidered." *Politics and Society* 43, no. 2 (2015): 151–180.

Shorto, Russell. *The Island at the Center of the World.* New York: Doubleday, 2004.

Siverson, Randolph M., and Harvey Starr. "Opportunity, Willingness and the Diffusion of War." *American Political Science Review* 84, no. 1 (1990): 47–67.

Slantchev, Branislav, and Ahmer Tarar. "Mutual Optimism as a Rationalist Cause of War." *American Journal of Political Science* 55, no. 1 (2011): 135–148.

Smith, Adam. *An Inquiry into the Nature and Causes of the Wealth of Nations.* Edited by Edwin Cannan. Chicago: University of Chicago Press, 1981. First published 1776.

———. *The Theory of Moral Sentiments.* Edited by D. D. Raphael and A. L. Macfie. Vol. 1 of *The Glasgow Edition of the Works and Correspondence of Adam Smith.* Indianapolis: Liberty Fund, 1982. First published 1759.

Smith, Alastair. "Alliance Formation and War." *International Studies Quarterly* 39, no. 4 (December 1995): 405–425.

Specht, W., and K. Fischer. "Vergiftungsnachweis an den Resten einer 900 Jahre alten Leiche." *Archiv für Kriminologie* 124 (1959): 61–84.

Spruyt, Hendrik. *The Sovereign State and Its Competitors.* Princeton: Princeton University Press, 1996.

Stark, Rodney. *For the Glory of God.* Princeton: Princeton University Press, 2003.

———. *How the West Won: The Neglected Study of the Triumph of Modernity.* Wilmington, DE: Intercollegiate Studies Institute, 2014.

———. *The Rise of Christianity.* Princeton: Princeton University Press, 1996.

Stasavage, David. *The Decline and Rise of Democracy: A Global History from Antiquity to Today.* Princeton: Princeton University Press, 2020.

———. "Representation and Consent: Why They Arose in Europe and Not Elsewhere." *Annual Review of Political Science* 19 (2016): 145–162.

———. "Was Weber Right? The Role of Urban Autonomy in Europe's Rise." *American Political Science Review* 8, no. 2 (2014): 1–18.

———. "When Distance Mattered: Geographic Scale and the Development of European Representative Assemblies." *American Political Science Review* 104, no. 4 (2010): 625–644.

Stephen, James. *Lectures on the History of France.* New York: Harper and Brothers, 1855.

Svolik, Milan. *The Politics of Authoritarian Rule.* New York: Cambridge University Press, 2012.

Swanson, Robert. *Promissory Notes on the Treasury of Merits: Indulgences in Late Medieval Europe.* Leiden: Brill, 2006.

Sweeney, James Ross, and Stanley Chodorow, eds. *Popes, Teachers, and Canon Law in the Middle Ages.* Ithaca, NY: Cornell University Press, 1989.

Taylor, Hannis. *The Origin and Growth of the English Constitution.* New York: Houghton, Mifflin, 1889.

Tellenbach, Gerd. *The Church in Western Europe from the Tenth to the Early Twelfth Century* (1936). Translated by Timothy Reuter. Cambridge: Cambridge University Press, 1993.

Thiebault, Paul. *Pope Gregory XI: The Failure of Tradition.* Lanham, MD: University Press of America, 1986.

Tilly, Charles. *Coercion, Capital, and European States: 990–1992.* Rev. ed. Cambridge, MA: Wiley-Blackwell, 1992.

———. "Reflections on the History of European State Making." *The Formation of National States in Western Europe,* edited by Charles Tilly, 3–83. Princeton: Princeton University Press, 1975.

Toynbee, Arnold. *A Study of History.* Oxford: Oxford University Press, 1946.

Tuchman, Barbara. *The March of Folly.* New York: Alfred A. Knopf, 1984.

Undset, Sigrid. *Kristin Lavransdatter.* Translated and edited by Tiina Nunnally. London: Penguin Books, 2005.

Van Caenegem, R. C. *The Birth of the English Common Law.* 2nd ed. Cambridge: Cambridge University Press, 1988.

van der Donck, Adriaen. *A Description of New Netherland.* Translated by Diederik Willem Goedhuys. Lincoln: University of Nebraska Press, 2010.

Vasquez, John. *The War Puzzle.* Cambridge: Cambridge University Press, 1993.

Wahl, Fabian. "Political Participation and Economic Development: Evidence from the Rise of Participative Political Institutions in the Late Medieval German Lands." *European Review of Economic History* 23 (May 2018): 193–213.

Waltz, Kenneth. *Theory of International Politics.* Reading, MA: Addison-Wesley, 1979.

Wang, Yuhua. "Betting on a Princeling." *Studies in Comparative International Development* 52, no. 4 (2017): 395–415.

———. "Sons and Lovers: Political Stability in China and Europe Before the Great Divergence." Working paper, Harvard Department of Government, October 3, 2017.

Weber, Max. *Economy and Society.* Edited by Guenther Roth and Claus Wittich. Translated by Ephraim Fischoff. New York: Bedminster Press, 1968.

———. *The Protestant Ethic and the Spirit of Capitalism.* New York: Charles Scribner and Sons, 1930.

Weingast, Barry R. "Adam Smith's Industrial Organization of Religion: Explaining the Medieval Church's Monopoly and Its Breakdown in the Reformation." Working paper, Stanford Department of Political Science, October 18, 2015.

Weinstein, Donald. *Savonarola: The Rise and Fall of a Renaissance Prophet*. New Haven: Yale University Press, 2011.

Wesson, R. *State Systems*. New York: Simon and Schuster, 1978.

White, Lynn. *Medieval Technology and Social Change*. Oxford: Oxford University Press, 1962.

Wood, C. T., ed. *Philip the Fair and Boniface VIII*. New York: Holt, Rinehart and Winston, 1967.

World Intellectual Property Indicators 2019. Geneva: World Intellectual Property Organization, 2019.

Wright, Georgia Sommers. "The Reinvention of the Portrait Likeness in the Fourteenth Century." *Gesta* 39, no. 2 (2000): 117–134.

Yue, Ricci P. H., Harry F. Lee, and Connor Y. H. Wu. "Trade Routes and Plague Transmission in Pre-Industrial Europe." *Scientific Reports* 7, no. 1 (2017): 12973.

INDEX

a clero et populo, 74, 76, 264

Abbo, Abbot of Fleury, 47

accountable government, 8, 90, 197,
    199–201, 232, 233, 235, 246
  in American colonies, 255–256
  concordats and, 218–230
  today, 273–276, 280, 291–292
  war and, 210–216, 217–218

Acton, Lord, 27, 31, 33

Adalbert of Mainz, Bishop, 69

advowson, 140

Africa, 18, 20, 20 (fig.), 22 (fig.), 23, 159

Agnes of Merania, 99

Alberic III, Duke of Tusculum, 41

Alexander III, Pope, 81–82, 151

Alexander VI, Pope, 110

alum, 133–134

American Revolution, 255

Americas, 18

Amiens, bishopric of, 99

Anacletus II, antipope, 128, 142

Anastasius IV, Pope, 152

anathema, 139

Anthelm, Bishop of Belley, 81–82

antipopes, 41, 58, 82, 128, 142

Aquinas, Thomas, 199, 200

Argentina, 7

Arnold of Brescia, 70, 71, 180, 209

Arras, bishopric of, 99

Article 64 (Treaty of Westphalia), 204,
    205, 206, 207

Article 65 (Treaty of Westphalia), 204,
    205, 206

Article 67 (Treaty of Westphalia), 204,
    205–206, 208–209

artwork (religious and secular), 54–57,
    56 (fig.), 196 (fig.), 263
  current distribution of, 259–260
  distance from Rome and, 122–123,
    122 (fig.), 197
  rise of secularism and, 195–197

Asia, 280, 281

assize of darrein presentment, 153

assize of mort d'ancestor, 153

assize of novel disseisin, 153

assize of utrum, 153

Ausculta fili (papal bull), 180

Australia, 22, 255

Austria, 7, 105, 231, 273

authoritarianism, 273, 274

Avignon papacy, 102, 114, 118, 174,
    176–180, 183, 184, 187, 189, 190,
    192–193, 194, 248
  beginning of, 83, 97, 105, 155
  diocesan wealth and, 174–176, 177–179
  emergence of new ideas during, 200
  end of, 111
  inside option exercised by, 87, 93
  interlude between Concordat
    of Worms and (*see* concordat
    interlude)
  length of, 97
  papal nepotism and, 142, 143, 185, 262
  scriptural texts not questioned by, 257
  secularism and, 97–98, 106–107, 195
Aztecs, 24

banking, 119, 134, 136, 145
Bartlett, Robert, 133
Basel (Switzerland), 105
Battle of Hastings, 202
Beaumaris Castle, 150
Belgium, 7, 9–10, 105, 231, 255, 273
Benedict IV, Pope, 32
Benedict VIII, Pope, 41
Benedict IX, Pope, 41–43, 46, 51, 55,
    56–58
Benedict X, Pope, 46
Benedictines, 130, 132, 133
Beno, cardinal priest of Santi Martino and
    Silvestro, 52
Benson, Robert, 71
Bernard of Clairveaux, 128, 133,
    134–135, 142
Bible, 6, 161, 185
Bill of Rights (US Constitution), 256
bishops
  canonical age for, 35
  gamble on, 169–174

  impact of division of loyalty in, 50
  power of, 287–288
  selection criteria and process, 80–89
  selection of preconcordat, 73–78
  tenure of, 87, 240–246, 244 (fig.), 248
  as vicars of Christ, 44
  wealth of deceased, 138–139
  See also concordat game; Concordat of
    Worms; diocesan wealth; Investiture
    Controversy; secularization of
    bishops
Bismarck, Otto von, 5
Black Death (bubonic plague), 96, 158,
    181, 182, 188, 195
blast furnace, 131
Blum, Léon, 6
Bohemia, 111
Boniface VIII, Pope, 72, 137, 154–155,
    178, 179–180, 197, 200
  Ausculta fili, 180
  Clericis laicos, 155, 211
  Ineffabilis amor, 179
  Unam sanctam, 155, 179, 199
borders (state), 203, 204, 206
Borgia family, 185–186
Brittany, Duchy of, 210
Bruges (Flanders), 230, 231
bubonic plague. *See* Black Death
Burgundy, 66, 67
Buringh, Eltjo, 149
Bury St. Edmunds, 154
Byzantine emperor, 55, 59, 260, 261
  Crusades and, 156
  Investiture Controversy and, 40–41, 43
Byzantine Empire, 19, 28–29

Cadfael, Brother, 253–254
Calixtus II, Pope, 8, 59, 65, 69, 71, 79, 93,
    141, 208, 266

game theoretic analysis of choices, 13
Lateran Council presided over by, 138
caloric potential of diocesan land
  preconcordat, 77–78, 77 (fig.)
  quality of life today and, 270–272,
    271 (fig.)
  secularization of bishops and,
    107–108, 108 (fig.)
Calvin, John, 168
Calvinism, 112
Calvino, Italo, 224–225, 240, 241
Canada, 22
canon 1 (Lateran Council), 140
canon 2 (Lateran Council), 140
canon 3 (Lateran Council), 138
canon 4 (Council of Nicaea), 44
canon 4 (Lateran Council), 139
canon 5 (Lateran Council), 138–139
canon 9 (Lateran Council), 139
canon 10 (Lateran Council), 140
canon 13 (Lateran Council), 143
canon 16 (Lateran Council), 141
canon 21 (Lateran Council), 138, 144
canon 25 (Council of Chalcedon), 72, 127
canon 25 (Lateran Council), 143
canonical age, 35
capitalism, 5–6, 130, 146, 290–291
cardinal-nephews, 34, 184, 264
cardinals, 33–34, 184
Carolingian dynasty, 55–56
Carrion Comfort (Hopkins), 253
Carthusians, 81, 133
Carus-Wilson, E. M., 131
castle construction, 147–151, 148 (fig.)
Cathars, 101
cathedral and church construction,
    136–137, 136 (fig.), 145, 147, 148
    (fig.), 149–151
Catholic Church, 1, 3, 6, 204, 257

child molestation scandals, 264–265
diplomacy and, 239
expansion of institutional advantage, 19
French break with, 174–176, 194
maneuvers to combat secular
    economic growth, 137–151
maneuvers to influence economic
    growth, 124–137
Orthodox Church break with, 59–60
reform contemplated by, 183–195
remeasurement of land owned by, 133
seizure of land owned by, 154
testing readiness to rebel against,
    176–183
three reasons for drift from religious
    mission, 27–28
See also bishops; concordat(s);
    Concordat of Worms; Concordats
    of London and Paris; Investiture
    Controversy; popes/papacy;
    punishment (by church/papacy)
Cecco d'Ascoli, 112
Celestine III, Pope, 99
celibacy (for clergy), 138
Charlemagne, Holy Roman emperor, 34,
    55, 59, 175
Charles the Bald, 55
Charles University, 110
Chartres Cathedral, 151
Chaucer, Geoffrey, 119, 210, 214
child molestation scandals, 264–265
China, 7, 228
    divinity of ruler assumed in, 24
    innovation in, 281
    per capita income in, 18, 20, 20 (fig.),
        21, 23
Christianity
    dawn of, 18–19
    Nestorian, 24

Christianity (*continued*)
  Orthodox, 59–60
  scientific questioning of scriptural texts,
    257
  See also Catholic Church
Christopher, Pope, 31, 32
Cistercians, 128, 129, 130, 133
Cîteaux (Burgundy), 128
Clement II, Pope, 42–43, 45, 51
Clement V, Pope, 97
Clericis laicos (papal bull), 155, 211
climate change, 119
coercion, 216, 220–224, 226–227
Cold War, 265
College of Cardinals, 46, 47, 49, 185
Cologne Cathedral, 151
Colonna family, 185
Commercial Revolution, 119, 158–161,
    163, 177, 196, 287
common law (English), 256
competition, 16, 24, 257, 258–265, 289,
    290, 291
conciliar movement, 184, 185, 188,
    201
concordat(s)
  accountable government and, 218–230
  bishop selection prior to, 73–78
  defined, 3
  dioceses covered by, 105
  quality of life prior to, 15, 17–21
  quality of life today and, 265–280
  as a step toward modern sovereignty,
    202–210
  terms of, 60–73
concordat game, 145, 146, 169, 171, 192,
    194, 219, 226, 229
  accountability of government and, 225,
    227, 230, 232, 235, 246, 274
  conciliar movement and, 184

  current day implications of, 266, 271,
    272, 274
  economic growth and, 124, 125, 126,
    129, 145, 146, 152, 162, 164, 165,
    168
  key implications of, 89–93
  rules of, 78–89
  secularism spread and, 106, 108, 109,
    113, 115, 116, 118, 121, 123
  third outcome of, 96–98, 123, 168,
    176, 183, 184, 188, 193
concordat interlude, 110, 114, 122, 137,
    189, 200
  Commercial Revolution and, 160–161
  Crusades during, 156–157
  current relevance, 253, 263–264,
    266–267, 269–270, 274, 276, 278,
    280, 281, 282, 291
  economic growth during, 124,
    125–126, 131, 137, 162, 163–164,
    165, 167
  end of, 105
  excommunications during, 101–103
  gamble on vacant sees during, 169, 170
  papal nepotism during, 52, 84,
    261–262
Concordat of London (1107), 60–61,
    103
  See also Concordats of London and
    Paris
Concordat of Worms (1122), 2–4, 44,
    50, 51, 52, 54, 55, 56, 59, 89, 95, 98,
    141, 147, 162, 218, 248, 250
  accountable government set in motion
    by, 201
  circumstances precipitating, 28
  Commercial Revolution and, 158–159
  Concordats of London and Paris
    foreshadowing, 61

current impact of, 9–11, 257, 260, 266,
269, 281, 286, 288

enduring lesson of, 292

European life prior to, 15

feudalism end given impetus by, 204

game theoretic analysis of, 79

implications of fiduciary responsibility
granted by, 203, 206

innovation and, 281

interlude between Avignon papacy and
(*see* concordat interlude)

long-term consequences for church, 71

monarchical tenure correlated with,
245

papal nepotism and, 261

parliament creation influenced by,
238–239

power implications of, 70

signing of, 2

terms of, 64–73

text of, 65–66

three stipulations of, 8

titular role importance in, 208

Concordats of London and Paris (1107),
8, 15, 50, 59, 66–67, 89, 95, 208,
248

circumstances precipitating, 28

Commercial Revolution and, 158–159

current impact of, 257, 266, 269, 286,
288

enduring lesson of, 292

feudalism end given impetus by, 204

monarchical tenure correlated with,
245

papal nepotism and, 261

signing of, 2

terms of, 60–64

confession, 144

confessors' manuals, 144

Confirmatio cartarum, 212–213, 222,
255–256

Constantine, Holy Roman emperor, 16,
25, 29, 43, 45, 47, 48, 54

Constantinople, 19, 29, 40

Constitution, US, 256

Constitution of Liberty, The (Hayek), 167

Constitutions of Clarendon, 140, 226

construction (religious and secular),
147–151, 148 (fig.)

corporations, 119

corruption
of the papacy, 28, 31, 32–33, 262, 263,
264–265

today, 266, 267, 276, 278–280, 279
(fig.)

Council of Basel, 184, 201

Council of Chalcedon, 68, 72, 127, 169,
170, 209

Council of Constance, 97, 111, 112,
188

papal nepotism and, 185, 186, 262

risk to papal authority and, 183–184

Council of Nicaea, 48, 73, 105, 138

canon 4, 44

winning coalition size and, 262–263,
264

Council of Trent, 184–185, 186, 187,
188, 192

Council of Troyes, 134

courts, 153

credit, 150

Crescenzi family, 41

Crescenzi-Ottaviani, Giovanni de'. See
Sylvester III, Pope

critical test, 271

Crusades, 134, 136, 156–158

curia, 49, 97

curia regis, 152–153

Cyprian of Carthage, Bishop, 40, 264
Czech Republic, 7, 105

Damasus I, Pope, 185
Dante Alighieri, 200
darrein presentment, 153
De monarchia (Dante), 200
De ordinando pontifice (Anonymous),
    44–45
De potestate regia et populi (Quidort),
    199–200
Declaration of Independence (US),
    213
Defender of the Faith (title), 182
Defensor pacis (Marsilius of Padua), 200
Delaware, 255
democracy, 11, 213, 265, 266, 267,
    273–276, 275 (fig.), 292
Denmark, 215
Dietrich I von Hengebach, Archbishop of
    Cologne, 81, 82, 109
diocesan wealth, 85–90, 91, 92–93,
    167–168
  break from church and, 174–176
  Concordats of London and Paris on,
    61, 63
  current impact of, 266–272, 268 (fig.),
    273–278, 277 (fig.), 280, 282–284,
    283 (fig.), 285 (fig.), 289
  data for analysis of, 107
  distance from Rome and, 123,
    187–191
  king's point of view on nominees and,
    85–86
  preconcordat control of, 75–78
  Protestant Reformation and, 193–194,
    193 (fig.)
  readiness to rebel against church and,
    177–179, 181–183, 182 (fig.)

secularization of bishops and,
    104–105, 107–109, 113–118, 114
    (fig.), 120, 121
  vacant sees and, 171, 172–174, 173
    (fig.)
diplomacy, 224, 239, 248
  See also negotiation
distance from Rome, 109–113, 249
  accountable government and, 219,
    220, 232, 233
  artwork subjects and, 122–123, 122
    (fig.), 197
  economic growth and, 162, 163–166,
    226
  readiness to rebel against church and,
    187–191, 195
  secularization of bishops and, 115–116,
    121
  of vacant sees, 170–171, 172–174, 173
    (fig.)
Dolcino, Fra, 112

eastern Europe, 23, 118, 120, 175, 274,
    276
East-West schism, 59
economic growth, 90, 92–93, 119–166,
    167–168, 265, 290–292
  accountable government and, 225–230
  Crusades and, 156–158
  entrepreneurial monastic orders and,
    128–134
  explanations offered for, 119–120
  maneuvers to combat secular, 137–151
  maneuvers to influence, 124–137
  political clout and, 120–124
  Protestant movement and, 187–191,
    191 (fig.)
  secular maneuvers for, 151–155
  See also wealth

ecumenical council, 184

Edward I, King of England (also Duke of Aquitaine), 178, 197, 211–214, 215, 222, 225

Edward the Confessor, 202

Egypt, 7

Ekelund, Robert, 147

Engelbrektsson, Engelbrekt, 215, 221

Engels, Friedrich, 5

England, 5, 6, 7, 105, 204
  American colonies of, 255–256
  basis of monarchy in, 202
  common law of, 256
  current impact of concordats in, 9–10, 273
  diocesan wealth in, 182–183, 182 (fig.)
  diplomacy and, 239
  economic growth in, 123, 152
  French war with, 197, 211–214
  legal reforms in, 152–154
  readiness to rebel against the church, 180–181, 182–183, 182 (fig.), 194, 195

Epistle to the Magnesians, 44

Eric of Pomerania, King of Sweden, Denmark, and Norway, 215

Estates General (France), 179, 222, 226

Estates General (Sweden), 215

Eudes de Sully, Bishop of Paris, 99

Eugene III, Pope, 128, 152

Europe
  eastern, 23, 118, 120, 175, 274, 276
  economic decline in, 17–21, 280, 286–287
  northern, 2, 87, 106, 120, 123, 168, 194, 195, 249
  northwestern, 119
  per capita income in, 17–23
  population growth in, 165
  quality of life preconcordat, 15, 17–21
  quality of life today, 265–280
  southern, 2, 106, 120, 123, 192, 249
  unique feature of, 24–25
  wealth: 800-1517, 174–175, 175 (fig)
  western (*see* western Europe)
  Western settler offshoots of (*see* Western settler offshoots)

European exceptionalism. *See* Western exceptionalism

Eusebius, 54

excommunication, 38, 91, 138–139, 179, 200, 213, 288
  of Dietrich I, 81, 109
  distance from Rome and, 109–110
  of Henry IV, 52, 82
  of Henry V, 52, 69, 82
  of Otto IV, 81
  of Philip II, 99
  of Philip IV, 72
  for political *vs.* religious reasons, 100–103, 101 (fig.)
  of Sergius III, 32
  of Sylvester III, 41
  of Waldo, 112

exports, 133–134, 154–155

fascism, 276

feudalism, 204, 206, 214

First Barons' War, 104

First Crusade, 156

First Lateran Council, 138, 139, 140, 141

Flanders, 197, 230–231, 232, 233

Florence, 110

Flotte, Pierre, 179

Food and Agriculture Organization (UN), 270

Formosus, Pope, 31

Fourth Crusade, 156, 157

Fourth Lateran Council, 143, 144, 147, 149, 151, 154, 190, 191 (fig.)

France, 3, 6, 7, 10, 105, 187, 190, 204
basis of monarchy in, 202
current impact of concordats in, 273
diocesan wealth in, 97, 174–176, 175 (fig.), 177–179
diplomacy and, 239
economic growth in, 123, 152, 154–155
English war with, 197, 211–214
Holy Roman Empire shift of base from, 33
interdiction experience in, 99–100, 109, 139–140
population of, 190
Protestant movement in, 185, 192
readiness to rebel against church, 176–180, 194
secularism in, 96, 97–98, 118
Western settler offshoots of, 255, 256
See also Avignon papacy

Frederick I, Holy Roman emperor (Frederick Barbarossa), 82, 151

freedom, 2, 3, 16

fulling machine, 131

game theory, 12–14
See also concordat game

Gascony, 211, 212

Genghis Khan, 17, 24

Gerard of Burgundy, 46

Gerard Segarelli, 112

Gerhoh of Reichersberg, 70

Germany, 5, 6, 7, 61, 105, 176, 255
artwork subjects in, 197
current impact of concordats in, 9–10, 273, 274
diplomacy and, 239

Holy Roman Empire shift of base to, 33, 55
Protestant movement in, 185, 187, 191

Ghent (Flanders), 230, 231

Gift of Pepin, 30

Gilchrist, John, 146

Gniezno (Poland), 105

Gratian, Johannes. *See* Gregory VI, Pope

Gratian of Bologna, 130

Great Famine, 182, 195

Gregory II, Pope, 28–29

Gregory VI, Pope, 49, 76
deposition of, 25, 42–43, 46, 51, 59, 100
sale of papacy to, 41–43, 57, 58

Gregory VII, Pope, 46–49, 51, 52–55, 57, 58, 60, 69, 71, 160
coalition of, 47–49, 48 (fig.), 54, 264
death of, 59

Guido of Burgundy (Archbishop of Vienne). *See* Calixtus II, Pope

Guido of Ferrara, 53

Gutenberg, Johannes, 6

Gutenberg Bible, 6, 161

Harold II, King of England, 202

Hayek, Friedrich, 167, 289, 290

heavy plow, 119, 189

Henry I, King of England, 60–61

Henry II, King of England, 140, 152–154, 226

Henry III, Holy Roman emperor, 25, 42–43, 51, 71, 100

Henry IV, Holy Roman emperor, 52–53, 57, 59, 60, 82

Henry V, Holy Roman emperor, 8, 59, 71, 79, 93, 266
excommunication of, 52, 69, 82
game theoretic analysis of choices, 13

terms of concordats and, 62–66, 68, 70–71

Henry VIII, King of England, 181, 182, 192

Henry of Lausanne, 101

heresy, 100, 101, 110, 111, 112, 186, 187, 200

Hildebrand of Sovana. *See* Gregory VII, Pope

Hitler, Adolf, 16, 273

Hobbes, Thomas, 18

Holy Roman emperor, 8, 128, 201, 204
 election of, 202
 war with the papacy, 47–58

Holy Roman Empire, 8, 24, 175
 base shift to Germany, 33, 55
 creation of, 19, 123, 258
 Crusades and, 157
 population of, 190
 Protestantism and, 194
 rise of, 48–49
 secularism in, 96, 97, 118

honesty (societal), 278–280

Honorius II, Pope, 134

Hopkins, Gerard Manley, 253

Hostiensis, 144

Huffman, Joseph, 239

Hugh of St. Victor, 70, 86, 208

humanities, Nobel Prizes in, 266, 284, 285 (fig.)

Hungary, 228

Hunt, Edwin, 152

Hus, Jan, 110–112, 192

Iconoclast Movement, 25, 28–29, 259, 261

Ignatius, Saint, 44

Incas, 24

India, 18, 23

indulgences, 35, 145

Industrial Revolution, 158

Ineffabilis amor (papal bull), 179

Ingeborg of Denmark, 99

inheritance rights, 153

Innocent II, Pope, 128, 129, 141–142

Innocent III, Pope, 44, 72, 81, 103–104, 137, 154
 Crusade initiated by, 156
 interdiction of French realm and, 99–100, 109

innovation, 11, 16, 106, 280–286

inside option, 83, 87, 93, 168, 183

interdiction, 82
 adverse consequences of, 102
 of Dietrich I, 81
 distance from Rome and, 111
 French experience with, 99–100, 109, 139–140
 of Prague, 111

interregnums. *See* vacant sees/ interregnums

Investiture Controversy, 50, 51, 54, 60, 64–73, 74, 78, 82, 89, 92, 93, 128, 169, 175, 194, 203, 218, 219, 287, 289
 artwork before and during, 55, 56 (fig.)
 catalyst for, 15, 43, 58
 causes and impact of, 39–47
 Crusades during, 156
 defined, 28
 monastic orders in the wake of, 130
 papal nepotism and, 52, 56, 142, 261
 punishment by church before and after, 100–103
 resolution of (*see* Concordat of Worms)
 royal grants to cities during, 239
 secularization of bishops during, 115

Ireland, 228
Islam, 19, 145, 260, 289
  Byzantine Empire invaded by, 28, 41
  Crusades and, 134, 156
  expansion of, 17, 21
  per capita income in world of, 18, 21
  Spain dominated by regimes of, 175
Italy, 66, 67, 105, 175, 176
  Crusades and, 157, 158
  current impact of concordats in, 273, 274
  diocesan wealth in, 181–183, 182 (fig.)
  economic growth in, 123
  per capita income in, 18
  population of, 190
  readiness to rebel against the church, 180–183, 182 (fig.), 194
Ivo, Bishop of Chartres, 69

James of St. George, Master, 150, 151
Japan, 23, 24, 281
Jerome, Saint, 132, 185
Jerome of Prague, 112
Jerusalem, 156
Jesus Christ, 17, 18, 20, 24, 25, 44, 134
Jews, 145
John, King of England, 72, 102–104, 154, 202
John IX, Pope, 32
John X, Pope, 32
John XI, Pope, 31
John XII, Pope, 34
jury system, 153–154
Justinian, Holy Roman emperor, 262

Kalmar Union of Denmark, Sweden, and Norway, 215
kings. *See* monarchs
"king's ransom," 214

Knights Hospitaller, 128, 134
Knights Templar, 128, 134–136, 145
Korea, 281

labor and laborers, 130–132, 249, 286
Labour Party (Britain), 6
Lambert, Holy Roman emperor, 32
land
  caloric potential of (*see* caloric potential of diocesan land)
  expansion of work on, 151–152
  remeasurement of church's, 133
  seizure of church's, 154
Langton, Stephen (Archbishop of Canterbury), 103–104
Lateran councils, 137–151
  First, 138, 139, 140, 141
  Fourth, 143, 144, 147, 149, 151, 154, 190, 191 (fig.)
  Second, 138–143, 142 (fig.), 153
  Third, 143, 145, 153
Lateran Synod, 64
Latin America, 23, 256
Lavant (Slovenia), 105
Le Goff, Jacques, 132, 133, 144
Lebus (Poland), 105
legal reforms, 152–154
Leo III, Byzantine emperor, 28–29
Leo III, Pope, 34, 59
Leo V, Pope, 31, 32
Leo VI, Pope, 32
Liber censuum, 71
life expectancy, 257, 266, 267, 276–278, 277 (fig.), 280
literacy, 6, 257
Lombards, 29
Lothair I (son of Louis the Pious), 55
Louis VI, King of France, 176
Louis VII, King of France, 176

Louis the Pious, 55

Louisiana Territory, 255, 256

Luther, Martin, 3, 6, 100, 105, 110, 123,
    168, 179, 189, 190, 194, 197, 262,
    264, 273
  death of, 184
  impact of ideas, 195
  ninety-five theses of, 192, 248
  safe passage to Rome declined by, 112

machinery, 131–132, 165, 257

Maddison, Angus, 17

Maddison Project, 17–18, 280

Magna Carta, 102–104, 212

maltolt, 211, 213

Marozia (Theophylact's daughter), 31,
    32

marriage, 6, 161
  alliances via, 220, 225, 227, 249, 290
  forbidden for clergy, 138, 140

Marsilius of Padua, 200

Marx, Karl, 5

Maryland, 255

Mayas, 24

Mecca, 17

Medici family, 110, 185–186

Medina, 17

Merlin, 254

Middle East, 18, 19, 20, 20 (fig.), 21, 22
    (fig.), 23

monarchy
  anointment of monarchs by popes, 38
  concordats signed by (*see*
    concordat(s); Concordat of Worms;
    Concordats of London and Paris)
  election of rulers, 202
  hereditary rule in, 202–203
  parliaments' impact on, 238–248
  self-interest in, 11–15

tenure of monarchs, 240–248, 242
    (fig.), 244 (fig.), 246 (fig.), 250
  two bodies of the king concept, 68, 208

monastic orders, 128–134

moneylenders, 145
  See also usury ban

Mongolia, 24

mort d'ancestor, 153

movable type, 161

Muhammad, 17

Murray, James, 152

Muslims. *See* Islam

Mussolini, Benito, 273

Napoleonic Code, 256

national assemblies. *See* parliaments

negotiation, 215–216, 220–224
  See also diplomacy

nepotism, papal. *See* papal nepotism

Nestorian Christianity, 24

Netherlands, 5, 7, 105, 152, 228, 231
  artwork subjects in, 197
  current impact of concordats in, 9–10,
    273
  Western settler offshoots of, 255, 256

New Amsterdam charter, 256

New Netherlands, 255

New York City, 256

New York State, 255

New Zealand, 22, 255

Nicholas I, Pope, 52

Nicholas II, Pope, 46

Nigeria, 7

ninety-five theses, 192, 248

Nobel Prizes, 266, 282–284, 283 (fig.),
    285 (fig.)

nonexceptional monarchs, 241

Normandy, Duchy of, 210

North Africa, 18, 21, 159

northern Europe, 2, 87, 106, 120, 123, 168, 194, 195, 249

northwestern Europe, 119

novel disseisin, 153

Norway, 215

oaths, 69, 72, 103, 208

Old World Trade Route Project, 107

Olomouc (Czech Republic), 105

Orsini family, 33

Orthodox Church, 59–60

Otto I, Holy Roman emperor, 34, 51, 55

Otto IV, King of Germany (later Holy Roman emperor), 81

Ottonian dynasty, 34, 50, 51

outside option, 83, 93, 96, 123, 168, 181, 183

papacy. *See* popes/papacy

papal curia. *See* curia

papal nepotism, 259, 260–262

birth of, 30–35

decline in, 50–52, 50 (fig.), 53, 55, 56–57, 83–84, 186, 196, 261–262

Lateran II's condemnation of, 141–143, 142 (fig.)

resurgence of, 185–186, 186 (fig.), 262, 263

timeline of, 34 (fig.), 261 (fig.)

Papal States, 27, 29–35, 39, 54, 105, 171, 186, 258

creation and territory of, 29–30

papacy regains control of, 201, 261

population of, 190

Papareschi, Gregorio. *See* Innocent II, Pope

Paris, bishopric of, 99

parliaments, 1, 90, 93, 162, 201, 214, 216, 217–218, 222, 225, 250, 265, 273

concordats' influence on creation of, 227–230, 229 (fig.)

English, 212–213

impact on monarchs, 238–248

rubber stamp or real, 233, 234, 235–238, 247

secularism, wealth, and, 230–235, 234 (fig.)

Paschal II, Pope, 60–64, 69, 128, 129

patent filings, 281

Patricius Romanorum (title), 29

Patrimony of Saint Peter, 29

patronage, 153

Paul I, Pope, 30

Peltzer, Jörg, 39

Pepin the Short, King of the Franks, 29–30, 34, 38, 51

per capita income

in 2000, 22 (fig.), 23

from 1960-2018, 265, 267, 280, 284

change over time, 17–23, 20 (fig.)

religiosity indicators and, 290

Peter, Saint, 16, 33, 34, 38

Peter of Bruys, 112

Peter's pence, 38

Philip I, King of France, 60–62, 97

Philip II, King of France (Philip Augustus), 72, 99–100, 102, 109, 139, 154, 202

Philip IV, King of France (Philip the Fair), 97, 137, 168, 176, 178, 179–180, 182, 183, 187, 192, 194, 197, 199, 200, 260

excommunication of, 72

exports to Rome cut off by, 154–155

government accountability increased by, 222, 226

war with England and, 211, 213, 214

Philip the Good, Duke of Burgundy, 231

Phoenicians, 7

Pierleoni family, 142

Pignatelli, Bernardo. *See* Eugene III, Pope

Pilgrims, 255

Plaisance, Bishop of, 63, 69

Poland, 105

Pomerania, Duchy of, 210

popes/papacy

    altered tides of political power, 258–265

    Avignon (*see* Avignon papacy)

    conciliar movement and (*see* conciliar
      movement)

    Constantinople's loss of control over
      selection, 29

    corruption of, 28, 31, 32–33, 262, 263,
      264–265

    maneuvers to increase political power,
      35–39

    murders and unexplained deaths,
      31–32

    nepotism and (*see* papal nepotism)

    punishment by (*see* punishment (by
      church/papacy))

    restoration of supremacy, 184

    return to Rome, 185–186

    sale of papacy, 41–43, 57, 58

    self-interest in, 11–15

    war with Holy Roman emperor, 47–58

Popular Front government (France), 6

Portugal, 105, 118, 159, 175, 255, 256,
    274, 276

power, 8–11, 287–289

    altered tides of, 258–265

    Concordat of Worms implications, 70

    papal, 31, 32–33, 35–39

    proposal, 71, 73

    regalian rights and altering the balance
      of, 67–68

    separation of, 200

Poznań (Poland), 105

Prague, 110–111

preexceptional monarchs, 241

Prestwich, Michael, 211–212

prince-bishops, 68

printing press, 161

property rights, 153, 204, 206

proposal power, 71, 73

prosperity, 2, 3, 8, 11, 106

    See also economic growth; wealth

Protestant Reformation, 3, 6, 87, 110,
    132, 146, 178, 179, 196, 248, 264

    beginning of, 105, 123, 157, 163

    circumstances leading to, 184–195

    outside option exercised during, 83, 93

    papal nepotism and, 262

    scriptural texts not questioned by, 257

    work ethic and, 106, 226

Protestant work ethic, 106, 130, 191, 226

public goods, 37, 76

punishment (by church/papacy), 71–72,
    82–83, 91–92

    assessment of costs, 109–113

    changing use of, 98–104

    See also excommunication; interdiction

quality of life

    preconcordat, 15, 17–21

    today, 265–280

Quidort, Jean, 199–200, 203, 225

regalian rights, 63, 70, 73, 79, 84–85, 95,
    121, 169, 203, 208, 209–210, 287

    balance of power altered by, 67–68

    defined, 60

    importance of, 60–61

    Treaty of Westphalia on, 207, 209

Reims Cathedral, 151

religious tolerance, 8, 11, 106

Renaissance, 260
Richard the Lionhearted, 154
Robin Hood, 253, 267
Robinson, I. S., 55–56
Roman Empire, 24
  Christianity adopted by, 19
  fall of, 3, 7, 19, 39, 44
  success of, 18–19
  See also Holy Roman Empire
Rome, 40
  Constantinople's loss of control of
    papal selection in, 29
  distance from and church punishment
    (*see* distance from Rome)
  papacy return to, 185–186
Runnymede, 103, 104
Russia, 105

Sabina, bishopric of, 41
saeculum obscurum, 31, 32, 261
Saisset, Bernard (Bishop of Pamiers), 179
Saladin, 156
sale of time, 145
salvation, 37, 38, 40, 76, 99, 191
  Crusades and, 134
  monopoly control of by church, 35, 72,
    93, 169, 183, 192, 195, 196, 287
  sale of time and, 145
Savonarola, Girolamo, 110, 111–112,
    181–182, 192, 195
Saxony, 53
Scandinavia, 118, 187, 188
Schimmelpfennig, Bernhard, 46, 49
science, 3, 106, 257, 266, 282–284
  See also technology
Scotland, 211
Second Crusade, 134, 157
Second Lateran Council, 138–143, 142
    (fig.), 153

secularism, 8, 11, 90, 93, 95–118, 201,
    265, 270, 287
  altered tides of power, 258–265
  of bishops (*see* secularization of
    bishops)
  changing use of church punishment
    and, 98–104
  Commercial Revolution and, 159–161
  costs of church punishment and,
    109–113
  Crusades and, 158
  economic growth and, 124–155,
    159–161, 167
  monarchical tenure and, 245, 248
  parliaments and, 230–235, 234 (fig.)
  rise of, 195–197
  today, 276–278
secularization of bishops, 10, 104–109,
    113–118, 114 (fig.), 117 (fig.), 120,
    121
  Commercial Revolution and, 159–161
  data available on, 105–107
  economic growth and, 124–126, 137,
    161–166, 163 (fig.)
  preconcordat, 75–78, 77 (fig.)
  tenure in office and, 246
selectorate, 36, 37
Seljuk Turks, 156
Senlis, bishopric of, 99
Sergius III, Pope, 31–32
Sicily, 105, 118, 159
Sigismund, King of Germany (later Holy
    Roman emperor), 111
simony, 42, 46, 74, 76, 140
Slovenia, 105
Smith, Adam, 5
Social Democratic Party (SPD)
    (Germany), 6
socialism, 6

Soissons, bishopric of, 99

southern Europe, 2, 106, 120, 123, 192, 249

southern Italy, 105

sovereignty. *See* state sovereignty

Soviet Union, 23, 276, 289

Spain, 105, 118, 159, 175, 255, 256, 274, 276

spending authority, 236–238, 247–248

St. Denis monastery, 62

St. Peter's Basilica, 63

Stalin, Joseph, 16

Stark, Rodney, 145, 146

state building, 215, 216–218, 247

state size, 232–233, 235–236

state sovereignty, 73, 169, 200, 202–210, 249

States-General (Bruges), 231

Stephen, James, 97

Stephen II, Pope, 29, 30, 51, 261

Stephen VII, Pope, 32

Suger, Abbot of St. Denis monastery, 62–63, 64

Suitger of Bamberg, Bishop. *See* Clement II, Pope

Summa theologica (Aquinas), 199

Sutri, 63

Swanson, Robert, 145

Sweden, 215

Switzerland, 105, 187, 228, 281

Sylvester III, Pope, 41, 43

synod of 1059, 46

Synod of Sutri, 41–42

Synod of Vienne, 69

"Tale of Melibee, The" (Chaucer), 119, 210

taxation, 128, 129, 211–213, 215, 222, 225

of church/clergy, 154, 155, 211, 213

Flemish revolt against, 230–231, 232

parliaments' influence on, 236–238, 247–248

Teb Tengerri, 24

technology, 119, 131–132, 134, 278

See also machinery; science

Teutonic Order, 134

Theodora (Theophylact's daughter), 31

Theophylact I, Count of Tusculum, 31, 32

Theophylactus of Tusculum. *See* Benedict IX, Pope

Third Crusade, 157

Third Lateran Council, 143, 145, 153

Thirty Years' War, 177, 178, 186, 194, 196, 203, 204, 259, 262

See also Treaty of Westphalia

Tilly, Charles, 215, 216, 218

tithes, 129, 140, 145

trade-route prevalence

Commercial Revolution and, 158–160

Crusades and, 156–158

French dioceses and, 174–176, 178

innovation and, 284

parliament creation and, 229

preconcordat, 77–78, 77 (fig.)

Protestant movement and, 190

quality of life and, 267, 270–272, 271 (fig.)

secularization of bishops and, 107, 108–109, 125–126, 137, 162, 163

traditional monarchs, 241, 242 (fig.), 243, 245

transparency, 3, 276, 278–280

Transparency International, 278, 280

Treaty of Westphalia, 178, 203, 204–206, 210, 248, 260

Article 64, 204, 205, 206, 207

Article 65, 204, 205, 206

Article 67, 204, 205–206, 208–209
trial by ordeal, 153–154
Tusculum family, 31–32, 33, 41, 46, 76
two bodies of the king concept, 68, 208
Tyre, 7

Unam sanctam (papal bull), 155, 179, 199
United States, 22, 213, 255–256, 281
Urban II, Pope, 156
usury ban, 136, 143–151, 148 (fig.)
utrum, 153

vacant sees/interregnums, 75, 78, 82–85,
        87–88, 92, 127, 196, 204, 206, 209
    adverse consequences of, 80
    gamble on, 169–174
    rules for filling, 79
van der Donck, Adriaen, 256
Veneto region of Italy, 105, 118, 176
Venice, 105, 175
vertical water wheel, 119, 134
Vicarius Christi, 44
Victor IV, antipope, 82

Waldensians, 101, 112
Waldo, Peter, 110, 112, 192
Wales, 211
Walter de Teye, 212
war, 208, 220, 221, 224, 250, 290
    accountable government and,
        210–216, 217–218
    monarchical tenure and, 247, 248
    parliaments and the ability to wage,
        236–238
    state building and, 215, 216–218, 247
Wazo of Liège, Bishop, 45
wealth, 8–11
    accountable government and,
        219–220, 225–230

monarchical tenure and, 240, 241–243,
        245, 246, 248
    parliaments and, 230–235, 234 (fig.)
    See also diocesan wealth; economic
        growth; per capita income
Weber, Max, 5, 106, 130, 226
Wenceslas IV, King of Bohemia, 111
western Europe, 15, 273, 276, 280
    Crusades and, 157
    economic growth and, 120
    innovation in, 281
    per capita income in, 17–23, 20 (fig.),
        22 (fig.)
Western exceptionalism, 1–2, 3, 5–25, 50,
        113, 201, 257, 258, 286, 289, 292
    beginning of the growth of, 106,
        116–118
    concordat game place and, 93
    economic growth and, 120
    importance of explaining, 1
    unexpectedness of, 17–23
    unsubstantiated explanations for, 5–8,
        250
Western Schism, 97, 111, 174, 183, 184,
        185, 194
Western settler offshoots, 254–256
    accountable government in, 255–256,
        292
    innovation in, 281
    per capita income in, 22, 22 (fig.), 23
Wichmann of Magdeburg, Archbishop,
        151–152
William, Duke of Normandy, 202
William II, King of England, 202
windmill, 134
winning coalition, 35–38, 263 (fig.)
    accountable government and, 226,
        227, 228–229
    defined, 36

democracy and, 292
of Gregory VII, 47–49, 48 (fig.), 54,
   264
rewards for, 37
size of, 36–38, 47–51, 48 (fig.), 54,
   228–229, 261, 262–265, 291, 292
wool merchants, 211, 213
work ethic, 106, 130, 132, 191, 226, 227,
   291
World Bank, 23

World War I, 265, 273
World War II, 265
writs, 153
Wroclaw (Poland), 105
Wycliffe, John, 110, 111–112, 192

Yassa, 24
Ypres (Flanders), 230

Zachary, Pope, 29

Bruce Bueno de Mesquita is the Julius Silver Professor of Politics at New York University. He is a member of the American Academy of Arts and Sciences and the author of twenty-three books, including *The Dictator's Handbook* (with Alastair Smith).

PublicAffairs is a publishing house founded in 1997. It is a tribute to the standards, values, and flair of three persons who have served as mentors to countless reporters, writers, editors, and book people of all kinds, including me.

I. F. STONE, proprietor of *I. F. Stone's Weekly*, combined a commitment to the First Amendment with entrepreneurial zeal and reporting skill and became one of the great independent journalists in American history. At the age of eighty, Izzy published *The Trial of Socrates*, which was a national bestseller. He wrote the book after he taught himself ancient Greek.

BENJAMIN C. BRADLEE was for nearly thirty years the charismatic editorial leader of *The Washington Post*. It was Ben who gave the *Post* the range and courage to pursue such historic issues as Watergate. He supported his reporters with a tenacity that made them fearless and it is no accident that so many became authors of influential, best-selling books.

ROBERT L. BERNSTEIN, the chief executive of Random House for more than a quarter century, guided one of the nation's premier publishing houses. Bob was personally responsible for many books of political dissent and argument that challenged tyranny around the globe. He is also the founder and longtime chair of Human Rights Watch, one of the most respected human rights organizations in the world.

•   •   •

For fifty years, the banner of Public Affairs Press was carried by its owner Morris B. Schnapper, who published Gandhi, Nasser, Toynbee, Truman, and about 1,500 other authors. In 1983, Schnapper was described by *The Washington Post* as "a redoubtable gadfly." His legacy will endure in the books to come.

Peter Osnos, *Founder*